*A*frican
*F*olktales *in*
T H E
*N*ew *W*orld

Folkloristics

❋

A L A N   D U N D E S , General Editor

African Folktales in THE New World

WILLIAM BASCOM

❋ *Indiana University Press*

BLOOMINGTON & INDIANAPOLIS

$\frac{4}{0}\sigma$

Illustration by Obiọra Udechukwu

The paper used in this publication meets the minimum requirements of American
National Standard for Information Sciences—Permanence of Paper for Printed
Library Materials, ANSI Z39.48-1984.

∞™

Manufactured in the United States of America

Library of Congress Cataloging-in-Publication Data

Bascom, William Russell, date
    African folktales in the New World / William Bascom.
        p.   cm. — (Folkloristics)
    XXV, 243
    "First appeared in Research in African literatures from 1976 to
1982"—Foreword.
    Includes bibliographical references and index.
    ISBN 0-253-31128-4 (cl). — ISBN 0-253-20736-3 (pa)
    1. Afro-Americans—Folklore. 2. Tales—United States—History and
criticism. 3. Tales—Africa—History and criticism. 4. Blacks—
America—Folklore. 5. Tales—America—History and criticism.
I. Title. II. Series.
GR111.A47B37   1992
398.2'08996073—dc20   91-46789

2 3 4 5   01 00 99 98

c. 1

✳ C O N T E N T S

F O R E W O R D

✳

Alan Dundes

This is not a book of jolly folktales from Africa designed to be read by or to young children seeking entertainment at bedtime or on a rainy day. Rather it is a set of technical essays, each devoted to one or more traditional narratives found in Africa and also in the New World. These essays, which first appeared in *Research in African Literatures* from 1976 to 1982, represent the completed portion of the last major research project of the late William R. Bascom, an eminent authority on African art and African folklore. The project was intended to demonstrate through the use of the comparative method the existence and nature of African and African-American folktales.

In order to appreciate the magnitude and importance of Bascom's unique achievement, it is first necessary to have some understanding of the comparative method as it is employed by folklorists. This critical method was developed in Europe rather than in Africa, but Bascom's application of the method to African data shows its utility outside of Europe. Then, following a brief consideration of African folk narrative scholarship in general, I shall attempt to place the whole project in historical perspective by discussing the longstanding debate over the origins of African-American tales and how Bascom came to undertake the project in the first place.

The comparative method has been at the heart of folkloristics, the scientific study of folklore, from the discipline's inception at the beginning of the nineteenth century. Folklore, no matter what the genre, is rarely confined to a single culture. Rather the "same" folktale or proverb is to be found in some variant form in adjacent cultures and perhaps even in cultures far distant in time and space. While it is true that few if any items of folklore can be shown to be universal in the sense of existing among *all* peoples, past and present, on the face of the earth, it is also the case that the areal or temporal distribution of a particular item of folklore can be ascertained through rigorous and meticulous scholarship. Thus folklorists can demonstrate the spread of Indo-European folktales from India to Ireland, or the diffusion of an ancient tale from Asia to native American cultures.

Each piece of folklore has its own particular geographical area of existence.

The difficulty lies in tracking all the known versions of that piece of folklore. Such a task requires vast knowledge and patience. The knowledge in question includes polyglot skills so as to be able to read reports of folklore written in a bewildering variety of languages. In the case of African folk narrative, for example, there is no one individual who could possibly be conversant with every single African native language—they number in the hundreds. But even to read folktale texts in the colonial languages in which many of these African tales were first reported requires a knowledge of Afrikaans, Arabic, English, Flemish, French, German, Portuguese, and Spanish, among others.

One peculiarity of the comparative method as practiced by folklorists stems from the assumed genetic or cognate relationship understood to exist between the items compared. In other words, when a folklorist compares and contrasts versions of a given tale type, it is taken for granted that these versions are historically related—they go back to a common ancestral form of that same tale.

This has been the convention ever since the Grimm brothers first published their celebrated *Kinder- und Hausmärchen*, the initial volume in 1812, the second in 1815. In fact, the Grimms were quite surprised to discover that many of the "German" folktales they had collected from their informants were the "same" stories as had been collected by Basile in Naples in his posthumously published (1634–1636) *Il Pentamerone* nearly two centuries earlier.

The Grimms dutifully mentioned parallels, that is, cognates, to their tales in the individual notes they published with the folktales. This model was followed thereafter. Felix Liebrecht (1812–1890), for example, published various comparative notes on tales and some of these essays he gathered together in his volume *Zur Volkskunde* (1879). Perhaps the most famous and indefatigable annotater of folktales in the nineteenth century was Reinhold Köhler (1830–1892), the librarian of the Ducal Library in Weimar. Evidently, Köhler read every book of folktales he could lay his hands on, and he made note of which particular tales—or as modern folklorists would say, which tale types—were contained therein. Köhler published comparative notes on folktales in various philological and folkloristic periodicals. Many of these notes were later gathered and published in his *Aufsätze* (1894) and his *Kleinere Schriften* (1898–1900). Köhler's incredible erudition is perfectly obvious in those collections of folktales which he was asked to annotate. A classic case would be Laura Gonzenbach's *Sicilianische Märchen* (1870), for which Köhler provided elaborate comparative notes. These notes were deemed so valuable that more than twenty-five years later they were republished in the leading folklore journal in Germany (Köhler 1896). Köhler also compiled the notes for Bladé's *Contes populaires* (1874) among other folktale collections. In France there was another great nineteenth-century comparativist, namely French folklorist Emmanuel Cosquin (1841–1919), whose comparative notes to his two-volume anthology *Contes populaires de Lorraine* (1886) were equally impressive.

A direct result of the comparative research on European folktales begun by the Grimms and continued by Liebrecht, Köhler, and Cosquin was the appearance of the *Verzeichnis der Märchentypen*, the first tale type index, published in 1910 by Finnish folklorist Antti Aarne (and twice revised, 1928 and

1961, by American folklorist Stith Thompson) and the monumental five-volume set of comparative notes to the tales contained in the Grimm canon by folklorists Johannes Bolte and Georg Polivka. This major achievement of folkloristics scholarship, the *Anmerkungen zu den Kinder—u. Hausmärchen der Brüder Grimm* (Leipzig, 1913–1931), remains to this day the primary source of the comparative study of Indo-European folktales. Bolte and Polivka were able to build on the strong foundation provided by nineteenth-century comparativists such as Köhler and Cosquin. The comparative study of such tales culminated in the development of the so-called Finnish historic-geographic method, which began by assembling as many versions of a given tale type as possible. (For details of the Finnish method, see Krohn 1926, Korompay 1978, Goldberg 1984, and Honko 1985a and b.) Warren Roberts based his comparative study of Aarne-Thompson tale type 480 on more than 900 versons of the tale of "The Kind and the Unkind Girls."

The splendid achievements of European folklorists with respect to folktale studies have unfortunately not been duplicated outside of the Indo-European orbit. There is no published native American tale type index for North, Central, and South America; there is no published pan-African tale type index—despite periodical pleas or plans for such (Arewa 1967, Crowley 1970, Tucker 1980). What this means is that it is extremely difficult for the average anthropologist or Africanist to locate parallels (cognates) for any tales which might be collected in the field. Even though there are literally thousands of texts of African folktales in print (cf. Bascom 1964), one cannot expect a typical field anthropologist to wade through dozens of arcane missionary periodicals in various foreign languages searching for possible versions of particular tales.

The situation in African folk narrative scholarship is therefore more akin to that which prevailed in the latter part of the nineteenth century with respect to European folktales. There is a handful of collections of African folktales with modest comparative notes and several key doctoral dissertations which survey selected portions of the total African narrative corpus (cf. Klipple 1938, Clarke 1958, Arewa 1966, Lambrecht 1967, and Haring 1982; for the West Indies, see Flowers 1952).

Even though comparative folkloristics may have lagged in the study of African folk narrative, there has long been an interest in African folklore. This is demonstrated by a number of short survey articles which offered at least token coverage of African folktales (e.g., Stanley 1893, Ellis 1894, Werner 1896, Seidel 1896, Werner 1906 and 1914, up through Herskovits 1961 and Ben-Amos 1975a), but most of these have been superseded by Ruth Finnegan's comprehensive *Oral Literature in Africa*, which includes substantial discussion of prose narrative (1970:315–88). The only major criticism of Finnegan is her stubborn preference for the oxymoronic term "oral literature" over "folklore." "Literature" by both etymology and referent means "writing." Hence there can be no such thing as "oral literature." The very term reflects an unfortunate longstanding literary bias among would-be folklorists who make literature primary and folklore secondary—and often derivative from supposed elitist classical literary anthologies of folklore. Such is the case in India, for example.

Chronologically and logically, oral tradition has everywhere preceded written materials. Accordingly, it is literature which is derived from folklore, *not* the other way round. The leading French specialists in African folktale, Denise Paulme (1972, 1975, 1976, 1977a and b) and Geneviève Calame-Griaule (1970) also seem to spurn the term "folklore" in favor of "littérature orale."

A full-fledged history of African folktale research has yet to be written. In the meantime, one can find details of the nineteenth-century interest by British folklorists in African folk narrative (Dorson 1968:349–71) and indications of the extraordinary collections of narratives made by German nineteenth-century missionaries and colonial administrators (Finnegan 1970:32–34). Some of the earliest considerations of African folktales were made by missionaries who made no secret of their plans to find Christian morality in such tales (cf. Meinhof 1928).

The veritable plethora of publications containing African folk narratives is of such dimensions as to make the individual scholar dependent upon bibliographical aids (such as Scheub 1977 and Görög 1981—for the New World, Szwed and Abrahams 1978) and survey essays (e.g., Horálek 1972 and especially Bascom 1964).

A very positive development in the study of African folk narrative is that African scholars themselves are investigating their own oral traditions. No longer can African folklore scholarship be considered solely as the vestiges of a colonialist enterprise. For a listing of theses on folk narrative written at the University of Yaounde in Cameroon, see Tala 1984:98. See also the works of Mofokeng 1954, Camara 1978, Okpewho 1983, Okafor 1983, Ndong 1983, and N'Da 1984 as typical examples of Africans studying African folk narrative.

Some of the early interest in African folk narrative among American folklorists stemmed from a concern with the possible origins of African-American folktales. The scholarly debate about folktale origins had originally centered on the tales of Uncle Remus published by Joel Chandler Harris (cf. Crane, Ellis, Gerber, Dundes, Piersen, and especially Baer). Racist bias was unfortunately a factor in the arguments that ensued. Some "scholars" maintained that African-Americans were an "imitative" people and must have borrowed their tales from either native Americans or Euro-Americans (for details, see Dundes 1965).

For any given African-American folktale, whether it is or is not one of those included in the Uncle Remus canon, there is only a limited number of possibilities with respect to its origin: (1) The tale developed here in the New World and therefore would have no analogues in Africa, Europe, or native North America. (2) The tale is found in Africa and in the African diaspora but is not found in Europe or among American Indians. This would clearly be an African/African-American tale type (it is this kind of tale which is the subject of this volume). (3) The tale is found in Europe but is not found in Africa nor among American Indians. Such tales told by African-Americans would appear to be European tale types circulating in African-American oral tradition. (4) The tale is not found in Africa or in Europe but is found in native American tradition. Such a tale type would seem to be a native American tale which was borrowed by African-American taletellers.

One would be well advised to keep in mind that storytellers are not so concerned as folklorists with the origins of the tales they tell. For a storyteller, a good tale is a good tale and deserves telling for that reason. It is the folklorist, the academic, who is intellectually curious about where a particular tale may have come from. The point is that for such scholars there are empirical and often laborious means available to rule out and to ascertain possible if not probable paths of folktale diffusion.

Toward the last quarter of the twentieth century, the debate about the origins of African-American folktales was suddenly resuscitated. Two champions emerged to represent the opposing sides of the argument. Richard M. Dorson (1916–1981), director of the Folklore Institute at Indiana University and the leading American folklorist of his generation, maintained that African-American tales in the United States were almost entirely of European origin, while William R. Bascom (1912–1981), the senior anthropological folklorist and the acknowledged expert on African folklore in the world insisted that many African-American tales were demonstrably of African origin.

The two disputants knew one another well. Dorson, his three Harvard degrees (of which he was inordinately proud) notwithstanding, never felt he had been adequately trained for his chosen career in folklore and so in 1952, thanks to an ACLS Faculty Study Fellowship, he spent a postdoctoral year at Northwestern University to study with Melville J. Herskovits and Herskovits's prize pupil, William R. Bascom. Ever since the appearance of Herskovits's *The Myth of the Negro Past* in 1941, American scholars had come to realize the significance of the cultural retentions of the African diaspora in the New World, and this meant folklore. In Herskovits's words, "More attention has been paid to folklore than to any other aspect of New World Negro life" (1958:272). Northwestern University became an important center for such studies. Bascom, after becoming Herskovits's first doctorate in Anthropology in 1939, stayed on at Northwestern University as a faculty member until moving to a professorship at the University of California, Berkeley, in 1957, where he became director of the Lowie Museum of Anthropology. (For a useful overview of Bascom's distinguished career, see Ottenberg 1982.)

Dorson and Bascom had very different personalities. Dorson, a New Yorker, was much more argumentative and was never happier than when he was attacking someone for what he believed was sloppy scholarship or an error in folkloristics methodology. His enjoyment of intellectual disputes was evident in his great disappointment when no one criticized (or even bothered to comment upon) his 1959 paper "A Theory for American Folklore." The "theory" boiled down to the (reasonable) idea that American folklore could best be studied against the background of American history (Dorson's own background!). He was so upset that he eventually reviewed the theory himself in 1969. His delight in academic debates is also manifest in one of his most memorable contributions to the history of folkloristics, his witty summary of the often acrimonious Lang-Müller exchanges in "The Eclipse of Solar Mythology."

Bascom, in contrast, was born in the midwest and was a patient, gentle soul who basically disliked confrontation. He much preferred to let his data and his many writings speak for themselves. Many of the classic definitive statements about general folklore theory and method were penned by Bascom (cf. 1953, 1954, 1955, 1957, 1973b, 1977, 1983), but his very special interest within folkloristics was the folklore of Africa (cf. 1964, 1972, 1973a, 1975). Despite his dislike of conflict, Bascom ably defended himself against Dorson's "accusations" (one essay (1975) called Bascom "misguided"). The present volume essentially substantiates the position Bascom advocated all along, namely, that African tale types were to be found in the New World.

In some ways the argument resulted from the two protagonists talking past one another. Dorson claimed he was arguing for a European origin *only* for the folktales he personally had collected from African-American communities in Michigan and Arkansas, whereas Bascom was interested in the more general issue of African-American folktales in the New World, not just those tales in Dorson's collections. In any case, something very positive did result from the dispute: Bascom's series of essays on individual African tale types.

It was certainly the debate with Dorson about the origins of African-American folktales which prompted Bascom to look into the question of African and African-American folktale cognates more closely. For many years Bascom, like Köhler before him, had made an effort to see every new collection of African folktales that appeared, and he took careful notes on the contents of each such volume. The resulting index-card file constituted a virtual private tale type index of African folktales. As an Africanist Bascom was admittedly more concerned with African tales than with African-American tales per se, but as a result of the public disagreement with Dorson, his former student and longtime friend, he decided to widen his horizons to investigate African-American tale collections in addition to the African collections.

By the time of his retirement as director of the Lowie Museum of Anthropology and as Professor of Anthropology at Berkeley in 1979, he had already been working on his new ambitious project. He decided to settle the African versus European origins question once and for all and to settle it on the basis of empirical, irrefutable evidence. Accordingly he began to make an all-out search for parallels for a total of ninety-nine folktales. This was a formidable task. It is hard enough to search for parallels for a single folktale, but to search simultaneously for ninety-nine different folktales was an extraordinary enterprise. Yet he thoroughly enjoyed it all. It was like a combination scavenger hunt and quest for buried treasure. Each tale represented a separate challenge. However, since he was seeking so many parallels at the same time, he could hardly consult any collection of African or African-American folktales without finding some texts of interest.

As Bascom began to amass more and more evidence, he started to publish his findings in a remarkable series of essays from 1976 to 1982. Fortunately,

Bernth Lindfors, then editor of *Research in African Literatures,* immediately recognized the importance of Bascom's comparative research, and he gladly published these essays just as soon as he received them. Nonfolklorists or folklorists not familiar with African folklore may not fully appreciate the magnitude of Bascom's achievement. Locating fifty to a hundred versions of a tale may look easy after reading Bascom's essays, but in the context of comparative work in African folk narrative scholarship it is definitely not. Early survey essays concentrated upon comparing different animal tricksters in different parts of Africa (cf. Hattingh 1944–1945), although Alice Werner in the first decade of the twentieth century remarked that the story in which the hare induces the hyena and ostrich to sell their mothers is found all over Bantu Africa (1906–1907:80; cf. 1915:61). Later studies (e.g., Pelton 1980) concentrate on one particular narrative character such as the trickster. But the purely comparative studies of African folk narratives are extremely limited in number and scope. There is Abrahamsson's excellent comparative study of the origin of death myths in Africa, first published in 1951, Loots's 1961 unpublished doctoral dissertation in Afrikaans (a historic-geographic study of Aarne-Thompson tale type 275A, "Hare and Tortoise Race: Sleeping Hare"), Paulme's 1977 study of Aarne-Thompson tale type 175, "The Tarbaby and the Rabbit" (cf. Werner 1899), and Paulme and Bremond's 1980 disucssion of 61 African versions of Aarne-Thompson 291, "Deceptive Tug-of-War" (which confirms my 1965 contention that this tale is African, not European—and is very probably related to the African-American rhetorical technique of "signifying" to the extent that one trickster figure dupes two victims into fighting one another). Paulme and Bremond were apparently unaware that this same tale type had already been studied comparatively on the basis of some thirty-seven texts by Sophonia M. Mofokeng in her unpublished doctoral dissertation (1954:6–122). Mofokeng also carries out comparative investigations of Aarne-Thompson tale type 5, "Biting the Foot" (1954:123–241), and what she calls "The Stone Motif" (cf. Motif K 1035. Stone [hard fruit] thrown into greedy dupe's mouth) in the same dissertation (1954:242–84).

One of the reasons Professor Bascom enjoyed his retirement so much was that he was free to devote all his energies to a major project worthy of his particular expertise and experience. This freedom did not last. Just as he completed some twenty-two essays, he was advised to have elective surgery to repair a faulty heart valve, and sadly the complications which occurred following open-heart surgery led to his untimely death on September 11, 1981. (By some eerie coincidence, this was the same day that Richard M. Dorson died. He had suffered a heart attack followed by a long period of coma.) The encyclopedic knowledge of African folk narrative that William Bascom possessed went with him. The project came to an abrupt end to await a time when some new student of African and African-American folk narrative will take up the challenge.

It is a pity that Professor Bascom did not have an opportunity to revise his essays before publication in book form. He would almost certainly have

wanted to add references to the tales he considered. Whether it was a matter
of referring to just one more text of "The Talking Skull" (Cransac 1935,
Pradelles de Latour 1990) or whether it was a more substantive matter of
taking into account structural (Bremond 1977) or psychoanalytic (Krüger-
Kahloula 1984a and b) studies of "Inside Cow's Belly," Bascom's high personal
standards of scholarship would have required him to be as inclusive as humanly
possible.

For the same reason, he might have wished to consult some of the earlier
parallel research carried out by Brazilian folklorists. For example, Arthur
Ramos devoted one chapter of his book *O Folk-Lore Negro do Brasil* to
folktales with African origins (1935:159–92), and Gustavo Barroso wrote an
entire essay on the lucky shot that kills game through the animal's ear, head,
and foot, a tale which corresponds to Bascom's "Deer's Hoof and Ear" (Barroso
1927). Other scholars who matched individual Afro-Brazilian folktale texts
with African parallels included Rodrigues (1932:247–316), Carneiro (1937),
and Ribeiro (1939:41–56). Bascom was familiar with Latin American scholarship in Africanisms and in fact was very much inspired by the Cuban
researchers Lydia Cabrera (1972) and Fernando Ortiz (1951) as well as Brazilian
specialist Roger Bastide (1959), among others. Of course, there is a world of
difference between matching single folktale texts and the truly massive documentation provided by Bascom's studies of individual tale types. Some of
the tales Bascom considered had long been thought to be African in origin,
but guesses and assertions are one thing, and convincing empirical proof is
quite another.

I decided to entitle this volume *Africn Folktales in the New World* even
though Bascom says two of the twenty-two narratives discussed are myths
("Oba's Ear" and "Moon Splits Hare's Lip") rather than folktales. These two
"myths" were not included in Bascom's own series entitled "African Folktales
in America" (see Bascom 1965 for the standard articulation of the generic
differences among myth, folktale and legend.)

Bascom did not write a preface specifically for this volume, but in one of
the last public lectures he delivered, the Archer Taylor Memorial Lecture,
presented to members of the California Folklore Society on April 4, 1981, he
included a description of the project he was then engaged upon. After re-
marking that he seemed to have a propensity to take on ambitious long-term
scholarly enterprises, he also noted with well-deserved pride that he had
managed to complete most of them, specifically *Ifa Divination* in thirty-one
years (1938–1969) and *Sixteen Cowries* in twenty-nine years (1951–1980). Then
he observed "I have my teeth into another big project," referring to the research
then in progress. As the title of that lecture, "Perhaps Too Much to Chew?"
prophetically suggested, he did not live to see this last project through to
completion. The portion of that Memorial Lecture which described the project
has been borrowed to serve as an author's preface (Bascom 1981:289–92).
Bascom's own account of his project cannot be improved upon.

Now while it may be perfectly true that the emphasis in African folkloristics

as in folkloristics generally may be said to have moved away from considerations of texts to studies of context and performance; that is, the concern
is with process rather than product, with story*telling* rather than story (cf.
Finnegan 1967, Ben-Amos 1975b, Okpewho 1990), it is also true that texts
will never go out of style. Ultimately, the scholarly interest in storytelling
should lead to a better understanding of the content and function of stories.

In the same way, one might contend that the nineteenth-century quest for
origins has become somewhat passé, having yielded precedence to such
twentieth-century issues as structure, function, and meaning. Evidence to the
contrary is provided by a continuing steady stream of studies of African survivals or retentions in the New World (cf. Dalgish 1982, Thompson 1984, Elder
1988, and Holloway 1990).

The parallel texts so assiduously assembled by Bascom and then published
seriatim may strike those readers no longer involved with the comparative
method or the search for origins as old-fashioned research. Perhaps it is. Still,
this series of essays constitutes a truly major contribution to our knowledge
of African and African-American tale types. Until such time as we have
something comparable to a five-volume Bolte-Polivka series of notes on African tales or a comprehensive pan-African tale type index, this volume of
African folktale parallels will have to suffice. At the very least, it shows that
the concepts of type and motif, so central to folkloristics, do apply perfectly
well to African data. Moreover, folklore scholars still interested in texts—and
that should mean *all* bona fide folklorists—have reason to be eternally grateful
to William Bascom for his unequalled knack for locating, translating, and
summarizing hundreds of fascinating texts, many of which were well concealed
in the most obscure and recondite sources. Although it is terribly disappointing
that he was not able to complete his original plan to document the African
origins of an additional seventy tale types, folklorists, especially Africanists,
can take pride in the present volume, which does demonstrate the incontro-
vertible existence of nearly two dozen African tale types. This last lesson
taught by William Bascom has such ample and gratifying detail that the
African identity of these tales simply cannot be questioned.

R E F E R E N C E S

Abrahamsson, Hans
  1977 *The Origin of Death: Studies in African Mythology.* New York: Arno Press.
Arewa, E. Ojo
  1966 A Classification of the Folktales of the Northern East African Cattle Area by
       Types, unpublished doctoral dissertation in Anthropology, University of Cali-
       fornia, Berkeley. Published by Arno Press in 1980.

1967 On Devising a New Arrangement for African Tale Types. *Southern Folklore Quarterly* 31:262–73.

Baer, Florence E.
1980 *Sources and Analogues of the Uncle Remus Tales.* FFC 228. Helsinki: Academia Scientiarum Fennica.

Barroso, Gustavo
1927 *Atraves dos Folk-Lores.* São Paulo: Comp. Melhoramentos de S. Paulo.

Bascom, William
1953 Folklore and Anthropology. *Journal of American Folklore* 66:283–90.
1954 Four Functions of Folklore. *Journal of American Folklore* 67:333–49.
1955 Verbal Art. *Journal of American Folklore* 68:245–52.
1957 The Myth-Ritual Theory. *Journal of American Folklore* 70:103–114.
1964 Folklore Research in Africa. *Journal of American Folklore* 77:12–31.
1965 The Forms of Folklore: Prose Narratives. *Journal of American Folklore* 78:3–20.
1969 *Ifa Divination: Communication between Gods and Men in West Africa.* Bloomington: Indiana University Press.
1972 Cinderella in Africa. *Journal of the Folklore Institute* 9:54–70.
1973a Folklore and the Africanist. *Journal of American Folklore* 86:253–59.
1973b Folklore, Verbal Art, and Culture. *Journal of American Folklore* 86:374–81.
1975 *African Dilemma Tales.* The Hague: Mouton.
1977 Frontiers of Folklore: An Introduction. In William R. Bascom, ed., *Frontiers of Folklore,* American Association for the Advancement of Science Selected Symposium 5. Boulder: Westview Press. Pp. 1–16.
1980 *Sixteen Cowries. Yoruba Divination from Africa to the New World.* Bloomington: Indiana University Press.
1981 Perhaps Too Much to Chew? *Western Folklore* 40:285–98.
1983 Malinowski's Contributions to the Study of Folklore. *Folklore* 94:163–72.

Bastide, Roger
1959 *Sociologia do folclore brasileiro.* São Paulo: Ed. Anhembi.

Ben-Amos, Dan
1975a Folklore in African Society. *Research in African Literatures* 6:165–98.
1975b *Sweet Words: Storytelling Events in Benin.* Philadelphia: Institute for the Study of Human Issues.

Bladé, Jean-François
1874 *Contes populaires recueillis en Agenais.* Paris: J. Baer.

Bremond, Claude
1977 The Clandestine Ox: The Transformation of an African Tale. *New Literary History* 8:393–410.

Cabrera, Lydia
1972 *Cuentos negros de Cuba.* 2nd ed. Madrid: Ramos, Art. Graf.

Calame-Griaule, Geneviève
1970 Pour une étude ethnolinguistique des littératures orales africaines. *Langages* 18: 22–47.

Camara, Sory
1978 Tales in the Night: Toward an Anthropology of the Imaginary. In Alan Dundes, ed., *Varia Folklorica.* The Hague: Mouton, Pp. 91–121.

Carneiro, (Antonio Joaquim) Souza
1937 *Os mitos africanos no Brasil.* São Paulo: Companhia Editora Nacional.

Clarke, Kenneth W.
1958 A Motif Index of the Folktales of Culture Area V West Africa. Unpublished doctoral dissertation in folklore, Indiana University.

Cosquin, Emmanuel Georges
1886 *Contes populaires de Lorraine,* comparés avec les contes des autres provinces de France at des pays étrangers. 2 vols. Paris: F. Vieweg.

Crane, T. F.
   1880–1881 Plantation Folk-Lore. *Popular Science Monthly* 18:824–33.
Cransac, G.
   1935 Légende de la tête qui parle: conte du pays Bornuan. *Bulletin de la Société des Recherches Congolaises* 21:111–16.
Crowley, Daniel J.
   1962 Negro Folklore; An Africanist's View. *Texas Quarterly* 5:65–71.
   1970 A Tale Type Index for Africa. *Research in African Literatures* 1:50–52.
   1977 *African Folklore in the New World.* Austin: University of Texas Press.
Dalgish, Gerard M.
   1982 *A Dictionary of Africanisms: Contributions of Sub-Saharan Africa to the English Language.* Westport, Conn.: Greenwood Press.
Dorson, Richard M.
   1955 The Eclipse of Solar Mythology. *Journal of American Folklore* 68:394–416.
   1959 A Theory for American Folklore. *Journal of American Folklore* 72:197–215.
   1968 *The British Folklorists: A History.* Chicago: University of Chicago Press.
   1969 A Theory for American Folklore Reviewed. *Journal of American Folklore* 82:226–44.
   1972 Africa and the Folklorist. In Richard M. Dorson, ed., *African Folklore.* Garden City: Anchor. Pp. 3–67.
   1975 African and Afro-American Folklore: A Reply to Bascom and Other Misguided Critics. *Journal of American Folklore* 88:151–64.
   1977 The African Connection: Comments on 'African Folklore in the New World' *Research in African Literatures* 8:260–65.
Dundes, Alan
   1965 African Tales among the North American Indians. *Southern Folklore Quarterly* 29:207–19.
   1971 The Making and Breaking of Friendship as a Structural Frame in African Folk Tales. In Pierre Maranda and Elli Köngäs Maranda, eds., *Structural Analysis of Oral Tradition.* Philadelphia: University of Pennsylvania Press. Pp. 171–85.
   1976 African and Afro-American Tales. *Research in African Literatures* 7:181–99.
Elder, J. D.
   1988 *African Survivals in Trinidad and Tobago.* London: Karia Press.
Ellis, A. B.
   1894 West African Folk-Lore. *Popular Science Monthly* 45:771–83.
   1895–1896 Evolution in Folklore: Some West African Prototypes of the Uncle Remus Stories. *Popular Science Monthly* 48:93–104.
Finnegan, Ruth
   1967 *Limba Stories and Story-Telling.* Oxford: Clarendon Press.
   1970 *Oral Literature in Africa.* Oxford: Clarendon Press.
Flowers, Helen Leneva
   1952 A Classification of the Folktale of the West Indies by Types and Motifs. Unpublished doctoral dissertation, Indiana University.
Gerber, A.
   1893 Uncle Remus Traced to the Old World. *Journal of American Folklore* 6:245–57.
Goldberg, Christine
   1984 The Historic-Geographic Method: Past and Future. *Journal of Folklore Research* 21:1–18.
Gonzenbach, Laura
   1870 *Sicilianische Märchen.* 2 Vols. Leipzig: W. Englemann.
Görög, Veronika
   1981 *Littérature oracle d'Afrique noire: Bibliographie analytique.* Paris: G.-P Maisonneuve et Larose.

Haring, Lee
1982 *Malagasy Tale Index.* FFC 231. Helsinki: Academia Scientiarum Fennica.
Hattingh, S. C.
1944–1945 Die Teerpopsprokie in Afrika. *Tydskrif vir Volkskunde en Volkstaal* 1:13–19.
Herskovits, Melville J.
1958 *The Myth of the Negro Past.* Boston: Beacon Press.
Holloway, Joseph E., ed.,
1990 *Africanisms in American Culture.* Bloomington: Indiana University Press.
Honko, Lauri
1985a Zur Quellengeschichte der finnischen Erzählforschung. *Fabula* 26: 104–123.
1985b Zielsetzung und Methoden der finnischen Erzählforschung. *Fabula* 26:318–35.
Horálek, K.
1972 Afrikanische Märchen in neuen Übertragungen. *Fabula* 13:167–80
Kipury, Naomi
1983 *Oral Literature of the Maasai.* Nairobi: Heinemann Educational Books.
Klipple, May Augusta
1938 African Folktales with Foreign Analogues, unpublished doctoral dissertaion in English, Indiana University.
Köhler, Reinhold
1894 *Aufsätze über märchen und volkslieder.* Johannes Bolte and Erich Schmidt, eds. Berlin: Weidmann.
1896 Zu den von Laura Gonzenbach gesammelten sicilianischen Märchen. *Zeitschrift für Volkskunde* 6:58–78, 161–75.
1898–1900 *Kleinere Schriften.* 3 Vols. Johannes Bolte, ed., Weimar: E. Felber.
Korompay, Bertalan
1978 *Zur Finnischen Methode: Gedanken eines Zeitgenossen.* Helsinki.
Krohn, Kaarle
1926 *Die folkloristische Arbeitsmethode.* Oslo: Instituttet for sammenlignende kulturforskning. Published in English translation as *Folklore Methodology.* Austin: University of Texas Press, 1971.
Krüger-Kahloula, Angelika
1984a *Die List des Schwacheren: Motivgeschichte und Anthropologie der Afro-Amerikanischen Erzahltradition.* Frankfurt: Campus.
1984b The Sad Fate of Mr. Fox in the Cow's Belly: Stability and Transformation in an Afro-American Folktale. *Cahiers de Littérature Orale* 14:97–124.
Lambrecht, Winifred
1967 A Tale Type Index for Central Africa. Unpublished doctoral dissertation in Anthropology, University of California, Berkeley.
Liebrecht, Felix
1879 *Zur Volkskunde.* Heilbronn: Henninger.
Lindfors, Bernth
1970 Approaches to Folktale in African Literature. *The Conch* 2(2):102–111.
Loots, W. J. G.
1961 Die Herkoms, ontwikkeling en verspreiding van die reisiesverhale. 2 Vols. Unpublished doctoral dissertation, University of Witwatersrand.
Meinhof, Carl
1928 Afrikanische Volkskunde in ihrer Bedeutung für uns. *Niederdeutsche Zeitschrift für Volkskunde* 6:65–69.
Mofokeng, Sophonia M.
1954 The Development of Leading Figures in Animal Tales in Africa. Unpublished doctoral dissertation, University of Witwatersrand.
N'Da, Pierre
1984 *Le conte Africain et l'education.* Paris: Editions l'Harmattan.

Ndong, Norbert
1983 *Kamerunische Märchen: Text und Kontext in ethnosoziologischer und psychologischer Sicht.* Artes Populares Studia Ethnographica et Folkloristica 8. Frankfurt am Main: Verlag Peter Lang.
Okafor, Clement Abiaziem
1983 *The Banished Child: A Study in Tonga Oral Literature.* London: The Folklore Society.
Okpewho, Isidore
1983 *Myth in Africa.* Cambridge: Cambridge University Press.
1990 *The Oral Performance in Africa.* Ibadan: Spectrum Books Limited.
Ortiz, Fernando
1951 *Los Bailes y el Teatro de los Negros en el Folklore de Cuba.* Habana: Ediciones Cardenas.
Ottenberg, Simon
1982 The Anthropology of William R. Bascom. In Simon Ottenberg, ed., *African Religious Groups and Beliefs: Papers in Honor of William R. Bascom.* Meerut: Archana Publications. Pp. 3–14.
Paulme, Denise
1972 Morphologie du conte Africain. *Cahiers d'études Africaines* 12:131–63.
1975 Typologie des contes Africaines du decepteur. *Cahiers d'etudes Africaines* 15:569–600.
1976 *La mère dévorante: Essai sur la morphologie des contes africains.* Paris: Gallimard.
1977a The Impossible Imitation in African Trickster Tales. In Bernth Lindfors, ed., *Forms of Folklore in Africa.* Austin: University of Texas Press. Pp. 64–103.
1977b Le puits des animaux ou La main prise. *Cahiers de littérature orale* 2:60–102.
Paulme, Denise, and Claude Bremond
1980 Le conte du 'Jeu de la corde' et la ruse de la 'peau pourrie' en Afrique Noire. *Cahiers de littérature orale* 8:49–77.
Pelton, Robert D.
1980 *The Trickster in West Africa: A Study of Mythic Irony and Sacred Delight.* Berkeley and Los Angeles: University of California Press.
Piersen, William D.
1971 An African Background for American Negro Folktales. *Journal of American Folklore* 84:204–14.
Pradelles de Latour, Charles Henry
1990 "Le Crâne qui parle", ou la réversibilité de la parole. In Veronika Görög-Karady, ed., *D'un Conte . . . à l'autre.* Paris: Centre National de la Recherches Scientifique. Pp. 563–72.
Ramos, Arthur
1935 *O Folk-Lore Negro do Brasil: Demopsychologia e Psychanalyse.* Rio de Janeiro: Civilização Brasileira.
Rattray, R. S.
1928 Some Aspects of West African Folk-Lore. *Journal of the Africa Society* 28:1–11.
Ribeiro, João
1939 *O Elemento Negro: Historia—Folklore—Linguistica.* Rio de Janeiro: Record.
Roberts, Warren E.
1958 *The Tale of the Kind and the Unkind Girls: AA-Th 480 and Related Tales.* Berlin: Walter De Gruyter and Co.
Rodrigues, (Raymundo) Nina
1932 *Os africanos no Brasil.* São Paulo: Companhia Editora Nacional.
Scheub, Harold
1977 *African Oral Narratives, Proverbs, Riddles, Poetry and Song.* Boston: G. K. Hall.

Seidel, A.

  1896 Die volksliteratur der Afrikaner. *Aus Allen Weltteilen* 27:347–54, 409–414.

Stanley, Henry M.

  1893 African Legends. *Fortnightly Review* 53:797–828.

Szwed, John F., and Roger D. Abrahams

  1978 *Afro-American Folk Culture: An Annotated Bibliography of Materials from
       North, Central and South America and the West Indies.* 2 Vols. Philadelphia:
       Institute for the Study of Human Issues.

Tala, Kashim Ibrahim

  1984 *An Introduction to Cameroon Oral Literature.* Yaounde.

Thomspon, Robert Farris

  1984 *Flash of the Spirit: African and Afro-American Art and Philosophy.* New York:
       Vintage.

Tucker, Elizabeth

  1980 Toward a Computerized Type Index for African Tales: Some Theoretical Con-
       siderations. *Research in African Literatures* 11:356–67.

Werner, Alice

  1896 African Folklore. *Contemporary Review* 70:377–90.

  1899 The tar-baby story. *Folklore* 10:282–93.

  1906–1907 Language and Folklore in West Africa. *Journal of the African Society* 6:
       65–83.

  1914 Some Notes on East African Folklore. *Folklore* 25:457–75.

  1915 Some Notes on East African Folklore. *Folklore* 26:60–78.

A C K N O W L E D G M E N T S

✳

My thanks to Bernth Lindfors for first proposing this volume and to Berta Bascom for her continued encouragement and support, the same encouragement and support which made it possible for every William Bascom project to make its way into print.

P R E F A C E

✳

My new project, another apparently endless one, is a series of articles on "African Folktales in America" that is appearing in *Research in African Literatures* (Austin, University of Texas Press). I became interested in this project when I read Richard M. Dorson's statement that African motifs are rare in the United States, even in Joel Chandler Harris's Uncle Remus tales.

In 1880 Harris challenged J. W. Powell's claim that some of the Uncle Remus tales were borrowed from North American Indians. Harris agreed with H. H. Smith who a year earlier had said, "One thing is certain. The animal stories told by the negroes in our Southern States and in Brazil were brought by them from Africa."

As a student of Herskovits I had thought that this century-old debate had been settled long ago. But Dorson says that in his own collection of over one thousand Negro narratives, primarily from Michigan and Arkansas, there is only one motif that surely came from Africa. Not even one tale type or even one folktale! And while he says that it "comes straight from West Africa," he adds, "But this case is exceptional." However, "The Talking Skull Refuses to Talk," as I call it, which formed the basis of my first article[1] in this series, is a folktale and a tale type.

I began this project with very little knowledge of Afro-American folktales, but in this first article I said, "I believe that I can show that more than twenty folktales must have come to the United States from Africa rather than from Europe." I now think that the number will exceed fifty. In fact, I am currently examining ninety tale types. Some of these will probably have to be eliminated for one reason or another, but others may be added. A number of them are found in the Uncle Remus tales and in Dorson's own collection.

Fortunately I did have some familiarity with the literature on African folktales. This grew out of my search for parallels to the verses of Ifa and Sixteen Cowries divination, my article on "Folklore Research in Africa"[2] and my book on *African Dilemma Tales.*[3] But there is a large, scattered, and growing number of published African folktales that have to be reexamined. I have made only a beginning with these African folktales.

The literature on Afro-American folktales in the United States is far less extensive, but I decided to include all of the Americas. This is because the existence of the same tale types in other areas to which African slaves were transported, such as the Antilles, adds weight to the argument for the African sources of tale types in the United States. I am confining my interest to tale types and excluding simple motifs.

There are, in addition, many tale types from Africa that are known in the Americas only outside of the United States, but I am only incidentally interested in them and Dorson agrees that many of them came from Africa. The point at issue is whether folktales found in the United States came here from Europe or from Africa.

My method is simple. I search the literature for folktales that have been recorded in Africa and in the United States. I then look for them in Aarne and Thompson's *The Types of the Folktale* and in the six volumes of Thompson's *Motif-Index of Folk-Literature*. If I do not find such a tale type in either of these two indexes, which provide good coverage of Indo-European folktales, I conclude that it could not have come from Europe and must have come from Africa. If European analogues do, in fact, exist, the burden of proof rests on those who maintain that the source is not Africa.

I am not concerned with ultimate origins. Indeed my method is of no help with tale types that are found both in India and in Africa and could have originated in either continent. However, where there are only African and American versions, and no European or Indian analogues are cited in these indexes, the tales probably did originate in Africa.

This is purely a library research project, but it is based on the field recordings of many scholars. Some students and colleagues have seen it as a personal attack on Richard M. Dorson, but it is not. I see it as a possible way of helping to end the century-old debate about the African sources of American folktales. The evidence has been sitting on library shelves, waiting to be analyzed. It is a challenge that I have not been able to resist.

Fifty, or even a hundred tale types from Africa do not represent a majority of the folktales in the repertoire of the Negroes of the United States. This repertoire includes folktales that originated here as well as others that came from Europe. In addition there are large numbers of folktales that are known in Europe as well as in Africa and the United States. Again my method is of no help with these tales which could have come from Europe, or from Africa, or from both continents. But if fifty tale types must have come from Africa instead of only one, the chance that these tales also came from Africa is increased fifty-fold.

Moreover these African folktales in the United States are not confined to blacks. They are found in collections of Anglo-American, Hispanic-American, Franco-American, and American Indian folktales as well, and the same is true in other parts of the New World. For this study to be complete, every folktale recorded in Africa, North and South America, the Antilles, and the African Islands should be examined, truly an endless task. Fortunately, however, it is not necessary to cite every African or American example of a particular folktale to make my point.

It is not easy to answer the question, "How do you know that these folktales were not carried from America to Africa?" I rest my case on two factors:

first, the fact that the population movement was predominantly in the opposite direction because of the slave trade, and second, because of the distribution of the tales on both sides of the Atlantic ocean. For example, I have found twenty versions of "Inside Elephant's Belly" in Africa, from Sierra Leone in the west to Gabon and Mauritius in the east. The seven United States versions come from the Cape Verde Islanders of New England and five southern states. The thirty-eight Antilles versions come from the Bahamas in the north to Trinidad in the south. The distribution in the Americas is easily accounted for by the slave trade; but how can American contacts with Africa account for the distribution in that continent? Moreover if this tale type originated in America, why is it found only among immigrants from African islands and in these five southern states?

I have no way of knowing how many of these folktales are still current in the United States. Several were published as recently as 1978 in Daryl Cumber Dance's *Shuckin' and Jivin'*, including "The Talking Skull Refuses to Talk," but others undoubtedly are no longer told. In any event they constitute a contribution to our national heritage because they have been preserved in books by Joel Chandler Harris, Elsie Clews Parsons, Alcée Fortier, Richard M. Dorson, and others. I believe that it is important, not only for folklorists and Afro-Americans, but for all Americans and for Africans to recognize the African contribution to American folklore.

N O T E S

1. William Bascom, "African Folktales in America: 1. The Talking Skull Refuses to Talk," *Research in African Literatures*, 8 (1977), 266–91.
2. William Bascom, "Folklore Research in Africa," *Journal of American Folklore*, 77 (1964), 12–31.
3. William Bascom, *African Dilemma Tales* (The Hague, 1975).

*A*frican
*F*olktales in
THE
*N*ew *W*orld

O N E

✳

Ọba's Ear: A Yoruba Myth in Cuba and Brazil

As my professor, the late Melville J. Herskovits, emphasized, Afro-American studies can shed light on Africa. The myth of Ọba's ear is a case in point. The myth itself began with the Yoruba people in Nigeria, but my encounter with it began in Cuba.

This is not a folktale, told as fiction—not an Uncle Remus tale. It is a sacred Yoruba myth, told as fact, about a Yoruba goddess who is still worshipped in Cuba and Brazil. The principal points that I wish to make are that this Yoruba myth has survived in the Americas in readily recognizable form, and that it could only have originated among the Yoruba of West Africa.

Perhaps I should preface this article by stating that I have no intention of disparaging Yoruba religion. The Yoruba, French, Spanish, and Portuguese texts are available for anyone to see, and I have translated them as accurately as I can. The two final Yoruba texts, in particular, were tape-recorded and then transcribed and translated by Yoruba men, and they provoked gales of laughter from Yoruba listeners.

In Havana in 1947, Berta, my wife, first heard the Yoruba myth of how Ọba cut off her own ear (Aarne-Thompson O). Ọba was cooking yam porridge (*amalá*), the favorite food of her husband, Shango. She was stirring and stirring it, when Oshun came to her house. Oshun asked, "What are you cooking?" "Yam porridge for Shango." Oshun said, "It will please him more if it has one of your ears." So Ọba cut off her ear and cooked it in the porridge. When Shango ate it, he got his real strength. Ọba took off her kerchief and showed him that she had cut off her ear because she loved him so much. Shango got mad and left her. He went to live with Oshun, which is what Oshun wanted. This is why Ọba covers her left ear with her hand when she dances.

Shango is a Yoruba God of Thunder, and the two women are goddesses of the River Oshun, which flows past Oshogbo, Nigeria, and the River Ọba,

Reprinted from *Research in African Literatures*, 7 (1976), 149–65.

which is a tributary of the River Oshun that flows past Ogbomosho. Oya, who appears in other versions of this myth, is goddess of the River Oya, which is the River Niger. In Yoruba belief, all three goddesses were wives of Shango.

In 1948 when we went together to Cuba, half a dozen informants told us this myth in fragmentary form. A composite of these accounts would go as follows. Shango was the lover of Oshun, but the husband of Oba, and Oya was trying to take him away from Oba. Shango did not like Oba's cooking, but Oya was a very good cook. She told Oba to cut off an ear and cook it with okra stew (quimbombo) for Shango. Oba did so in order to keep Shango at home, and she covered the wound so that Shango would not see that her ear was missing. But Shango saw the ear in his stew and was angry, and never wanted Oba again. She left in shame, and he took Oya as his wife.

Only two of the six informants mentioned who advised Oba to cut off her ear; both named Oya. In one of the versions, Oshun was said to be Shango's senior wife and Oba was his junior wife. A seventh informant told a quite different myth in which Oya cut off Oba's ear when the two women were fighting.

Two more complete versions from Cuba have been published by Lydia Cabrera.[1] Changó had three wives, Obba, Oshún, and Oyá. Obba was the first of the three wives—the senior wife, the legitimate wife, and the respected wife. Her jealousy and the perfidious advice of Oshún, according to some, or Oyá, according to others, condemned her to live apart from her husband, who held her in great esteem, but who stopped living with her in marriage because she gave him her ear to eat.

Obba hoped that Changó would be faithful. One day she complained to Oshún that he did not spend much time with her. Oshún asked, "Do you want Changó to remain quietly at home?" "How much I would like that!" "Well then, cut off an ear, make okra stew (cararú) with yam porridge (amalá) and your ear, and give it to Changó to eat. When he swallows it and has it inside of him, he will love you much more." And Obba cut off an ear, made okra stew, and called Changó.

Changó was with Oyá. "Do you hear? Obba is calling me. I am going." Upset, Oyá said, "She is your favorite!" "She is my wife, I respect her." Obba had set the table. "Eat." Obba had her head covered with a white kerchief. "What's the matter, Obba? Why aren't you eating?" "I have no appetite." "Why are you sad?" "I never see you."

Changó finished and left. He went to see Oshún who told him, "Is it possible that a man as elegant as you are is not ashamed to live with a woman with a physical defect?" "What woman?" "Obba." And all was revealed. Changó tore off the white cloth with which she had covered her head and saw that she was lacking an ear. "What have you done, Obba! I will not abandon you, you are my senior wife; but as you have mutilated yourself, I will not live in your house any more."

The narrative continues with an episode in which Obba is confused with

Oyá, and ends with the following: when Obba dances, she dances holding her hands to her head, concealing her ears. Cabrera's second version follows.

When Yemayá (Yemoja, Shangó's mother) was talking with Obba, she told her what a glutton Changó was, and the quantities of corn meal and okra stew that had to be cooked for him. They were married, but Changó abandoned her. He left and spent many days away from home. Changó didn't want anything but drumming (*batá*) and feasting. In one of his absences, Elegguá (Ẹlẹgba, Eshu) told Obba to give a feast; he looked for Changó and took him to the drumming that Obba prepared.

Oyá went to look for him to take him from the feast, but Changó was having a good time; he showed Oyá the head of a ram, and she fled in fright. As a sacrifice, and to "tie" Changó to her, Obba cut off her ear and put it in the okra stew (*quimbombó*). But Changó saw the ear floating in the stew, and he left. Then Obatalá covered Obba's head with a white kerchief, which she never takes off. These two goddesses were enemies from then on. Obba, who adores Changó, has never pardoned Oyá, who was the one who advised her about the ear. She lives apart, hiding her missing ear. Very respected, she takes care of her husband's house (*ilé*). But the sweetheart, the official concubine of the God of Thunder, is as jealous as his wife, Obba.

A somewhat different Cuban version was published by Lachatañeré.[2] Oba was the legitimate wife of Shangó, in charge of domestic affairs. She accompanied him on all his military expeditions in order to take care of his diet, which consisted of *amala* (corn meal with *quimbombó* and ram meat). One day Shangó went to a war that lasted a very long time. It was the war that he had with Ogún. Oba, as usual, followed her husband with the provisions.

The war was prolonged and, when he had the opportunity, Shangó went to Oba to regain his strength with the *amala*. With surpassing care, Oba employed her culinary art to satisfy the immeasurable appetite of her husband. But the battle continued. It continued so long that provisions became scarce, and it was increasingly difficult for Oba to find the ingredients of *amala*. But Oba multiplied her efforts. She sharpened her wits, and Shangó was never lacking for *amala*. But the day came when her efforts were in vain. Her cleverness failed. Oba could not find any ram meat to add to the *amala*. But, being a woman of great strength, Oba did not yield to misfortune. This time the corn meal was bubbling in the pot without meat, and Oba had the strength to cut off her two ears and add them to the pot. Thus Oba, who was a very beautiful woman, ceased being beautiful, and her spirits failed. She locked herself in her room and cried. "Ah, I am a repugnant woman without ears. Ah, I am the wife who has stopped being beautiful." That same day Shangó arrived with an erection and claimed his wife. "Oba, I have won the war. Come and share the victory with your husband." Oba remained silent. Beside himself, Shangó demanded the immediate presence of his wife, but Oba remained silent. Furious, the warrior went to search for her and found her stretched on the floor; he tried to pick her up, and found that she was lacking both ears. "Ah, wife, without *etí* (ears), I do not love you any more," exclaimed

Shangó, and he fled from the place. In a little while Oba recovered and ran through the plains howling. "Ah, I am a woman without ears. Ah, I am a woman who has stopped being beautiful." And she went into the woods, always with the same lament. Oba shed so many tears that she turned into a river.

In Brazil the myth of Qba's ear was first reported in 1937 by Edison Carneiro, but with Qba confused with Qya.[3] I have not been able to see this early account,[4] but, as Roger Bastide notes, the error is corrected in a subsequent publication.[5] Óbá does not have one ear. She was a wife of Xangô, less loved than the others, and she believed the words of the favorite wife, Yansā (Qya), who told her that she had to cut off her ear to win the affection of Xangô. In dancing she conceals her left ear with her copper shield, with leaves, or simply with her hand.

According to another Brazilian version published by Pierre Verger,[6] Shango had many wives, and he spent his days and nights with them in turn; but he especially loved Oshoun, who knew how to please him with her kindness and voluptuousness. Pretty and coquettish, she used all the weapons of a woman to keep a man. This was not without exciting the jealousy of her co-wives, and Oba, less favored, came one day to ask her what was the secret that assured her the favors of their husband, Shango. Oshoun explained that the way to a man's heart is his stomach, and that her secret was to serve him his favorite food. Not without malice, she added that as a good co-wife she would show Oba how to prepare a certain soup at which Shango marveled, and she invited her to return a few hours later.

Oba returned at the appointed time. Oshoun had tied a cloth around her head that concealed her ears, and she had cooked a soup in which two mushrooms were floating. Oshoun showed them to Oba, telling her that they were her ears, which she had cut off and put into the pot; she added that Shango would be enchanted with it. Soon Shango arrived, ate the soup, found it excellent, and went to bed with Oshoun. Some days later the time came for Oba to take care of Shango. She followed the advice of Oshoun, cut off an ear, and cooked it in a soup for Shango. He showed no pleasure in seeing Oba disfigured and covered with blood, and he found the dish that she served repugnant.

At that moment Oshoun appeared, having removed the cloth from her head; her ears were intact, and she began to mock Oba. Furious, Oba threw herself at her rival, and a battle ensued. Shango flew into a rage, shot fire from his mouth, and thundered at his wives, who fled in fright and turned themselves into the two rivers that bear their names today. One must never mention the name of Oba when crossing the River Oshoun, lest she drown you immediately. Similarly, one must not speak of Oshoun when crossing the river Oba. These two rivers flow into each other, and at their confluence the waters are extremely agitated and beat furiously against each other in remembrance of their past adventure.

A third Brazilian version has been published by Roger Bastide.[7] Xangô had three wives, Yansan (Ọya), Oxun (Ọshun), and Obá, but Oxun was the favorite wife and Obá the abandoned one. The unhappy goddess (*orixa*), not knowing how to win the affection of her husband, one day asked Oxun how she was able to share Xangô's bed so easily. Malicious Oxun told her that she had a medicine, and, concealing her head in a cloth so that Obá could not see her lie, she said that she had cut off her ear to cook it in Xangô's okra stew (*cararú*). By eating it, he had made an unending erotic alliance with her. Then Obá cut off her ear and cooked it in her husband's food; but Xangô had hardly taken a bite of his stew when he rejected it in disgust and had Obá called to learn what she had put in the dish to make it so bad. Obá came, disfigured and bleeding, all in tears. Xangô exploded in anger. He sent his third wife away, having become too ugly to arouse his desire. When Obá manifests herself in the *candomblés* of Bahia, which is only rarely, she covers her left ear with leaves, or she conceals her head under a colored cloth.

Cuban and Brazilian versions of the myth are cited briefly in Bascom.[8]

Not having heard this myth in Nigeria, I enquired about it when I returned there with Mrs. Bascom in 1950-51, before the versions of Cabrera, Verger, and Bastide had been published. As in Cuba and Brazil, there are apparently not many worshipers of Ọba in Nigeria, but I did find three informants who knew the myth about her ear. A Shango (*Sàngó*) worshiper in the town of Mẹko said that Ọya, Ọshun, and Ọba (*Ọya, Õsun, and Ọbà*) were the three wives of Shango. Ọba was the one who cut off her ear to make stew when Ọya told her to do so, and Shango drove her away.

A priest of Ọba in Ọyọ said that Ọba, Ọshun, and Ọya were all wives of Shango. Ọba was the senior wife, but Shango loved Ọya, his junior wife, more than he loved Ọba. Ọya told Ọba to cut off her ear and cook it in okra stew (*ọbè ilá*) so that Shango would love Ọba as much as he loved her. Ọba cut off part of her left ear, and when Shango found it in his stew he drove her away, saying that he would have nothing more to do with her. In possession Ọba dances with her hand over her left ear, and he himself also dances in that fashion. The River Ọba rises near the village of Igbọn, where she was born and where she became a deity, but her principal place of worship is Ogbomọshọ.

At Ogbomọshọ the priest of Ọba confirmed that Igbọn, on the road to Ilorin (about ten miles from Ogbomọshọ), where Ọba became a deity and turned into the River Ọba, is near the river's source, and that since the wars of the last century Ogbomọshọ has been her principal place of worship. He said that Ọba and Ọya were wives of Shango, but Ọba left him and married Ajagún at Igbọn. One of Ọba's praise names is "Ọba, who owns (red) parrot tail feathers and who fights on the left side" (*Ọba eleko a ja osi*). He confirmed that Ọba covers one ear with her hand in possession, but he said that he did not know why; and when told the myth, he said that he did not know it.

As told by Ọshun worshipers at Ilesha, it was Ọshun who caused Ọba to cut off her ear. Ọba was the senior wife of Shango, and when Shango married Ọshun, Ọba did all the housework for her, as Yoruba women do for seven days to show respect for the new wife. Ọba made the fire, cooked the food, swept the floor, and so on. One day Ọba asked Oshun to do something, and Oshun answered that Ọba could not ask her to do anything. One day Ọba asked Oshun why Shango loved her more than herself. Oshun had put blood from a pigeon on her ear and had wrapped her head in a headtie. She told Ọba that when she cooked bean stew (gbẹgiri) for Shango she cut off a piece of her ear and put it in the stew. So Ọba cut a piece of her ear and put it in Shango's stew, and Shango saw it. Ọba told him how his junior wife had said that he liked stew that way, but Shango drove Ọba away. Ọba and Oshun are still enemies, and if a person takes water from the River Ọba and puts it into the River Oshun, they will meet great trouble.

A version recorded at Oshogbo, Nigeria, by Pierre Verger[9] says that Ṣango had three wives, Ọya, Ọsun, and Ọba. Ọsun made very good food for Ṣango, and he loved her very much. One day she played a bad trick on Ọba, who always sought to obtain cooking secrets that would assure her Ṣango's love. Ọsun put a large flat mushroom in the shape of an ear in the soup for Ṣango, and he went into ecstasies over the excellence of the meal. Ọba went to find Ọsun and found her with a kerchief tied over her head, concealing her ears; she asked what Ọsun had done to prepare such a good dish. Ọsun replied that she had cut off her ears and had put them in the soup. Desiring to enter into Ṣango's good graces, when her turn came to make the food, Ọba cut off an ear and cooked it in the soup. Ṣango found the ear in his dish and cried, "What is this? I can't eat that!" and flew into a rage. When Ọsun removed the kerchief tied over her head and showed Ọba her two ears intact, Ọba was furious and started to beat her. Ọsun became a river, and Ọba became another river. At the place where they meet, the water is always agitated. If one crosses one of the rivers, one must not mention the name of the other on pain of drowning. And whence the saying, Ọba ma bọsun, "You cannot sacrifice to Ọba and Ọsun at the same time." (I would translate this as "Ọba does not sacrifice to Oshun.")

There is also a Yoruba proverb that says, "We don't give the child of Ọba to Oshun" (A ki gbe ọmọ Ọba fun Ọsun).

A second Yoruba version recorded by Verger[10] at Ouidah in Dahomey says that Ṣango had three wives, Ọya, Ọsun, and Ọba. Ọsun and Ọba were always fighting. One day Ọba was with Ṣango while Ọsun was doing the cooking. Ọba told Ọsun that it was the wish of Ṣango that his food be cooked on a fire made with banana trunks; the fire could not be lit, and when Ṣango returned his meal was not ready. Ṣango was angry. Later it was the turn of Ọsun to be with Ṣango. In revenge she told Ọba that it was the wish of Ṣango that Ọba's ear be used in preparing his food. When Ṣango returned, he again became angry and fought the jealous wives.

A Yoruba version of the myth reported by Harold Courlander does not mention Ọba.[11] Shango had many wives, including Oya and Oshun. Oya was a good cook, but Oshun's cooking did not please Shango at all, and Oya envied Oshun's beauty. The day of the annual festival was approaching, and as usual Shango would provide a feast. He appointed Oya and Oshun to prepare the food. Oshun asked Oya to tell her how she made her food so tasty. Oya said, "Have you never noticed that I always wear my headdress low to cover my ears?" She said that she had cut off her ears to use as a special ingredient in the food. Oshun cut off her ears and put them in soup. When it was served, one of the guests found her two ears in his bowl and fled in horror. Everyone saw the ears and departed. In disgust and anger, Shango summoned Oya and Oshun. Oya told what Oshun had done, and Shango removed Oshun's headdress. Oshun accused Oya of having cut off her ears also, but when Oya's headdress was removed her ears were unmutilated.

Finally, toward the end of our 1950–51 fieldwork, a diviner recited two versions of the myth into a tape recorder. He belonged to the cult of Orishala at Ǫyǫ, but he had been trained in divining with sixteen cowries in the town of Igana, where he was born. He agreed to tape all the verses for sixteen cowry divination that he knew, and when he finished he recorded a number of myths. They were recorded in Yoruba, transcribed, and translated.

Both versions of the myth are obviously based on a divination verse, with the names of the mythical diviners (given in quotation marks) interrupting the narrative, but it was not included by him as a verse for sixteen cowry divination. They are told in poetic rather than prose form, and they include an episode not previously encountered. Ifa and Ǫrunmila are names of the Yoruba God of Divination.

"The child learns to buy a knife;
"The child buys a very sharp one"
They were the ones who divined for Shango.
He took Ǫba as a wife
And chose Ǫya as a concubine.
"The vine clings to the tree at the bottom
"And climbs up to the top"
They were the ones who divined for Ǫba
Who was the favorite wife of Shango.
She said, "This husband, how will he love me,
"That he will never leave me,
"That he will love me
"And will not love anyone else?
"What should I do?"
And she went (to the diviners),
And they said, "What is it?"
"What should I use in cooking stew?
"What should I use in cooking stew for a husband
"So that he will love me?"
"An ear is what one should cook stew with for a husband,
"So that he will love one."
"Ha! An ear?"
They said, "Yes."

"Can you help me cut it?"
They said, "Yes."
She said they should cut it,
And they cut it;
They cut it.
After they cut off her ear
She cooked it for Shango,
And he ate it.
Inevitably after a while
Ọrunmila took Ọba from Shango.
When he had taken her, what then?
"Wherever you are going
"I will go with you"
Was the one who divined for Ọya
Who succeeded Ọba.
She said she would follow Ọrunmila,
And Ọrunmila married her.
"Little things are what we are seeing;
"A big thing is coming, father of them all"
Was the one who divined for Ọrunmila.
Ifa again said he would marry Ọshun.
After he married Ọshun, what then?
He married Ọshun.
Well, Ọba was his senior wife,
But Ọba was the one who washed the dishes;
Ọba was the one who ground the pepper;
Ọba was the one who cooked the food.
The senior wife!
Ọya just sat down.
After a while Ọya said, "I will open something for you to see,"
And Ọba trembled in fright.
Then Ọshun arrived,
And one day
Ọshun watched them and watched them.
She called Ọba and asked,
"Why is it that you act like this?"
She said, "This is how Ọya frightens me.
"She says she will open something for me to see."
Ọshun said, "You must not grind pepper any more.
"Aren't you the senior wife?
"Well then, can't she grind pepper for me
"As you are grinding pepper for her?"
Ọshun came.
When Ọya called, Ọba, come and do this,"
Ọshun would say, "You must not do it."
Ọya would say, "I will open something for you to see."
Ọshun said, "What do you have to open?"
Ọya said, "I will open it for you to see."
"Well," Ọshun said, "Open it now.

"Whatever you have to open, open it.
"Today you will open it!
"If you don't open it, you must not leave."
When Ọya opened her skirt
There were sixteen vaginas under her waist,
And all of them were emitting smoke.
When Ọya opened her skirt thus
Ọshun said, "Is that all?"
When Ọshun opened her skirt,
Sixteen, sixteen times sixteen vaginas
Were under her waist,
And Parrots' tail feathers were her pubic hair,
Bright red.
Ọba and Ọya fled in fear.
Ọba fled;
Ba! Ba! Ọba was the first to fall down,
And Ọba became a river.
Gba! Gba! Ọya fell down,
And she too became a river.
And Ọshun also fell down,
And she became a river.
That was the day that those three fell down
And that they became rivers.
"The child learns to buy a knife;
"The child buys a very sharp one"
They were the ones who divined for Ọrunmila.
Ifa took Ọba as a wife
And chose Ọya as a concubine.
"The vine clings to the tree at the bottom
"And climbs up to the top"
Was the one who divined for Shango
When he married Ọya and married Ọba.
"Little things are what we are seeing;
"A big thing is coming, father of them all"
They were the ones who divined for Ọrunmila.
Ifa was going to marry Ọshun.
That is where these three became rivers.

In this first version it seems that Ọba's diviners were the ones who told her to cut off her ear; in the second it is Ọya. The first version contains several inconsistencies, but they need not concern us here. The second version follows.

"The child learns to buy a knife;
"The child buys a very sharp one"
Cast for Ọrunmila.
Ifa took Ọba as a wife
And chose Ọya as a concubine.
"The vine clings to the tree at the bottom
"And climbs up to the top"

Cast for Orunmila.
Ifa was courting Oshun.
Orunmila took Oba as wife
And they were living together.
After a while
Ifa took Oya from Shango
And married Oya.
When Orunmila took Oya as a divorceé
Oba was the one who ground pepper for her.
Oba was the one who pounded yam flour;
Oba was the one who pounded yam loaf;
She was the one who prepared food.
Oba was the one who fetched water,
Who swept the house,
And who polished the floor.
Oshun was coming to visit,
And when Oshun came to visit Orunmila,
She was watching them from head to foot (lit., hands and feet).
She said, "You, Oba,
"What is the matter? Who is the senior wife?"
Oba said, "I am,
"But I don't know what is the matter with my husband.
"He loves Oya too much."
When Oba asked Oshun,
Oshun said she should go and ask Oya.
When she asked Oya,
Oya said, "Ha! Your husband cannot love you,
"You who have been with him all these days
"And did not cook your ear for him
"And give it to him to eat.
"If you cut your ear for him
"He will love you."
Oba said they should cut off one of her ears,
And Oba gave it to her husband.
(She told Oshun), "This is what she said,
"You, Oshun, this is what she said."
Oshun said, "Go and do it,"
And she did so.
Oshun said, "I am coming."
When she came
She married Orunmila.
When Oya told Oba to grind pepper,
Oshun would say, "Don't grind it."
When she told her to go to the river,
Oshun would say, "Don't go."
When she said, "Sweep the floor,"
Oshun would say, "Don't sweep it."
When she said she should polish the floor,
Oshun would say, "Don't polish it."

Ọya threatened, "I will open something for you to see."
Ọshun said, "What do you have to open for me to see?
"What do you have?"
Ọshun said, "Open what you have.
"What you have to open, open it."　　.
When Ọya did so,
She opened her underskirt slowly like this
And from below fire was smoking.
Sixteen vaginas were under her waist
And they were smoking.
Ha!" Ọshun said, "Is that all?"
She said, "I dare you to wait and see mine!"
When Ọshun opened hers slowly like this,
There were sixteen, sixteen times sixteen vaginas.
Parrots' tail feathers were her pubic hair;
They were bright red.
Ọba fled, Ọya fled,
And Ọshun ran after them.
Ọba was the first to fall down,
And Ọba became a river.
Ọshun also fell down and she became a river.
That was the day that these three became rivers.

Some folklorists still maintain that few, if any, African folktales are known in America. While they may be referring only to the United States, they speak of America. But here is a myth about which there can be no question. As told in Cuba and Brazil, it had an African, and specifically a Yoruba, origin. It is Ọba who cut off her ear in all sixteen versions, with the single exception of Courlander's, whose informant seems obviously to be mistaken. The variants differ, even within Cuba, or Brazil, or West Africa; but it makes little difference whether the ear was cooked in stew, soup, or porridge, or whether Ọba was tricked by Ọya or Ọshun. Both of the two latter variations are probably legitimate and, as a hypothesis, I would suggest that worshippers of Shango credit Ọya with the trick, while Ọshun worshippers claim the credit for their own deity; for others, it depends on which variant they heard.

In its different versions, the myth explains and validates various religious beliefs and ritual practices, including the tabus on mixing the waters of the Ọba and Ọshun rivers and on mentioning the name of one when crossing the other; why Ọba and Ọya, or Ọba and Ọshun, are enemies; how Ọba, Ọya, and Ọshun turned into rivers and became river goddesses; and why Ọba dances with her hand on her ear or with her ears covered with leaves or a cloth.

I

Ọmọ kóbẹ rà;
Ọmọ rà jónijóni
Àwọn ló dá fún Ṣàngó.
Ó gbé Ọbà níyàwó

Ó sì lọ yan Ọya lálè.
Wònrànwọ́nrán dìmọ́gi nílẹ̀
Ó ba dórí
Àwọn ló dà fùn Ọbà
Tí ṣe àyò Ṣàngó.
Òn, ọkọ yi bí o ti ṣe fẹ́ràn òn,
Tí kò fi ní kọ̀ òn lẹ̀,
Tí yió fi fẹ́ràn òn
Ti kò fi lè fẹ́ ẹlòmíràn mọ́?
Òn tí lè ṣe?
Ó sì lọ,
Wọn ní kiní?
Kí lọ̀ fi sebẹ̀?
Kí là fí sebẹ̀ fún ọkọ
Tí fi fẹ́ràn ẹni?
Etí ni à fí sebẹ̀ fún ọkọ,
Tí fí fẹ́ràn ẹni.
Ha! Etí?
Ó ní hin.
Ẹ ó a lè bá òn ke?
Wọn ní han nù.
Ó ní wọn ó ke,
Ni wọn bá ke;
Ni wọn bá ke.
Kí wọn ó ké etí nù un
Ọbà bá sè fún Ṣàngó,
Ó bá jẹ ẹ.
Dandan nà nīgbàtí yio pé
Òrúnmìlà ó gba Ọbà lọ́dọ̀ Ṣàngó.
Nīgbàtí yi ó gba títítí ńkọ́?
Níbi ò nrè
Ma bá ọ lọ
Nló dá fún Ọya
Ló tẹ̀lé Ọbà.
Ó ní a fi bí òn na tẹ̀lé Òrúnmìlà,
Òrúnmìlà fẹ́ ẹ.
Kékèké là ńrí;
Ńlá ǹbọ̀, baba gbogbo wọn
Nlo wá dá fún Òrúnmìlà.
Ifá tún ni òn-ó fẹ́ Ọṣun.
Nīgbàtí yí ó fẹ́ Ọṣun ńkọ́?
Ó fẹ́ Ọṣun.
Bẹ̀ e ní Ọbà ni ìyálé,
Ọbà ní fọ̀wo;
Ọbà ní lọta;
Ọbà ní sè oṅjẹ.
Iyálé!
Ọya a jókó.
Bó bá pé Ọya a ní òn ó mọ̀ ṣí ǹkan,

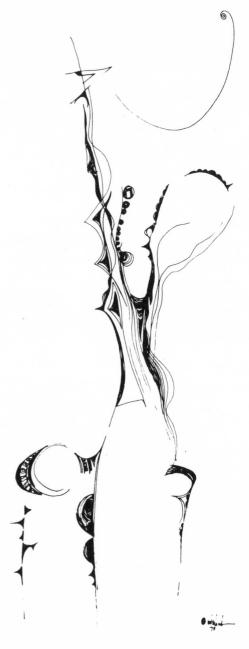

Ọbà a mọ gbọn.
Nīgbà tó ṣe Ọ̀ṣun dé,
Nīgbà ó dijọ́ kan
Ọ̀ṣun wò wọn títítí.
Ó wá pé Ọbà
È ti rí tí ìwọ fi nṣe bá un?
Ó ní bí tí ṣe nù un.
A ní òn ó ṣí ǹkan.
Ó ní ọ ò gbọdọ̀ lọta mọ́.
Ṣe bí ìwọ nìyálé?
Njẹ kí òn nà ó mọ wá lọta fún òn
Bí ìwọ ti ńlọta un?
Ọ̀ṣun dé.
Bí Ọya bá pé Ọbà o wá ṣe báyí,
Ọ̀ṣun a ní ọ̀ gbọdọ̀ ṣe.
Ọya a ní òm ó ṣí ǹkan hàn ọ́.
Ọ̀ṣun a ní kiní ọ ní tí ọ ṣī?
A ní òn ó ṣi hān.
Họ́wù! Ọ̄ṣun nī ṣi níbẹ̀ un.
Ntí o bá ni tọ̀ ṣi, ṣí i.
Lóni lọ̀ ṣi!
Bí ò ṣi o gbọdọ̀ lọ níbẹ̀ un.
Nīgbà Ọya o ṣi
Ọ̄bò mẹ́rìndílógún ní ńbẹ nídí rẹ̀,
Gbogbo ẹ̀ ní nrúná.
Ti Ọya ọ ṣiṣọ
Ọ̀ṣun ní ó di ení.
Nīgbàtí Ọ̀ṣun ó ṣi pè ẹ̀ báyí,
Mẹ́rìndílógún, mẹ́rìndílógún ọ̀nà mẹ́rìndílógún
Ní ńbẹ nídí rẹ̀,
Èkó ódẹ ni irun rẹ̀,
Ó wá bẹ yò ò.
Ọbà òn Ọya bá họ.
Ọbà họ;
Bà! Bà! Ọbà ló kọ́ lù ilẹ̀,
Ọbà di odò.
Gbà! Gbà! Ọya nà lùlẹ̀,
Òn nà di odò.
Ni Ọ̀ṣun nà bá lùlẹ̀,
Ló bá di odò.
Nijọ́ nà ni àwọn mẹ́tẹ̀ta bá lúlẹ̀
Tí wọn di odò.
Ọmọ kọ́bẹ rà;
Ọmọ rà jónijóni
Āwọn ló dá fún Ọ̀rúnmìlà.
Ifá gbé Ọbà níyàwó
Ó lọ yan Ọya lálè.
Wọ̀nrànwọ́nrán dìmọ́gi nílẹ̀
Ó ba dé orì

Ló dá fún Ṣàngó
Tó fẹ́ Ọya tó sì fẹ́ Ọbà.
Kékèké là ńrí;
Nlánlá ńbọ̀, baba gbogbo wọn
Àwọn ló dá fún Òrúnmìlà.
Ifá ó fẹ́ Òṣun.
Ibi tí wọn mẹ́tẹ̀ta gbé di odò nù un.

II

Ọmọ kọ́ ọbẹ rà;
Ọmọ rà jónijóni
Dá fún Òrúnmìlá.
Ifá gbé Ọbà ní ìyàwó
Ó yan Ọya lálè.
Wọ̀nrànwọ́nrán dìmọ́ igi nílẹ̀
Ó ba dé orí
Dá fún Òrúnmìlà.
Ifá nṣe òrẹ Òṣun.
Òrúnmìlà ó gbé Ọbà níyàwó nù un
Wọn ńbá aiyé wọn lọ.
Nĩgbàtí o ṣe
Ifá gba Ọya lọ́dọ̀ Ṣàngó
Kó fẹ́ Ọya.
Nĩgbàtí Òrúnmìlà ó mú Ọya lópó
Ọbà ní nlọ ata fún Ọya.
Ọbà ní gúnlùbọ́;
Òn ní gúnyán;
Òn ní rokà.
Ọbà ní pọnmi,
Ní gbálè,
Ní palé.
Òṣun nwā nwa wá,
K'Òṣun o ma wá Òrúnmìlà wa nun,
Nwò wọn l'ọ́wọ́, nwò wọn lésẹ̀.
Ò ní iwọ Ọbà
È ti jẹ́? Tani ìyálé?
Ọbà ní òn ni,
Ò o sì wá mọ ntóse ti ọkọ òn.
Tí o ṣe fẹ̀ràn Ọya tó bá un.
Nĩgbàtí Ọbà ó bi Òṣun,
Òṣun ní kó lọ bi Ọya.
Nĩgbàtí yió bi Ọya
Ọya ni Ha! Ọkọ ò lè fẹ̀ràn ìwọ,
Iwọ tí o ti dé ọ̀dọ̀ rẹ̀ látijọ́ yi
Tí ọ fi etí sebẹ̀ fun
Kí o fun jẹ.
Tí o bá fi etí sebẹ̀ fun
Yió fẹ̀ràn rẹ.
Ọbà ní kí wọn ó fá òn letí kan,

Ọbà sì fi fún ọkọ.
Bó ti wí nìyi,
Iwọ Òṣun bó ti wí nìyi.
Òṣun ní lọ rè ṣe bẹ́ ẹ̀,
Ò sá ṣe bẹ̀ ẹ̀ nù un.
Òṣun ní òn bọ̀ wá.
Nīgbàtí yió wa
Ò wá fẹ́ Òrúnmìlà.
Bí Ọya bá ní kí Ọbà ó lọta,
Òsun a ní kí ó mọ́ lọ̄.
Tí ó bá pé kó lọ odò,
A ní kí ó mọ́ lọ.
Bó ní gbálẹ,
A ní kí ó mọ́ gba.
Bí ó pé ki ó pa ilé,
A ní kí ó mọ́ pa.
Ònó mọ̀ ṣí nkan nàn ọ.
Kí lọ ó a ṣí hàn òn?
Kí lọ ní?
Òṣun ní ṣí on tí o ní.
Òn ti ọ o ṣí ọ ní ṣi.
Nīgbàtí Ọya ó ṣe,
Ọya ṣí tòbí ẹ̀ pé ẹ báyí
Gbogbo abẹ́ ẹ̀ ni iná ńrú.
Òbò mẹ́rìndílógún ní ńbẹ ní ìdí Ọya
Iná ní ńrú níbẹ̀.
Ha! Òṣun nnà ní kíni?
Ó ní ọ ò yó a dúró ọ wò tòhun!
Nigbàtí Òṣun ó ṣí ti ẹ̀ pé báyí,
Mẹ́rìndílógún, mẹ́rìndílógún ọ̀nà mẹ́rìndílógún.
Èkó ídẹ ló i ṣe irun rẹ̀;
Ni iho ẹ bẹ sò.
Ọbà ọ Ọya ọ,
Òṣun nà gbá yá wọn.
Ọbà ló kọ́ lùlẹ̀,
Ló bá di odò.
Òṣun nà bá lùlẹ̀ ló bá di odò.
Ijọ́ tí àwọn mẹ́tẹ̀ta ti wọn dodò nù un.

NOTES

1. Lydia Cabrera, *El Monte. Igbo Finda, Ewe Orisha, Vititi Nfinda*, 2d ed. (Miami: Colección del Chicherekú, 1968), pp. 224–26.
2. Romulo Lachatañeré, "El Sistema Religioso de los Lacumís y otra Influencias

Africanas en Cuba. III," *Estudios Afrocubanos*, 5 (1945–46), 208. A similar version, discovered too late to be included in this analysis, has been published by Mercedes Cros Sandoval in *La Religion Afrocubana* (Madrid: Playor, 1975), pp. 211–12.

3. Roger Bastide, *Le Candomblé de Bahia (Rite Nagô)*, Le Monde d'Outre Mer, Passé et Présent, Première Série, Études V (1968), p. 176.

4. Edison Carneiro, "Xango," in *Novos Estudos Afri-Brasileiros*, ed. G. Freyre et al., Biblioteca de Divulgação Scientifica, IX, Civilização Brasileira (1937), pp. 143–44.

5. Edison Carneiro, *Candomblés de Bahia*, Publicações do Museu do Estado, No. 8 (1948), p. 46.

6. Pierre Verger, *Dieux d'Afrique, Culte des Orishas et Vodouns à l'ancienne Côte des Esclaves en Afrique et à Bahia, la Baia de tous les Saints au Brésil* (Paris: Paul Hartmann Éditeur, 1954), pp. 185–86.

7. Bastide, pp. 176–77.

8. William Bascom, *Shango in the New World*, Occasional Publication of the African and Afro-American Research Institute, No. 4 (Austin: The University of Texas at Austin, 1972), p. 14.

9. Pierre Verger, *Notes sur le Culte des Oriṣa et Vodun à Bahia, la Baie de tous les Saints, au Brésil et à l'ancienne Côte des Esclaves en Afrique*. Mémoires de l'Institut Français d'Afrique Noire, No. 51 (1957), p. 413.

10. Ibid.

11. Harold Courlander, *Tales of Yoruba Gods and Heroes* (New York: Crown Publishers, 1973), pp. 87–90.

T W O

✳

The Talking Skull Refuses to Talk

In this article I will try to establish as a fact, beyond dispute, that the folktale which I call "The Talking Skull Refuses to Talk" was brought to the United States from Africa. It is the tale that Dorson has said "comes straight from West Africa."[1] However, my documentation of this statement is not therefore unnecessary; nor is it simply an antiquarian search for African "survivals" in the New World; nor is it racist.[2] It is, I submit, important not only for Afro-Americans, but for folklorists, for Africans, and for all Americans to recognize the African contributions to America's folklore.

The recent revival of the almost century-old debate about African origins of Afro-American folktales, particularly those found in the United States, would seem to have been due in large part to Dorson's claim that they are rare. In his *American Negro Folktales*, which deals only with the United States, he says, "The first declaration to make is that this body of tales does not come from Africa. It does not indeed come from any one place but from a number of dispersal points, as the comparative notes make clear. Many of the fictions, notably the animal tales, are of demonstrably European origin. Others have entered the Negro repertoire from England, from the West Indies, from American white tradition, and from the social conditions and historical experiences of colored people in the South. Only a few plots and incidents can be distinguished as West African. Each tale has to be studied separately to discern its history."[3]

Then he says, "Comparing the motifs known in West African folktales with those in my own collection, I have found a correspondence of only about ten percent. Of the twenty-two African motifs found in the over two hundred motifs in my tales, only one is not known in Europe. This is K1162 (an index to these motifs appear on p. 380), 'Dupe tricked into reporting speaking skull, is executed for lying,' which does provide an African core to one popular American Negro tradition. But this case is exceptional."[4] This is, of course, the motif or tale type in question.

Reprinted from *Research in African Literatures*, 8 (1977), 266–91.

Motifs are one things, tale types another.[5] A comparison of motifs is no substitute for a study of tale types. As Dorson himself has said, "Each tale has to be studied separately to discern its history."[6] Crowley, who suggests that Dorson's estimate might be lowered to 9 percent, says that "motifs are notoriously untrustworthy, and a fairer count will not be possible until one can compare whole tale types."[7] Piersen, who challenges both estimates, concludes that "the motif method is suggestive but not precise for examining the origins of Afro-American or Negro folklore."[8] And, speaking of Tale Type 15, "The Theft of Butter (Honey) by Playing Godfather," Dundes says, "It will take a full-fledged comparative study of the Tale Type to determine the possible origins and paths of diffusion of the tale."[9] It is such a study of one folktale or tale type that I present here.

As I will demonstrate, "The Talking Skull Refuses to Talk" is not simply a motif but a folktale and, really, a tale type. Speaking of it, Piersen says that "Dorson reported just one American Negro tale not known in Europe and with only an African analogue—K1162"[10] in Dorson's collection. As far as I am aware, this is the *only* motif that Dorson concedes has come to the United States from Africa. The twenty-one other motifs with African analogues also have European analogues and in his view, presumably, were derived from Europe, or at least their African origins are dubious.

As I reread his statements, quoted above, it seems clear to me that Dorson is saying that the African contribution to the folklore of the United States is *completely* negligible—it constitutes only this one exceptional motif that is not known in Europe—not 10 percent, but only one motif out of over two hundred in his collection.

Later, however, he seems to concede that a second folktale also came to the United States from Africa, although this is not clear from the context of his statement, "Who can deny obvious ubiquities, like Tar-baby?"[11] Nor is it clear that he concedes the five other folktales which "do constitute the core of the case for African origins."[12] These tales appear in his *American Negro Folktales* as No. I, "Who Ate Up the Butter" (AT15), No. 7, "Rabbit and Bear Inside the Elephant," No. 9, "Race Won by Deception: Relative Helpers" (AT1074), which he entitles "Rabbit and Hedgehog," No. 10, "Mr. Rabbit and Mr. Frog Make Mr. Fox and Mr. Bear Their Riding-Horses" (a combination of AT4 and AT72 involving both courting and feigned sickness), and No. 72, "Why the Negro Has Kinky Hair."

I propose a series of articles dealing with folktales recorded in the United States that I believe are unquestionably of African origin. Not having previously investigated Afro-American folktales systematically, I do not know how many tales this series will include. However, without controversial tales with many African and many European analogues, such as "Kind and Unkind" (AT480) or "The Race Won by Deception" (AT1074), I believe that I can show that more than twenty folktales must have come to the United States from Africa rather from Europe.

I start with "The Talking Skull Refuses to Talk" not simply because Dorson admits that it comes from Africa, but to demonstrate that it is a tale type, and not just a motif, and also to show the kind of documentation that can be provided, in some instances, for African origins. Other folktales will have far less documentation, but I believe that the African analogues will be convincing. They will include some other folktales in Dorson's collection, and more than a few from the tales of Uncle Remus, despite the fact that Dorson has said that Joel Chandler Harris "makes the quite erroneous statement about origins, still largely credited, 'One thing is certain—the negroes did not get them from the whites: probably they are of remote African origin.'"[13] On the contrary, some of the Uncle Remus tales cited by Harris in 1883, and by Gerber in 1893, came to the United States from Africa.[14]

I shall concentrate on folktales recorded in the United States, but I shall include analogues reported elsewhere in the Americas for two reasons. Most importantly, their existence in these other areas to which African slaves were imported addes weight to the argument for the African sources of these tales. Secondly, Dorson has concluded, and *a priori* I agree, that the New World repertoire falls into two groups of stories: the Atlantic and Caribbean Islands and northeastern South America, pointing toward Africa, and the plantation states of the Old South of the United States, pointing toward Europe and Anglo-America.[15] It is to provide the basis for a test of this conclusion that these data are partially assembled here. To my surprise, it is not supported by the folktale in question; thus far I have found only one version from the Antilles and South America, but eighteen versions from the United States, both north and south.

I am not concerned with the question of ultimate origins—African, European, Indian, or other. Some of these folktales may have come to Africa from India, or perhaps they traveled in the opposite direction; but this is a separate issue. In the case of "The Talking Skull Refuses to Talk," it should be noted that the evidence suggests an African, rather than an Indian or European, origin. I am primarily concerned, however, with folktales that came to the United States from Africa.

It should be noted that Dorson's estimate is biased in several ways. First, as he notes, his (and Crowley's) comparisons are based on Kenneth W. Clarke's unpublished dissertation, "A Motif Index of the Folktales of Culture Area V, West Africa." Many African slaves came to the New World from this area, the Guinea Coast; but it is only one of Herskovits's nine African culture areas. If the Mediterranean littoral, with its European cultural affinities, is included as Culture Area X, both estimates are based on only about 3 percent of the African continent, without considering the African islands, which I am including here.

Second, Dorson's 10 percent estimate is based only on his own collection (of over one thousand narratives), primarily from Michigan and Arkansas. The many other collections of Negro folktales from the United States will certainly increase the number known to have come from Africa, but I cannot predict how this will affect the percentage estimates.

Third, although he writes about *American Negro Folktales*, many of the folk narratives in his collection are not folktales. Well over a third of the 165 narratives in *Negro Folktales in Michigan* appear to be memorats or personal reminiscences.[16] Accounts of African witches who ride their victims are to be found, not in collections of folktales, but in the ethnographic literature. Dorson's conversation about witches[17] hardly even qualifies as a folk narrative.

However, Dorson regards *all* prose narratives as folktales, including memorats, legends, and myths. He says that "professional folklorists—such as Stith Thompson in *The Folktale*—conceptualize folktale to cover all kinds of oral traditional prose narratives."[18] I seriously doubt that many professional folklorists hold this view.

As Piersen has noted,[19] the Aarne-Thompson tale type index can be misleading in the search for African origins. Because it specifically disclaims any real coverage of Africa,[20] it would be a mistake to conclude that if any American folktale is not found in this index, it is not known in Africa. Aside from occasional citations of African sources, its limited coverage of African folktales is based on May Augusta Klipple's unpublished dissertation, "African Folk Tales with Foreign Analogues." As its title clearly states, this study deliberately does not include the many African folktales not found outside Africa. Moreover, it would also be a mistake to conclude that all of the New World folktales in the Aarne-Thompson index came from Europe because, as Crowley has noted,[21] some of them have analogues in Africa, but not in Europe. And again it would be a mistake to conclude that all of the New World motifs in Stith Thompson's *Motif-Index of Folk-Literature*[22] came from Europe. For the motif in question here, B210.2, it gives only "U.S. Negro: Baughman."

On the other hand, because of its comprehensive coverage of Indo-European folklore, the Aarne-Thompson index is an invaluable resource when searching for European analogues. If it cites none, one may conclude that a given tale type has not been recorded in Europe. If European analogues do, in fact, exist, the burden of proof rests on those who maintain their source is not Africa.

In a very real sense it is going at things backwards to start with a control of the Afro-American folktale literature and then search the African literature for analogues, if only because of its widely scattered nature and the absence of an African tale type index. Even Clarke's motif index for the Guinea Coast can only be an introductory guide because of its limited geographical coverage. It seems more prudent to start with some degree of control of the African folktale literature and then to look for analogues in the United States and Europe, using the indexes of Aarne-Thompson and Baughman.[23]

Baughman, however, has deliberately given only a partial coverage of Afro-American folktales. Many well-known tales are not mentioned, including AT157, "Learning to Fear Men," which Dorson says is the Negro folktale most commonly encountered in the United States.[24] But Baughman does include "The Talking Skull Refuses to Talk" under Motif B210.2, "Talking animal or object refuses to talk on demand. Discoverer is unable to prove his claims: is beaten." For it he mentions five Negro versions, without giving their sources, and cites Randolph ([3] in the summaries that follow) with Herbert Halpert's comparative notes.[25] Halpert cites Frobenius and Fox [6], Fauset [19], Dorson [20], Parsons [24], Hurston [25], Botkin [33], Brewer [34], Botkin [35], Fauset [36], Courlander and Herzog [38], and Dobie [42]. Dorson cites only Baughman's five unidentified versions, Frobenius and Fox [6], Hurston [25], Randolph [31] with Halpert's comparative notes, and Barker and Sinclair [38]. Only two African folktales ([6] and [38]) are included in these citations.

Dorson also cites an Igbo folktale under Motif E632.1, "Speaking bones of murdered person reveal murder," but as Piersen has suspected and as I have previously stated, this is a different tale type,[26] and it is also common in Africa. Dorson adds that his Michigan tale [20] brings to mind Type 720, "My Mother Slew Me, My Father Ate Me," where birds or flies reveal a murder. This again is manifestly a different tale type.

A shortcoming of some investigations into the question of African origins is that the African literature has not been researched with the diligence of Elsie Clews Parsons, Martha Warren Beckwith, Melville Jean Herskovits, and May Augusta Klipple. To be sure, some of the analogues they cited are not convincing; but at least these references should have been checked out to determine their relevance.

Some scholars have also been content to cite only a few African analogues, and they have done so only by volume and page number. The latter is also true of the analogues cited by Parsons, Beckwith, and Herskovits. Many of these references are to publications that are not readily available, even to other folklorists, and are in foreign languages so that many readers cannot judge how convincing the parallels are. In order that the reader may be able to judge for himself, I will, in most instances, be presenting the tales in the form of summaries or abstracts.

I have previously cited fourteen African versions, with full texts for three that come from Ifa divination verses ([9], [10], and [27]), but with no summaries for the others.[27] Two additional Ifa verses are given here in full for comparison with these three. The first [7], told by an Ifa diviner in Ifẹ, Nigeria, in 1965 has not been published. It was recorded on a typewriter as translated into English by an interpreter and is not a word-for-word rendition. The second [8] is available only in a typewritten manuscript in Yoruba and has not been published in English.

There are several versions of the tale type under consideration or, if you prefer, several related tale types. The first is "The Talking Skull Refuses to Talk," which Dorson concedes came straight from Africa. The second is "The Talking Animal Refuses to Talk," and the third is "The Singing Tortoise Refuses to Sing." Dorson, Baughman, and Halpert all seem to agree that the three versions constitute a single tale type. It is immaterial to me whether they constitute one, two, or three tale types. I will present the three versions separately, but in this series I will count them as only one tale type.

The distinctive feature of these folktales is not that the skulls or animals can talk (or sing), but that later they *refuse to talk*. Many things talk in African folktales that have no relationship to these folktales, including tales of talking skulls.[28] Kenneth W. Clarke has said it well, "All animals speak, and they speak in almost every story."

There are only three of the forty-three tales noted below in which the skull or animal does not specifically refuse to talk or sing, and all three can be safely considered to be derivatives. The singing turtle in Texas [42] simply disappears temporarily, returning to sing, "Don't tell all you see." Similarly, the Haitian tortoise [43] escapes, but returns to sing, "Uncle Pierre Jean talks too much." In Dorson's Arkansas version [23], the tale is cleverly intertwined, as he says, with another tale type, "Dividing Souls." John is beheaded because Old Master hears nothing at the cemetery, but the skeleton head then tells John, "I told you something that got me here would get you here. You talk too much."

The usual result of the refusal to talk is that the person who reported the talking skull or animal is killed or beaten, but there are examples where it finally talks or sings, and saves him. Many of these folktales conclude with the skull or animal saying something to the effect that "You talk too much," or "Your big mouth killed you." In the United States, the African tortoise often becomes a turtle, terrapin, or cooter. Incidentally, this series of historically related folktales neatly illustrates how the African chief or king has been replaced, in the United States, by the Old Master or the boss.

Finally, before turning to the abstracts of the African and New World versions of this folktale, it should be understood that none of these three similar patterns appear in Aarne and Thompson's tale type index and only United States Negro versions are cited in Thompson's motif index. Thus they could not have come from Europe or from India.

My twenty-four African versions came from Senegal (Fulani), Mali (Malinke), Ghana (Unspecified and Ashanti), Togo (Tem), Nigeria (Unspecified, Nupe, Yoruba, and Efik), Angola (Kimbundu), Zaire (Kongo and Nyanga), Tanzania (Swahili), Malawi (Yao), and Zambia (Lamba). The eighteen United States versions come from Pennsylvania, Michigan, Arkansas, Oklahoma, Texas, Mississippi, and North Carolina, plus Courlander's two unspecified examples. One version comes from Haiti. Undoubtedly, there are other examples that I have missed.

A. The Talking Skull Refuses to Talk

1. (Fouta Senegal: Fulani) A man came upon the head of a man who had been killed by a lion. He asked what had happened. The head said, "My tongue is what put me here." The man went to the village and told the people that he had talked with the head of a dead person. They denied it, and the affair grew to the point where the king investigated it. The man told his story again and said that if the head did not reply the king should kill him. They

went to the head and the man repeated, "What brought you here?" but the head did not answer. He asked again but there was no reply. He picked up the head and spoke into its ear, and the head answered, "My tongue." The man asked the people, "Did you hear?" The king decided to take him away and kill him. As they left, the head called to the man to come. He came back and it said, "Is it not my tongue that put me here?" The head called to the people and spoke to them, and the man was freed. Later he told the king that as long as he lived he would not lie, be afraid, or be jealous. The king tested him on the last two points by having him ambushed and by having men sleep with his two wives. He survived the ambush, and he had his wives feed the two men. (Gaden, pp. 164–69)

2. (Mali: Malinke) A man said that the king could kill him if he found him jealous, telling a lie, or showing cowardice, and he passed the three tests that the king set for him in ways similar to those in the preceding tale [1]. In explaining why he never lied, he told the following. One day I found a human skull on the path and asked how it came there. The skull replied, "Because I talked so much." In the next town I told the chief who said, "You lie." I said, "Let two people come with me and see." He said, "If you are lying, your head will be cut off." We went back, but when I asked the skull why it was there it did not answer. I asked three times, but it did not answer. They bound me and drew a saber to kill me. I asked, "Why did you speak yesterday, and why don't you speak today?" The skull said, "The mouth, the mouth." The others heard and released me, and reported it to the chief. Since then I never lie. (Frobenius [1922], pp. 84–90)

3. (Togo) a hunter saw a skull, whitened with age, in the forest. He asked, "What brought you here?" The skull replied, "Well, what brought you here?" The hunter was frigntened to hear the skull speak, and he ran back to the village. He told the chief what had happened. The chief said, "You lie! A skull cannot speak." The hunter said, "If I am lying, I will die." The chief sent his people to the skull with the hunter, saying that if it did not speak, he was to die. The hunter repeated his question to the skull, but it did not answer and he was killed. The people reported that the hunter had lied and had been killed. When they left, the skull said to the hunter, "What brought you here?" The hunter answered, "My mouth." (Frobenius, "Volksdichtungen" [1924])

4. (Nigeria: Hausa) Following a lengthy narrative about how a barber revealed that there was a horn on the king's head (AT782), the barber was driven from the king's land. On his way through the forest, he saw a human skull, white and dry. He asked, "Who brought you here?" The skull answered, "It was my mouth that brought me here." The barber returned to the king and told what had happened. The king said, "You lie." The barber said, "If it is not true, kill me." The king's people went back to the skull with the barber, but it did not speak. The barber was brought back to the king and was killed. But it was his mouth that killed him with so much talk. (Mischlich [1929])

5. (Nigeria: Hausa) A traveler came upon a severed head on a tree stump. It said, "Whatever you do, learn to keep your mouth shut." The man ran to town in terror and told the chief what had happened. The chief said that the man would be rewarded if his story was true, but if it was false he would be beheaded. The man returned to the stump with the chief's executioner and attendants, but the head remained silent. The executioner drew his sword and cut off the man's head. Then the head spoke, "I told him to keep his mouth shut." (Johnston [1966], pp. 78–79)

6. (Nigeria: Nupe) A hunter found a human skull in the forest and asked, "What brought you here?" The skull answered, "Talking brought me here." The hunter ran and told the king that he had found a skull that talked. The king did not believe him and sent a guard to see if his story was true, with orders to kill him if it was not. All day long the hunter begged the skull to speak, but it remained silent and the hunter was killed. When the guard had left, the skull asked, "What brought you here?" The hunter's head replied, "Talking brought me here." (Frobenius, "Volkerzählungen," [1924], pp. 150–51)

7. (Nigeria: Yoruba) "A chicken with few feathers lays few eggs so it will see feather to cover them" was the one who divined for Earth, child of Idere Akoko. They said he should be careful not to eat too much and die in the bush. When Earth ate and ate, he died in the bush called Oko Amuta. When people wanted to plant ochra, they cleared the bush and found his skull and hung it on a tree. When the ochra was ripe, it was the time of the Edi festival. On the fourth day of the festival, the farmer sent an indentured servant to pluck his ochra at Oko Amuta. When the servant met Earth's skull, he said, "You, Earth, everyone in town is eating and drinking, but you stay here." The skull replied, "Is it just today or yesterday that I have been here? The ochra that you have come to pluck, pluck it and leave without so much talk." When the servant returned to town, he said that he had seen a skull speaking in the farm where he had gone to pluck ochra. People were surprised and ten of the king's bodyguards (Ogungbẹ) and ten of his messengers (Ẹmẹsẹ) were sent back with him. He said that if the skull did not speak, they should take their sword from its scabbard and cut off his head. When they got to the farm, he called, "Skull, Skull of Oko Amuta, Skull, Skull," but it did not answer. They took the sword and cut off his head. As they were leaving, the skull called them and said, "The man who came to pluck ochra, did not pluck it and go. He began to say they were dancing in town and eating and drinking. I said, 'Is it just today or yesterday that I have been here?'" When they heard this, they ran back to town and reported it. They said that if it were not so when they got back to the farm, they should be killed as the first man was killed. When they returned, they called, "Skull of Oko Amuta, Skull, Skull of Oko Amuta," but the skull did not answer. The bodyguards and the messengers were beheaded. As the others turned to leave, the skull spoke again, "Come here. First they sent a servant to pluck ochra; he did not do it but began to ask questions. Next the king's bodyguards and messengers came, and they began to ask questions." The same thing happened again and again,

and many people were killed. When very few people were left, they said Ọrunmila should go to Oko Amuta. Ọrunmila divined and was told to buy a ewe, roasted yams, and a white cloth. Ọrunmila took them to the farm and spread out the white cloth. He put sixteen *ọdundun* leaves on it and crushed them. He set the skull on the leaves, covered it with the white cloth, and carried it home. When he reached the top of the laterite, he said, "A flood of rain water unites; it reaches the top of the laterite, it becomes divided" (Agbara fidi sọkọn, o de ori yangi o di otu yagba). Then Lọwa, Jaran, and all the other palace chiefs came out and shouted, "Heeee, Aiye rele-oooo." They dug a hole in the ground, put leaves in it, put the skull on the leaves, and buried them. Until today, at midnight on the fourth day of the Edi festival, the Otu priests go there and sacrifice to it. We say, "We are going to sacrifice to Earth." (Bascom [1965])

8. (Nigeria: Yoruba) Parakọda were the ones who cast Ifa for Ọlọbẹde of Ipetu. They said that he should offer one he-goat and the knife that was in his hand before he went to farm. He refused and did not offer them before he went to farm. Ọlọbẹde of Ipetu finished working on the farm and he was coming home in the evening; he turned aside to a plant to pick its fruit. As he reached his hand out to pick it, he heard a skull speaking, saying, "Don't touch me. Don't touch me. Don't you see me?" Ọlọbẹde of Ipetu was frightened; he ran home. He reported to the king that he saw a skull on the farm, and it was speaking. He asked that the king send someone to go and look at it. The king said, "I don't believe that a skull can speak." Ọlọbẹde insisted; he said, "Well, I am certain that the skull that I saw was speaking. If you don't find it so, let the king kill me." The king sent two people to follow him. When they reached the plant, Ọlọbẹde did as he had done before, so that the skull would speak. The skull did not speak. The two messengers that the king of Ipetu had sent killed Ọlọbẹde there as the king had commanded. As they turned to go home, the skull said, "Thank you very much. I am so pleased." The messengers returned home and reported to the king what their eyes had seen and what their ears had heard. To make a long story short, many people perished because of this matter; those that perished because of it were almost a hundred people. The town elders went to Ọrunmila to tell him about it and to ask what they should do to end this calamity. Ọrunmila named a sacrifice for them: a she-goat, a chicken, 44,000 cowries, and the leaves of Ifa (*wọrọ* leaves). They heard and they sacrificed. Then Ọrunmila said that they should take the skull from the plant, put it in a coffin, and put the leaves of Ifa on it. He said that they should cover it and give it a proper burial. Wherever they found a property marker, they should not touch the property. He warned the children and the people, "You must not touch the marked property." (Epega, pp. 14–16)

9. (Nigeria: Yoruba) Earth refused to make a sacrifice so that she would live to see her son become king. She died in the farm, and the forest grew up and covered her grave. No one remembered where it was, and her son grew and became king. One day a farmer was hoeing yam heaps, and his

hoe chopped Earth's skull. It cried out, "Did you chop me with your hoe?" The farmer dropped his hoe and ran to tell the king that he had seen a talking skull. He said that the king should send someone back with him, and that if the skull did not talk, they should cut off his head. The king sent the Ogboni society, and when the skull refused to talk, they cut off the farmer's head. When they turned to go, the skull asked, "Did you kill someone?" The Ogboni reported to the king what they had seen, and he sent his bodyguards back with the Ogboni. Again the skull refused to speak and the Ogboni were killed. When the bodyguards turned to go, the skull again asked, "Did you kill someone?" This time the king sent his messengers and his priests to make an atonement. The priests took a ewe, a white cloth, and other materials when they went. They poured palmwine and the blood of the ewe on the skull, and when it had eaten, it said it was Earth and they should carry it home. They carried it home in the white cloth, having learned that it was the king's mother. (Bascom [1969], pp. 428–33)

10. (Nigeria: Yoruba) Earth refused to make a sacrifice so that Alaba, his mother, would live to see him become king. Alaba died in the presence of her indentured laborer, who knew that she was buried at the base of a tree. Earth grew up and became king. When the indentured laborer had repaid his debt, he used to make fun of Alaba when he passed her grave, saying, "Skull, are you looking at the tree in Alaba's farm?" One day the skull answered, saying, "Laborer of Alaba, when you go to the farm you should keep your mouth shut." The man went to the king and said he had seen a talking skull, and that if they went there and it did not talk, they could cut off his head. The king sent his bodyguards and messengers, and when the skull refused to talk, they cut off the man's head. Then the skull asked, "Why did you kill him?" They replied, "Why did you not answer before?" The skull said, "His big mouth killed him." When this was reported to the king, he sent his priests to make an atonement. (Bascom [1969], pp. 436–39)

11. (Nigeria: Efik) A young man stumbled over a skull. Annoyed, he hit it with his staff, saying, "You, skull, you died of your foolishness." The skull answered, "If I died of my foolishness, then soon you will die of your cleverness." Startled, the young man rushed home and told the elders he had seen a skull that spoke to him. They did not believe him, having passed by the skull many times. The youth said that the skull would speak when he beat it, and that they could kill him if it didn't. The people went with him to the skull. He beat it with his staff, saying, "You, skull, you died of your foolishness," but the skull did not speak. He tried again and failed, and was put to death. Then the skull spoke, saying, "It is as I said, foolishness killed me, and cleverness has killed you." (Jablow [1969])

12. (Angola: Kimbundu) A young man found a skull by the path. Everyone used to pass by it, but he struck it with a staff, saying, "Foolishness has killed you." The skull replied, "Foolishness has killed me. Smartness will kill you." The youth went back home and told the elders, who said, "You have told a lie. All of us have passed by the head, but we never heard it speak." He said,

"Let us go. If it does not speak, cut off my head." When they got there, he beat the head saying, "Foolishness has killed you," but the head kept silent. He did so again, and when there was no answer, the crowd said, "You lied," and they cut off his head. Then the skull said, "Foolishness has killed me. Smartness has killed you." The people said, "We have killed him unjustly. The head has spoken." (Chatelain [1894])

13. (Zaire: Kongo) A man found a skull in an abandoned village. He asked the cause of its death, and it replied, "Of what do we not die? We die from water, we die from illness." The man went on to the next village and told the elders he had found a skull that replied when he questioned it. Saying that it was a lie, they asked, "Will it respond if we question it?" "Yes." "If it doesn't answer, what should we do?" "If I have lied, kill me." The elders went to the abandoned village and questioned the skull; it did not reply. They returned to the man and began to beat him, saying that he was going to die. The chief arrived and asked what was happening. He was told, and the man begged for pity. The chief had a youth bring a spear and kill him. His body was carried away and left unburied. (van Wing and Scholler [1940], pp. 41–44)

14. (Zaire: Nyanga) Trapping rats in the forest, a boy saw the teeth of a dead man. He asked, "What made you die?" The set of teeth replied, "It is what came out of my mouth that killed me." The boy did not tell his companions. He went and told the elders who came there with him. They told him to talk to the teeth as before, but the teeth refused to talk. They said he had lied and killed him. Then the teeth said to the boy, "I told you that I brought death upon myself. Now you have thrust it upon yourself." That is why if you see something you should call your comrades to see it also. (Biebuyck and Mateene [1970])

15. (Tanzania: Swahili) A man found the head of a man, long dead, in the plains. He struck it and the head said, "You are not good. If a man dies, say to him, 'Slowly.'" The man went home and said he had found a talking head. The people said, "You are a liar." He said, "If the head doesn't talk, you can kill me." They went to the head and he struck it, but it said not a word. The people killed the man, and then the head said, "Do you see what I told you? If a man dies, say to him, 'Slowly,' Now you are as dead as I am." The people said, "We have killed our friend for nothing." (Lademann, Kausch, and Reuss [1910])

16. (Malawi: Yao) A chief's headman, "Mr. Mouth," saw a skull by the path. Half intoxicated with hemp, he kicked it, saying, "Who killed you?" The skull answered, "Mr. Mouth." Frightened, he kicked it again and then went to tell the chief what had happened. The chief and his people returned with the headman, but the skull did not answer when he did as before. The chief said that the headman was not to be trusted and had him killed. (Stannus [1922])

17. (Malawi: Lamba) A man drunk with beer came upon a skull and asked, "What killed you?" The skull replied, "That mouth of yours will do the same to you." The man ran to the village and told the chief what he had seen. The

chief said, "Lies!" and told his people to go with the man and kill him if the skull didn't speak. The man talked to the head, but it wouldn't speak. The people said he was lying and killed him. As they were leaving, the skull said, "Look at the man you have killed. He came and asked what killed me. And I said, 'That mouth of yours will do the same to you.' And see, he is dead." (Doke [1927])

18. (United States) Walking home, a slave kicked a white, dry skull in the grass and it rolled out into the open. He apologized and was about to put it back, when it sang. He asked how it got there, and the skull replied, "My big mouth did this to me." The slave ran home and told his master what had happened. The master and other people went back with him. The slave asked the skull to speak and sing, but it didn't make a sound. The master said that the slave had been drinking, gave him a good whipping, and left him to sober up. When he had gone, the skull sang its song, and the slave asked, "What took you so long?" The skull replied, "My big mouth did this to me. Your big mouth did this to you too." (Courlander [1957], pp. 74–75)

19. (Pennsylvania) A man who talked too much saw a skull on the road and asked, "What are you doing here?" The skull answered, "Tongue brought me here and tongue will bring you here." The man told others, but they didn't believe him. He said that if the skull didn't talk, they could cut off his head. They went to the skull, but it did not talk, so they cut off his head. As his head rolled on the ground, the skull said, "I told you tongue brought me here and tongue is what brought you here." (Fauset [1928])

20. (Michigan) John was walking in the woods and saw a skeleton. He said, "This looks like a human. I wonder what he's doing out here." The skeleton said, "Tongue is the cause of my being here." John ran and told Old Master, who didn't believe him. They went back with many other people, but the skeleton wouldn't talk. So they beat John to death. Then the bones said, "Tongue brought us here, and tongue brought you here." (Dorson [1956], pp. 62–63; [1967], pp. 147–48)

21–22. (Michigan) Dorson mentions two additional texts of this tale [20] from Adelle Leonard and Iola Palmer (Dorson [1956], p. 212; [1967], p. 147)

23. (Arkansas) John ran to tell Old Master about the Devil and God dividing souls in the cemetery and fell over a skeleton head. He asked, "What are you doing here?" and the skeleton head replied, "Same thing got me here will get you here." John went on and told Old Master about what was happening in the cemetery. Old Master didn't believe him but went there with him, saying that if it were not true he would cut off John's head. When they got to the cemetery, the two slaves who had been dividing apples were gone and they heard nothing. Old Master cut off John's head and the skeleton head turned over and said, "I told you something that got me here would get you here. You talk too much." (Dorson [1958], pp. 48–50; [1967], pp. 146–47)

24. (North Carolina) A man found a "skeleton of a man's head" and asked why it was there. It replied, "Mouth brought me here. Mouth's going to bring you here." The man went to town and told what had happened, and a crowd

followed him back. The skull did not speak, and the others fell on the man and beat him. Then the skull said, "Didn't I tell you your mouth would bring you here?" (Parsons [1917])

25. (Florida) A man named High Walker could make the bones and skulls in a boneyard rise up, shake themselves, and lie down again. Another man sold himself to the Devil and lay down with the skulls and bones. His flesh disintegrated and only his skull and bones were left. High Walker came to this man's skull and kicked it, telling it to rise and shake itself. Finally the skull said, "My mouth brought me here, and if you don't mind, yours will bring you here." High Walker went and told his white folks, but the white man didn't believe him. High Walker said, "Come with me. If it doesn't speak, you can chop my head off." They went back and he kicked and kicked the skull, but it said nothing. So the white man cut off his head. Then the skull said, "See that now. I told you that mouth brought me here and if you didn't mind, it would bring you here." (Hurston [1969], pp. 219-20; reprinted in Botkin [1966], pp. 717-18)

B. The Talking Animal Refuses to Talk

26. (Nigeria) One day a man's sheep talked. He ran and told the king, but the king would not believe him. The king told him to bring the sheep, and that he would be beheaded if it could not speak. When the man brought his sheep, it did not say anything. The king ordered his soldiers to cut off the man's head; but when they were about to do so, the sheep cried out, "Spare my master! Do not cut off his head!" Everyone was astonished, and the king ordered the soldiers to set the man free. (Anonymous [1930], pp. 14-16; translated in Anonymous [1949], pp. 16-18)

27. (Nigeria: Yoruba) Chief Lọwa offered a sacrifice so that empty boasting would not cause him disgrace. When someone told the king that Lọwa had a ewe that talked like a human being, the king sent for him and asked if it were true. Lọwa said it was true, and the king told him to bring the ewe in four days. He said that if it talked he would give Lọwa half his possessions, but if it did not, Lọwa would be roasted over a fire. When the day came, Lọwa brought the ewe. He talked and talked to it, but it refused to answer. They threw Lọwa to the ground, bound him, and began to pass him slowly back and forth across the fire. On the third pass, the ewe asked, "Are you killing someone?" The people shouted, "The ewe is talking!" and the king gave Lọwa half of all his possessions. As Lọwa was taking his ewe home, he asked, "Why did you let them pass me over the fire three times?" The ewe replied, "Should I have answered the very first time, and let you get all this wealth without any suffering? If one becomes rich through trade, do we not see its scars on one's body?" (Bascom [1969], pp. 528-33)

28. (Zaire: Kongo) A hunter caught a leopard in his trap. He said to the leopard, "Stupidity has brought you to this fate." The leopard replied, "It is stupidity that brought me here. Cleverness will bring you here too." The hunter

hurried to the village and told the people what had happened, but they said, "He lies." He said, "If I lie, I will leave the village." They went back to the trap with him, but the leopard did not speak. The people returned to the village, leaving the hunter behind. The hunter asked the leopard, "Why didn't you speak, when you spoke before?" The leopard said, "It is my stupidity that brought me here. It is your cleverness that brought you here." (Courlander [1963], pp. 64–66)

29. (United States) John went fishing and took a nap. He heard someone calling his name and saw a blacksnake. It said it was trying to be sociable because "Aren't we both black? You might as well say we are kin." John ran back to his boss and told him what had happened. The boss said that they should go back and see. When they got to the snake, it didn't say a word. The boss said that John had let him down and left. John asked the snake, "Why did you make me a liar?" The snake said, "John, you let *me* down. I spoke only with you, and you had to go and tell a white man." (Courlander [1976], pp. 441–42)

30. (Michigan) While plowing, John's mule said it was tired of working. John ran to his boss and told him what had happened. His boss didn't believe him and sent him back to work again. The same thing happened and again he told his boss. His boss went back with him, threatening to hang John if the mule didn't talk. It didn't, and John refused to plow any more. He heard his boss tell his wife that John was going crazy, and they would have to shoot him. Then the mule said, "See, I told you you talk too much. I could have told you that the boss would never believe it." (Dorson [1954]; [1956], pp. 63–65; [1967], pp. 149–51)

31. (Arkansas) A blabbermouth who told only the truth found a turtle in the road. It said, "You talk too damn much." He ran to town and told people, but they laughed in his face. He said, "Come with me and I'll show you." When they got there, the turtle didn't say a word. The people were mad because they had walked a long way in the hot sun, and they kicked the man into a ditch and left him there. Then the turtle spoke, "Didn't I tell you? You talk too damn much." (Randolph [1953]; [1957], pp. 3–5)

32. (Arkansas) John saw a turtle sitting on a log in the bayou. It said to him, "Black man, you talk too much." The second time it did so, he ran back and told Old Master what had happened. Old Master went back with John, saying that if the turtle didn't talk, he would give John a good beating. John begged the turtle to talk, but it didn't say anything. So Old Master took John to the house and gave him a good beating. When John went back to the bayou, the turtle said, "Black man, didn't I tell you you talked too much?" (Dorson [1958], pp. 50–52; [1967], pp. 148–49)

33. (Oklahoma) A nigger found a terrapin by the spring and asked it what had brought it there. It replied, "Teeth and tongue brought me here, and teeth and tongue will bring you here." He ran to tell his master and they went back to the spring. He asked the terrapin what had brought it there, but it wouldn't say a word. His master told him that he would get in trouble for telling a

lie. The next day he saw the terrapin and it said the same thing again. Soon afterwards he was lynched near the place he had seen the terrapin. (Botkin [1968], p. 7)

34. (Texas) A slave saw a big bullfrog and threw a pebble at it. The frog said, "Don't do that. Let's be friends." After that the frog said good morning to him every day. Hoping to gain his freedom, the slave eventually told his master, who didn't believe him. He told the slave that he would give him his freedom if it were true, but if not, he would give him the worst beating he had ever had. They went to the frog, and the slave said good morning to it. The frog did not answer, and the master took the slave back to the house and gave him a severe whipping. The next morning the frog returned the slave's greeting. The slave asked why it hadn't said anything the day before. The frog replied, "Because I told you the other day, nigger, you talk too much." (Brewer [1932])

35. (Mississippi) A colored man went to chop a cotton field in return for food. He met a cooter that said to him, "Nigger, you talk too much." He ran back to the big house and told the white man what had happened. He said that if the cooter didn't talk, the white man could cut his throat. They went back to the cooter, but it didn't say anything. So the white man whipped the colored man and left him there. Then the cooter said, "Nigger, I told you you talk too much." (Percy [1941], pp. 294–96; reprinted in Botkin [1949], p. 510)

36. (Alabama) A Negro found a turtle near a pond and said good morning to it. It returned his greeting, and he said that he didn't know it could talk. It said, "That's what I say about you niggers, you talk too much." The man went back to the house and told his master, who said he was just lying. He insisted, and the master said he would go to see the turtle, but that if it didn't talk he would beat the Negro half to death. The Negro greeted the turtle but it didn't say anything. He begged the turtle, but it wouldn't talk. His master took him to the house and beat him. Afterward the Negro went back and asked the turtle why it hadn't answered. The turtle answered, "Well, that's what I say about you niggers, you talk too much anyhow." (Fauset [1927])

37. (North Carolina) A man came upon a terrapin that said to him, "One day you shall be free." The man went to his master and told him what had happened. The master said he would go there with him, but if the terrapin didn't talk, he would whip the man to death. The terrapin didn't talk, and the slave was almost whipped to death. Then the terrapin said, "It's bad to talk too much." (Parsons [1917], p. 177)

C. Singing Tortoise Refuses to Sing

38. (Ghana) A hunter in the forest heard singing accompanied by sweet music. When he looked through the branches, he saw a tortoise playing a tiny harp and singing, "It is man who forces himself on things, not things which force themselves on him." He returned time and time again to listen,

and finally persuaded her to return with him so he could enjoy her singing every day. She agreed on the condition that she would sing to him alone. However, the hunter could not keep his secret, and finally the word reached the chief. The hunter was called before the Assembly, but no one would believe what he told them. He said that he would bring the tortoise and if she didn't sing, he was willing to die. The next day he brought the tortoise and everyone gathered round to listen, but no song came. He tried in vain to coax her to sing, and was beheaded. Then the tortoise spoke, explaining, "He brought his punishment on himself. I lived happily in the forest, singing my little song, but he was not content to come and listen to me. He had to tell my secret to all the world." (Barker and Sinclair [1917], pp. 119–21; retold in Courlander and Herzog [1947], pp. 65–71)

39. (Ghana) A hunter in the forest heard someone singing and playing a stringed instrument. Following the music, he found a tortoise sitting on a stone with an instrument such as he had never seen. He returned time and time again to listen to the music. Finally he persuaded the tortoise to go home with him, but on the condition that he tell no one. The hunter gave his promise but, hoping to become wealthy, he told others that he had a singing tortoise. The word reached the ears of the chief, who summoned the hunter, and he confirmed that he had a singing tortoise. "Do you mean that a tortoise— the most silent of all animals—can sing?" asked the chief. "Yes, and it can also play," the hunter answered. Everyone laughed at him, but the chief ordered him to bring the tortoise to perform for him. The hunter said that if it did not sing he would forfeit his life. The next day the hunter brought the tortoise and its instrument. He told it to sing for the chief, but it did not sing. He told it that he would lose his life if it did not sing, but it did not sing. The people waited until sundown and then the hunter was beheaded. Then the tortoise sang its song. The people shouted, "The tortoise sings! The hunter spoke the truth! We have killed him even though he spoke the truth." The tortoise said, "You are not to blame. The hunter sentenced himself. I lived happily in the forest singing my little song. I went home with him, but he broke his promise to me." Then it took its instrument and went slowly back to the forest. Since then no one has heard a tortoise singing. (Joslin [1952], pp. 267–79)

40. (Ghana) Breaking a tabu, a hunter went hunting on Friday. He found a turtle playing a guitar and singing. He took it home with him and, breaking another tabu, he told people that it could sing and play the guitar. The chief said he would cut off the hunter's head if he fooled the people who had assembled to hear the turtle. The hunter ordered the turtle to sing, but nothing happened. He repeated his command, but the turtle just sat there. The hunter was taken away and executed. Then the turtle began to play its guitar and sing, "Don't trouble trouble till trouble troubles you." Since then, no hunter has hunted on Friday. (Addo [1968], pp. 31–32)

41. (Ghana: Ashanti) A hunter heard the sound of music in the forest. Creeping toward it, he saw a tortoise playing a small accordian and singing gaily. He told the tortoise he would take it home to play and sing there. The

tortoise said it could not refuse, since the hunter had a gun, but warned him that he would have only himself to blame if there were trouble. The hunter told the chief about the tortoise and asked him to assemble his people to hear it. The chief said that if the hunter lied, he would lose his head. When the people assembled, the hunter begged the tortoise to play and sing, but it just turned its head away. The people laughed and the hunter was led to the executioner. As his head rolled on the ground, the tortoise picked up its accordian and sang, "Trouble does not look for man; it is man who looks for trouble." The hunter was given a grand funeral—after all, he had spoken the truth—and the tortoise was taken back to the forest. (Appiah [1967], pp. 33–36; summarized in Appiah [1968], p. 128)

42. (Texas) While fishing, a boy saw a turtle crawling on a log in the river. It had a banjo, and it began picking and singing. The boy ran home and told his father, who gave him a thrashing for telling a lie. Finally the boy persuaded his father to go and see the turtle playing the banjo and singing. When they got there, the turtle was not to be seen, and the father was about to administer another thrashing. Then, all at once, they heard music and saw the turtle on the log, picking its banjo and singing, "Live in peace. Don't tell all you see." (Dobie [1932])

43. (Haiti) Given feathers by the birds so that he could fly away with them if the farmer came, a tortoise ate with the birds in a garden. But when the farmer came, the birds took back their feathers, and the tortoise was caught. As Pierre Jean, the farmer, was going to beat it, the tortoise began to sing, "What a tragedy, I have no wings!" The farmer liked the song and put the tortoise in a box and took it home. The President heard about the tortoise and made the farmer a bet: he would get 100,000 *gourdes* if the tortoise sang, but he would be shot if it did not. Meanwhile the farmer's wife let the tortoise escape into the river, while trying to get it to sing. She put a lizard in the box, and it did not sing for the President. When the box was opened, the President called the farmer a cheat and ordered that he be taken back to the river and shot. Just as they were about to shoot the tortoise sang, "Uncle Pierre Jean talks too much. Stupidity doesn't kill a Haitian, it makes him sweat!" The President heard, and the farmer was released and given the money. (Courlander [1960], pp. 179-81; [1976], pp. 70-71)

BIBLIOGRAPHY

Addo, Peter Eric Adotey
1968 *Ghana Folk Tales: Ananse Stories from Africa.* New York, Exposition Press.
Anonymous

1930 *African Folk Tales. Book II.* Lagos, Church Missionary Society's Bookshop; London, Longmans, Green.

1949 *Itan Arǫsǫ ti Afrika. Iwe Keji.* London, Longmans, Green.

Appiah, Peggy

1967 *Tales of an Ashanti Father.* London, André Deutsch.

1968 *The Children of Ananse.* London, Evans Brothers.

Barker, W. H., and Sinclair, Cecilia

1917 *West African Folk-Tales.* London, George C. Harrap.

Bascom, William

1965 Field notes.

1969 *Ifa Divination: Communication between Gods and Men in West Africa.* Bloomington, Indiana University Press

Biebuyck, Daniel P., and Mateene, Kahombo

1970 Anthologie de la Littérature Orale Nyanga. *Académie Royal des Sciences d'Outre-Mer, Classe des Sciences Morales et Politiques,* N.S. 36:192–95.

Botkin, B. A.

1949 *A Treasury of Southern Folklore.* New York, Crown.

1966 *A Treasury of American Lore.* New York, Crown. ([1944]

1968 *Lay My Burden Down.* Chicago, University of Chicago Press. [1945].

Brewer, J. Mason

1932 Juneteenth. *Publications of the Texas Folk-Lore Society* 10:48–50.

Chatelain, Heli

1894 Folk-Tales of Angola. *Memoirs of the American Folk-Lore Society* 1:242–43. Reprinted in Harold Courlander, *A Treasury of African Folklore.* New York: Crown, 1975, p. 301.

Courlander, Harold

1957 *Terrapin's Pot of Sense.* New York, Henry Holt.

1960 *The Drum and the Hoe.* Berkeley, University of California Press.

1963 *The King's Drum and Other African Stories.* London, Rupert Hart-Davis.

1976 *A Treasury of Afro-American Folklore.* New York, Crown.

Courlander, Harold, and Herzog, George

1947 *The Cow-Tail Switch.* New York, Henry Holt.

Dobie, J. Frank

1932 Footnote to Brewer's version [35]. Juneteenth. *Publications of the Texas Folk-Lore Society* 10:50.

Doke, Clement M.

1927 Lamba Folk-Lore. *Memoirs of the American Folk-Lore Society* 20:176, 177.

Dorson, Richard M.

1954 More Tales of John Blackmore. *Western Folklore* 13:256–58.

1956 *Negro Folktales in Michigan.* Cambridge, Mass., Harvard University Press.

1958 *Negro Tales from Pine Bluff, Arkansas, and Calvin, Michigan.* Indiana University Folklore Series No. 12.

1967 *American Negro Folktales.* Greenwich, Conn., Fawcett.

Epega, D. Onadele

n.d. If a—Amǫna Awǫn Baba Wa. Ode Rěmǫ, Imǫlě Oluwa Institute. VIII, pp. 14–16.

Fauset, Arthur Huff

1927 Negro Folk Tales from the South [Alabama, Mississippi, Louisiana]. *Journal of American Folk-Lore* 40:263.

1928 Tales and Riddles Collected in Philadelphia. *Journal of American Folk-Lore* 41:536–37.

Frobenius, Leo

1922 Erzählungen der Mande. *Atlantis* 8:84–90. Reprinted in Leo Frobenius, *African*

Nights. Black Erotic Folk Tales, trans. Peter Ross. New York: Herder and Herder, 1971. Pp. 189–96.

1924 Volkserzählungen und Volksdichtungen aus dem Zentral-Sudan. *Atlantis* 9:150–51. Translated in Leo Frobenius and Douglas C. Fox, *African Genesis.* New York: Stackpole Sons, 1937. P. 236. Reprinted in Harold Courlander, *A Treasury of Afro-American Folklore.* New York: Crown, 1976. P. 583.

1924 Volksdichtungen aus Oberguinea. I Band. Fabuleien Dreier Völker. *Atlantis* 11:234–35.

Gaden, Henri
1913 *Le Poular. Dialecte Peul du Fouta Sénégalais. Vol. I.* Collection de la Revue du Monde Musulman. Paris, Ernest Leroux.

Hurston, Zora Neal
1969 *Mules and Men.* New York, Negro Universities Press. [1935]

Jablow, Alta
1961 *Yes and No: The Intimate Folklore of Africa.* New York, Horizon Press. Also published as *An Anthology of West African Folklore.* London: Thames and Hudson, 1962. Source unidentified.

Johnston, H. A. S.
1966 *A Selection of Hausa Stories.* Oxford, Clarendon Press.

Joslin, Mike
1952 *Anansi Sem. Spindelsagor fràn Guldkusten.* Stockholm, LTs Förlag. Reprinted in Mike Joslin, *Märchen von der Goldküste,* trans. Anni Carlson. Munich: Nymphenburger, 1960. Pp. 177–89.

Lademann, Gebhard; Kausch, Ludwig; and Reuss, Alfred
1910 Tierfabeln und andere Erzählungen in Suaheli. *Archiv für das Studium deutscher Kolonialsprachen* 12:83.

Mischlich, A.
1929 Neue Märchen aus Afrika. *Veröffentlichungen des Staatlichsächsischen Forschungsinstitutes für Völkerkunde in Leipzig* 9:115–19.

Parsons, Elsie Clews
1917 Tales from Guilford County, North Carolina. *Journal of American Folk-Lore* 30:176–77.

Percy, William Alexander
1941 *Lanterns on the Levee.* New York, Knopf.

Randolph, Vance
1953 A Folktale from Arkansas. *Tennessee Folklore Society Bulletin* 19:102–03.
1957 *The Talking Turtle and Other Ozark Folk Tales.* New York, Columbia University Press.

Stannus, Hugh
1922 The Wayao of Nyasaland. *Harvard African Studies* 3:322.

van Wing J., and Scholler, Cl.
1940 *Legendes des Bakongo-Orientaux.* Brussels, Bulens.

NOTES

1. Richard M. Dorson, *American Folklore* (1959; rpt. Chicago: Univ. of Chicago Press, 1962), p. 188.

2. Ibid., p. 185.

3. Richard M. Dorson, *American Negro Folktales* (Greenwich, Conn.: Fawcett, 1967), pp. 15–16.

4. Ibid., p. 16. There are obvious errors here, as K1162 does not appear in Dorson's index to his motifs and, in Stith Thompson's Motif Index, K1162 reads, "Man persuaded to go to store with scythe. Is tied up as madman." As Dundes (see note 9) points out, Dorson probably refers to Kenneth Clarke's K1162+, but the motif is more accurately identified by Baughman and by Thompson as B210.2, "Talking animal or object refuses to talk on demand. Discoverer is unable to prove his claims: is beaten." See note 19. Elsewhere, Dorson ([1956] p. 212; [1967], pp. 147, 148, 381) correctly identifies the motif as B210.2

5. Motifs are only elements of a folktale. As defined by Stith Thompson in *The Folktale* (New York: The Dryden Press, 1946), p. 415, a tale type "is a traditional tale that has an independent existence. . . . A *motif* is the smallest element in a tale having a power to persist in tradition." Two or more tale types may be combined in a single narrative, but they are separate tale types if they have been told by themselves. Many of the tale types that I will consider, including this one, are sometimes combined with other tale types.

6. Dorson, *American Negro Folktales*, p. 16.

7. Daniel J. Crowley, "African Folktales in Afro-America," in *Black America*, ed. John Szwed (New York: Basic Books, 1970), p. 203.

8. William D. Piersen, "An African Background for American Folktales?" *Journal of American Folklore*, 84 (1971), 212–13.

9. Alan Dundes, "African and Afro-American Tales," *Research in African Literatures*, 7 (Fall 1976), 191–92.

10. Piersen, p. 213.

11. Richard M. Dorson, "African and Afro-American Folklore. A Reply to Bascom and Other Misguided Critics," *Journal of American Folklore*, 88 (1975), 160.

12. Ibid., p. 157.

13. Dorson, *American Folklore*, p. 176.

14. Joel Chandler Harris, *Nights with Uncle Remus* (Boston and New York: Houghton Mifflin Company, 1883), pp. xvii–xxvii; A. Gerber, "Uncle Remus Traced to the Old World," *Journal of American Folk-Lore*, 6 (1893), 245–57.

15. Dorson, *American Negro Folktales*, p. 17.

16. Richard M. Dorson, *Negro Folktales in Michigan* (Cambridge, Mass.: Harvard Univ. Press, 1956), nos. 52–63, 65–97.

17. Ibid., pp. 139–44; *American Negro Folktales*, pp. 238–43.

18. Dorson (1975), p. 152.

19. Piersen, pp. 210–11.

20. Antti Aarne and Stith Thompson, *The Types of the Folktale*, FF Communications No. 184 (1961; rpt. 1964), p. 7.

21. Daniel J. Crowley, "Extra-European Folktale Areas of the World: A Tabular Analysis," *Preprint Series* (Mimeographed) (Bloomington, Ind.: Folklore Students Association), vol. 1:1 (1973), 33.

22. Stith Thompson, *Motif-Index of Folk-Literature*, vols. 1–6 (Bloomington: Indiana Univ. Press, 1955–1958).

23. Ernest W. Baughman, *Type and Motif Index of the Folktales of England and North America*, Indiana University Folklore Series No. 20 (1966).

24. Dorson, *American Negro Folktales*, p. 16.

25. Halpert says, "Reports of this story from English-speaking white informants are rare. The story is usually told by Negroes, and I believe it is of African origin" (Vance Randolph, *The Talking Turtle and Other Ozark Folk Tales* [New York: Columbia Univ. Press, 1957], p. 179).

26. Piersen, p. 213; William Bascom, *Ifa Divination: Communication between Gods and Men in West Africa* (Bloomington: Indiana Univ. Press, 1969), p. 136.

27. Bascom, pp. 136-37, 428-31, 436-41, 528-33.

28. E.g., René Guillot, *Contes d'Afrique,* Numéro spécial du Bulletin de l'Enseignement de l'A. O. F. (1933), pp. 81-82; Leo Frobenius, "Die Atlantische Götterlehre," *Atlantis,* 10 (1926), 294-96; Elphinstone Dayrell, *Folk Stories from Southern Nigeria, West Africa* (London: Longmans, Green, 1910), pp. 38-41, 98-103; Labi Tawaba and Tamundel Mubele, *Qui la Sortira de Cette Pierre?* Ceeba Publications, series 2, vol. II (1974), 50-57.

The Talking Skull Refuses to Talk: Addenda from Portuguese Sources*

In his article on African folktales in America in *RAL,* 8 (Fall 1977), William Bascom expressed his surprise at finding only one version of the tale of the skull in the Antilles and South America, a version having been reported from Haiti. As a matter of fact, at least three versions from northern South America are to be found in the literature, that is in the non-English literature, adding strength to the assumption that the tale was carried to the Americas from Africa.

Luís de Câmara Cascudo, the Brazilian folklorist who is well known to some Americans, published three Brazilian versions of the tale in his classic comparative study, *Trinta "estórias" brasileiras* (Porto, Portugal: Portucalense Editora, 1955), pp. 71-75. The first, "Quem perde o corpo é a língua" (The tongue is the body's ruin), was told to Cascudo, like the other twenty-nine stories in his book, by his old nurse, a white woman and, to use his words, "a humble, illiterate Shahrazad." She grew up in the coastal region of Rio Grande do Norte, where African influences are ancient and powerful. Her version tells of a hunter who is beaten up by his companions when the skull fails to repeat in their presence what it has told him: The tongue is the body's ruin.

The second version, reproduced from Théo Brandão's *Folclore de Alagoas* (Maceío: Ramalho, 1949), also comes from northeastern Brazil. It was told first to Brandão's great-great-great-grandfather in his childhood by a black female slave. Here "a man" walking along a path knocks on a skull with his cane, asks it what killed it, and receives the answer, "The tongue." Considered to be a liar, the man ends up by being beheaded on the king's orders.

The third version was given to Cascudo in 1951 by Braga Montenegro, a well-known writer from Ceará, another northeast Brazilian state. Braga Montenegro heard it from his great-grandmother. According to his version, a young nobleman comes upon the skull while hurrying to a reception at the royal palace and kicks it out of his way. A voice issues from the skull, saying,

*This addenda by Gerald M. Moser is reprinted from *Research in African Literatures,* 9 (1978), 256-57.

"What killed me was my tongue." This young man likewise loses his head, for the skull refuses to talk again until it is too late.

Cascudo quotes a fourth version that might have come from Portugal. He found it in Viriato Padilha's *O livro dos fantasmas* (Rio de Janeiro: Quaresma, 1925). Nevertheless, he concludes: "There seems to be no reason to doubt that the tale came to Brazil with the black African slaves. The obvious question yet to be answered is where on the black continent did it originate? The oral literature of the Arabs contains many tales about talking skulls that reply to the questions of saints, prophets and wise men. I don't know any [Arabian] version that resembles our written ones, but there are elements common to both. Until further information turns up, we must be content with the evidence of its having traveled to Brazil with the Bantus and Sudanese" (*Trinta "estórias" brasileiras*, p. 74; the translation is mine).

Cascudo reported the same findings in a later book, *Made in Africa* (Rio de Janeiro: Editora Civilização Brasileira, 1965), pp. 96–98, in which he traced the African origins of many things in Brazilian culture while he was on a study trip to Angola. In this book he added another Angolan version (Oscar Ribas, 1961) to Chatelain's version of 1894. To these two I could add a third Kimbundu version, published in 1918 by Domingos Van-Dúnem ("A Caveira," in *Novo Almanach de Lembranças Luso-Brasileiro para 1919* [Lisbon, 1918], pp. 22–23). Cascudo also refers to a version which Henri Junod collected among the BaRonga of Mozambique. And there may be more.

In short, the tale of the talking skull is well attested in northeastern Brazil, as well as in southern Africa. If a lesson may be drawn, it is that it will pay folklorists to read the literature that exists in Portuguese.

The Talking Skull Refuses to Talk: More Addenda*

I am grateful to Gerald M. Moser for calling my attention to the three Brazilian and three additional African versions of this tale. As I said, "I shall concentrate on folktales recorded in the United States, but I shall include analogues reported elsewhere in the Americas . . . ," "these data are partially assembled here," and "Undoubtedly, there are other examples that I have missed."

My coverage was obviously incomplete, and I have subsequently found two more versions of the talking animal that refuses to talk. In the first, from the United States, a Negro told his boss to come and see a talking alligator. When it refused to talk, the boss kicked him on his behind and went back to the big house. Then the alligator said, "Just like a Negro! I said good morning to YOU, and you had to go tell a white man!" (Langston Hughes and Arna Bontemps, *The Book of Negro Folklore* [New York: Dodd, Mead & Company,

*This addenda by William Bascom is reprinted from *Research in African Literatures*, 9 (1978), 258.

1958], 505–06; I assume that this tale is reprinted, but I have not been able to locate the original source).

In the second version, from Jamaica, a talking monkey agreed to accompany a man if he promised to tell no one that it could talk. Together they came to Jamaica, the one place in the world where no one told tales. The man could not keep the secret and was accused of spoiling the island by telling a tale. He protested that he was telling the truth and was ordered to bring the monkey before the judge. In court the monkey whispered in his ear so that no one else could hear, "So this is your word of honor?" and refused to say another word. The judge ordered the man to gather up the tale and do away with it, and he sent to Anancy for help. Anancy bought the tale for a bag of shillings, and then made up an unbelievable tale of his own. When the judge heard of this, he had both Anancy and the man brought to court. When he heard Anancy's tale, the judge smiled and ruled that telling tales was not that bad, and it was good for Jamaica to have them like other countries (F. Turenne des Prés, "The Tale–A West Indian Folk Story," *Phylon*, 13 [1952], 293–97).

T H R E E

＊

Trickster Seeks Endowments; Measuring the Snake; Challenging Birds (Insects) to Fill a Container; Milking a Cow (Deer) Stuck in a Tree

I have adapted my first title from that of Elsie Clews Parsons, "Rabbit Seeks Endowments" [76]. As we shall see, it covers a group of related folktales that combine a number of motifs (and tale types) in various ways, making it difficult to treat them separately. It is perhaps best known in the Ashanti version in which Ananse, the spider, seeks the right to have folktales known as "Ananse stories" [14–15, 17–21]. This version is found only in Ghana and does not seem to appear in the New World, but other versions have been reported in Africa from Gambia to Zaire, with many variations in both Africa and the Americas.

Most commonly , the trickster seeks wisdom, cunning, or power in Africa [1–2, 6–8, 10, 12, 22, 24–26, 29], the United States [32–33, 41–43, 50, 52, 56–57], and elsewhere in the New World [64–76]. With six exceptions [22, 42–43, 69–70, 73], these thirty-four tales end with him being told that he is already smart enough, or something to that effect. A similar ending is also found in seven tales involving different quests [9, 13, 44–46, 58, 61].

A third commmon pattern involves the trickster's attempt, usually successful, to win a bride. This is found in Africa [3–5, 13, 23], the United States [35, 45–47, 49, 53, 59], and in the Dominican Republic [63].

In other African versions the trickster wants to become king [9, 11], or seeks two extra legs [16] or a child [28], or no quest is specified [27]. In the United States he wants a tail [54] or a long tail [37, 39–40, 44], large eyes [38], food [30, 36], to have a means of offense [58], or no quest is specified [31, 34, 48, 51, 55]. Elsewhere in the New World he wants to become king [61], asks to be larger [60, 77–78], or he seeks a reward of money and wins a bride [62].

Reprinted from *Research in African Literatures*, 9 (1978), 216–55.

To achieve his goal, the trickster must obtain one or more things. Told to bring a snake or its teeth, he pretends to measure it in Africa [1-4, 6-9, 11, 14-17, 20-22, 29], the United States [30-32, 37-38, 41-42, 45, 50, 53, 56-58], and Guadeloupe [57], or he captures it in some other way [18; 33, 35, 43, 59; 62, 75, 78]. In Africa the snake is usually a boa or python, in the United States a rattlesnake, in Guadeloupe a big snake, and in Colombia it is simply a snake.

Another task is to bring a wild animal or its teeth or tusks. In Africa this usually involves the leopard [4-8, 14-15, 17, 20-21] or elephant [5, 10, 12-13, 23-26], but also the lion [3, 16, 28] hyena [1, 2?], or jackal [11]. In the United States it is the alligator [30, 32, 39, 41-42, 44-46, 48-49, 53-54, 56, 59] or, in two instances, the elephant [32, 49]. Elsewhere in the New World it is the crocodile or alligator [63-64, 66, 69, 71, 77], lion [75], elephant [78], or gorilla [74]. This is accomplished in a variety of ways.

A third task is to bring a gourd or sack full of birds or insects (hornets, yellow-jackets, wasps, bees, gnats, flies, or ants). He accomplishes this by challenging them to fill his container in Africa [1-2, 5-6, 9-11, 14-16, 18, 29], the United States [30, 37, 42, 45, 47, 54-57], and elsewhere [62, 67, 69?], or he does so by other means [7-8, 17, 19-21; 35, 38-41, 44, 46, 52, 58; 73, 76, 78].

In Africa the trickster also obtains the milk of the wild African buffalo or "bush-cow" [1-2, 11-13, 25-26, 28], lion [10], deer [9], antelope [27], or cow [29], in the United States the milk of a deer [46] or cow [34, 51], and elsewhere the milk of a wild cow [64-66, 69], mean cattle [73], or a pig [70]. Usually he tells the animal that it doesn't have enough milk [2, 9-11, 29; 73], or he milks it when it is stuck in a tree [12-13, 25, 27-28; 34, 46, 51; 64, 66, 69].

In Africa he must also bring the tears of a lion [24-25], hippopotamus [10], serpent [12], or elephant [28]; in the United States the tears of a deer [37, 40, 44, 47, 53]; and in Trinidad the tears of a tiger [76].

Many other tasks are prescribed, but one or more of these five are found in all but five of the seventy-eight narratives presented here. In one tale the trickster secures the meat of an alligator, panther, and elephant [36], in another the skins of an alligator, tiger, and monkey [55], and in a third the skins of an alligator, tiger, and three monkeys [61]. In two tales [68, 72] he brings the tooth of Zamba (unidentified), as he does in two others [66, 70] in which he also brings milk. Despite the variety of the trickster's quests and tasks and other differences in details, there can be little doubt that these folktales are historically related.

The tasks of bringing Zamba's teeth, fish scales, buzzard and rooster feathers, and peas, and ringing the devil's bell have no counterparts in these African folktales and may well be New World inventions. The same is true of the incident of the alligator telling the trickster, usually the rabbit disguised as a squirrel, how it can be killed [30, 45, 48, 54, 56, 59, 61, 63, 77].[1]

The attempt to kill the trickster after he has completed his tasks [44; 66, 73-76] is found in one of the African versions [24], and the breaking of the animal's tooth by slipping or sliding [64-66, 68, 70-71] is found in another

[10]. Breaking the animal's tooth or tusk by tying it to a tree is found in both the United States [32] and Africa [25].

The incident of burning a load on an animal's back or head [32, 36, 74–75] is found in two different African folktales from the Fulani of Mali and the Beni Mtir Berber of Morocco. In the former, Baby Hare said that his father's elephant would have cut a hundred bunches of straw and put them on its back for him to ride on. Elephant cut a hundred bunches of straw, put them on its back, and told Hare to mount. Hare mounted, struck his flint and steel, lit the straw, and jumped down. Elephant went into the forest, set it on fire, and died.[2] In the latter, after other incidents, Jackal told Crow to help him load wood on Lion's back. When they had done so, Crow asked if he could mount, and Lion let him do so. Jackal gave Crow a match and told him to set the wood on fire. Crow did so and flew off. Lion was burned, and they ate him. Another incident follows.[3]

The dung of a dog [68–69] comes from a different African folktale, to be discussed later, as do the incidents of the trickster's hole answering [47] and of his tying an animal to a tree because of a storm [60–61, 76–77].

"Trickster Seeks Endowments" does not appear in Aarne and Thompson's *The Types of the Folktale*. Certainly it is not AT331, "The Spirit in the Bottle," or AT592, "The Dance Among Thorns," which have been cited. A reference to Barker and Sinclair's folktale from Ghana [14] is given under motif K717, "Deception into bottle (vessel)," but the description of this motif does not fit these folktales: "Insects (or a spirit) having escaped from a bottle are told they cannot return. They accept the challenge and go back into the bottle." One relevant motif would seem to be K711.0.1, "Birds enticed into bag," but the only reference given for it is to North American Indians. Another is H1151.6, "Task: Stealing elephant's tail (tusk)," for which the only references are to different folktales, and these are African. The most relevant motif is H1154.6, "Task: Capturing squirrel or rattlesnake," but as Dundes has already pointed out,[4] the only reference given for this motif is to a tale in *Nights with Uncle Remus* [50].[5] Since there are no references to similar tale types or motifs from Europe or India, these folktales must have come from (and originated in) Africa.

This is no new discovery. In 1893, Gerber cited an analogue, which I have not yet located, of this Uncle Remus tale [50] from the Wolof of Senegal or Gambia. In it, Hare "comes to the Creator desiring to be more cunning. God asks him to catch some sparrows in his calabash. After he has done this, God tells him to go off, for if he complied with his request, he would upset the world." Compared to several other tales he considered, Gerber said that in this case the similarities between the African and American versions are "not quite so close, though still beyond doubt."[6]

In 1943, Parsons cited eleven African parallels [3–6, 10, 14, 17–20, 24] to her versions from the Antilles [65–76], as well as versions from Mexico [60] and the Bahamas [62], fourteen from Virginia, South Carolina, and Georgia

[36–43, 49–50, 52–55], and five from the Hitchiti, Natchez, and Creek Indians [30–31, 56–58].[7]

Dundes gives this as the first of his "African Tales among the North American Indians," adding versions from the Seminole [59] and Potawatomi (unavailable). He says, "It is clearly not a European tale type," and concludes that "this is a popular West African tale type which diffused to southeastern American Indian groups via American Negro tradition in which the tale is also common. The tale is *not* found among the majority of American Indian tribes and as Gerber pointed out in 1893, it is hard to imagine that an American Indian tale diffused to many parts of Africa by those few American Negroes who returned to Africa. In short, the American Indian origin theory for this particular tale is untenable."[8]

Thus it has been argued that if Afro-American folktales did not come from Europe, they must have come from the American Indians, and the debate over this theory is also nearly a century old. In 1883, Joel Chandler Harris challenged J. W. Powell's support of the American Indian origin theory, saying, "it is impossible to adduce in support of such a theory a scintilla of evidence that cannot be used in support of just the opposite theory, namely that the Indians borrowed their stories from the negroes." And as Dundes has noted, Harris cited his tale in which Rabbit seeks out old Witch Rabbit [50] as one which was "undoubtedly borrowed from the negroes" by the Creek Indians [58].[9]

Courlander has also said that a version of this tale type from Georgia [52] and another from Guadeloupe [64] are "direct descendants of an Ashanti explanation of how Anansi, the spider trickster, came to be the owner of all tales" [21].[10] In view of its wide African distribution, one may question its Ashanti origin, but not that it came to America from Africa.

However, further investigation reveals that this composite tale type includes several other tale types, each of which occurs by itself and thus "has an independent existence."[11]

    III. Measuring the snake [22]

    IV. Challenging birds (insects) to fill a container [55]

    V. Milking a cow (deer) stuck in a tree [34, 51]

As we have seen earlier, all three of these tale types are found in both the United States and Africa, but not in either Europe or India. A fourth tale type, "Bringing an alligator's tooth," is also found by itself [48, 63, 71] but is not relevant here because I have not found an African version.

My twenty-nine African versions come from Gambia (Mandinka), Sierra Leone (Temne), Liberia (Unspecified and De), Ivory Coast (Wobe), Mali (Fulani and Malinke), Upper Volta (Mosi), Ghana (Unspecified, Ashanti, and Ewe), Nigeria (Hausa, Bura, and Igbo), and Zaire (Mbala); there is also the Wolof tale summarized by Gerber. The thirty from the United States come from Oklahoma (Hitchiti and Natchez Indians), Louisiana (Chitimacha Indians), Mississippi, Alabama, Virginia, South Carolina, Georgia (Negro and Creek

Indians), and Florida (Seminole Indians); to these may be added the Pota-
watomi tale cited by Dundes. Nineteen others come from Mexico, Guatemala
(Chuh Indians), Bahamas, Dominican Republic, Guadeloupe, Marie Galante,
Les Saintes, Dominica, Martinique, Saint Lucia, Grenada, Trinidad, Venezuela
(Warao Indians), and Columbia; in addition, although we have not yet found
a published version, Berta M. Bascom recalls having heard "Trickster Seeks
Endowments" in Cuba.[12]

1. (Gambia: Mandinka) Hare went to God and asked for cunning. God
told him to bring a gourd full of weaver birds, a gourd full of buffalo milk,
a live python, and a live hyena. He took a gourd to the weaver birds, arguing
with himself as to whether or not they could fill it. They went into the gourd
until it was full, and Hare closed its mouth. He went to a buffalo that had
given birth, arguing with himself as to whether she would fill his gourd with
milk. The buffalo let him milk her until the gourd was full. He went to a
python with a long bamboo, arguing with himself as to whether or not it
would be long enough. The python lay down by the bamboo and Hare tied
it to the bamboo. He sent word to a hyena that God was going to give a
charity. The hyena went with Hare and carried the python to God. God asked
Hare how he had gotten the four things, and Hare told Him. God told him
to go away, saying that if He added to Hare's cunning he would also catch
human beings. (Gamble, n.d.)

2. (Gambia: Mandinka) Hare went to God to beg for cunning. God told
him to bring a live python, a gourd full of weaver birds, and a gourd full of
wild-buffalo milk. Hare took a long piece of bamboo and went to a python,
saying to himself that it would not be long enough. The python asked who he
was arguing with, and he said that his people said that the bamboo was longer
than it was. The python agreed to let Hare measure it, and Hare tied it to the
bamboo. Hare took a gourd and went to the weaver birds, saying to himself
that they would fill it. He opened the gourd and the birds filled it. He tied the
gourd shut and went to a suckling buffalo, saying his doubting words. Buffalo
gave milk and filled the gourd. Hare went to a hyena and said that God wanted
to make a charity and wanted the hyena to be present. Hare took the python,
the milk, and the birds, and went with the hyena to God. God asked Hare,
and Hare explained everything. God said that the cunning that Hare had was
enough, and that if He added to it, hare would cause a lot of trouble even to
humans. (Anonymous [1955], p. 4; translated in Gamble, n.d.)

3. (Sierra Leone: Temne) To win a bride, Spider was told by her mother
to bring lion's teeth with fresh blood on them, palm wine from a sass-wood
tree [which does not give wine], and a boa constrictor. Spider made a fire
and a bench nearby, and invited the animals to come one by one to warm
themselves. When a lion came he put leaves on the fire. The smoke made the
lion close its eyes and open its mouth, and Spider knocked out its teeth with
a hammer and took them to the girl's mother. He chopped a hole in a sass-
wood tree and hung a pot by the hole. Then he stole palm wine, rubbed some
in the hole, and filled the pot. He got a man to take down the pot and they

carried it to the mother. The man confirmed that the palm wine came from a sass-wood tree. Spider took a long stick to a boa and told it that he and a friend argued about whether it was as long as the stick. The snake lay down beside the stick and Spider tied the snake to it, saying that this would make the snake straight. Spider took the boa to the mother and married her daughter. (Cronise and Ward [1903], pp. 40–49)

4. (Sierra Leone: Temne) Spider said he would marry a woman who would take as her husband only a person without a scar. Her family told him to bring the skin of a snake, and he took the cast of a snake that had just shed its skin. They said he should bring a leopard tooth, and he scratched a leopard until it slept and then knocked out a tooth. They said he should bring wine from the iroko tree [which does not give wine], and he tapped palm wine in a calabash and hung it on the iroko tree. They said he should bring a live python, and he got the python to measure its length against a stick and tied the python to it. They said he should bring a bush-cow, and he made a fire and killed it as it warmed itself. They said he should bring a camel, and he borrowed one. They said he should bring a ground-squirrel, and he dug one up. They said he should bring a hippo, and one hippo helped him tie up another. They said he should bring dancers, and he gave them tobacco and promised them a tip. They went with him, so the family gave him his wife. (Thomas, Part III [1916], pp. 7–10)

5. (Sierra Leone: Temne) A woman said that whoever married her daughter must bring a cage full of wild geese, a live elephant, and a leopard's tooth. Many people, large animals, and small animals tried and failed. When Spider's turn came, he took a cage to the river and, pretending to be arguing with himself, told the wild geese that he had a bet that they could not fill the cage. They entered it, he closed the door, and he took them to the woman. The next day he went to an elephant and told it that it could not come to town even when they beat a drum. He put a stick in the elephant's ear and turned it; it felt nice and the elephant went to town with him. The next day he made a big fire and invited all the animals to come and warm themselves. The leopard sat where smoke was going into its mouth, and Spider knocked out a tooth. He took it to the woman who gave him her daughter in marriage. (Thomas, Part III [1916] pp. 84–86)

6. (Liberia) Nymo went to a Bush-Doctor and begged him for wisdom. The Bush-Doctor told him first to bring a python, all the rice-birds, and a leopard's tooth. Nymo took a long stick and told a python that the Bush-Doctor said it was not as long as the stick. When the python stretched out by the stick, Nymo tied it to the stick and took it to the Bush-Doctor. He made a large basket and took it to the rice farms. He told the rice-birds that the Bush-Doctor said that they were less numerous than the sparrows and could not fill the basket. They flew into the basket and Nymo carried them to the Bush-Doctor. Holding a club behind his back, he told a leopard that the Bush-Doctor said its teeth were not as white and strong as elephant's. The leopard opened its mouth to show off its teeth, and Nymo knocked out

a tooth with his club and ran with it to the Bush-Doctor. The Bush-Doctor said, "You are wise enough. It would be unsafe to make you wiser." (Bundy [1919], pp. 416–17)

7. (Liberia) Hare went to God to ask for wisdom. God said he must first bring two leopard teeth dripping with blood. Hare invited a leopard to dinner and complimented it on its beautiful teeth. The leopard opened its mouth and Hare struck it with a club, knocking out two teeth. He took them to God, who said he must bring the most poisonous snake in the forest. Hare took a stick and went around the forest measuring animals. When a snake asked him what he was doing, he said God had asked him to find out which was the longest animal in the forest. The snake said it was, and asked to be measured. Hare placed his stick beside the snake and tied it at each end and in the middle. He took the snake to God, who said he must bring all the little birds. Hare made a strong cage and went to the little birds. He told them that a snake would eat them that night, and that they should sleep in the cage where they would be safe. They went into the cage, and Hare took them to God. God told him that anyone who had as much wisdom as he had needed no more. (Baharav [1965], pp. 40–41)

8. (Liberia: De) Hare went to God to ask for wisdom. God told him to bring two leopard teeth dripping with blood. Hare praised a leopard's strong, white teeth, the leopard opened its mouth wider, and Hare knocked out two teeth with a club. He took them to God, who told him to bring the most poisonous snake in the forest. Hare put marks on a stick and went around measuring animals. A poisonous snake asked what he was doing, and Hare said God wanted to know which was the longest animal. The snake let itself be measured, and Hare tied it to the stick. He took the snake to God, who said he must bring all the little birds. He took a cage to the birds and told them to sleep in it because a snake was planning to eat them. They went into the cage and Hare took them to God. God said, "Anyone who has so much wisdom needs no more." (Pinney [n.d.], pp. 90–92)

9. (Ivory Coast: Wobe) God told the animals he would make king the one who could find a snake the exact length of a stick and fill one gourd with deer milk and another with small birds. Many animals tried and failed. When Hare's turn came, he told the birds that God had made fun of their number, saying that there were not enough to fill his gourd. When they flew into it, he took them home. He told a deer that God had said that no deer could fill a gourd with milk. The deer filled the other gourd, and Hare took it home. He told a snake that God had made fun of its small size, saying that the stick was longer than it was. When the snake lay by the stick, Hare tied it to the stick and took the snake home. When he brought the three things, God said that Hare was the most cunning of all animals, and recompensed him by giving him speed in running. That is why hares are rarely caught. (Girard [1967], pp. 317–18)

10. (Mali: Fulani) Long ago God decided to give Hare cunning. He told Hare to bring him a calabash of lion milk, a calabash of hippopotamus tears,

a sack full of birds, and an elephant tusk. Hare told a lioness that the entire village had said that she could not nourish her child with her own milk, and that he had been sent to learn if this was true. The lioness told Hare to milk her, and he filled his calabash with milk. She said he should take it and show the villagers. Hare went to the river and told a hippopotamus that the horse and the donkey both said that their son was larger than its son. The hippopotamus showed Hare its son, and Hare said that he had been deceived. Hare said that he knew that the hippopotamus's father was dead. The hippopotamus began to weep, and Hare caught its tears. Hare told the birds that the villagers said that all of them could not fill his sack. They went in, filling the sack, and Hare tied it shut. Hare told an elephant that people said it could not slide. The elephant told him to moisten the ground. Hare did so, and the elephant slid. It slid again, but tumbled and its tusks stuck in the ground. Hare took a tusk and went with all the things to God. God tapped Hare's forehead and said, "You surpass all the animals of the forest in cunning." After the tap on the forehead, Hare became small as he is today. (le Brun [1919–20], pp. 193–95)

11. (Mali: Malinke) God told Hare that to become king he must bring a calabash full of flies, a calabash full of gnats, a snake bound to a stick, milk of the African buffalo, and a fettered jackal. Hare went to an elder who refused to help him, saying that God told lies. Hare went to the flies and told them that God said there were not enough flies to fill a calabash. They went into his calabash and he closed it when it was full. He did the same to the gnats. He took a bamboo pole and told a snake that God said it was not as long as the pole. The snake told him to tie its head and tail to the pole, which Hare did. The snake said Hare should release it, but Hare said that God would not believe him unless he saw it. Then he went to a buffalo and said that God said it had no milk. The buffalo told Hare to milk it, and he filled his calabash with milk. Jackal offered to serve as Hare's horse. Hare saddled it and carried everything to God. God said that there was one more thing: he must come by a path on which there was neither Monday nor Friday. Hare went back to the elder. The elder said that God had tricked Hare because there is no path without Monday and Friday. Meanwhile the jackal escaped and the gnats and flies made holes in their calabashes and flew away. (Frobenius, "Erzählungen," [1922], pp. 151–53)

12. (Upper Volta: Mosi) Hare asked the Sky God to show him many tricks. He was told he must bring buffalo milk, serpent tears, and an elephant tusk. He found an elephant and told it that he thought that it was larger than a tree, but people said that it was smaller. The elephant stood on its hind legs to show that it was larger, but the tree broke and the elephant fell, breaking a tusk. Since it was no longer of any use, the elephant let Hare take the tusk. He found a viper and, when it was away, killed its children. When it returned Hare told it not to cry because it would have other children. The viper cried and Hare gathered its tears in a calabash. He took a bowl of salt and millet meal to a buffalo near a baobab tree. He pretended to butt the tree and gave

the food to the buffalo, saying that it had fallen from the tree when he butted it. The buffalo took a long run and butted the tree so hard that its horns stuck in the trunk. Hare said that he would try to release the horns with milk. He milked the buffalo, but could not release the horns. Hare left with some of the milk, leaving the buffalo stuck to the tree. When Hare brought the three things, the Sky God said, "What good would it be to give you other tricks? You have enough already." (Tauxier [1917], pp. 414-15)

13. (Upper Volta: Mosi) Dwarf Antelope said that he would give his beautiful daughter in marriage to the one who brought the milk of an African buffalo, a panther hide, and an elephant tusk. Hare heard and took some spicy food to a buffalo. The buffalo liked it and wanted more. Hare said that it came from a tree, and that the buffalo could get more if it butted the tree with its horns. The buffalo ran full force at it, and its horns stuck in the tree. Hare milked the buffalo and took a calabash of milk to Dwarf Antelope. Hare asked panther to go swimming with him, taking red pepper in his wallet. They took off their clothes and went into the water. Saying that he had forgotten something, Hare went back and rubbed the panther's clothes with red pepper. When the panther couldn't put on its spotted clothes, Hare offered to wash them, but instead he took the hide to Dwarf Antelope. Then he went to the elephants and, looking up at the sky, said he saw something beautiful. When the elephants said they couldn't see anything, Hare told them to climb on top of each other so that the top elephant could see it. When they did so, Hare burned the foot of the elephant on the bottom, and the elephant on top fell, breaking its tusk. Hare took the tusk to Dwarf Antelope, saying, "Now, give me your daughter." Dwarf Antelope replied, "I cannot give her to you. You have showed me that you are exceptionally smart. I am also exceptionally smart. If our families intermarry and a child is born, it would be as smart as God, and that would not be good." (Frobenius, "Erzählungen," [1922], pp. 228-32)

14. (Ghana) Anasi, the spider, went to the chief of the gods, Nyankupon, and asked that all tales told by men might be known as Anansi stories instead of Nyankupon stories. He was told that his wish would be granted if he brought a jar full of live bees, a boa constrictor, and a tiger [i.e., leopard]. He took a jar and, pretending to be arguing with himself, went to the bees and told them that he and God had been arguing because God said that bees could not fly into the jar. They flew into it, Anansi sealed it, and he sent it to God. He took a long stick, and again pretending to argue with himself, told a boa constrictor that he had been arguing with God's people because they said that it was not as long as the stick. He asked to meausure the boa and it laid itself out straight. Anansi tied it to the stick and sent it to God. Then he took a needle and thread and sewed up his eye. He told a tiger that this made him see wonderful things, and the tiger wanted to see them too. He sewed up the tiger's eyes and led him to Nyankupon, who granted Anansi's request. (Barker and Sinclair [1917], pp. 29-31; reprinted in Lee [1930], pp. 24-25)

15. (Ghana) Spider went to God to ask that folktales be called Anansi stories instead of Nyankupon stories. He was told to bring a python, a leopard, and a large pot full of bees. He took a large pot and, pretending to be arguing with himself, he went to the bees and told them that he and God had been arguing because God said there were not enough bees in the world to fill the pot. The bees flew into the pot, and Anansi covered it and told the ants to carry it to God. Spider cut a long pole and told a python that he and God had been arguing because God said that the python was shorter than the pole. The python stretched out to its full length beside the pole and let Spider bind it to the pole to get a true measurement. Then he went to a leopard after spinning a web with which he covered his eyes. He told the leopard that this made him see beautiful visions, and leopard wanted to see them also. Anansi tied the leopard's eyelids shut and removed his own web so that he could see. He led the leopard and an elephant carried the python. They went to God who gave Spider the privilege of having all folktales be called Anansi stories. (Joslin [1952], pp. 31–49; [1960], pp. 7–24)

16. (Ghana) Wanting to be different from other insects, Spider went to God and asked for two extra legs. God told him to bring a black python, a pot with a million bees, and a lion. Spider took a long bamboo stick and, pretending to be arguing with himself, went to a python. He told the python that his wife said that it was longer than the stick, but that he said that it was not. The python offered to be measured and stretched out beside the stick. It said that to keep from wiggling it must be tied to the stick, and Spider tied it. Next he took a large calabash and went to the grassland, talking to himself about how all the bees in the world could not fill it. This made the bees mad and they swarmed into the calabash, and Spider closed it. Then he took a strong rope and asked a lion its weight. He laughed at the answer, saying that it could not possibly weight that much because he could lift it with one hand. The lion was tied so that Spider could lift it, and Spider refused to untie it. He took the three things to God and was given two extra legs, but people laughed at him so much that he now hides in the corners of houses. (Addo [1968], pp. 42–45)

17. (Ghana: Ashanti) Ananse, the spider, went to Nyankupon, the Sky-God, to buy his stories. He was told that they could be bought only with the python, leopard, fairy, and hornets. Spider said that he would add his mother. He took a palm branch and went to a python, pretending to be arguing with himself. He said that he and his wife were arguing because she said that the branch was longer than it was. The python stretched itself out and Spider tied it to the branch and took it to the Sky-God. Spider took a gourd full of water and went to a swarm of hornets. He poured some of the water on the hornets and some on himself. Then he cut a plantain leaf and covered his head. He told the hornets that it was raining and invited them into the gourd. They flew in and Spider closed it and took them to the Sky-God. Then he trapped a leopard in a pitfall and caught a fairy with a tarbaby, and took them to the Sky-God, along with his mother. The Sky-God gave

all his stories to Ananse and said that they should be called Spider-stories. (Rattray [1930], pp. 54–59; retold in Radin and Sweeney [1952], pp. 25–27, and Radin [1970], pp. 25–27)

18. (Ghana: Ashanti) Spider, Ananse, went to the Sky God, Nyame, and asked what it would cost to have the tales called "Nyame's stories" to be known as "Ananse's stories." Nyame said he must bring one of the little folk of the forest, a serpent, and some ants. Spider took a pot and went to the ants and said that he had been told that they could not fill it. They went inside and he closed the pot and took it to Nyame. Spider took food into the forest for the little folk; he caught one, put it in a bag, and took it to Nyame. He took a long stick to a serpent and played a game of "attach me" and "release me" with it. Then next day Ananse tied the serpent to the stick and did not release it. He took the serpent to Nyame who granted that "Nyame's stories" should be known as "Ananse's stories." (Herskovits and Herskovits [1937], pp. 53–55)

19. (Ghana: Ashanti) Ananse went to Nyankompon, the Sky God, and asked that stories be called "Ananse's stories." Nyankompon said that he must bring a serpent, ants, and one of the little folk of the forest. He caught two little folk with a tarbaby, a wooden figure covered with latex, and took everything to Nyankompon who granted his request. [The narrative does not tell how he captured the serpent and the ants.] (Herskovits and Herskovits [1937], pp. 55–56)

20. (Ghana: Ashanti) Ananse went to Nyame, the Sky God, and asked if the stories could be called "Ananse's stories." Nyame said yes, if Ananse brought a boa, gnats, and a leopard. He took a bottle to the gnats and told them that if it rained they could go inside it to keep dry. He went home to get water and scattered it, shouting that rain was coming. The gnats went into the bottle and Ananse corked it and took it to Nyame. He took a long stick and went to a boa, pretending to argue with himself whether it would be the same length. He told the boa that he had made a bet that it would be longer than the stick. The snake lay down by the stick, but the stick was longer. Ananse told the snake he would tie it to make it longer. He tied the boa and took it to Nyame. He went to a leopard and played "tying and loosing" with it. When leopard's turn to be tied came, Ananse did not release it. He took the leopard to Nyame who said that the stories should be named after Ananse. (Herskovits and Herskovits [1937], pp. 56–57)

21. (Ghana: Ashanti) Anansi, the spider, wanted to own all the stories known in the world. He went to Nyame, the Sky God, and offered to buy them. He was told that he could if he brought hornets, a python, and a leopard. He cut a small hole in a gourd and threw water from a large calabash on himself and on the hornets, putting the calabash on his head as if protecting himself from a storm. He invited the hornets into the gourd and plugged up the hole with grass. Next he cut a pole and some strong vines and, pretending to be arguing with himself, he went to a python. He told it that he and his

wife had been arguing because she said that it was shorter than the pole. The python stretched out to its full length beside the pole and let Spider bind it to the pole. Then he dug a pitfall in the forest in which the leopard was trapped. He made a spring snare which the leopard tied to its tail in order to get out, but when the leopard hung in the air, Spider killed it with his weapons. He took the things to the Sky God who gave him the stories which since then have been known as Anansi stories. (Courlander and Prempeh [1957], pp. 3–8; reprinted in Courlander [1976], pp. 586–87)

22. (Ghana: Ashanti) A messenger was sent to ask God to save a village from a python. God said that they should ask Spider, who boasted about how wise he was, and promised to give him more wisdom if he succeeded. Spider agreed to help. He cut down a young tree and many lianas and went to the river where the python was. The villagers brought food that the python liked and Spider invited it to eat. Then he asked the python to be measured. It stretched out beside the tree and Spider tied it to the tree. Spider called the villagers and chopped the python to bits. God was annoyed, but kept his word. He threw of pot of wisdom at Spider, hitting him in the waist. That is why Spider has such a narrow waist. (Appiah [1967], pp. 11–18)

23. (Ghana: Ewe) The king said that the one who brought him an elephant tusk could marry his daughter. All the men tried and failed. Spider mixed meal with honey and gave it to an elephant to eat. The elephant asked where he had gotten it and Spider told it to thrust its tusk into a large bone. When it did so, Spider said that a hunter was coming. The elephant tried to free itself and lost its tusk. Spider took the tusk to the king and was told that he could marry the maiden on the eighth day. That day the king set another task [unspecified]. Spider performed it and took the maiden home. There he told her to fetch water in her hands. She refused and ran back to her father. (Spiess [1919], pp. 24–25)

24. (Nigeria: Hausa) A woman told Spider she would teach him more cunning if he brought some tears of a lion, an elephant tusk, and the skin of a dingo. Spider lay down on the traders' road, pretending to be dead. Traders passed by, noting that Spider had died. Spider ran ahead of them and lay down again on the road. One trader decided to go back for the first spider so that he could eat both. He set down his load of salt, which Spider took, and the trader could not find either spider. Spider put the salt on a rock for an elephant to eat. While she was eating, the rock broke her tusk and Spider took it. He went to the dingos and told them to make fun of the elephant because of her broken tusk. They sang a song mocking her, and Spider told her what they were doing. He told her to kill the dingos and flay them. She did so and Spider took their skins. Saying that he had medicine for a lion's sore eyes, Spider put pepper in them. The lion wept and Spider collected the tears. He took the things to the woman, who told him to get under a calabash so that she could teach him more cunning. When she went out to get a stone, Spider came out and hid by the door. She smashed the calabash with the

stone, saying she would kill Spider. Spider asked, "What about your calabash?" She replied, "If I taught you more cunning, you would destroy everybody." She drove Spider out, and he ran away. (Tremearne [1910], pp. 358–60)

25. (Nigeria: Hausa) Spider asked a Malam to teach him cunning. The Malam told him to bring an elephant tusk, lion tears, the skin from a hyena's forehead, and bush-cow milk. Spider found a bush-cow and said they had been arguing as to whether its horns could pierce a baobab tree. The bush-cow butted the tree and couldn't pull its horns out. Spider said that if he sprinkled milk on the horns they might come out, but they didn't and he took the milk. Spider told an elephant that there would be a hunt the next day and that it should hide in a shrine where the hunters would not come. He also said that the elephant must not move, so he lashed its tusk to a tree. The next day Spider came beating a drum and crying that everyone should meet at the shrine. The elephant gave a violent start, leaving its tusk tied to the tree, and Spider took it. He told a lion that the elephant was ill and led it to the elephant, whose mouth was swollen. The lion began to cry, and Spider caught the tears in a gourd. He told a hyena about the elephant's plight, and when the hyena went there it began to rejoice. This made the lion mad, and it killed the hyena. Spider took some skin from the hyena's forehead and went to the Malam with it, the lion's tears, the elephant's tusk, and the bush-cow's milk. The Malam said that Spider had enough tricks already, and sent him away. (Edgar, vol. II [1911] no. 12; translated in Edgar, n.d.)

26. (Nigeria: Hausa) Spider asked a Malam for medicine to make him clever. The Malam said he must first bring milk of the African buffalo. Spider went into the forest and lay down under a large tree. A tree spirit struck him and he ran aside. A buffalo passed by and was struck; it fell and could not get up. Spider milked it and took the milk to the Malam, who told him to bring the tusks of an elephant. Spider made food of rice and honey and gave some to an elephant. The elephant asked where such fine food came from. Spider ran to a stone and rubbed it all over with the food, and then led the elephant to it. He told the elephant that the food was under the stone and that it must lift the stone with its tusks. Its tusks broke and Spider took them to the Malam. The Malam now said that he must bring the livers of a jackal, a leopard, a lion, and a snake. Spider bought a cow and invited these animals to a feast. He told the jackal to divide the meat and jackal did so. [The episode that follows is told as a separate tale type.] As they ate, the jackal looked at the leopard greedily. This angered the leopard and they began to fight, knocking sand into the lion's eyes. This angered the lion who killed both of them, but it stepped on the snake. The snake bit the lion and they both died. Spider took their livers to the Malam who said that God had given Spider more intelligence than He had given him, a Malam. He told Spider to go away because he needed no medicine. (Frobenius, "Volkserzählungen," [1924], pp. 366–67)

27. (Nigeria: Bura) Squirrel challenged Roan Antelope to make a hole through a baobab tree, but Antelope asked Squirrel if he could do so. Squirrel

ate a hole on one side of the tree, and a second hole on the other side. When Antelope saw the two holes, she said she could do that too. Antelope backed away and rushed at the tree, sinking her horns deep into it. She could not pull them out, and Squirrel came every day to milk her. Other episodes follow. (Helser [1934], pp. 85–89)

28. (Nigeria: Igbo) A man who wanted a child went to a wizard. He was told to bring buffalo milk, elephant tears, a lion's tooth, a monkey's tail, and a lion's brains. Rabbit [i.e., Hare] offered to help him. Rabbit challenged a buffalo to run through thick bushes. Its horns stuck in a tree and the man milked it. They met an elephant mourning the death of its son. Rabbit said that the tears of a prince should not fall on the ground, and caught them in a bowl. Rabbit told the elephant that the lions and monkeys were laughing because it was weeping.The elephant attacked a lion and broke one of its teeth, and it caught a monkey's tail with its trunk and pulled it off. Rabbit went away and the lion attacked a donkey, but the donkey kicked and cracked open the lion's skull. The man took everything to the wizard who made a medicine and the man's wife bore a son. When the son grew up, he caught Rabbit and bought the donkey, and took care of them because they had helped his father. (Vernon-Jackson, "Book One," [1963], pp. 54–57)

29. (Zaire: Mbala) Rat told Gazelle, "I want to be as cunning as you are." Gazelle said he must bring a vase full of live birds, a calabash of fresh milk, and a serpent. Rat went to some birds, asked them if they could fill his vase, and closed it when they were inside. He went to a cow and asked it if it could fill his calabash with milk, and it did. He went to a snake, asked to measure its length, and tied the snake to a piece of wood. When he returned with the three things, Gazelle said, "If I teach you to be cunning, you will be more cunning than I am." (Lumbwe Mudindaambi [1973], pp. 162–65)

30. (Oklahoma: Hitchiti Indians) Rabbit asked an old man for food and was told to bring an alligator. He went to the river and told an alligator that it was needed to fashion a wooden spoon. The alligator followed him and he beat it with a stick, but it escaped into the water. Rabbit turned himself into a squirrel and told the alligator that he had been sent to find why it had not gone to fashion the spoon. He said Rabbit was a fool and had treated the alligator badly. The alligator followed him and told him that if Rabbit had hit it on the hip and the back of the head it would have been killed. Rabbit did this and took the alligator to the man, who told him to bring a sack full of ants. He went to the ants and told them that people were saying that they could not fill his sack. They said they could and went in, and Rabbit took them to the old man. He told Rabbit to kill a rattlesnake and bring it to him. Rabbit sharpened a stick and told a rattlesnake that people were saying that it was about the length of the stick, but that he thought it was longer. The snake stretched out and Rabbit began measuring it, but when he got to the back of its head he stuck the stick through it and took it to the old man. The old man pulled his ears, stretching them straight up, and slapped his cheeks, making them flat. (Swanton [1929], pp. 104–05)

31. (Oklahoma: Natchez Indians) After several incidents, the animals sent Rabbit to get a rattlesnake, hoping that he would be killed. Rabbit sharpened a long stick and told a rattlesnake that many said it was long, many said it was short, and they had sent him to measure it. The snake straightened out and Rabbit began measuring it; then he stuck the stick into its head and killed it. He took the snake to the animals, but they said they had told him to bring it alive and gave him another task, to make the water run straight in the channel. (Swanton [1929], pp. 230–34)

32. (Louisiana: Chitimacha Indians) Rabbit went to God and asked Him for more power. He was told that he had power enough already and was set three tasks to prove it. He was told to bring the canine teeth of an alligator, and when the alligator was asleep, he tied its canine teeth to a tree and set fire to the grass about it. The alligator woke up and gave such a jerk that it pulled out its teeth. Rabbit took them to God and was told to bring an elephant tusk. Rabbit went to the home of an elephant and began cutting hay. When asked what he was doing, he said he was cutting hay and would share it with the elephant if it carried the hay home. Rabbit tied a rope to one of the elephant's tusks to lead him, and they started off. It began to rain and they went under a tree to keep dry. Rabbit tied the rope to a limb and set fire to the hay on the elephant's back. It tried to jump from under the burning hay and its tusk was broken off. Rabbit took the tusk to God and was told to bring a rattlesnake. He took a stick and laid it beside a sleeping rattlesnake. It woke up and asked what he was doing. Rabbit said he wanted to measure it and that he must tie it to the stick because it was crooked. He tied it to the stick and carried it to God who said, "You see that you are clever enough and don't need any more power." (Swanton [1917], pp. 475–76)

33. (Mississippi) Rabbit was the smartest animal in the woods, but he wasn't satisfied. He went to the king of the animals and asked for more sense. The king said he must bring him peas from a man's garden. He pried a board off the garden fence and took peas to the king. The king said that Rabbit was smart, but that he must bring him a buzzard's tail feather. Rabbit had a fox play dead, and when the buzzard, the undertaker, tried to carry it home, Rabbit snuck up behind the buzzard and pulled out a handful of tail feathers. He took them to the king, who told him he must bring a rattlesnake's poison fangs. Rabbit took a ball of sweetgum and covered it with partridge feathers. He tied it to a string and dragged it past a rattlesnake's home. Thinking it was a little partridge, that rattlesnake bit it, and its teeth stuck in the gum and wouldn't come loose. Rabbit said that the only way to get the rattlesnake loose was to break the teeth. He did so and took the ball of sweetgum with the teeth in it to the king. The king said, "There's no use in you asking for more sense. I just am not going to give you more because you have too much already." (Sale [1929], pp. 32–38)

34. (Alabama) Rabbit wanted a drink, but he knew that it would be no use to ask Cow for milk because she had refused him last year, and when his

wife was sick, too. Cow was grazing under a persimmon tree whose fruit was not ripe enough to fall. After they had exchanged greetings, he asked her to hit the tree with her head and knock down some persimmons. Cow tried, but no fruit fell. Cow went to the top of a hill and ran against the tree so hard that her horns stuck in it. She asked Rabbit for help, but he said he wasn't strong enough. Rabbit went home and brought his wife and children, and the milked Cow. (Carmer [1934], pp. 168–69; reprinted in Hughes and Bontemps [1958], pp. 4–5)

35. (Alabama) Rabbit wanted a wife, but all the animals refused to let him marry their daughters. He put on his best clothes and went to the king and asked to marry his daughter. The king said that he must show how smart he was by bringing a bag full of blackbirds and two teeth from a live rattlesnake. He took a bag and, pretending to be arguing with himself, he went to some blackbirds. He told them that there was a big discussion about whether quails or blackbirds were heavier. The blackbirds went into the bag to be weighed, and Rabbit tied it shut. Then he went to a rattlesnake and told it that people said that it had a crooked back. The snake straightened itself out, but Rabbit said there was a crook in the middle which he could fix. He cut a long pole and tied the snake's head and neck to it. He took pincers out of his pocket and pulled out the two big front teeth. He took the teeth and the blackbirds to the king, who told him to bury a bag full of money. Rabbit took the bag away and opened it. Two big dogs came out and chased him. If he had had a tail they would have caught him, but he had already lost it. (Courlander [1957], pp. 60–64)

36. (Virginia) To get alligator meat for his wife, Rabbit went to the creek and played his harp and sang. An alligator came out to dance and Rabbit struck it with a club, but it went back into the water. Rabbit killed a squirrel, dressed in its skin, and played his harp again. This time when the alligator came out, Rabbit killed it and took it to his wife. To get panther meat for her, he built a fire in the woods and blew a horn. When the panther came, Rabbit said it could eat him if it came through the fire. The panther did not know about Rabbit's tar-baby in the fire, and was caught and died. Rabbit took it to his wife. To get elephant meat for her, he told an elephant that it could not carry a stack of hay, a can of oil, a box of matches, and himself on its back. The elephant said that it could and was loaded. Rabbit poured the oil on the hay, lit it with a match, and got down. The elephant died and Rabbit took some of the meat to his wife. (Bacon and Parsons [1922], pp. 277)

37. (South Carolina) Rabbit went to Father for a long tail and was told to bring the blackbirds from a fig tree. He told the blackbirds that his bag had said they could not fill it, and all flew in. He took them to Father who said he should bring a rattlesnake. He told a rattlesnake that his pole had said it was longer than the snake. The snake lay down beside the pole and allowed Rabbit to tie it to the pole. Then Father said that Rabbit must bring a bottle of deer tears. He told a deer that a tree had said it was larger than the deer's head. To measure it, he tied the deer to the tree and choked it until its tears

filled his bottle. When father received the bottle of tears, he told Rabbit that if he were given a long tail he would destroy the whole world. (Christensen [1969], pp. 32–34)

38. (South Carolina) Rabbit complained to God that his eyes were too small. God told him to bring six blackbirds, but not six mocking-birds. Rabbit took a cage and sang that it could hold six blackbirds, but not six mocking-birds. Six blackbirds went into the cage and Rabbit took them to God. God sent him to bring two rattlesnake teeth. Rabbit took a string and told a rattlesnake that a man said it was not as long as the string. Rabbit put the string around the snake's neck to measure it, drew it tight, and choked the snake to death. He knocked out its teeth and carried them to God. God gave him big eyes. (Parsons, "Sea Islands," [1923], pp. 14–15)

39. (South Carolina) Rabbit and Wolf went fishing. Rabbit ate all the fish and Wolf cut off his tail. Rabbit went to God to get a long tail. God said he would give it to him if he brought an alligator tooth. Rabbit took a guitar or banjo, went to the creek, and began to play and sing. All the alligators came out to dance, and Rabbit killed one of them and took its tooth. Next God told Rabbit to catch five blackbirds. Rabbit went to them and told them to rest in his hands. They did, and Rabbit took them to God. God gave Rabbit [a long tail and] a box, telling him not to open it until he had crossed the creek. Rabbit didn't obey; he opened the box and thirty bulldogs came out and bit off his tail again. (Parsons "Sea Islands,' [1923], pp. 15–16)

40. (South Carolina) Rabbit went to God and asked for a long tail. God told him that he must bring deer tears and blackbirds. He went to some blackbirds and said he could fill his sack by himself, and he filled it with wind. The blackbirds flew into the sack and he took them to God. He told a deer that he could run through a tree, although he only slipped around it. The deer tried and killed itself when it struck the tree, and Rabbit got its tears. He took them to God and was given a long tail. God gave him a box and a hatchet and told him to open the box in an oat field. When he opened it, two dogs and a bulldog came out and cut off his tail. (Parsons, "Sea Islands," [1923], p. 16)

41. (South Carolina) Rabbit went to God and asked for more sense. God told him that he must bring a flock of partridges, a rattlesnake, and an alligator tooth. He took a stick to a rattlesnake and asked to measure it. He tied the snake's tail and head to the stick and carried it to God. Then he bet some partridges that they couldn't eat all the peas in his calabash. The partridges entered the calabash; Rabbit covered it and took them to God. Then he went to the riverside with fiddlers and sang, and the alligators danced. He killed one and pulled out its tooth and took it to God. God refused to give him any more sense and drove him away, saying that he had too much sense already. (Parsons, "Sea Islands," [1923], pp. 16–17)

42. (South Carolina) Rabbit went to God for some wisdom. God told him He would give him wisdom if he brought an alligator tooth. Rabbit took a guitar to a pond and began to play and sing. An alligator came out to dance,

and Rabbit killed it and took its tooth to God. God told him to bring a bag full of blackbirds. Rabbit bet the blackbirds that they could not fill up his bag. They flew into it and Rabbit carried them to God. God told him to bring a rattlesnake tooth. Rabbit took a stick to a rattlesnake and said that some of the boys had bet it wasn't longer than the stick. The rattlesnake measured itself against the stick and Rabbit tied it to the stick and took its tooth to God. God gave Rabbit a box and told him not to open it until he got to an open field. Rabbit opened it before he got there. Two dogs jumped out of the box and bit off his tail. (Parsons, "Sea Islands," [1923], pp. 17–18)

43. (South Carolina) Rabbit is so wise because he asked God to give him plenty of tricks. God told him to bring a rattlesnake tooth. Rabbit took pincers and went into the swamp. He bet a rattlesnake that it couldn't lie down beside a log with its head at one end and its tail at the other and let him put the pincers into its mouth. The snake took the bet and lay down. Rabbit tied its head and tail to the log, jerked out a tooth, and took it to God. God was angry with him and ran him out of the place. (Parsons, "Sea Island," [1923], p. 18)

44. (South Carolina) Rabbit went to God to ask for a long tail like those of Cow and Horse, to brush away sandflies and other insects. God told him to bring a bag full of blackbirds, an alligator's eye-teeth, and a calabash full of deer tears. He went to a place where men were burning grass off the rice fields, and when the birds flew away and lit on the ground he caught them and put them in his bag. Then he went to the river and sang and played his fiddle. An alligator came out of the water, praised his singing, and asked him to teach it to sing like he did. He told the alligator to close its eyes and open its mouth. He propped its mouth open with a piece of wood and knocked out both eye-teeth with a hammer. He told a deer that it couldn't jump as high as a goat could. The deer jumped over a bush, then over a taller bush, and then landed in the fork of a tree it tried to jump over. Rabbit said that dogs were coming and the deer struggled and cried. Rabbit caught its tears in a calabash and, leaving the deer in the tree, took everything to God. God said Rabbit was smart, but he looked vexed and told him to sit under a pine tree. Rabbit moved away from the tree and God sent a flash of lightning that made kindling of the tree. As Rabbit fled, God said, "You're so smart! Get a long tail yourself." (Stoney and Shelby [1930], pp. 175–92)

45. (South Carolina) Rabbit asked to marry the king's daughter. The king said he could if he brought a bag of blackbirds, a rattlesnake tooth, and an alligator tooth. Rabbit took a bag and bet some blackbirds that they couldn't fill it. They flew into the bag and Rabbit tied it shut and took them to the king. Rabbit met a rattlesnake, remarked on how large it was growing, and asked to measure it. It lay down beside Rabbit's stick and Rabbit tied the snake to the stick to straighten it out. He took out its tooth and carried it to the king. Rabbit went to a pond and called to an alligator to come out of the water. Playing a game of going through Rabbit's legs, he hit the alligator with a stick, but it escaped into the water. Rabbit killed a squirrel, dressed

in its skin, and went back to the alligator. It complained that Rabbit was mean because he had hit it with a stick. It said it was glad that Rabbit hadn't hit it on the side, because it would have been dead. Rabbit hit it on the side, killed it, and took a tooth to the king. The king said that Rabbit was too smart. Rabbit said that the king should either give him his daughter or give him trouble. Saying he would give him trouble, the king gave Rabbit a bag and told him not to open it until he was in a big field. When Rabbit opened the bag, three hound dogs jumped out and ran after him. One of the dogs bit off Rabbit's tail, and it has been short to this day. (Johnson [1968], pp. 142–44; reprinted in Cothran [1972], pp. 70–72)

46. (South Carolina) Rabbit asked to marry Man's daughter, and Man said he must bring nine blackbirds. Rabbit took a sack and his fiddle and went to a field of blackbirds. He began to fiddle and stick his head in and out of the sack as if he were getting something good out of it. King blackbird asked what he was doing, and Rabbit bet that nine blackbirds couldn't do it without touching the sack. Nine blackbirds flew into the sack and he tied it up and took them to Man, who told him to bring the tooth of a live alligator. Rabbit took his fiddle to the river and began to play. An alligator thought the music was nice, and Rabbit offered to teach it to dance. He told the alligator to sashay around, close his eyes, and go between his legs. When the alligator did so, Rabbit knocked out a tooth and took it to Man, who told him to bring deer milk. He took a pail and his fiddle to a tree and began to jump back and forth through a hole in the tree. He bet a deer that it couldn't do the same. While Rabbit played his fiddle, the deer tried; but the hole was too small and the deer was wedged in it. Rabbit milked the deer and took a pail of milk to Man. Man said, "If you are that smart, you are smart enough to marry any man's daughter without asking for her." Rabbit took the girl riding, and her father saw her no more until he met her while traveling. (Work Projects Administration, South Carolina [1941], pp. 12–17)

47. (South Carolina) Rabbit was told that he could marry the king's daughter if he brought deer tears. He bet a deer that it couldn't put its head through a rope. When it did so, Rabbit pulled the rope so tight that the deer cried. Rabbit caught the tears in a bottle and took it to the king, who said he must bring a sack full of blackbirds. He found a flock of blackbirds and bet them that they could not fill his sack. They did so and Rabbit took them to the king, who said he must bring the fang of a rattlesnake. Rabbit asked a rattlesnake to open its mouth so that he could get a fang, but it crawled away. Rabbit went home to his hole. He called to the hole, but it said nothing. He said, "That's mighty strange. My hole doesn't say anything." He called again and the hole said, "Huh!" Rabbit said, "I knew something was in my hole." (Work Projects Administration, South Carolina [1941], p. 17)

48. (South Carolina) Rabbit took his guitar to a pond and began to play. An alligator came out of the pond and Rabbit told it to dance through his legs. Rabbit hit it on the head with a hammer, but it jumped into the pond. The next morning Rabbit came back dressed as a squirrel. The alligator came

out of the pond and said that Rabbit had played the same tune the day before, and then had hit it on the head with a hammer. It added that if Rabbit had hit it on the knot, it would have been killed. The "squirrel" said that Rabbit always played dirty tricks and that the alligator should dance for him. When the alligator went through his legs, Rabbit hit it on the knot and killed it. He took its tooth and carried it to the king. (Work Projects Administration, South Carolina [1941], pp. 4–5)

49. (Georgia) Rabbit went to an African herb doctor for love magic. The man said he needed an elephant tusk, an alligator tooth, and the bill of a rice-bird to make a charm bag. Rabbit induced an elephant to show its strength by pulling up a small pine tree, destroying a sapling, and getting its tusk stuck in a large pine tree. Rabbit got its tusk and took it to the African. He told an alligator that they should make a good road to the creek. The alligator liked the idea and began to sweep the ground with its tail while Rabbit beat the bush with a cane. Rabbit hit the alligator, knocking out a tooth, and took the tooth to the African. He asked a rice-bird if it could fly. The bird flew when the wind blew and then flew around inside a house where there was no wind. Rabbit shut the door, caught the bird, and took it to the herbalist. The herbalist made a charm bag for him, and Rabbit married his girl. (Harris [1883], no. 34; [1955], pp. 261–64)

50. (Georgia) Because he felt that he couldn't fool other animals any more, Rabbit went to Witch Rabbit for help. She told him to bring her a squirrel. He put a bag over his head and went to a squirrel's tree and knocked two stones together. The squirrel asked what he was doing, and he said he was cracking nuts. The squirrel came into the bag, and Rabbit carried it back to Witch Rabbit. She told him to bring a rattlesnake. He took a noose and told a rattlesnake that he wanted to measure it, because the bear said it was only three feet long. The snake straightened out and Rabbit measured it. He slipped the noose over its head and took it back to Witch Rabbit, who said, "If you get any more sense, you'll be the ruination of the whole settlement." (Harris [1883], no. 35; [1955], pp. 264–68)

51. (Georgia) Rabbit badly wanted a drink. He determined to try his hand with Cow, knowing that she would give him no milk because she had refused him more than once, and when his wife was sick, at that. After they had exchanged greetings Rabbit said that there were some persimmons in a tree, and asked Cow to butt the tree and shake them down. Cow butted the tree, but the persimmons were green and none fell. After two more unsuccessful tries, she ran at the tree and butted it so hard that one of her horns stuck in it. She asked Rabbit to help her, but he said that he couldn't climb. He said he would bring Bull, but instead he went home and returned with his wife and children. all carrying pails. They milked Cow and left her stuck in the tree. During the night she got loose, but in the morning she stuck her horn back in the tree. When Rabbit came she chased him, but he escaped. (Harris [1880], no. 9; [1955], pp. 28–32)

52. (Georgia) Rabbit went to a Conjure Man to learn how to make people

believe that he was wiser than everyone else. He learned many things, but when he asked for full knowledge, the Conjure Man said that he had sense enough. Rabbit kept begging and the Conjure Man said that he must bring a live rattlesnake. Rabbit took a long stick and bet a rattlesnake that it was not as long as the stick. The snake stretched itself out and Rabbit put the stick beside it, slipped a noose around its neck, and tied it to the stick. He took the snake to the Conjure Man who said that if he could fool a rattlesnake, he had all the sense he needed. But Rabbit begged for more and was told to bring a swarm of yellow-jackets. Rabbit took a large calabash, cut a hole in it, put honey inside it, and tied it on long pole. He found a yellow-jacket nest and put the calabash nearby. The yellow-jackets smelled the honey and went into the calabash. Rabbit stopped up the hole and took the yellow-jackets to the Conjure Man. The Conjure Man told him that he was the smartest of all animals, and would become smarter every day. Then he marked Rabbit with a tuft of white hair between his eyes so that all would know that he had the best sense in his head. (Jones [1925], pp. 111–13; reprinted in Courlander [1976], 478–79)

53. (Georgia) The king said that his daughter would marry the man who brought the eye-teeth of an alligator and tears of a deer. Rabbit went to the river and played his fiddle, singing a funny song. An alligator came out of the river to listen, and when it laughed with its eyes shut, Rabbit knocked out one of its eye-teeth. Rabbit trapped a deer in a pitfall and told it that dogs were coming. The deer began to cry and Rabbit caught its tears in a calabash. He took the tears and the tooth to the king and married the king's daughter. (Jones [1925], pp. 132–33)

54. (Georgia) Rabbit asked a man for a tail and was told to bring a bag full of blackbirds. Rabbit bet the blackbirds that they couldn't fill his bag. They flew in and took them to the man. The man told Rabbit that that wasn't enough for a tail; he must bring an alligator. He asked an alligator to carry him across a pond and hit it on the head with a stick, but the alligator did not die. The next day he dressed in a squirrel's overcoat and asked the alligator to carry him across. When they started off, the alligator said that Rabbit had struck it on the head, but if he had struck it on the tail he would have killed it. Rabbit struck it on the tail and killed it. (Work [1919], p. 404)

55. (Georgia) Rabbit and Fox went hunting. Rabbit told Fox to shoot all the birds on the ground, but not those that flew into a tree. They found blackbirds which flew into a tree. Rabbit bet them that they couldn't fill his sack. They all flew into the sack and Rabbit closed it. Fox didn't have any. (Work [1919], pp. 404–05)

56. (Georgia: Creek Indians) Rabbit went to the Master and asked him for wisdom. He was told to fill a sack with small red ants. Rabbit told the ants that the Great Master had said that they could not fill his sack. They filled it and he took them to the Master, who told him to bring a rattlesnake. Rabbit told the snake that the Master said it was not as long as his stick. The snake said, "Measure me," and lay down by the stick. Rabbit ran the sharp end of

the stick into its head and carried it to the Master, who told him to bring an alligator. Rabbit went to the lake and told an alligator that they wanted it to get timbers for a scaffold on which to roast an ox. The alligator followed Rabbit who struck it with a club, but it escaped into the water. Rabbit returned and told the alligator that Rabbit was a mean person. The alligator followed him again and told how it had been beaten in the wrong place. Rabbit asked where a blow would hurt it, and the alligator said that if it were struck across the hips the blow would finish it. Rabbit struck it across the hips and carried the dead alligator to the Master who said, "You have more sense now than I could give you." (Swanton [1929], pp. 58–59)

57. (Georgia: Creek Indians) Rabbit asked Christ for more knowledge and was given a sack to fill with blackbirds. He told some blackbirds that people said that they were too few to fill the sack. They flew into the sack until it was full, and Rabbit carried them to Christ. Christ told Rabbit that he would be given more knowledge if he brought a rattlesnake. Rabbit made a sharp arrow and told a rattlesnake that Christ said it was not as long as the arrow. The snake let Rabbit measure it, and Rabbit ran the arrow through it and carried it to Christ. Christ said, "If I gave you any more knowledge, you would set the world on fire," and threw Rabbit into a brier thicket, saying that that would be his home. (Swanton [1929], pp. 59–60)

58. (Georgia: Creek Indians) Rabbit went to the Life Controller and complained that he had no offense, and could only run when attacked. He was told to bring a rattlesnake. He told a rattlesnake that the Life Controller had ordered him to measure it. The snake stretched itself out beside Rabbit's stick, and Rabbit tied its head and tail to the stick. He carried it to the Life Controller, and was told to bring a swarm of gnats. He told some gnats that he had been sent to count them, and that he would do so as they flew into his bag. They flew in and Rabbit took them to the Life Controller, who said, "See what you have done by means of the faculties I have bestowed on you. Use them and you will fulfill your destiny." (Swanton [1929], pp. 60–61)

59. (Florida: Seminole Indians) Rabbit wanted to marry, but everyone said that he must first kill an alligator. He made friends with an alligator and then hit it on its body with a big stick; but it was not hurt and went into its hole. Disguised as a squirrel, Rabbit came back to the alligator, which told him how Rabbit had tried to kill it but didn't know how. Rabbit asked where a blow would hurt the alligator and was told on its head and back. Rabbit hit it with a stick and killed it. He cut off its tail and took it to the people, but they said he must kill a rattlesnake. He went to the hole of a rattlesnake and hit it on the head with a stick. He brough the dead snake back, but was told he must chop down a large tree with one blow. He got a woodpecker to peck all around the tree and felled it with one blow. He won his bride, but wanting two wives he chopped her in two and killed her. (Greenlee [1945], p. 144)

60. (Mexico) Having escaped from a lion, Rabbit went to God and asked to be made larger. God told him to bring an alligator skin, a tiger skin, and a monkey skin. He went to a stream and leaped about, frisking in the sand.

An alligator tried to do the same, but could not bend. Rabbit killed it with a blow to its neck and took its skin. He met a tiger and began to weep bitterly. When the tiger asked why he was crying, he said that a strong wind was coming and he wanted to be tied to a tree. The tiger asked to be tied first, and when Rabbit found that it could not break the rope, he hit the tiger on the head with a big stick, killing it, and took its skin. He met a monkey and told it that he was looking for someone to play his large musical instrument. They set off together, but the monkey became tired. They stopped and the monkey fell asleep. Rabbit killed it with a kick to the head and took the three skins to God. God said to Rabbit, "If you have killed these animals and taken their skins, what would you do if I should make you equal to them? Although I have created you small, I have given you wiles, cleverness, and agility. If I should make you equal to other animals, you would tear them to pieces. I can grant your wish in one way only." God caught Rabbit by the ears, making them longer, and then flung him away. (Anonymous [1927], pp. 144–50)

61. (Guatemala: Chuh Indians) Rabbit and Lion argued as to which of them should be King of the Animals, and they brought the case before God. God said to Rabbit, "Lion is very strong, but you are very clever. If you will bring me the skins of an alligator, a tiger, and three monkeys, you can be king." Rabbit took a ball and played with it by a river. An alligator asked what he was doing, and Rabbit invited it to play with him. They played for a while, and then Rabbit hit the alligator on the head with a stick. The alligator said that it would not play any more, because if Rabbit hit it on the tail it would die. Rabbit went to another river and played with another alligator. He hit it on the tail, killing it, and took its skin. He fastened hollow calabashes to trees where a tiger lived, turning their openings toward the wind so that made a great noise in them. He met the tiger and said, "Do you hear the howling wind? There is going to be a great storm that will blow us away. We must tie ourselves to the trees." The tiger asked to be tied, and Rabbit tied it. Then he killed it and took its skin. Rabbit then sat under a tree and played guitar. The monkeys were delighted with the music and asked how they could reward Rabbit. He asked them to help him spread his net, and their claws became entangled in it. He killed them and took their skins. Rabbit took all the skins to God, but when God heard his story, he seized Rabbit by the ears and shook him, saying "You are very clever, but you are a rogue, not worthy to be King of the Animals." That is why Rabbit has long ears. (Kunst [1915], pp. 353–54)

62. (Bahamas) The queen agreed to give Jack five hundred dollars if he killed a snake. Jack told the snake that people said it couldn't go into a slipnoose. When it did, he tightened the noose and soldiers cut the snake to pieces. The queen said she had one more trial for him. If he could kill all the rice-birds in the corn field, he could marry her daughter. Jack told the rice-birds that people said that they couldn't fill up a basket. The rice-birds went into the basket and Jack closed it. He took them to the queen and married her daughter. (Edwards [1942], pp. 94–95)

63. (Dominican Republic) The king told Juan that he could marry his daughter if he brought an eye-tooth of an alligator. Juan went to the edge of the sea and played his violin and sang. When an alligator came, he gave it a drink. Then he played and sang, and gave it another drink. The alligator was so drunk that it told Juan that it would be knocked out if it was hit on the head. Juan took a stick and knocked it out and pulled out a tooth. He took it to the king and married the king's daughter. (Andrade [1930], pp. 58–59)

64. (Guadeloupe) Rabbit asked God for much wisdom, and God told him to bring the scales of a great ocean fish, the milk of wild cow, and two teeth from a living crocodile. Rabbit played his drums on the sea shore, and small fish came out to dance, then larger fish, and finally the great fish came but would not leave the water. Rabbit asked the great fish to drum while he danced, and then he drummed while it danced. Rabbit lay down while the great fish watched over him, and then it lay down while he watched. He killed the fish and took its scales to God. Rabbit climbed a large tree in the woods and called for a wild cow to come. He told her that he had bet that she was not strong enough to knock over the tree. The cow charged the tree and her horns stuck it. When Rabbit was sure that she could not pull free, he came down and milked her and took the milk to God. Rabbit soaped a crocodile's trail down a hill and placed a large rock at the bottom. He called to the crocodile that there was a dead rabbit for him to eat and lay down as if he were dead. The crocodile slipped on the soap, slid down the hill, and crashed into the rock, knocking out two of its teeth. Rabbit took the teeth to God, who said that he already had great wisdom and that he would not add to his cleverness. (Courlander [1976], pp. 92–93)

65. (Guadaloupe) Rabbit asked God for wisdom, and God told him to bring the skin of a wild pig, the milk of a wild cow, Zamba'a teeth, and a scale of the big fish. Rabbit drummed on the shore and the little fish began to dance, but he rejected them. The big fish fell on the sand. Rabbit threw sand at it and a scale dropped off and Rabbit took it. Rabbit put flour and syrup in a coconut and offered it to a wild cow, asking for some milk to improve the dish. The cow let Rabbit tie and milk her. Rabbit proposed to Zamba that they race down a hill. He soaped the course and put a big rock at the bottom. Zamba hit the rock and a tooth fell out, and Rabbit asked for it for his child to play with. Rabbit taught a wild pig a song about Zamba's tooth, and then told Zamba that the pig was singing about him. He told the pig to pull out a hair and he took it and the other things to God, who said, "You are wiser than I, begone." (Parsons [1933–43], Part II, pp. 1–2; Part III, p. 17)

66. (Guadaloupe) Rabbit asked God for wisdom, and God told him to bring the milk of a wild cow and two alligator teeth, and to ring the devil's bell. Rabbit made two holes in a tree and climbed up to eat its fruit. A cow came and asked Rabbit to throw down some fruit, and Rabbit told her to butt the tree. Her horns were caught in the holes, and Rabbit milked her. He took an elastic bag to the devil and told him he could not go into it. The devil and

all of his family went into the bag, Rabbit tied it up and rang the devil's bell. He soaped a hill and put rocks at the bottom. He challenged an alligator to a race. The alligator slipped, fell against the rock, and lost its teeth. Rabbit took the things to God. God gave him a gourd and told him he would find wisdom under it at the end of the garden. Rabbit went under the gourd for a few minutes, and then climbed a tree. A clap of thunder crushed the gourd into the dust. Rabbit told God he was wiser than God, and God replied, "Then why did you come to ask me for wisdom?" (Parsons [1933–43], Part II, pp. 2–3; Part III, pp. 17–18)

67. (Guadaloupe) Rabbit asked God for power, and God told him to bring a scale of a big fish, a long snake, and a pecking bird with all her little ones. Rabbit took a drum to the shore and little fish came to dance. He pretended to die, and the big fish said they must carry him home. On the way he killed the big fish and took its scale. Rabbit took a big stick into the woods saying, "Yes, he will be as long as this. No, he will not be as long." A snake said, "Yes, I am as long." It stretched out alongside the stick and Rabbit bound it to the stick. Then Rabbit talked to his basket, saying, "Yes, she will fill it. No, she will not fill it." A bird and her little ones entered the basket. Rabbit took everything to God who said, "Rabbit, you are cleverer than I." (Parsons [1933–43], Part II, p. 5; Part III, p. 18)

68. (Marie Galante) Rabbit asked God for wisdom, and God told him to bring Zamba's tooth, the hair of a wild pig, and dog's dung. Rabbit greased a hill with soap and told Zamba that it was a short cut. Zamba fell and broke a tooth. Rabbit took it, saying he would give it to his child as a souvenir. He told Zamba that the wild pigs were jeering at him because he had lost a tooth and suggested that Zamba pull out their hair. Rabbit followed Zamba and picked up the hair. He hid in a tree and waited for a dog to pass, but the first dog was too big. A very thin, weak dog came and they got into a fight and Rabbit defecated. He took the dung and other things to God, who said he would burn every dead Zamba, every dead wild pig, and every dead dog. Rabbit said that when two men get into a fight you don't know which one has defecated. God said, "You are wise enough" and, seizing him by the ear, flung him away. That is why Rabbit's ears are long. (Parsons [1933–43], Part II, pp. 255–56; Part III, p. 19)

69. (Les Saintes) Rabbit asked God for a little wit, and God told him to bring a gourd full of soucriers [birds?]. Rabbit told the soucriers that they could not fill his gourd, and they all went into it. God told Rabbit to bring an alligator tooth, the milk of a wild cow, and the dung of a dog. Rabbit invited all the animals to a dance and an alligator cried out to show off its beautiful teeth. Rabbit broke off a tooth with a stick and ran away. He told a wild cow that if she butted a tree it would fall down. Her horns stuck fast and Rabbit offered to pull them out if she let him milk her, which she did. He met a dog, they fought, and Rabbit defecated. He carried the things to God who said that the dung was not that of a dog. Rabbit said, "Two men

fight and defecate and you don't know whose it is." (Parsons [1933–43], Part II, p.233; Part III, p.19)

70. (Les Saintes) Rabbit asked God for wit, and God told him to bring milk from his pig, three of Zamba's teeth, and to ring the devil's bell. Rabbit gave the pig syrup and milked it. To Zamba he proposed a game of going up stairs, and soaped the stairs. Zamba slipped and broke three teeth, and Rabbit took them. To the devil he proposed a game of being tied in a sack, and while the devil was tied inside he rang the devil's bell. Rabbit went to God who caught him by the ear and said, "There's your wit." That is why Rabbit has such big ears. (Parsons [1933–43], Part II, p. 233–34; Part III, p. 19)

71. (Dominica) Rabbit asked God for a little wit, and God told him to bring an alligator tooth. Rabbit put okra on a flat rock and sang for the alligators to dance. One of them slipped and fell on its mouth. Rabbit knocked out its tooth with a nail driver and took it to God. God seized him by the hair and shook him saying, "Get out, you have enough wit; you don't need any more." (Parsons [1933–43], Part I, p. 378; Part III, p. 16)

72. (Dominica) Rabbit asked God for a little wit, and God told him to bring Zamba's tooth. Rabbit told a wild pig that Zamba had spoken ill of him and suggested that he break Zamba's tooth. They invited Zamba to a dance, shut him up in a pen, and broke his tooth. Rabbit carried it to God who told Rabbit to tell him the names of seven men. When he did so, God said, "Get out. You are too smart." (Parsons [1933–43], Part I, pp. 378–79; Part III, pp. 17, 176)

73. (Martinique) Rabbit asked God for wit so that he would be smarter than he was. God told him to bring a glass of milk from cattle so mean that they would charge a shadow. When the king of the herd asked Rabbit why he was crying, he replied that God had said that she could not fill his little glass with milk. The cow let Rabbit milk her and he took the milk to God. He asked for wit and God gave him a box to be filled with blackbirds. Rabbit put a little meal in the box and told some blackbirds that God said that they could not eat it. When they went into the box, he closed it and carried them to God. God promised to give him wit, and gave him a gourd and a guava. He told Rabbit to go under the gourd at noon and eat the guava, but Rabbit got Tiger's child to do so. A clap of thunder smashed the gourd and Rabbit said, "God, so this is the wit you gave me!" God grabbed him by the ears and threw him into a hutch. From that day we always see rabbits in a hutch. (Parsons [1933–43}, Part I, pp. 162–63; Part III, p. 16)

74. (Saint Lucia) Rabbit asked God for more sense and was told to bring the gold teeth of Mistress Gorilla, who was in the family way. Rabbit told her that if he did not eat God's big cow, God would keep a rope around his neck for ninety-nine days. She proposed that they gather trash from the cane field to roast the cow and then eat it together. Rabbit loaded the trash on her head and set fire to it. She fell and broke her gold teeth, and Rabbit took them to God. God told him to get under a calabash and to take sense when

it came. Rabbit ran up a tree and a thunderbolt smashed the calabash. God told Rabbit that he had enough sense and should be content, that he was the smallest but had more sense than all the other animals. (Parsons [1933–43], Part I, pp. 128–29; Part III, p. 16)

75. (Grenada) Rabbit asked God to give him sense, and God told him to bring the biggest serpent. Rabbit told the serpent that God had sent him, patted its neck, and strangled it with twine. God told him to bring the teeth of the biggest lion in the woods. Rabbit told the lion that God's straw house was leaking. The lion gathered grass and Rabbit tied it on its back. He set the grass on fire with gasoline and a match, and the lion burned up. He took its teeth to God who said, "All the sense you have, and you want more!" God gave Rabbit a calabash and dropped a thunderstone on it. Rabbit ran away bawling. "God! God! I have more sense than you!" (Parsons [1933–43], Part I, p. 73; Part III, pp. 15–16)

76. (Trinidad) Rabbit asked God to give him wit, and God sent him to bring a gourd full of wasps. Pretending to be arguing with himself, Rabbit told the wasps that a man had said that they could not go into his gourd. They went in, and Rabbit stoppered the gourd and carried them to God. God sent Rabbit for tiger tears. He took a paper marked with charcoal and gave it to a tiger, but the tiger said it could not read. Rabbit said that God sent word that a storm was coming and that all the big animals must tie themselves to a big tree so that they would not be harmed. The tiger asked to be tied. Rabbit tied it and beat it with a stick until it wept. He carried its tears to God, who told him to go under a box and he would give him wit. When God turned his back, Rabbit came out and hid. God sent a thunderbolt that crushed the box. Rabbit laughed, saying that if he were not so smart he would have met his death. God grabbed him by his ears and tossed him away. Since then Rabbit's ears have been long. (Parsons [1933–43], Part I, pp. 1–2; Part III, p. 15)

77. (Venezuela: Warao Indians) Because he was small, Rabbit asked God to stretch him out a little. God told him to bring a jaguar paw and a crocodile tooth. Rabbit went to a river and called a crocodile. He told it that it should not go when the old ones called it. The crocodile said it would not go that day, but that it would go the next day. The next day the crocodile came and Rabbit hit it with a stick. It nearly died, but went back into the water. The following day Rabbit returned and the crocodile told him that a tree had fallen on it and that it had nearly died, but if a pole fell on its hand it would die. The next day Rabbit returned, killed the crocodile, and pulled out a tooth. He began tying some lianas and a jaguar asked what he was doing. Rabbit said that a cyclone was coming, and that he was tying himself so that he would not go with the wind. The jaguar said it should be tied first. Rabbit tied it, cut off a paw, and took the paw and the teeth to God. God stretched his ears but refused to stretch his body, saying that if He did so he would cause his companions much suffering because he deceived them. (Wilbert [1964], pp. 175–80; [1969], pp. 213–20)

78. (Colombia) Rabbit went to God and asked why he was so small, wanting to be made larger. God told him to catch an ant, wasp, snake, elephant tusk, and rooster feathers. He made a small hole in a calabash and went to the ants, arguing with himself, saying, "Nothing can fit in it. I cannot fit in it." An ant asked what he was saying, and he said that he had an argument with a man who said that no one could get into the calabash. The ant went inside and Rabbit covered the hole. Telling the same story, he went to the wasps and then to the snakes. A wasp went in with all her family, and a snake went into the calabash also. He went to a rooster and pretended that he was dead. The rooster pecked and pecked at him and when it came to Rabbit's anus, he tightened it and caught the rooster. The elephant was very fond of honey, and Rabbit told it where there was a bees' nest. When the elephant stuck its tusk in the tree, Rabbit said that the police were coming. The elephant ran away, leaving its tusk in the tree. Rabbit took everything to God and asked to be made larger. God pulled his ears and asked him to look at his shadow and see how big his ears were. Rabbit looked and saw how big he was. (Mason [1930], pp. 217–18)

B I B L I O G R A P H Y

Addo, Peter Eric Adotey
    1968 *Ghana Folk Tales: Ananse Stories from Africa.* New York, Exposition Press.
Andrade, Manuel J.
    1930 Folk-Lore from the Dominican Republic. *Memoirs of the American Folk-Lore Society* 23.
Anonymous
    1927 Por que tiene largas las orejas el tio conejo. Why Uncle Rabbit Has Long Ears. *Mexican Folkways* 3.
Anonymous
    1955 Sanding Na Nyameng Dano Allah Ya. *Kibaro,* October–December.
Appiah, Peggy
    1967 *Tales of an Ashanti Father.* London, André Deutsch.
Bacon, A. M., and Parsons E. C.
    1922 Folk-Lore from Elizabeth City County, Virginia. *Journal of American Folk-Lore* 35.
Baharav, Gene
    1965 *African Folktales Told in Israel,* Second Series. Haifa, Mt. Carmel International Training Center.
Barker, W. H., and Sinclair, Cecilia
    1917 *West African Folk-Tales.* London, George G. Harrap.
Bundy, Richard C.
    1919 Folk-Tales from Liberia. *Journal of American Folk-Lore* 19.
Carmer, Carl
    1934 *Stars Fell on Alabama.* New York, Farrar & Rinehart.
Christensen, A. M. H.

1969 *Afro-American Folk Lore.* New York, Negro Universities Press. [1892]
Cothran, Jean
   1972 *The Whang Doodle. Folk Tales from the Carolinas.* Columbia, South Carolina, Sandlapper Press.
Courlander, Harold
   1957 *Terrapins' Pot of Sense.* New York, Henry Holt.
   1976 *A Treasury of Afro-American Folklore.* New York, Crown.
Courlander, Harold, and Prempeh, Albert Kofi
   1957 *The Hat-Shaking Dance and Other Tales from the Gold Coast.* New York, Harcourt, Brace.
Cronise, Florence M., and Ward, Henry W.
   1903 *Cunnie Rabbit, Mr. Spider, and the Other Beef.* London, Swan Sonnenschein.
Edwards, Charles L.
   1942 Bahama Songs and Stories. *Memoirs of the Americna Folk-Lore Society* 3. [1895]
Edgar, Frank
   1911–13 *Litafi na Tatsuniyoyi na Hausa,* vols. I–III. Belfast, W. Erskine Mayne.
Edgar, Frank
   n.d. Hausa Folk Tales and Miscellanea, Vol. I–III, trans. Neil Skinner, *Mss.*
Frobenius, Leo
   1922 Erzählungen aus dem West-Sudan. *Atlantis 8.*
   1924 Volkserzählungen und Volksdichtungen aus dem Zentral-Sudan. *Atlantis 9.*
Gamble, David P.
   n.d. *Mss.*
Girard, J.
   1967 Dynamique de la Société Ouobé. *Mémoires de l'Institut Fondamental d'Afrique Noire 78.*
Greenlee, Robert F.
   1945 Folktales of the Florida Seminole. *Journal of American Folklore 58.*
Harris, Joel Chandler
   1880 *Uncle Remus: His Songs and His Sayings.* New York, D. Appleton.
   1883 *Nights with Uncle Remus.* Boston and New York, Houghton Mifflin.
   1955 *The Complete Tales of Uncle Remus.* Compiled by Richard Chase. Boston, Houghton Mifflin.
Helser, Albert D.
   1934 *Education of Primitive People.* New York, Fleming H. Revell.
Herskovits, Melville J., and Herskovits, Frances S.
   1937 Tales in Pidgin English from Ashanti. *Journal of American Folk-Lore 50.*
Hughes, Langston, and Bontemps, Arna
   1958 *The Book of Negro Folklore.* New York, Dodd, Mead.
Johnson, Guy B.
   1968 *Folk Culture on St. Helena Island, South Carolina.* Hatboro, Pennsylvania, Folklore Associates. [1930]
Jones, Charles G.
   1925 *Negro Myths from the Georgia Coast.* Columbia, South Carolina, The State Company.
Joslin, Mike
   1952 *Anansi Sem. Spindelsagor fran Guldkusten.* Stockholm, LTs Förlag. Reprinted in Mike Joslin, *Märchen von der Goldküste,* trans: Anni Carlsson, Munich, Nymphenburger, 1960.
Kunst, J.
   1915 Some Animal Fables of the Chuh Indians. *Journal of American Folk-Lore 28.*
le Brun, Joseph
   1919–20 Recueil de fables et de chants en dialecte *Hal Poular. Anthropos* 14–15.

Lee, F. H.
 1930 *Folk Tales of All Nations*. New York, Conrad-McCann.
Lumbwe Mudindaambi, Ng.
 1973 Pourquoi le coq ne chante plus? Mythes mbala 2. *Ceeba Publications*, Serie II 8.
Mason, J. Alden
 1930 Cuatro cuentos colombianos. *Journal of American Folk-Lore* 43.
Parsons, Elsie Clews
 1923 Folk-Lore of the Sea Islands, South Carolina. *Memoirs of the American Folk-Lore Society* 16.
 1933–43 *Folk-Lore of the Antilles, French and English. Memoirs of the American Folk-Lore Society* 26, Parts I–III.
Pinney, Peter
 n.d. Legends of Liberia. Mimeographed.
Radin, Paul, and Sweeney, James Johnson
 1952 African Folktales and Sculpture. *Bollingen Series* 32. Pantheon Books. Reprinted in Paul Radin, *African Folktales*. Princeton, New Jersey, Princeton University Press, 1970.
Rattray, R. S.
 1930 *Akan-Ashanti Folk-Tales*. Oxford, Clarendon Press.
Sale, John B.
 1929 *The Tree Named John*. Chapel Hill, University of North Carolina Press.
Spiess, Carl
 1918–19 Fortsetzung der Fabeln über die Spinne bei den Ewe am Unterlauf des Volta in Westafrika. *Mitteilungen des Seminars für Orientalische Sprachen zu Berlin* 21, Part III; 22, Part III.
Stoney, Samuel Gaillard, and Shelby, Gertrude Mathews
 1930 *Black Genesis*. New York, Macmillan.
Swanton, John R.
 1917 Some Chitimacha Myths and Beliefs. *Journal of American Folk-Lore* 30.
 1929 Myths and Tales of the Southeastern Indians. *Bureau of American Ethnology Bulletin* 88.
Tauxier, L.
 1917 *Le Noir du Yatenga*. Paris, Émile Larose.
Thomas, Northcote W.
 1916 *Anthropological Report on Sierra Leone*, Parts I–III. London, Harrison and Sons.
Tremearne, A. J. N.
 1910–11 Fifty Hausa Folk-Tales. *Folk-Lore* 21–22.
Vernon-Jackson, Hugh
 1963 *More West African Folk Tales. Book One*. London: University of London Press.
Wilbert, Johannes
 1964 Warao Oral Literature. Instituto Caribe de Anthropologia y Sociologia, *Monography* 9.
 1969 Textos Folkloricos de los Indios Warao, University of California, Los Angeles, *Latin American Series* 12.
Work, Monroe N.
 1919 Folk-Tales from Students in the Georgia State College. *Journal of American Folk-Lore* 32.
Work Projects Administration, South Carolina
 1941 *South Carolina Folk Tales*. Compiled by Workers of the Writers' Program of the Work Projects Administration in the State of South Carolina. Bulletin of University of South Carolina.

N O T E S

1. Nevertheless this motif does occur in an African folktale involving Crocodile as ferryman. Joseph Schönhärl, *Volkskundliches aus Togo* (Dresden & Leipzig: C. A. Kochs, 1949), 58–63; reprinted in Carl Meinhof, *Afrikanische Märchen* (Jena: Eugen Diederichs, 1921), 201–205. Cf. [54].

2. Joseph le Brun, "Recueil de fables et de chants en dialecte *Hal Poular,*" *Anthropos,* 14–15 (1919–20), 186–88.

3. E. Laoust, "Contes Berbères du Maroc," *Publications de l'Institut des Hautes Études Marocaines,* 50 (1949), Part I, pp. 23–24, Part II, pp. 33–34.

4. Alan Dundes, "African Tales among the North American Indians," *Southern Folklore Quarterly* (1965), 212.

5. Because of the many editions of the Uncle Remus books with varying pagination, references to Joel Chandler Harris's folktales will be by tale number for the first editions, and page numbers for the 1955 edition compiled by Richard Chase.

6. A. Gerber, "Uncle Remus Traced to the Old World," *Journal of American Folk-Lore,* 6 (1893), 249. [Gerber's Wolof analogue which Bascom could not locate has since been identified convincingly by Emil A. Magel who found it in Abbé Boilat's *Grammaire de la langue Woloffe,* published in Paris in 1858. See Emil A. Magel, "The Source of Bascom's Wolof Analogue 'Trickster Seeks Endowments,'" *Research in African Literatures,* 10 (1979), 350–58.]

7. Elsie Clews Parsons, "Folk-Lore of the Antilles, French and English," *Memoirs of the American Folk-Lore Society,* 26, Part III (1943), 15. Parsons also mentions as "slightly suggestive" a tale from France that I find to be quite different (E.-H. Carnoy, "Littérature orale de la Picardie," *Les Littératures Populaires de Toutes les Nations* [1883], 247–51).

8. Dundes, pp. 212–13.

9. Joel Chandler Harris, *Nights with Uncle Remus* (Boston and New York: Houghton Mifflin, 1883), pp. xxviii–xxix, 208.

10. Harold Courlander, *A Treasury of Afro-American Folklore* (New York: Crown, 1976), pp. 92–93, 478–79, 586–87.

11. I will admit that distinguishing these three additional tale types may seem to be a cheap way of inflating the number of African folktales in the United States. I did not do so in an earlier draft of this article, as I did not in "The Talking Skull Refuses to Talk." I do so now in self-defense. If I did not, I might be faulted for not recognizing a tale type when I see one.

12. A Cuban version is to be found in Felix Coluccio, *Folklore de las Américas, primera antología* (Buenos Aires: El Ateneo, 1949), 159. Rabbit brought an eagle feather, lion tooth, and serpent egg to the Lord who said that he might be dangerous if he were larger. A version from Venezuela is to be found in A. Ernst, "Tío Tigre und Tío Conejo," *Zeitschrift für Ethnologie,* 20 (1888), 277. One from Puerto Rico is to be found in J. Alden Mason and Aurelio M. Espinosa, "Porto-Rican Folk-Lore," *Journal of American Folk-lore,* 40 (1927), 334. And there is a Lyele version from Upper Volta in Marcel Guilhem, *50 Contes et fableaux de la savane,* vol. II (Paris: Libel, 1962), 72–85. With these addenda, the totals are 31 from Africa, 30 from the United States, and 22 from elsewhere in the New World.

F O U R

✳

Bird's Head (Leg) under Its Wing

This folktale requires little discussion. It is well known in Africa and the United States and is one of those that Dundes has identified as having come to the United States from Africa.[1] Briefly, the usual pattern is that the dupe sees a bird with its head or leg tucked under its wing, has his own head or leg cut off, and dies. It is often the trickster who is duped.

The head is cut off in seventeen of the twenty-five African tales cited here and in nineteen of the twenty-three from the United States. The leg or foot is cut off in five African tales and in two from the United States. Other versions describe cutting off four feet [8], a foot, an ear, and the tongue [12], the head and a leg [23], two legs [28], and the head and three legs [38].

This tale does not appear in the Aarne-Thompson tale type index, but two entries in Thompson's motif index are relevant. Since no versions from Europe (or India) are cited, it must have come from (and originated in) Africa. One is motif J2413.4.1, "Fowl makes another animal believe he has had his neck cut off. . . . He has leg hidden under his wing." The only references cited here are to the Fang [4] and the Congo [7]. The other motif is J2413.4.2, "Fowl makes another animal believe he has had his neck cut off. He has his neck under his wing. . . ." The only references here are to the Thonga [25], Alabama [33], North Carolina [34], South Carolina [38], and Florida [48]. From the examples that follow, it is clear that these are not simply two motifs, but one or two tale types. I shall count them as one.

I have found only one version of this folktale in West Africa, in the interior of Nigeria [1]; and neither J2413.4.1 nor J2413.4.2 is listed in Clarke's motif index for the Guinea Coast.[2] This absence is significant because it effectively eliminates the possibility that the tale originated in America and was carried to Africa by freed slaves who returned to Sierra Leona, Liberia, and other parts of the Guinea Coast. Support for this conclusion is found in the fact that I have not yet found this tale in the Americas outside of the United States.

Reprinted from *Research in African Literatures*, 10 (1979), 59–74.

These two motifs are not listed in Flowers' index,[3] and Hansen's index[4] does not cite any versions of it under "Beheading," "Head," or "Leg."

My twenty-two African examples come from Nigeria (Tiv), Cameroun (Ewondo), Gabon (Fang), Zaire (Kongo, Boloki, Mongo, Kanyoka, and Luba), Kenya (Kamba and Giryama), Tanzania (Digo, Sandawe, and Mwanga), Malawi (Nyanja), and Mozambique (Ndau and Tsonga). The twenty-three tales from the United States come from Arizona (Hopi and Tewa Indians), New Mexico (Zia Indians), Louisiana, Mississippi, Alabama, North Carolina, South Carolina, Georgia, and Florida. I am sure that there are more.[5]

1. (Nigeria: Tiv) Hare went to visit Cock and found him asleep with his head tucked under his wing. Amazed, he cried out in alarm, "Cock, where is you head?" In a muffled voice Cock said that he had told one of his wives to cut off his head and place it on a pole so that he could watch his wives even if he went to sleep or went on a trip. Hare was impressed. He went home and told his senior wife to cut off his head and place it on a pole. She tried to dissuade him, but this enraged him. He beat her with a stick and commanded her to obey. So she cut off his head and fastened it to a long pole. When the other wives returned, they found Hare lying lifeless on the ground and a great wail arose. Cock offered to take all of Hare's wives, and they agreed. (Bergsma and Bergsma [1969], pp. 42–44)

2. (Cameroun: Ewondo) A man saw Parrot with one leg stuck under his wing and asked where the other leg was. Parrot replied that he had left it at home with his wife. The next morning the man tried to cut off his leg with an ax, but it slipped and fell to the ground, wounding him. Other incidents follow. (Atangana and Messi [1919], pp. 119–21)

3. (Cameroun: Ewondo) Elephant saw Parrot with one leg stuck under his wing and asked where it was. Parrot said he had cut it off so that it could protect the youths on the hunt. Elephant asked Parrot to show him the medicine to put on the wound, and Parrot did so. Elephant assembled his people for a hunt, saying that his leg would go along and protect them. He told them to cut off his leg and they took it with them. Elephant tried to cure his wound, but he died. (Atangana and Messi [1919], pp. 223–24)

4. (Gabon: Fang) Elephant visited his friend, Parrot, and found him standing on one leg with the other bent up and hidden under his feathers. He asked Parrot what he had done with his leg. Parrot said that his children had gone hunting with it. Elephant went home and told his children to prepare for a hunt. When they were ready he told them to saw off his leg. They cut it off and carried it with them on the hunt. When they returned their father was dead. Parrot was blamed; but he said he had not told Elephant to cut off his leg, and the charge was dismissed. (Nassau [1914], pp. 235–36)

5. (Zaire: Kongo) Fowl ground red peppers and mixed with them with water so that it looked like blood. He told his slaves that when Leopard came to collect a debt, they should say that his head had been cut off and taken to the farm to be combed and cleaned. Then he hid his head under his wing and told them to pour some of the pepper water on his neck. The slaves did

as they were told and Leopard believed them. Leopard invited people from many towns to come and see him perform the wonder. His head was cut off, but when it had been combed and cleaned it would not stick on Leopard's neck. (Weeks [n.d.], pp. 371-73)

6. (Zaire: Kongo) Chameleon took possession of Frog's house and children. Frog asked Elephant, then Leopard, and then Sparrows to evict Chameleon. Sparrows agreed to help. They took their drums to the house and began to dance with their heads under their wings. Chameleon wanted to imitate them. She cut off her head and fell dead. (Weeks [n.d.], pp. 445-46)

7. (Zaire: Boloki) Returning from a trading journey, Fowl hid one leg under his wing and said that he had sold it for two thousand brass rods. Hearing this, Hippopotamus said, "If Fowl received two thousand brass rods for his small leg, how much will I receive for mine?" So he went to town with some friends, and his leg was cut off and sold for a large number of rods. He bled to death, and another episode follows. (Weeks [1913], p. 205)

8. (Zaire: Mongo) Hen said to Genet, "Friend, let us cut off our feet so that we can walk well." Genet agreed and cut off all his feet, while Hen hid one foot under her wing. Then she lowered her foot and said that they should dance, but Genet did not have feet to dance. Genet was angry and they fought. (Hulstaert [1970], pp. 152-55)

9. (Zaire: Kanyoka) After another episode, Patridge's children sang and danced with their heads in their wings. Kamundi found them and said, "The song is nice. Cut off my head so that I can dance too." He put his head against a tree and they cut it off and ran away. Kamundi was dead. (de Clercq [1909], pp. 446-47)

10. (Zaire: Luba) Kite's children danced and sang, "We have cut off our heads. We have cut off our heads." (The audience joins in the song and imitates the dance and the cut-off head, holding their left arms over their heads and right hands on their hearts.) Kite's children sang, "We have cut off our heads. Cut your head off." Flying Dog's wife cut off the heads of her husband and her children. (Frobenius [1928], pp. 383-84)

11. (Zaire: Luba) After an incident in which Cock was killed, Cat went to visit his widow. She had her head under her wing and Cat asked her children where it was. They said she had left it in the field to chase birds while her body rested. Cat thought that was a good idea. He went home and told his wife to take her large knife and cut off his head. She did so, but instead of going to chase birds the head fell to the ground inert. (de Bouveignes [1934], pp. 65-172)

12. (Zaire: Luba) The Parakeets wanted to teach Tembiawoko, an eavesdropping animal, a lesson. One morning he came to listen at the door of mother Parakeet and heard her sharpening a knife. She told her children to tie her tightly and cut off her foot, ear, and tongue. She said her foot would enter the house without disturbing her, her ear would hear everything, and her tongue would persuade the whole world. Everyone knows that a parakeet's ear is so small that it is hidden by feathers, and Parakeet kept her tongue in her mouth and put her

foot under her wing as if her children had really cut them off. Then she cried, "Without having to go out, I know that Tembiawoko is outside. I know what he thinks without having to ask, and I am able to persuade him to cut off his foot, ear, and tongue without having to say anything to him." Tembiawoko went home and told his children to sharpen a knife, tie him tightly, and cut off his foot, ear, and tongue. They could not dispute their father's orders and did so. The Parakeets mocked him. (de Bouveignes [1934], pp. 115–20)

13. (Zaire: Luba) Hen left her husband and went to live in the fields. She made friends with Heron who gave her fish that he caught. One day Heron visited Hen and asked what she had done with her foot. She said she had cut it off and sent it to join the hunt. She said that this was an infallible way for the hunters to take much game. She told him that if he did the same, all the herons would catch many fish. Heron assembled the other herons and sent them to catch fish. He had his children cut off his foot and sent them to join the others. In the evening the herons returned without fish and were told that the next time would be better. The children tried to fasten on their father's leg but could not do so. Another incident follows. (de Bouveignes [n.d.], pp. 69–76)

14. (Kenya: Kamba) Hyena and Cock invited each other to drink beer. On the second round Hyena greeted Cock but Cock didn't utter a sound. As Cock had instructed her, his wife said that she had cut off his head and it had gone to drink beer, but the rest of his body was there. She told Hyena to wait until Cock returned. Hyena did so and Cock and Hyena drank beer together. The same things happened on the third round. Then Hyena invited Cock to drink beer and told his wife to cut off his head with a knife and tell Cock that his head had gone to drink beer but would return. She cut off his head and it fell down here and his body fell there. When Cock came she told him what she had been told to say. Cock said she had killed Hyena and took her as his wife. (Lindblom [1926], pp. 10–13)

15. (Kenya: Giryama) Hare went to visit his friend Cock and found him asleep with his head under his wing. Hare had never seen him like that before, but did not doubt Cock's wives when they said that he was in the habit of taking off his head and sending it with the herd-boys to pasture. They asked if Hare had never seen a man have his head cut off to go to pasture, while the man stayed at home. Hare said, "Never! But when the herd-boys come home, will he get up again?" The told him to wait and see. When the herd-boys arrived they were told to rouse their father. They did so and Cock welcomed his guest and they talked together. Hare wanted to know how it was done, and Cock told him it was quite easy if he wanted to do it. Hare accepted Cock's explanation and returned home anxious to try it the next day. In the morning he told his boys to cut off his head, bore through his ears and put a string through them to carry it more conveniently. They did so and his wives put his body on the bed. When Cock arrived and inquired about Hare, the women showed him the body lying on the bed. Cock said Hare was a simpleton but waited until the herd-boys returned. They struck

Hare, as he had told them, but he did not get up again. People mourned him, saying, "Such a clever man. And to have met his death through such a trifling thing." (Taylor [1891], p. 133; retold in Werner [1933], pp. 271–72)

16. (Kenya: Giryama) Cock told his wife to tell his friend Hare that his head had been cut off and had gone with his sons to the pasture. Hare came and saw Cock with his head under his wing and asked if Cock could still be alive. When the herd-boys returned, Cock sprang up and crowed. Hare told his wife to tell Cock the same thing and had her cut off his head and give it to his herd-boys. Hare died. (Werner [1965], pp. 5–8)

17. (Tanzania: Digo) Goat saw Cock with his head stuck under his wing. Hen told him that Cock had cut off his head and that it had gone to the pasture. She told Goat to wait until the herds returned. Goat waited and saw Cock with his head. When Cock went to visit Goat, Goat told the herdsmen to cut off his head and take it with them to pasture. They did so, and Cock was told to wait till the herds returned. But Cock said they had killed Goat. (Dammann [1935–36], pp. 228–31)

18. (Tanzania: Sandawe) After another episode, Hare visited Dove. He asked Dove's wife where his friend was. She said that his body had stayed, but that his head had gone to see his mother. Later Hare saw Dove with his head. Dove said that he had returned and that he would visit Hare in three days. Hare told his wife to sharpen his ax. When Dove came she cut off Hare's head. Dove saw it and went home. (Dempwolff [1916], pp. 162–64)

19. (Tanzania: Mwanga) After another episode, Cock hid his head under his wing when Rabbit came to call. His wife told Rabbit that she had cut off Cock's head and sent it to have the feathers plaited. Pretending that his head had been brought back, Cock took his head from under his wing. Rabbit asked his wife to do the same for him and was killed. (Dewar [1900], p. 129)

20. (Tanzania: Mwanga) Hare visited Cock and drank beer with him. Cock sang and danced and told his wife to cut off his head so that he could dance well. He went outside, stuck his head under his wing, and danced again. One day Hare drank beer alone. He told his wife to bring an ax, and he laid his neck against a tree trunk. She chopped off his head and he died. (Busse [1936–37], pp. 254–56)

21. (Malawi: Nyanja) When Swallow came to visit, Cock's wife told him that Cock had cut off his head, as he had had a great shock. Cock had put his head under his wing. When Cock went to visit, Swallow's wife told him that Swallow had cut off his head, as he had had a great shock. Swallow was dead. Another episode follows. (Rattray [1969], pp. 62–64, 142–45)

22. (Malawi: Nyanja) Little Fowl came to visit Big Fowl and found him with his head under his wing. He thought his head was cut off. When he came again, Big Fowl was showing his head. Little Fowl said, "Last time you had no head." Big Fowl said, "Yes, this time I have put it on." Little Fowl went home and told his brother to cut his head off. His brother did so and Big Fowl found Little Fowl dead. (Holland [1916], p. 163)

23. (Mozambique: Ndau) When Hare came to visit, Rooster's wife told him

that Rooster was in the house, but that his head and one leg had gone to drink beer. At first Hare did not believe it, but then he saw Rooster standing on one leg without his head. Hare went home and returned the next day. He asked Rooster how he had sent his head and leg to drink beer, and Rooster said that he had cut them off. Hare went home and told his wife that in the morning she should cut off his head and his leg. She said that he would die; but he insisted, and she did so. When Hare failed to rise, she told Rooster who said that he had thought that Hare was wise, but he was a fool. (Boas and Simango [1922], 179–80)

24. (Mozambique: Tsonga) When Hare visited Hen, he was told that she had gone fishing. Hare said, "But this headless fowl, is this not she?" The women said yes, but that only her head had gone fishing. Hen had hidden her head in her feathers. Hare was sent to look for Hen's head near the water, and while he was gone they bought fish and wet the fish lines. When Hare returned, Hen had taken her head out of her feathers. She said she had been waiting for him and gave him a fish. The next day Hen went to visit Hare and found everyone crying. They had prepared the fish lines and then cut off Hare's head. He was dead. (Junod [1896], pp. 39–40; [1897], pp. 135–36)

25. (Mozambique: Tsonga) After other episodes, Hen invited Hare to drink beer, and Hare saw Cock roosting with his head under his wing. He asked where Cock's head was, and Hen said he had cut it off and sent it round to invite their friends. Hare asked what kind of drugs were used for the operation, and Hen replied, "None. You just sharpen a knife well and cut your head off." When Hare invited Hen to drink beer, he cut off his head and killed himself. (Junod, vol. II [1913], pp. 213–17; translated in Junod, vol. II [1936], pp. 203–05; reprinted in Feldman [1963], pp. 152–55)

26. (United States) Rabbit saw Guinea Fowl one day but couldn't see his head although he looked and looked. The next day he met Guinea Fowl and asked him where his head had been. Guinea Fowl said he had left it at home for his wife to lick. Rabbit told his wife to cut off his head and lick it while he went out. She protested, but he insisted. So she chopped it off and Rabbit died. (Fauset [1927], p. 220)

27. (Arizona: Hopi Indians) Coyote met Eagle who was standing on one foot with the other foot hidden in his feathers. Coyote asked why he was standing on one foot, and Eagle said it was because he had cut one leg off. Coyote wanted to try and asked how he had done it. Eagle told him to lay his leg across a stone and strike it with a sharp stone. Coyote did so and cut off his leg. Eagle lowered his other leg, showing Coyote he had both legs. Then he flew away and Coyote limped off, probably perishing. (Voth [1905], pp. 198, 306)

28. (Arizona: Tewa Indians) Coyote saw hawk in a tree and asked why he had only one leg. Hawk said he was born that way and that he caught rabbits and deer because he had only one leg. He said that two legs bother a person and that Coyote was always hungry because he had four legs, which was too many. Coyote asked how he could have only one leg, and Hawk gave him a

knife. Coyote chopped off two legs; then Hawk showed that he had both legs. Coyote died. (Parson [1926], pp. 293–94)

29. (New Mexico: Zia Indians) Fox came upon Crow with one leg under his wing. Fox asked why he was crowing, and Crow said because he had lost a leg and was looking for someone to help him get another. Fox was going to make a leg out of dry cactus, but Crow started to hop around on one leg. He said he didn't need the other leg and could get along without it. Fox said he wanted to be like Crow and asked to have one front leg cut off. Crow asked him four times if he really wanted a leg cut off, and each time Fox said yes. Crow cut off Fox's leg and Fox screamed. Crow tied the wound with his feathers and then lowered his other leg. He told Fox that it had just grown back and that this might happen to Fox later on. (Espinosa [1936], pp. 89–90)

30. (Louisiana) Every evening Rabbit passed Turkey sleeping with his head under his wing. Curious, he finally stopped and asked Turkey if he had a head. When Turkey said yes, he asked where it was. Turkey said, "It is here." Rabbit could not see Turkey's head, and as he saw that Turkey did not want to show him where it was he ran home and said to his sister, "Do you know that turkeys take off their heads and go to sleep? And they can talk without their heads! I am going to do the same thing." Before his sister could say anything, Rabbit took an ax and cut off his head. His sister tried all ways to stick it on again but could not do so. (Fortier [1895], pp. 24–25; translated in Basset [n.d.], pp. 428–29, 442–43; reprinted in Botkin [1966], p. 674)

31. (Mississippi) Rabbit went to Turkey's house and found him with his head under his wing. He asked where his head was, and Turkey said he had cut it off and left it at home for his wife to make biscuits. Rabbit went home and told his wife to cut off his head. She protested, but he insisted. She chopped off Rabbit's head and he died. (Fauset [1972], pp. 219–20)

32. (Mississippi) Guinea Fowl used to hide his head under the green. Rabbit asked him where his head was, and he said that he had left it home for his wife to delouse. Rabbit told his wife to cut off his head and delouse it. She did so and his brother said, "What a pity for a damn fool!" (Fauset [1927], p. 220)

33. (Alabama) Rooster put his head under his wing and told Rabbit that he had left it at home for his wife to comb. Rabbit asked for a hatchet so that he could cut off his head and leave it at home, so that his wife could comb it and he could go with Rooster. He put his head on a block and chopped his head off. That was the last of him. (Richardson, Work, and Parsons [1919], p. 401)

34. (North Carolina) Rooster and Rabbit were farming. One day Rooster stayed home. Rabbit was in the field and Rooster was at the house. Rooster put his head under his wing and when Rabbit came, Rooster told him that his wife had cut off his head. Rabbit told his wife to cut off his head. She said that it would kill him, but he told her to cut it off. When she started cutting, he said, "Stop, stop!" (Parsons [1917], p. 190)

35. (South Carolina) Rooster told Fox to watch their potato patch while he

went home for dinner. Rooster came back with his head under his wing, saying that he had been home and his wife had cut off his head. Rabbit [sic] ran home and told his wife to cut off his head. Rooster took his head out from under his wing and said, "Rabbit is dead, but I'm still alive." (Parsons [1921], p. 7)

36. (South Carolina) Rabbit met Partridge and asked him where his head was. Patridge said that he had left it at home for his wife to look at. Rabbit went home and told his wife, saying that he too was going to leave his head home for her to look at. He told her to get an ax and cut it off, and she did so. Patridge fooled him; he had had his head under his wing. (Parsons [1921], p. 7)

37. (South Carolina) Fox and Rooster farmed together and each said he would outwit the other. One day Fox saw Rooster with his head under his wing and asked him what he was doing with his head cut off. Rooster said that he was having his wife wash and iron his neck and head for the frolic that night. Fox went home and told his mother to chop off his head and wash and iron it for the frolic. She didn't want to, but he threatened to tear her to pieces. Fox laid his head on the chopping block and she chopped it off. (Parsons [1921], p. 7)

38. (South Carolina) Rabbit saw that at night Rooster had only one leg and no head at all, but in the morning he had his head and two legs. He asked Rooster why he cut his head and leg off at night and put them back in the morning. Rooster said that he rested that way. Rabbit told his wife to cut off his three legs and head so that he could rest. When she did so, Rooster held up his leg and took his head from under his wing, saying, "I have my head." (Parsons, "Sea Islands" [1923], pp. 33–34; reprinted in Lee [1930], p. 107, and Weldon [1959], pp. 179–80)

39. (South Carolina) In winter Partridge would put his head under his wing. Rabbit saw him this way and asked where his head was. Partridge said he had left it at home with his wife. Rabbit asked how he got his head off. Partridge said he had his wife knock it off, but that she must not knock it off too hard. Rabbit told his wife to knock off his head, but not too hard; and she knocked off his head. She told Partridge that Rabbit didn't wake up. Partridge said she had knocked him too hard. (Parsons, "Sea Islands" [1923], p. 34)

40. (South Carolina) Partridge stole from Rabbit's and Fox's pea patch. One time he was in the patch when they came to look at the peas. Seeing Rabbit, Partridge ran into the road, put his head under his wing, and began to flutter. Rabbit ran home to his wife and said that Partridge had his head cut off and was having a fine time. He told his wife to cut off his head. She said that he would die, but he insisted. She cut it off, and he fell down dead. (Parsons, "Sea Islands" [1923], pp. 34–35)

41. (South Carolina) A man killed a partridge and put its head on the ground. Partridge took it and told Rabbit that he could cut off his head and

that Rabbit couldn't. Partridge put his neck under his wing and dropped the head. Rabbit cut off his head. (Parsons, "Sea Islands" [1923], p. 35)

42. (South Carolina) Rabbit saw Partridge with his head under his wing and asked him where his head was. Partridge said that he had left it at home so that his wife could comb it. Rabbit asked how it was done and was told that he just had to ask his wife to cut it off. Rabbit went home and told his wife to take an ax and chop off his head. His wife argued but finally gave in. Rabbit put his head on the block and his wife chopped it off. Rabbit was just as dead as he could be. (Johnson [1968], pp. 146–47)

43. (South Carolina) Rabbit made a whip of alligator's tail and hung it in a tree. Partridge took the whip home, returned to the tree, and put his head under his wing. Rabbit looked at him carefully and then started to run. Partridge called to him, and Rabbit asked where his head had been. Partridge said he had eaten a piece of alligator tail and his head had come off. He said he liked it with his head off, because he could leave his head in the house when it was cold or raining. Rabbit said he would take his head off too, and he told his wife to cut it off. He laid his head on the cutting block and she cut it off with an ax. (Work Projects Administration, South Carolina [1941], pp. 27–28)

44. (South Carolina) Partridge and Rabbit were going to a dance. Partridge was sitting on a stump with his head under his wing. He asked Rabbit if he could cut off his head, saying he was going to do so before they went to the dance. Rabbit went home and asked his wife, his mother, and his daughter to cut off his head, but they refused. Partridge came by and offered to do so. Rabbit put his head on a stump, and Partridge chopped it off with an ax. Partridge took his head out from under his wing and went to the dance, saying that he would bury Rabbit when he came back. (Work Projects Administration, South Carolina [1941], pp. 28–29)

45. (Georgia) Rabbit greased his hair, combed it carefully, and promenaded in front of Bear's house. Bear's wife asked Bear why he didn't look as nice as Rabbit. When they met, Bear asked Rabbit how he combed his hair so nice. Rabbit said he didn't comb it, but every morning his wife chopped off his head with an ax so that she could get at it good and then slapped it back on again, all combed. Bear asked if it didn't hurt or bleed, and Rabbit said hardly any. Bear went home and told his wife how Rabbit got his hair combed, and she was eager to try it. Bear put his head on a log and his wife cut it off. (Harris [1892], pp. 236–38; retold [1894], pp. 131–38; reprinted [1948], no. 5; [1955], pp. 861–63)

46. (Georgia) After other incidents, Crow noticed that all the birds had gone to sleep without their heads. He couldn't see a single bird with its head on and concluded that going to sleep with your head on had gone out of fashion. He didn't know that they had their heads under their wings. He asked Rabbit about it, and Rabbit said that the birds had their heads off because the mosquitoes were so bad. Rabbit offered to bring the doctor that took their

heads off for them, and he brought Wolf. Crow told Wolf that he wanted to be like the other birds. Wolf bit off Crow's head and carried him home. (Harris [n.d.], no. 8; [1955], pp. 640–47)

47. (Georgia) Rabbit was laughing at how Crow had lost his head, and Fox asked him why he was laughing. He told Fox and his wife how Crow hadn't known that taking off one's head when going to sleep was the fashion. He said he did so himself and found it more comfortable. When bedtime came, Fox said he was ready to have his head taken off if his wife would help him. She said that an ax looked scary, but it wouldn't hurt if it was the fashion. So she got the ax and chopped off Fox's head. She had to go to bed with her head on, and the next morning Fox didn't wake up. (Harris [n.d.], no. 9; [1955], pp. 647–53)

48. (Florida) Rabbit saw Rooster with his head tucked under his wing. When they met again, Rabbit said, "When I saw you the other day, your head was off. How was that?" Rooster said that he had his wife chop off his head so that he could sun it. Rabbit went home and told his wife to chop off his head, and that was the last of his head. (Parsons [1917], p. 226)

B I B L I O G R A P H Y

Atangana, Karl, and Messi, Paul
    1919 Jaunde-Texte. *Abhandlungen des Hamburgischen Kolonialinstituts* 24, Reihe B, *Völkerkunde, Kulturgeschichte und Sprachen* 14.
Basset, Réne
    n.d. Contes Populaires d'Afrique. *Les Littératures Populaires de Toutes les Nations*, Vol. 47, c. 1903.
Bergsma, Harold, and Bergsma, Ruth
    1969 *Tales Tiv Tell.* Ibadan, Oxford University Press.
Boas, Franz, and Simango, C. Kamba
    1922 Tales and Proverbs of the Vandau of Portuguese South Africa. *Journal of American Folk-lore* 35.
Botkin, B. A.
    1966 *A Treasury of American Folklore.* New York, Crown [1944].
Busse, I.
    1936–37 Inamwanga-Texte. *Zeitschrift für Eingeborenen-Sprachen* 27.
Curtis, Natalie
    1920 *Songs and Tales from the Dark Continent.* New York, C. Schirmer.
Dammann, Ernst
    1935–36 Digo-Märchen. *Zeitschrift für Eingeborenen-Sprache* 26.
de Bouveignes, Olivier (Nom-de-plum of Léon Guébels)
    n.d. *En écoutant conter les Noirs.* Namur, Grand Lacs.
    1934 *Ce que content les Noirs.* Bruxelles, Collection Durendal.
de Clercq, Aug.
    1909 Quelques légends des Bena Kanioka. *Anthropos* 4.
Dempwolff, Otto

1916 Die Sandawe. *Abhandlungen des Hamburgischen Kolonialinstituts* 34, Reihe B, *Völkerkunde, Kulturgeschichte und Sprachen* 19.

Dewar, Emmeline H.
1900 *Chinamwanga Stories.* Livingstonia Mission Press.

Espinosa, Aurelio M.
1936 Pueblo Indian Folk Tales. *Journal of American Folk-Lore* 49.

Fauset, Arthur Huff
1927 Negro Folk Tales from the South: Alabama, Mississippi, Louisiana. *Journal of American Folk-Lore* 40.

Feldmann, Susan
1963 *African Myths and Tales.* New York, Dell.

Fortier, Alcée
1895 Louisiana Folk-Tales in French Dialect and English Translation. *Memoirs of the American Folk-Lore Society* 2.

Frobenius, Leo
1928 Dichtkunst der Kassaiden. *Atlantis* 12.

Harris, Joel Chandler
1892 Brother Bear Learns to Comb his Head. *Dixie* 8, no. 4.
1894 *Little Mr. Thimblefinger and his Queer Country.* New York, McKinlay, Stone & Mackenzie.
n.d. *Told by Uncle Remus.* New York, Grosset & Dunlap. [1903]
1948 *Seven Tales of Uncle Remus,* Ed. Thomas H. English. Atlanta, Emory University.
1955 *The Complete Tales of Uncle Remus.* Compiled by Richard Chase. Boston, Houghton Mifflin.

Holland, Madeleine
1916 Folklore of the Banyanja. *Folk-Lore* 27.

Hulstaert, G.
1970 Fables Mongo. *Académie royal des Sciences d'Outre-Mer, Classe des Sciences morales et politiques,* NS 37, 1.

Johnson, Guy B.
1968 *Folk Culture on St. Helena Island, South Carolina.* Hatboro, Pennsylvania, Folklore Associates. [1930]

Junod, Henri A.
1896 *La Tribu et la Langue Thonga avec Quelques Echantillons du Folklore Thonga.* Lausanne, Georges Bridel.
1897 *Les Chants et les Contes des Ba-Ronga.* Lausanne, Georges Bridel.
1913 *The Life of a South African Tribe.* Vols. I–II. Neuchatel, Attinger Freres; London, Macmillan.
1936 *Mouers et Coutumes des Bantous. La Vie d'une Tribu Sud-Africaine.* Vols. I-II Paris, Payot.

Lee, F. H.
1930 *Folk Tales of All Nations.* New York, Coward-McCann.

Lindblom, Gerhard
1926 Kamba Tales of Animals. *Archives d'Etudes Orientales* 20:1.

Nassau, Robert H.
1914 *Where Animals Talk.* London, Duckworth.

Parsons, Elsie Clews
1917 Tales from Guilford County, North Carolina. *Journal of American Folk-Lore* 30.
1917 Folk-Tales Collected at Miami Fla. *Journal of American Folk-Lore* 30.
1921 Folk-Lore from Aiken, S.C. *Journal of American Folk-Lore* 34.
1923 Folk-Lore of the Sea Islands, South Carolina. *Memoirs of the American Folk-Lore Society* 16.
1926 Tewa Tales. *Memoirs of the American Folk-Lore Society* 19.

Rattray, R. Sutherland
    1969 *Some Folk-Lore Stories and Songs in Chinyanha*. New York, Negro Universities
        Press. [1907]
Richardson, Clement; Work, Monroe N.; and Parsons, Elsie Clews
    1919 Folk-Tales from Students in Tuskeegee Institute, Alabama. *Journal of American
        Folk-Lore* 32.
Taylor, W. E.
    1891 *Giryama Vocabulary and Collections*. London, Society for Promoting Christian
        Knowledge.
Voth, H. R.
    1905 *Traditions of the Hopi*. Publication 96, Anthropological Series 8. Chicago: Field
        Columbian Museum.
Weeks, John H.
    n.d. *Congo Life and Jungle Stories*. London, Religious Tract Society. [1911]
    1913 *Among Congo Cannibals*. Philadelphia. J. B. Lippincott.
Weldon Jr., Fred O.
    1959 Negro Folktale Heros. *Publications of the Texas Folklore Society* 29.
Werner, Alice
    1933 *Myths & Legends of the Bantu*. London, George G. Harrap.
    1965 Giryama-Texte. *Zeitschrift für Kolonialsprachen* 5. [1914–15]
Works Projects Administration, South Carolina
    1941 *South Carolina Folk Tales*. Compiled by Workers of the Writers' Program of
        the Work Projects Administration in the State of South Carolina. Bulletin of
        University of South Carolina.

N O T E S

1. Alan Dundes, "African and Afro-American Tales," *Research in African Litera-tures*, 7 (Fall 1976), 184.

2. Kenneth Wendell Clarke, "A Motif-Index of the Folktales of Culture Area V, West Africa," Ph.D. Dissertation, Indiana Univ., (1958).

3. Helen L. Flowers, "A Classification of the Folktales of the West Indies by Types and Motifs," Ph.D. Dissertaton, Indiana Univ., (1952).

4. Terrence Leslie Hansen, "The Types of the Folktale in Cuba, Puerto Rico, the Dominican Republic, and Spanish South America," *Folklore Studies* [Berkeley and Los Angeles, Univ. of California Press] 8 (1957), 172, 184, 187.

5. I have not yet had access to the Ndau tale (Curtis [1920], p. 48) cited by Parsons, "Sea Islands" (1923), 33 n. 2.

F I V E

✳

Inside Cow's (Elephant's) Belly

This is my first example of how misleading motifs can be. It is necessary to consider tale types and, beyond that, to examine the narratives cited to determine whether or not they are similar enough to be considered historically related. There are many narratives in which a character enters the belly of an animal, including Tom Thumb and Jonah and the whale, and those in which he does so in order to demand the return of food or an object. None of these, however, is similar to the tales considered here.

Usually one character takes another into a cow or elephant to cut meat from its stomach for food, warning him not to cut the heart; but the second character does so, and the animal dies. Many of the tales continue with the two characters, who are trapped inside the animal, hiding in its internal organs. People come and butcher the animal and throw away or wash the organ in which one of the characters is hiding; he comes out and accuses them of throwing dirty things on him and often tells them to beat the organ in which the other is hiding.

Dorson has recorded an excellent version of this tale type in Arkansas [19]. Except for cutting the heart, which is also lacking in some African versions [4, 8, 14], it is complete with all the other elements noted above, and even has the animals entering the belly when Elephant was laughing [5, 8–9, 11–12].

In the headnote to this tale, Dorson observes that Helen L. Flowers identified a number of West Indian versions of this tale type as an independent subtype of Open Sesame (AT676). He comments, however, that his tale is closer to Tom Thumb and Jonah and the whale. "This story clearly has closer affinities with the Thumbling-Petit Poucet complex, where the tiny hero is swallowed by a cow (see Grimm no. 45, 'Thumbling as Journeyman') or even with Jonah and the whale, than with Open Sesame, to which it is linked only by one stray motif."

Reprinted from *Research in African Literatures*, 10 (1979), 323–49.

As we shall see, AT676 does not fit our tale type, but the only connection between Dorson's Arkansas tale and Tom Thumb (AT700) or Jonah and the whale is also only a single motif: a character or characters inside an animal's stomach. Moreover, while Tom Thumb is swallowed by a cow (Motif F911.3.1) and Jonah is swallowed by a whale, the characters in these African and American folktales enter the animal voluntarily,[1] and they do so in order to carve out meat from its stomach.

Dorson does note that Flower's citations include Africa, and he cites a version [17] from Mauritius (not Senegal). He says of his Arkansas tale, told by Mrs. L. R. Toler, "The substitution of the elephant for the cow in the Toler text is curious." There is nothing curious when it is recognized that this tale came from Africa, where the animal involved is usually an elephant or a cow.

Clearly the tale type considered here is different from Tom Thumb, as described in Aarne and Thompson's *The Type of the Folktale:*

> 700 *Tom Thumb.* Plowing. The king buys the boy. In thieves' company. In the belly of the cow and of the wolf. Cf. Type 327B.
> I. *The Hero's Birth.* A childless couple wish for a child, however small he may be; they have a boy the size of a thumb [F535.1].
> II. *His Adventures.* [F535.1.1] (a) He drives the wagon by sitting in the horse's ear; (b) he lets himself be sold and then runs away; (c) he is carried up the chimney by the steam of food; (d) he teases the tailor's wife; (e[1]) he helps thieves rob a treasure-house; (e[2]) he betrays the thieves by his cries; (f) he is swallowed by a cow [F911.3.1], makes an outcry [F913], and is rescued when the cow is slaughtered; (g[1]) he persuades the fox who has eaten him to go to his father's house and eat chickens, or (g[2]) the wolf to go to his father's pantry; he then calls for help and is rescued.

It also differs from the tale type cited by Flowers, as described in Aarne and Thompson:

> 676 *Open Sesame.* A poor man observes robbers who enter into a mountain [F721.4]. Uses, like them [N455.3], the words "Open up" [D1552.2] and gets gold from the mountain [N512]. His rich brother tries to do the same thing but is killed [N471]. The rich brother lends his money scales to the poor brother; a piece of money remains in the scales and thus betrays the secret [N478]. When he is in the mountain he forgets the formula for opening it.

The motif of the password is common in the tales from the New World but occurs in only one African version [2]. It seems to have been added to the American tales rather than having been lost, as Dorson suggests, in the case of his Arkansas tale.

Actually, the folktales under consideration are closer to Part I (a) of AT68 than to either AT676 or AT700; however, the only references cited for AT68 and for its six component motifs are to India. Since no European references are cited, I conclude that these tales could not have come from Europe. This tale type is described in Aarne and Thompson as follows:

68 *The Jackal Trapped in the Animal Hide.* [F929.1, J2136.6.1, K565.2, K952.1.1, K1022.1.1, K1973].

I. *Entering the elephant.* (a) An elephant lets his friend the jackal enter his body to drink water. The jackal eats the internal organs and the elephant dies. The jackal is trapped in the carcass. (b) A jackal eats its way into a carcass which it finds and is trapped inside when the skin dries.

II. *Jackal and the God.* A god passes and the jackal challenges him to a rain-making contest. The god sends rain, the carcass swells, and the jackal escapes. (b) The jackal pretends to be a god and frightens people into bringing sacrifice and pouring water over the carcass.

India 12.

It should be noted that Dorson is not the only eminent folklorist who has mistakenly equated this tale type with AT700. Parsons, for example, cites Braga and Coelho for Portugal and Bolte and Polivka's comparative study in a footnote to her Bahamian tale [26] and in a later note [62] she adds Carnoy for France. All four of these references are clearly to the Tom Thumb tale type. Parsons also cites several African tales in which a character is swallowed by an animal and then kills it. I have excluded these, but they do not fit the pattern of either Tom Thumb or Jonah and may constitute another tale type which has also been found in the United States. I have also excluded Jekyll's Jamaican tale in which Annancy is trapped in a butcher shop because he took cow liver and then is rescued.

Nevertheless, nearly a century ago Crane cited Bleek's Herero or Damara tale as an analogue of the Uncle Remus version [24] of this type type,[2] although I exclude Bleek's tale here because Elephant swallows Tortoise. In 1893 Gerber identified the Uncle Remus tale as having come from Africa, citing a Temne homologue [1].[3] Gerber also noted that "certain traits that are especially prominent in the Southern story [24] occur in Africa only; there alone the animal or dwarf enters the cow or elephant voluntarily, there alone the warning with regard to the heart is found." Two years later Ellis gave an Akan homologue [13] to the Uncle Remus tale.[4]

Dundes also concludes that this tale type came to the United States from Africa, citing Crane, Gerber, and Ellis. As he says, "The point is that this African/Afro-American Tale Type has an identity of its own, and it is neither a subtype of Aarne-Thompson 676 nor a subtype of Aarne-Thompson 700, Tom Thumb."[5]

There are variations on the general pattern outlined above, including the many markedly different conclusions. Many apparently fragmentary tales end with the death of the cow or elephant or with the death or escape of the character trapped inside. In a number of tales only one character is inside the belly, but in some of these also he comes out to accuse people of throwing dirty things on him [2-3, 25, 34, 43, 45].

The names of some of the characters in the New World tales deserve mention because of their African associations. Anancy, Nancy, Annancy, or Anansi[6] in these tales is Ananse, Spider, the trickster in the folktales of the Akan of

Ghana and the Ivory Coast. Like other animal characters in African folktales, Ananse has obvious human attributes. Although sometimes conceived as a spider in the New World, in the Bahamas he is described as follows: "B'Anansi.—or Nansi, Boy Nasty, or Gulumbanansi, a trickster and hero, either boy, man, or monkey."[7]

As a slight digression I note that Dorson says, "Another noted folklorist, Martha Warren Beckwith, assembled a whole volume of Anansi the Spider stories in Jamaica, but Anansi fails to set foot in the United States," and elsewhere he says, "no Anansi stories are found in the United States."[8] Ananse in fact rarely appears in the United States, but these are typical overstatements. In one of the Uncle Remus tales, entitled "Brother Rabbit Doesn't Go to See Aunt Nancy," "de creeturs what wuz watchin' un her, seed wid der own eyes dat she wuz half 'oman an' half spider. She had sev'm arms an' no han's."[9] In his introduction to *Seven Tales of Uncle Remus* in which this tale appears, Thomas H. English comments, "the second of the sketches left in manuscript is notable in that it introduces a character called Aunt Nancy, identified as 'de granny er Mammy-Bammy-Big-Money,' 'de ole Witch Rabbit,' who is readily recognizable as Annancy, the spider hero of Jamaican folk tales."[10] There is, however, no suggestion of an African connection in "Brother Rabbit and Miss Nancy."[11]

In a tale from North Carolina, Ann Nancy scalds Buzzard's head, making him bald.[12] In Philadelphia Nancy rides Tiger, is caught by Tacoma's tar baby, boils Monkey, squeezes Greyhound who has stolen her fruit, and is beaten by Whip.[13] North of the United States, in Nova Scotia, Anancy, Nancy, Brer Nancy, or Brother Nancy appears, along with Tacoma.[14]

Tacoma, Tacoomah, Takoma, Tukoma, Tukuma, Toukouma, Tookerma, Tookerman, or Terycooma is Ntikuma, Ananse's son in Ghana.[15]

Bouqui, Buquí, Bouky, Boukee, Bookee, or Booky has sometimes been identified as *bouquin,* meaning old he-goat, old hare, or buck hare in French; but among the Wolof of Senegal and Gambia Bouki is Hyena, the stupid, perfidious dupe of Hare.[16] Bouki or Bouqui is not the Haitian trickster,[17] but the greedy dupe or foil of the trickster, Malice [35]. In the Bahamas he is described as "B'Booky.—the stupid, greedy, lascivious foil of B'Rabby, sometimes his brother or close friend, usually bigger in size, and conceived as a rabbit, goat, monkey, or as a human."[18]

Bookay is the password and name of the cow in Georgia [24]. In Nevis the password is "Open, Tukoma, open!" [47], and in Antigua it is "Open, Toukouma, open!" [50].

Rabby and, presumably, La Pain [22] and Lapén [37–38] refer to Rabbit. In tales from Guadeloupe [52–56], Marie Galante [57], Les Saintes [58], Dominica [59], and Trinidad [62] the French *lapin* is translated as *rabbit,* the American counterpart of the wide-spread African trickster, Hare.

I have not yet identified either Malice or Zamba, except for the fact that the former is a trickster [35] and the latter is a foil or dupe [52–55]. These two opposing roles, however, are not consistently played out in these tales, with the traditional trickster sometimes being duped while the dupe escapes [1, 33, 41, 56, 61].

My seventeen African versions come from Sierra Leone (Temne), Liberia (Bandi), Mali (Malinke), Ivory Coast (Anyi), Upper Volta (Mosi and Samo), Ghana (Akan), Nigeria (Bura), Rio Muni (Benga), Gabon (Mpongwe), and Mauritius. Tauxier notes that his tale [9] is also known by the Foulsés and Mandés. The seven from the United States come from New England (Cape Verde Islanders), Arkansas, Oklahoma (Caddo Indians), Louisiana, Virginia, and Georgia. Thirty-eight come from the Bahamas, Jamaica, Haiti, Dominican Republic, Puerto Rico, St. Thomas, Anguilla, Saint Martin, Saint Eustatius, Nevis, Antigua, Montserrat, Guadeloupe, Marie Galante, Les Saintes, Dominica, Saint Lucia, Grenada, and Trinidad.

1. (Sierra Leone: Temne) After blaming Anteater for killing a cow, Spider went with Mr. Taba to another of the king's cows. Spider told her to break wind and they went into her belly. Spider told Taba not to cut her heart and they filled their baskets with meat. Spider made the cow break wind again and they left. When they went another time Taba cut the heart and the cow died with both inside her. Spider hid by the liver and Taba hid in the rectum. The king's children found the dead cow and began to butcher it. Spider said they should not chop him and they were frightened; but they pulled Spider out with his basket and flogged him. Spider said that Taba was with him, but he didn't know where he had gone. When the children took the rectum to the brook to wash it, they shook it and Taba jumped out. He blamed the children for splattering him with cow dung and the king gave him new clothes. Spider was flogged with a palm frond, and this is why he has so many legs; then the king let Spider run away. (Schlenker [1861], pp. 44–57; translated in Bleek [1870], pp. 104–08)

2. (Sierra Leone: Temne) Frog went to the king's cow and said "Cow open." The cow opened its mouth and Frog jumped in and was swallowed. He cut much fat, being careful not to cut the heart. Then he repeated the password, came out, took the fat home, and cooked it. He invited Spider to eat with him, and Spider asked him where he had gotten the meat. Frog said he would take Spider there the next day. After incidents of mock sunrise, they went to the cow. When they were inside Frog warned Spider not to cut the heart and both took meat home. For several days Spider went by himself and finally he cut the cow's heart. The cow fell dead and Spider could not get out. People cut the cow open and gave the insides to children to wash. Spider jumped out and blamed them for throwing dirty things on him. They begged forgiveness, but Spider complained to the king. He was given the cow's head and two legs, and another episode follows. (Cronise and Ward [1903], pp. 231–39)

3. (Sierra Leone: Temne) After other episodes, Spider went into the belly of the chief's cow to cut its heart. It died and when people butchered it they gave the stomach to children to wash. As they did so Spider came out and accused them of throwing dirty things on his fine gown. They went to the

chief, who gave Spider all his cows because his things had been dirtied. (Thomas [1916], Part III, pp. 72–74)

4. (Liberia: Bandi) Spider crawled into a sorceress's cow and ate heartily. Another day he crawled in and ate again, and the cow died. The sorceress looked into the cow and saw Spider. He was beaten vehemently and ran away. (Germann [1933], p. 127)

5. (Mali: Malinke) Hyena played chess with Elephant. Each time that Elephant said "checkmate" he laughed and his anus opened. Hyena slipped into Elephant's belly and ate its fat. Hyena grew fat and [after other episodes] he took Hare with him. Hyena played chess with Elephant, was checkmated, and Hyena and Hare went inside Elephant's belly. Hyena showed Hare the heart and told him not to touch it because Elephant would die and their exit would be forever closed; but Hare did not follow Hyena's advice and Elephant died. Hare told Hyena to hide in the spleen while he hid in the intestine; but Hyena insisted on hiding in the intestine, saying that he was too large to hide in the spleen. The chief heard of Elephant's death and sent servants to cut him up. When the belly was opened they took out the spleen and threw it into the bush. Hare came out and cried, "Pay attention. You almost killed me with what you threw." The servants begged to be excused, saying that they had not known Hare was there. When they were about to take out the intestine, Hare said that he was sure that the one who had killed Elephant was in it. Hare told them to beat the intestine with sticks, and when he was sure that Hyena was dead, he left. (Montell [1905], pp. 45–49)

6. (Mali: Malinke) Hare went to a herd of cattle, crawled into the anus of a cow, and cut meat from its stomach. He took the meat home for his wife to cook, and Jackal's wife came for fire and smelled the meat. She extinguished the fire several times, each time returning for fire again. Finally Hare gave her some meat and she took it home to her husband. Jackal went to Hare who promised to take him along in the morning. After incidents of mock sunrise, they went to the cattle and entered one of the cows. Hare warned Jackal not to cut the heart, liver, or kidney, but Jackal did so and the cow died. Jackal hid in the maw and Hare hid in the blind-gut. People found the dead cow, began to butcher it, and threw the blind-gut away. Hare came out and blamed them for dirtying his clothes, and they promised him meat. He told them he had seen Jackal crawl into the cow. He said that Jackal had surely hidden in the maw and that they should beat it until he was dead. They did so, and other incidents follow. (Frobenius, "Erzählungen" [1922], pp. 121–24)

7. (Ivory Coast: Anyi) In a time of famine Ananzè, the spider, grew fat while all others grew thin. God noticed that his cow was growing thin, although he doubled, tripled, and quintupled its rations. Each night Ananzè was entering the cow's stomach and eating his fill. Hyena saw that Ananzè was growing fat and asked to go with him. Ananzè warned him repeatedly not to touch the heart, and they entered the cow and began eating. Hyena bit off the heart and swallowed it, and the cow fell dead. The word spread

and all except Ananzè and Hyena went to God to mourn. God ordered them to cut up the cow. A boy took the paunch, but it was heavy and he called others to help him carry it. When they threw it on the ground it burst and Ananzè appeared. He rebuked them for not having seen him. Hyena tried to escape but was beaten until his back was broken. From that day Hyena has the gait that we know. Other incidents are introduced by the author in the course of this narrative. (Dadié [1955], pp. 105–13)

8. (Upper Volta: Mosi) Hare and Elephant played checkers and Elephant won. In his joy Elephant laughed, lifting up his rear leg; and Hare entered his behind. He cut meat from Elephant's belly and came out. The next time Hyena went with Hare. They played checkers and Elephant won. Elephant laughed, lifting up his rear leg; and they went inside his belly. Hare made Hyena stay in the large intestine while he went into the small intestine. Then Elephant died and people cut him to pieces. They took the small intestine to empty it and Hare came out. He told them to take sticks and beat the large intestine, because the one who killed Elephant was there. They beat the large intestine, killing Hyena, and took Hyena and Elephant to eat. (Froger [1910], pp. 256–57)

9. (Upper Volta: Mosi) Elephant beat Hare at the board game [*warri*, *mancala*] and laughed so much that he opened his anus. Hare entered his stomach and cut a bag full of meat and fat which he took home to his wife. Hyena's wife came to visit her and saw her abundance of food. She told Hyena, chiding him for not bringing food. Hyena asked Hare where he had gotten the food and Hare told him. The next day they went together and when Elephant won the game and laughed, they both entered his stomach. Hyena cut Elephant's heart and Elephant fell dead, trapping them inside. A hunter saw Elephant's carcass and brought the villagers to butcher it. Hyena hid in the big intestine and Hare hid in the little intestine. When the people reached the intestines they gave the little one to children to clean in the bush. Hare escaped, bathed, and joined the people. Pretending to be a diviner, he told them that the one who had killed Elephant was inside the big intestine. They took sticks and beat it, killing Hyena. They gave some of the meat to Hare, who took it home to his wife. (Tauxier [1917], pp. 423–24)

10. (Upper Volta: Mosi) Elephant played the board game every day. One day Hare played against him and lost. Elephant was so happy that he danced for joy, and Hare noticed that his anus opened. He slipped in, cut meat, slipped out again, and hid the meat. They played some more and each time Hare let Elephant win so that he could get more meat. He took it home and came again every day to play the game with Elephant. One day Jackal came, smelled the meat, and threatened to kill Hare unless he told where he had gotten the meat. Hare promised to take Jackal along and the next morning they went to Elephant and let him win. Elephant danced for joy at having beaten them both, and they both slipped inside him. Hare warned Jackal not to cut the heart but Jackal cut it and Elephant died. A hunter saw Elephant's carcass and called the villagers to help him butcher it. Meanwhile Jackal hid

in the maw and Hare hid in the gall. When the people reached the gall they threw it away and Hare came out and cleaned himself. He went to the people and consulted his oracles to determine how Elephant had died. He announced that Elephant had been killed by something in his maw. He told them to beat the maw until the thing was dead. They beat it until they thought that Jackal was dead, but he was not and escaped. The hunter gave Hare some of the meat. (Frobenius, "Erzählungen" [1922], pp. 242–45)

11. (Upper Volta: Mosi) Hare played the board game with Elephant. Whenever Elephant won he laughed and rolled on the ground, opening his mouth wide. Hare entered into his belly, cut off some meat, and took it home to his family. Hyena noticed the meat and asked to accompany Hare. They went to Elephant and, as usual, Hare lost the game to Elephant's delight. When he opened his mouth they went into his belly. They had gathered much meat when Hyena saw the heart surrounded by fat. "Don't touch that," said Hare. "You might kill Elephant." But Hyena cut off Elephant's heart and his mouth closed. For three days they were trapped in Elephant's belly. Then they heard hunters coming to butcher Elephant, and Hare hid in the stomach while Hyena hid in the paunch. When Elephant was butchered, the hunters gave the stomach to a child to empty. He emptied it at a distance and saw Hare, who accused him of throwing its contents on him. The child apologized, saying that he had not seen Hare. They went back to the hunters who asked Hare if he knew who had killed Elephant. Hare said it was one of his (Hare's) enemies and told them to beat the paunch, and Hyena was beaten. (Guillot [1933], pp. 25–27)

12. (Upper Volta: Samo) During a famine Hare met Elephant who was discouraged. Hare said foolish things to cheer him up, and Elephant laughed so much that Hare could enter his body through his anus. Hare stuffed himself with Elephant's fat, took all he could carry, and came out. When Hyena asked where he had found so much food, Hare told him and they went to Elephant together. Hare made Elephant laugh and they both went into his stomach. Hyena tore off lots of fat and meat, and Hare told him not to touch the heart lest they be lost. Hyena did not listen to him and Elephant fell dead. All the doctors of the forest came to learn the cause of Elephant's death, and they began their autopsy. Hare wanted to hide in Elephant's stomach, but Hyena took that hiding place and Hare hid in the paunch. The doctors gave the paunch to the monkeys to empty, and Hare came out and accused them of soiling him. The monkeys bathed him and Hare told the animals to put the stomach aside and beat it with clubs. They did so and Hyena was beaten to death. (Guilhem, vol. I [n.d.], pp. 114–17)

13. (Ghana: Akan) Meat was scarce but the king had two cows that voided meat for him every day. Kwaku Anansi, Spider, and his friend, Kwaku Tse, went to the king and asked for meat, saying that they had seen his cows; but the king refused to give them any. They rubbed the cows' noses with a leaf that made them sneeze and, making themselves very small, they jumped into the mouths of the cows and were swallowed. They cut meat from the insides

of the cows and left it there. They next day the cows voided meat for the king, but it was not fresh. Spider warned his friend that if he cut the cow's belly or its heart it would die and he would not be able to get out. But he told him to cut the heart, saying that he should hide in the stomach and, when the cow was cut open, he should hide in the bowels. Then each of them entered the belly of a cow and cut its heart, and both cows died. When the king found his cows dead, he had his slaves cut them open and carry the paunches to the water side. When they threw the paunches into the water, Spider and Kwaku Tse came out covered with filth and accused the slaves of throwing the paunches on them. They went to the king and complained that the filth had spoiled their charms. To make new charms the king gave them the heads and hearts of the cows and some hair of his two wives. Another episode follows. (Ellis [1895–96], 97–103)

14. (Nigeria: Bura) Toward the end of a lengthy tale, Squirrel led Hyena to a dead elephant. They started to skin it but the elephant's children came, so they entered the corpse. Hyena hid in the stomach and Squirrel hid in the bladder. The young elephants decided to carry the corpse home. They cut out the bladder and threw it aside. Squirrel came out and asked who had poured water on him. The young elephants apologized, saying that they had not known he was there. Squirrel offered to divine to find out who had killed the elephant. He announced that the killer was inside the stomach and told the elephants to get large clubs and beat it. They did so, killing Hyena, and other incidents follow. (Helser [1930], pp. 217–23; [1934], pp. 77–82)

15. (Rio Muni: Benga) In a time of meat hunger Tortoise came to a giant goat. It invited him to enter and he went in through its aperture, cut fat, and came out. He took the meat home and Leopard's children learned of it. Leopard put ashes in Tortoise's bag and followed the trail. Together they went in through the goat's aperture, and Tortoise warned Leopard not the cut the goat's heart. Leopard cut it and the goat died, crying out so that the townspeople heard. They found the goat dead and began to butcher it. Meanwhile Leopard hid in the bowels and Tortoise hid in the bladder. When the people came to the bladder, they threw it away. Tortoise crawled out and asked who had thrown dirty water on his face. They apologized and Tortoise told them to spear the goat's stomach. Leopard was killed, and another incident follows. (Nassau [1914], pp. 202–07)

16. (Gabon: Mpongwe) After other episodes, Tortoise plotted to get even with Leopard by causing him to kill the enormous goat that allowed other animals to cut meat from inside its body, except for its heart. Tortoise took meat from the goat and let Leopard see it. Leopard asked where he had gotten the meat and Tortoise said he would take him there. When they reached the goat, Tortoise asked it for meat. Tortoise and Leopard went in through the goat's mouth, and Tortoise told Leopard to cut where he pleased, but not from the heart lest the goat die. He warned him repeatedly, but greedy Leopard cut the heart and the goat died. They couldn't get out and Leopard hid in the stomach and Tortoise hid in the gall-bladder. When the animals learned

that the goat was dead, they decided to cut and divide it. They set the stomach aside and told a child to throw the bitter gall-bladder away. As he did so Tortoise jumped out and blamed him for throwing the dirty gall-bladder in his face. The others apologized and invited Tortoise to share the meat. Tortoise asked, "What makes that stomach so big?" He told the animals to spear it, because the one who had killed the goat was in it. They killed Leopard with their spears, shouting that he had killed their goat. (Nassau [1914], pp. 30–37)

17. (Mauritius) King Elephant was old and useless. He went about with his mouth always open, and the animals thought he was smiling. Dry season came and Hare could find no food. When he saw Elephant's open mouth he jumped into it and crawled into the stomach. He began eating the tripe and he gnawed at the heart. Elephant fell dead and Hare could not get out. The animals found their dead king and prepared to bury him. Hare hid in the intestines and Ape had the intestines thrown away. Hare came out, cleaned himself, and joined the animals in mourning the king. (Baissac [n.d.], pp. 338–45; translated in Bemelmans [1941], pp. 65–66)

18. (New England: Cape Verde Islanders) Wolf's nephew, Pedro, used to go into a cow to eat. Wolf saw how fat Pedro was and asked to go with him, promising to eat only a little bit. Pedro took his uncle to the cow and said, "Cow, open my mouth" and they went in, and he said, "Cow, close my mouth!" After they had eaten a while Pedro said that it was time to go, but Wolf wanted to eat still more. Pedro went outside after telling Wolf the password, but when Wolf wanted to leave he said, "Cow, close my mouth!" The cow tightened up and Wolf could not get out. He began to eat again and when he ate in the line of the cow's heart, the cow fell dead. When the cow's owner came to skin it Pedro told him that there was something inside it, but he paid no attention. They took out the maw and shook it over a rock. Wolf dropped out and accused them of shaking that dirty thing over him. The man offered Wolf a quarter of the cow, but finally gave him the whole cow so that Wolf would not take him to court. Another incident follows. (Parsons, "Cape Verde" [1923], Part I, pp. 14–15; Part II, pp. 9–10)

19. (Arkansas) Rabbit had a bucket of lard and Bear wanted to know where he had gotten it. Rabbit said that Lion and Elephant were telling big tales and Elephant laughed so long and loud and opened his mouth so wide that he jumped in, got a bucket of fat, and jumped out again. Bear went with Rabbit to Elephant, and when he laughed they both jumped in and began tearing out fat. Elephant closed his mouth and Rabbit went into the bladder and told Bear to go into the melt [spleen]. Elephant died and his friends cut him open to see what his trouble was. When they came to the bladder they threw it down the hill. Rabbit jumped out and yelled, "Look out, don't throw your nasty mess on me." He asked what the trouble was and they said that Elephant was dead. Rabbit asked where the melt was and told them to beat it. They beat Bear into a jelly and found him dead. (Dorson [1958], pp. 18–20; [1967], pp. 81–83)

20. (Oklahoma: Caddo Indians) When Coyote was about to kill him, Rabbit asked Coyote to help him kill a buffalo. Rabbit led Coyote to a fat old buffalo and they climbed into its anus. Rabbit told Coyote to eat the buffalo's sides. They both began to eat and soon the buffalo fell dead. An old man began to butcher it. Rabbit told Coyote to hide in an intestine, and Rabbit hid in the bladder. When the man had cut up the buffalo he placed the intestines to one side, but threw the bladder into the bushes. Rabbit came out and escaped, but Coyote was discovered and killed. (Dorsey [1905], p. 99)

21. (Louisiana) Bouqui found Rabbit cooking meat and asked where he had found it. Rabbit said Bouqui was too greedy and rascally, but finally told him to take a bag and a knife, jump into the throat of the king's cow when it opened its mouth, and cut meat from inside its belly. He warned Bouqui not to cut near the cow's heart. Bouqui entered the cow as he had been told, but he cut a piece of meat near its heart. The cow fell down dead and Bouqui could not come out. People came and cut the cow open to see why it had died. They found Bouqui, cut out his bowels, and filled him with sand. Another incident follows. (Fortier [1888], pp. 127-28, 153-54; [1895], pp. 111-12)

22. (Louisiana) Bookee and La Pain used to eat inside a cow, and its owner noticed that it was growing thin. Bookee told La Pain not to eat the cow's heart, but one day La Pain bit the heart and the cow died. The owner found his cow dead and cut it open. La Pain hid in the pee bag and Bookee hid in the dung bag. The man threw the pee bag away and La Pain complained that he was throwing water on him. The man apologized. Then he took a stick and looked in the other bag where he found Bookee. He accused Bookee of eating his cow, and Bookee blamed La Pain. But the man tied Bookee to a post and stuck seven hot irons in his ass. (Fauset [1927], p. 242)

23. (Virginia) Rabbit had a butcher shop and everyone wondered where he got his meat. One rainy day he suggested to Wolf that they get some meat. By some curious means they got inside a cow and began cutting the meat. Rabbit saw the heart and told Wolf not to cut it or they would get no meat. Wolf agreed, but he accidentally cut the heart. The cow fell dead and they had a hard time getting out. Another episide follows. (Lemar [1896], pp. 185-86)

24. (Georgia) Rabbit found Fox cooking some nice beef and asked where he had gotten it. Fox said he would show him the next day. They went to a cow named Bookay and Fox shouted "Bookay." The cow opened its mouth wide and they jumped inside. Fox told Rabbit not to cut near the haslet, and they began cutting meat. Rabbit cut into the haslet and the cow fell dead. Fox said that he would go into the maul [maw?] and that Rabbit should go into the gall. The owner found the cow and began to cut it open to see what had killed it. Rabbit crept out of the gall and told him that the one who killed his cow was in the maul. The man took a stick and beat the maul until Fox was dead, and other episodes follow. (Harris [1880], no. 34; [1955], pp. 111-15)

25. (Bahamas) Rabby was looking for food and saw a big cow. He spanked

its bottom and said, "Open, Kabendye, open!" The cow's bottom opened and Rabby jumped in with his knife and pan. He cut his pan full of meat, gave the password, and jumped out. Bouki saw Rabby and asked where he had gotten the meat. Rabby told him about the cow and how to go inside, warning him not to cut one big thing lest the cow fall dead. Bouki went inside the cow and cut and cut, but he wasn't satisfied; he cut the heart and the cow fell dead and its bottom wouldn't open. People found the cow dead, cut it open, and took out its guts. Bouki was inside the maw, swelled up. A woman said to cut the maw open and when they did so Bouki jumped out without being seen. Bouki said that they had thrown nasty stuff on him, and they offered him half the cow. At first he refused, threatening to take the people to jail, but he accepted and went home with half of the cow. (Edwards [1891], pp. 53–54; [1942], pp. 77–78)

26. (Bahamas) Rabby used to go to a cow and the cow opened its belly and Rabby jumped in. Boukee came when Rabby was cooking the meat and asked where he got it. Rabby told him to come the next day and they went to the cow together. Rabby said, "Open, gobanje, open!" and they went inside the cow. Rabby showed Boukee the heart and told him not to cut it, but Boukee was so wild that he cut the heart and the cow fell dead. Rabby told Boukee to go into the maw and Rabby went into the gall. The owner found his cow dead and cut it open. He put the maw down and threw away the gall. Rabby jumped out of the gall and accused him of throwing the gall on his clean clothes. Rabby told the man to get a stick and beat the maw, and they beat Boukee until they almost killed him. (Parsons [1918], pp. 8–9)

27. (Bahamas) Boukee's wife complained that Rabby brought fresh meat while Boukee brought none. After an incident of mock sunrise Rabby took Boukee to the king's pasture. Rabby said, "Open, cabanje, open!" and a cow opened and they went inside. Rabby cut only a little basketful of meat, but Boukee wanted lots. Rabby came out, telling Boukee to say, "Open, cabanje, open!" when he wanted to come out; but when Boukee started to come out he said, "Shut, cabanje, shut!" The cow sealed up tighter each time he said it and then fell dead. When the king learned that his cow was dead, he told some men to butcher it. When a woman was washing the belly, Boukee jumped out and accused her of throwing it on him. The men gave Boukee half of the cow and twenty pounds. Another episode follows. (Parsons [1918], pp. 9–10)

28. (Bahamas) Boukee found Rabby cooking meat and asked where he had gotten it. The next day Rabby took Boukee to a cow and said, "Open, Ber Bajer, open!" Rabby went in and then Boukee gave the password and went in. Rabby told Boukee not to touch the "thing that was hanging up," but Boukee was greedy. He cut and cut until he cut the thing. He gave the password, but the cow shut up tighter. He stayed inside and that was the end of Boukee. (Parsons [1928], p. 497)

29. (Bahamas) A man asked his friend where he got meat. The friend took him to a cow and they went inside it. Cut, cut, cut. But one morning they went inside and the cow dropped down. (Parsons [1928], p. 497)

30. (Bahamas) Rabby and Bouky wanted fresh meat. They went to a cow and said, "Open, cabangy, open!" and went inside the cow with their knife and pan. Rabby told Bouky not to cut that red thing because he would kill the cow. Rabby filled his pan and came out, but Bouky was so greedy that he cut the cow's heart and the cow died. People threw the cow into the sea with Bouky inside; but they heard crying in the cow and brought it back. They cut the cow open and found a man [Bouky] inside, and he never tried that again. (Parsons [1928], p. 507)

31. (Bahamas) Jack [Rabby] used to go into a cow and cut out as much meat as he wanted, and his brother Booky wanted to go into the cow too. [Another episode intervenes.] Rabby went to the cow and said, "Open, Kafesya, open!" He went into the cow, cut out as much meat as he wanted, and came out. Booky was there and heard the password. He gave it and the cow opened and he went in. Rabby had told him that he must not cut the cow's heart because the cow would drop dead and not open. When it was time to come out Booky said, "Shut, Kafesya, shut!" and the cow shut up tight. Booky was angry and cut more and the cow dropped down dead. When the king found his cow dead he had a doctor cut it open to see what had killed it. He found Booky dead and they burned his body. (Crowley [1966], pp. 46–48)

32. (Bahamas) Devil and Rabby used to go inside a cow every morning and take out meat to cook. After an incident of mock sunrise they went to the cow and said, "Open Kabanya, open" and went inside and ate. Devil was so greedy that he cut until the cow dropped down dead, and Devil couldn't get out. The owner found the cow dead and cut it open. He caught Devil and beat him with a switch. (Crowley [1966], p. 73)

33. (Bahamas) Booky went to a cow and said, "Open Shebanja, open" and the cow opened. Booky went inside and cut out all the meat. Then he saw a red thing but didn't cut it. He went out and said, "Shut Shebanja, shut" and the cow shut up. Rabby was there and heard the passwords. He told the cow to open and went inside with a bucket. He cut all the meat and then he saw the red thing. He cut it and put it in his bucket, but the cow fell down dead and Rabby couldn't get out. The owner found the dead cow and they cut it open. They found Rabby crying in a tired voice, "Open Shebanja, open." The owner caught him and hung him over a fire. Another episode follows. (Crowley [1966], pp. 92–93)

34. (Jamaica) Anansi sent his child to Tacoomah's yard for fire. The child was given fat, which Anansi ate. Anansi asked where Tacoomah had gotten the fat and when he promised not to cause trouble Tacoomah agreed to take him along the next morning. On the way Tacoomah told Anansi to say "Open, sesema, open" and the cow would open its belly, and to say "Shut, sesema, shut" when he was inside. Then Anansi should cut fat from the cow's belly, but he mustn't cut the back-string because the cow would die. Both of them went to the cow, gave the passwords, cut meat and took it home. The next morning Anansi went by himself, gave the password, and entered the cow. He began to cut meat but he cut the back-string and the cow dropped dead.

Anansi hid in the maw and when the cow was butchered the owner told his daughter to wash the belly at the river. She threw it into the water and Anansi jumped out and accused her of throwing that nasty thing on him. Anansi was given a cow in payment, and another episode follows. (Beckwith [1924], pp. 26–27)

35. (Haiti) Malice entered the king's cow through its anus and cut meat. He told Bouqui that he must take a little sack like his own, but Bouqui brought thirty sacks. After he had filled fifteen, Bouqui made a bad cut and the cow fell dead. Malice went into the bladder and Bouqui went into the guts. When the cow was butchered, the bladder was thrown away. Malice came out all wet and accused them of wetting him. They let him buy the cow's skin and he told them to beat the guts. Bouqui came out covered with excrement and another episode follows. (Parsons [1933–43], Part II, pp. 479–80; Part III, p. 56)

36. (Haiti) Malice stole meat from inside the king's cow every day. One day he went into the cow with Bouqui. He told Bouqui not to cut the heart, but Bouqui was so hungry that he cut the heart first. (Parsons [1933–43], Part II, p. 481; Part III, p. 56)

37. (Dominican Republic) Buquí sent his son to Lapén's house for fire. Lapén gave the boy a piece of egg that his father ate when he got home. Buquí asked Lapén where he had found eggs. Lapén said that they were inside a cow and that they must not cut the cow's heart. Buquí entered the cow and cut her heart. The cow died with Buquí inside, but Lapén escaped. The owner opened the cow and did not find the heart, but he found Buquí. He made a fire and Buquí died in it. (Andrade [1920], p. 121)

38. (Dominican Republic) Looking for food, Buquí and Lapén found a very fat cow. Lapén said, "Let's go inside and eat the liver. But if you eat the heart the cow will die and we won't be able to get out." They went inside and ate. When Lapén was full he said that they should go out, because if the cow's owner came he would kill them. But Buquí was such a glutton that he stayed inside and kept on eating. The owner came and caught Lapén as he was coming out of the cow's mouth. When the owner said he would throw Lapén in the fire, Lapén said he was happy, but that he must not be thrown into the plants. The owner threw him into the plants and Lapén ran off. Buquí stayed inside and kept on eating. He saw the red heart and ate it and the cow died. When the cow was opened Buquí had drowned in the cow dung because he was a glutton. (Andrade [1930], pp. 121–22)

39. (Puerto Rico) Firefly asked Spider how she ate to become so fat. Spider did not want to tell him because Firefly was so greedy; but finally she told him to find the fattest ox, give the password, and go inside. Then he could cut meat, but he should not eat too much because the ox would die. Firefly took his knife and six bags, and when he was inside the ox, he filled his bags with meat. Then he cut the heart and the ox fell dead. When the owner saw his ox he told the king. The king said that they should skin the ox and distribute its meat among the poor. When they opened the ox they found the

six bags of meat and the knife, but Firefly did not come out until everyone had taken the meat. (Mason and Espinosa [1927], pp. 387–88)

40. (Puerto Rico) After another incident, Rabbit told Spider that in the morning they would go to the king's cows and give the password. Then Spider would enter a cow's mouth and cut off all the meat she wanted; but she must not cut the heart because the cow would die and she would not be able to come out. In the morning Spider gave the password, went into the mouth of the queen's cow, and cut very much meat. She saw the heart and cut it. The cow closed its mouth and Spider could not come out. Herdmen saw the dead cow and told the king. They cut the cow open and found Spider full of blood. They said that if she did not give them a hundred pesos they would denounce her. Spider gave them the money and they went to town and bought all that they needed. (Mason and Espinosa [1927], p. 388)

41. (St. Thomas) Anancy asked Tukuma where he got his nice meat. Tukuma took him to the king's cow which opened when he gave the password; but he warned Anancy not to be greedy and not to touch the heart. When Tukuma left Anancy stayed inside and cut the heart. The cow fell dead and did not respond to the password. The king had Anancy killed and put in his garden as an example of greed. (Meade [1932], p. 363)

42. (Anguilla) A man cut a hole in the king's cow, went inside and cut off all the fat. He told a friend where he got the meat, and the friend went inside the cow. He cut its windpipe and couldn't get out. People skinned the cow and gave the belly to an old woman to clean. When she cut the belly the man jumped out and dirtied her. When he said he would tell that she had killed the cow, she gave him her ring, her earrings, and everything she had. (Parsons [1933–43], Part II, p. 411; Part III, p. 56)

43. (Saint Martin) A man went to a cow and said, "Open, Caesar, open!" The cow opened and he went in and took out fat. While he was cooking it his brother came and asked where he got it. At first he refused to tell, saying that his brother would be caught, but then he told. The brother went and cut the thing he was told not to cut, and the cow died. People skinned the cow and gave the belly to an old lady. The brother jumped out of the maw and accused her of throwing the stinking cow belly on him. (Parsons [1933–43], Part II, p. 400; Part III, p. 55)

44. (Saint Martin) Tookerman went into an old cow every day and cut out meat. Raven asked where he got the meat and Tookerman took him along. He told Raven not to cut the thing going "tick-a-tick, tick-a-tick," but Raven cut it. The cow fell dead and Raven fell into the maw. Tookerman butchered the cow and gave the maw to an old lady. She threw it off a cliff, and Raven's neck was broken. (Parsons [1933–43], Part II, pp. 400–01; Part III, p. 56)

45. (Saint Eustatius) After other incidents including mock sunrise, Nancy took Tookerma to a cow, telling him not to cut the maw string. He told him to say, "Open, Goozie, open!" when he went in and "Shut up, Goozie, shut up!" when he came out. Nancy stayed outside while Tookerma went in and cut. When his bag was nearly full Tookerma said, "Open, Goozie, open!"

but the cow didn't open. He cut the maw string and the cow fell dead. People came and started to butcher the cow. When they emptied its belly, Tookerma accused them of throwing the guts on him and threatened to tell the manager. They gave him a quarter of the cow, but he said that that wasn't enough, so they gave him the whole animal. (Parsons [1933–43], Part II, pp. 378–79; Part III, p. 55)

46. (Nevis) Tacoma asked Nancy what he was cooking. Nancy said Tacoma would tell the others but he should come back in the morning. After incidents of mock sunrise, Nancy took Tacoma to a cow. Nancy went in first and cut his bag full. He told Tacoma not to cut the thing that went "tick, tack," but Tacoma cut it and the cow fell down dead. An old woman opened the belly in the bay and Tacoma came out. He accused her of throwing her nasty thing on him and demanded half. She gave him all. (Parsons [1933–43], Part II, p. 326; Part III, p. 55)

47. (Nevis) After other incidents, Lion took Turtle to a cow, telling him to say "Open, Tukoma, open!" He told Turtle he must not cut the main string, but Turtle cut it and the cow fell dead. The owner gave the belly to an old lady and when she opened it in the sea Nancy [sic] came out. He accused her of throwing the nastiness on him and said he would tell if she didn't give him half. (Parsons [1933–43], Part II, pp. 326–27; Part III, p. 55)

48. (Nevis) After other incidents including mock sunrise, Nancy and Lion went inside a cow through a hole in its side. Nancy told Lion not to cut the main string, but he did. The cow ran into the river and Nancy fell out the hole, messed up with the cow's filth. Ashamed, he told a man that the cow fell on him and messed up his clothes. (Parsons [1933–43], Part II, p. 327; Part III, p. 55)

49. (Nevis) After other incidents including mock sunrise, Lion took Nancy into a cow's belly and they cut meat. Nancy cut the main gut and both fell in the cow's belly. (Parsons [1933–43], Part II, pp. 327–28; Part III, p. 55)

50. (Antigua) When there was not much to eat Nancy went to a cow and said, "Open, Toukouma, open!" The cow's behind opened and Nancy went in and filled his sacks with meat. He gave the password, came out, and went home. Nancy gave a piece of meat to the daughter of Toukouma, who saw a bit of it sticking in her teeth. Toukouma went to Nancy and was told about the cow. Toukouma went to the cow, gave the password, and entered; but he was greedy and cut the main guts and the cow died. The owner cut the cow open, found Toukouma inside, and beat him. (Johnson [1921], pp. 53–54)

51. (Montserrat) Terycooma went to a cow and said, "Open, sheshame, open!" and when he came out he said, "Shut, memba, shut!" He took Nancy with him, telling him not to cut the one that went "peep pap, peep pap." But Nancy cut until the cow fell dead. Nancy gave Terycooma all he owned for the cow. (Parsons [1933–43], Part II, p. 292; Part III, p. 55)

52. (Guadeloupe) Lapin went into the belly of the king's cow and took fat. Zamba asked to go along with him, and Lapin said he should bring a very little gourd. When they arrived Lapin said, "Samiwo, open!" They went in

and Lapin said, "Samiwo, close!" Lapin warned Zamba not to cut the heart, but Zamba did so to fill his big gourd and the cow dropped dead. Lapin went into the bladder and Zamba went into the maw. When the king had the cow cut up they threw out the bladder. Lapin jumped out and reproached them for throwing the bladder on him, saying that he would tell the king. They found Zamba and took him to the king. They stuck a hot iron into Zamba's anus and he died. Lapin received one hundred francs and meat from the king, and when Zamba's wife asked him about her husband, Lapin denied that he had gone out with him. (Parsons [1933–43], Part II, pp. 13–14; Part III, p. 54)

53. (Guadeloupe) Lapin went into the belly of a cow and took fat. He took Zamba with him, telling him not to cut the bladder,[19] but Zamba cut it and the cow fell dead. Zamba went into the intestine while Lapin went into the bladder. When they cut the cow open they threw away the bladder; Lapin came out and accused them of throwing the bladder on him. When they found Zamba they asked who had brought him there. Zamba said it was Lapin, but Lapin turned himself into a black rabbit and said, "No, not I. It was grey." (Parsons [1933–43], Part II, pp. 14–15; Part III, p. 54)

54. (Guadeloupe) Lapin stole a cow of the king. Every evening he went inside and filled his little pot with meat, but on the third day the cow fell dead. Zamba came and smelled his meat and asked to be taken along. When they were inside another cow, Lapin said he would cut on the right side and that Zamba should cut on the left. Zamba cut too much and the cow fell dead. In the morning Lapin came out, but Zamba was caught and taken to the king. Zamba said that Lapin had been there with him, but he was whipped while Lapin hid. (Parsons [1033–43], Part II, p. 15; Part III, p. 54)

55. (Guadeloupe) Every evening Lapin went inside a cow and filled his little calabash with fat. Zamba went with him, taking a large calabash. Lapin said, "Zoubli, open!" and they went in. Lapin told Zamba not to cut the dark meat, but Zamba did so and the cow fell dead. Lapin was in the maw and Zamba was in the belly. When the king had the dead cow cut open, they caught Zamba; but when they washed the entrails, Lapin came out and reproached them for throwing excrement on him. They gave Lapin half of the meat, and other episodes follow. (Parsons [1933–43], Part II, pp. 15–16; Part III, p. 54)

56. (Guadeloupe) After another episode, Zamba entered the king's cow from behind and stole meat. Lapin asked where he got the meat and Zamba said that if Lapin were not so voracious, he would show him. Lapin pleaded, and the next morning they entered the cow. Zamba warned Lapin not to cut the nerves, but Lapin did so and Zamba sprang out. The cow fell dead as the king arrived. Zamba told the king that the cow's excrement had soiled his white clothes. When the king found Lapin in the cow's belly, Lapin accused Zamba; but the king did not believe him. The king had a hot iron thrust into Lapin from behind, and other incidents follow. (Parsons [1933–43], Part II, pp. 18–19; Part III, p. 54)

57. (Marie Galante) The king noticed that his cattle were growing thin.

Lapin and Zamba were going into them and taking all their fat. The king found a cow dead and cut it open. He threw the bladder, with Lapin inside, into the sea. Lapin came out and went back into the water. Then he went to the king and told him to open the intestines, and they found Zamba. Zamba accused Lapin, but the king had Zamba burned with a hot iron. (Parsons [1933–43], Part II, p. 262; Part III, p. 55)

58. (Les Saintes) Lapin and Zamba went inside the king's cow to take fat. After an incident of mock sunrise they went again. Lapin told the cow's tail to open and warned Zamba not to cut the heart. Another episode follows. (Parsons [1933–43], Part II, p. 236; Part III, p. 54)

59. (Dominica) Lapin was cutting meat from inside a cow. Tiger said he was hungry and Rabbit said he would show him where to go if he were not so voracious. They went to the cow and Lapin said, "Marie Jeane, open!" The cow opened and they both went inside. Lapin told Tiger not to cut the big thing hanging there, but Tiger cut the heart and the cow fell dead. When men came to quarter the cow, Lapin said he would go inside the bladder and the Tiger should go inside the guts. The men threw out the bladder and Lapin jumped out and complained of their wetting him. To keep Lapin from reporting to the king, they promised him the meat. They beat the guts and crushed Tiger. (Parsons [1933–43], Part I, p. 383; Part III, p. 53)

60. (Saint Lucia) Rabbit was cutting tripe from a cow every day. One morning Nancy told Rabbit to go inside. Rabbit cut tripe and gave it to Nancy. Rabbit went in again, and Nancy went home to cook after telling Rabbit to cut the heart and the liver. When Rabbit did that the cow dropped dead. The owner cut the cow open and found Rabbit, and another episode follows. (Parsons [1933–43], Part I, p. 125; Part III, p. 53)

61. (Grenada) Spider and Tiger went to a dead cow. Tiger took one sack, but Spider put two sacks in one. Spider would not leave until his sack was full, and the cow's owner caught him. Spider said that Tiger told him about the cow, but Tiger said the Spider stayed to fill two sacks in one. The owner killed Spider. (Parsons [1933–43], Part I, p. 76; Part III, p. 53)

62. (Trinidad) Lapin was stealing meat from inside Elephant's belly. Tiger sent a child to Lapin for fire, and Lapin gave the child a piece of meat. Tiger learned about the meat and proposed going with Lapin. Lapin told him to take a little sack, but Tiger took a big one. Lapin warned Tiger not to cut "what hangs there," but Tiger cut the heart and Elephant dropped dead. Lapin found Tiger dead inside Elephant, salted them both, and ate them. (Parsons [1933–43], Part I, p. 11; Part III, p. 53)

B I B L I O G R A P H Y

Andrade, Manuel J.
    1930 Folk-Lore from the Dominican Republic. *Memoirs of the American Folk-Lore Society* 23.

Backus, Emma M.
   1898 Animal Tales from North Carolina. *Journal of American Folk-Lore* 11.
Baissac, C.
   n.d. Le Folk-Lore de l'Île-Maurice. *Les Litteratures Populaires de Toutes les Nations.*
      27.
Beckwith, Martha Warren
   1924 Jamaica Anansi Stories. *Memoris of the American Folk-Lore Society* 17.
Bemelmans, Ludwig
   1941 *Hotel Splendide.* New York, The Viking Press.
Bleek, W. H. I.
   1870 *Reineke Fuchs in Afrika.* Weimar, Hermann Böhlau.
Cronise, Florence M., and Ward, Henry W.
   1903 *Cunnie Rabbit, Mr. Spider, and Other Beef.* London, Swan Sonnenschein.
Crowley, Daniel J.
   1966 I Could Talk Old-Story Good: Creativity in Bahamian Folklore. *Folklore Studies*
      17. Berkeley and Los Angeles, University of California Press.
Dadié, Bernard B.
   1955 *Le Pagne Noir, Contes Africains.* Paris, Présence Africaine.
Dorsey, George A.
   1905 Traditions of the Caddo. *Publications of the Carnegie Institution of Washington*
      41.
Dorson, Richard M.
   1958 Negro Tales from Pine Bluff, Arkansas, and Calvin, Michigan. *Indiana Uni-
      versity Folklore Series* 12.
   1967 *American Negro Folktales.* Greenwich, Conn., Fawcett.
Edwards, Charles L.
   1891 Some Tales from Bahama Folk-Lore. *Journal of American Folk-Lore* 4.
   1942 Bahama Songs and Stories. *Memoirs of the American Folk-Lore Society* 3.
      [1895]
Ellis, A. B.
   1895–96 Evolution in Folklore. *The Popular Science Monthly* 48.
English, Thomas H.
   1948 See Harris 1948.
Fauset, Arthur Huff
   1927 Negro Folk Tales from the South [Alabama, Mississippi, Louisiana]. *Journal
      of American Folk-Lore* 40.
   1928 Tales and Riddles Collected in Philadelphia. *Journal of American Folk-Lore*
      41.
   1931 Folklore from Nova Scotia. *Memoirs of the American Folklore Society* 24.
Fortier, Alcée
   1888 Bits of Louisiana Folk-Lore. *Transactions of the Modern Language Association
      of America, 1887* 3.
   1895 Louisiana Folk-Tales in French Dialect and English Translation. *Memoirs of the
      American Folk-Lore Society* 2.
Frobenius, Leo
   1922 Erzählungen aus dem West-Sudan. *Atlantis* 8.
Froger, Fernand
   1910 *Étude sur la langue des Mossi (Boucle du Niger).* Paris, Ernest Leroux.
Germann, Paul
   1933 Die Völkerstämme im Norden von Liberia. *Veröffentlichungen des Staatlich-
      sächsischen Forschungsinstitutes für Völkerkunde in Leipzig.* Erste Reihe, Eth-
      nographie und Ethnologie 1.
Guilhem, Marcel
   n.d.–1962 *50 Contes et Fableaux de la Savane,* vols. I–II. Paris, Ligel.

Guillot, René
    1933 Contes d'Afrique. *Numéro spécial du Bulletin de l'Enseignement de l'A. O. F.*
Harris, Joel Chandler
    1880 *Uncle Remus: His Songs and His Sayings.* New York, D. Appleton.
    n.d. *Told by Uncle Remus.* New York, Grosset & Dunlap. [1903]
    1948 *Seven Tales of Uncle Remus.* Edited by Thomas H. English. Atlanta, Emory University.
    1955 *The Complete Tales of Uncle Remus.* Compiled by Richard Chase. Boston, Houghton Mifflin.
Helser, Albert D.
    1930 *African Stories.* New York, Fleming H. Revell.
    1934 *Education of Primitive People.* New York, Fleming H. Revell.
Johnson, John H.
    1921 Folk-Lore from Antigua, British West Indies. *Journal of American Folk-Lore* 34.
Lemar
    1896 Brer Rabbit and Brer Wolf. *The Southern Workman* 25.
Mason, J. Alden, and Espinosa, Aurelio
    1927 Porto Rican Folk-Lore: Folk-Tales. *Journal of American Folk-Lore* 40.
Meade, Florence O.
    1932 Folk Tales from the Virgin Islands. *Journal of American Folk-Lore* 45.
Monteil, C.
    1905 Contes Soudanais. *Collection de Contes et Chansons Populaires* 28.
Nassau, Robert H.
    1914 *Where Animals Talk.* London, Duckworth.
Parsons, Elsie Clews
    1918 Folk-Tales of Andros Island, Bahamas, *Memoirs of the American Folk-Lore Society* 13.
    1923 Folk-Lore from the Cape Verde Islands. *Memoirs of the American Folk-Lore Society,* Parts I–II.
    1928 Spirituals and Other Folklore from the Bahamas. *Journal of American Folk-Lore* 41.
    1933–43 Folk-Lore of the Antilles, French and English. *Memoirs of the American Folk-Lore Society* 26, Parts I–III.
Rattray, R. S.
    1930 *Akan-Ashanti Folk-Tales.* Oxford, Clarendon Press.
Schlenker, C. F.
    1861 *A Collection of Temne Traditions, Fables and Proverbs.* London, Church Missionary Society.
Tauxier, L.
    1917 *Le Noir du Yatenga.* Paris, Émile Larose.
Thomas, Northcote W.
    1916 *Anthropological Report on Sierra Leone,* Parts I–III. London, Harrison and Sons.

NOTES

1. Frog is swallowed in one tale [2], but only after he has given the password and jumped into the cow's open mouth. In the Akan tale [13] Anansi and Kwaku Tse are

also swallowed, but only after making the cow sneeze and jumping into its open mouth.

2. T. F. Crane, "Plantation Folk-Lore," *The Popular Science Monthly,* 18 (1880–81), 828; W. H. I. Bleek, *Reynard the Fox in South Africa, or Hottentot Fables and Tales* (London: Trübner, 1864), pp. 27–29; W. H. I. Bleek, *Reineke Fuchs in Afrika* (Weimar: Hermann Böhlau, 1870), pp. 21–23.

3. A. Gerber, "Uncle Remus Traced to the Old World," *Journal of American Folk-Lore,* 6 (1893), 251.

4. A. B. Ellis (1895–96), pp. 97–103. In my summary of this lengthy version I have eliminated many of the irrelevant details.

5. Alan Dundes, "African and Afro-American Tales," *Research in African Literatures* 7 (Fall 1976), 190–91, 197.

6. Other variants include Hanansi, An'Nancy, and Aunt Nancy.

7. Crowley (1966), p. 29.

8. Dorson (1967), p. 17; *American Folklore* (1959; rpt. Chicago: Univ. of Chicago Press, 1962), p. 185.

9. Harris (1948), no. 7; (1955), pp. 865–67.

10. Harris (1948); (1955), p. 846.

11. Harris (n.d.), no. 16; (1955), pp. 709–14.

12. Backus (1898), pp. 288–89.

13. Fauset (1928), pp. 531, 532, 534, 535, 541.

14. Fauset (1931), pp. 45, 48, 49, 49, 50, 50.

15. Rattray (1930), pp. 4–5.

16. Fortier (1895), p. 94; Léopold Sédar Senghor and Abdoulaye Sadji, *La Belle Historie de Leuk-le-Lièvre* (London: George C. Harrap, 1965), pp. 10–11. [1953]

17. Dorson (1958), p. 19; (1967), p. 82.

18. Crowley (1966), p. 29.

19. The French text gives *boudin,* pudding; but Parson's abstract says, "Zamba cuts the cow's bladder."

S I X

＊

Deer's Hoof and Ear; Dog and Dog Head

For a change of pace I now present two folktales that are less well documented than those thus far considered. Both seem to be more common in the United States than in either Africa or other parts of the New World. The first concerns the killing of a deer with a single shot that passes through its hind hoof and its ear. The second concerns the trickster who claims that game has been killed by his dog head, rather than by the dog of his friend.

Furthermore, to my knowledge, it has not previously been suggested that either of these folktales came to America from Africa. I have not found them in either Aarne and Thompson's tale type index or in Thompson's motif index. Apparently there are no analogues from either Europe or India. Until someone produces such analogues, I conclude that these two tale types came to the United States from Africa (and originated there).

Deer's Hoof and Ear

1. (West Africa) After another episode, the wife of an Arab asked him to smash a deer's hoof and pierce its ear with a single arrow. He hit the deer's ear with a stone and the deer stopped to scratch it. Then with one arrow he pierced its ear and smashed its hoof. "Was that good?" he asked, and she said, "Yes." (de Zeltner [1913], pp. 242–43)

2. (Mali: Bambara) The Elders of a village met every day to chat. All told big lies except one who said nothing while his son sat near them listening. One day the boy said, "Father, all the elders tell lies. You alone say nothing. What is the reason?" His father said, "Since you speak thus, I will talk tomorrow." The next day he told the others, "One day I went hunting. I shot an arrow at a deer, and it fastened its foot and its ear together!" All began to cry at once, "You lie! You lie! It's not true!" The boy said, "Don't dispute

Reprinted from *Research in African Literatures*, 11 (1980), 175–86.

it. If he found the deer scratching its ear with its hind foot, it would be very possible." (Travélé [1923], pp. 61–62)

3. (United States) An old Virginia Colonel boasted that he had killed a buck by shooting it through its hind hoof, the ball passing out at its forehead. As his hearers doubted this, he called on his servant to verify his statement. The servant said, "As the deer raised his foot to scratch his head, Master's bullet passed through both." When the company had left the servant said, "For Heaven's sake, Master, when you tell another big lie, please don't scatter them so, because I had mighty hard work to bring them together." (Anonymous [1859], p. 282; reprinted in Botkin [1949], pp. 69–70)

4. (Pennsylvania) There was a slave who could lie about anything. His master told a friend that he once shot a deer in the hoof and the bullet came out through the deer's ear. His friend bet fifty dollars that it was not possible. The master asked his slave to explain how it happened. The slave said that a flea bit the deer on the ear and it put its hoof up to its ear to scratch it when his master shot. When the friend had gone, the slave asked his master not to get the lies so far apart next time. (Fauset [1928], pp. 548–49)

5. (Texas) A plantation owner was a magnificent storyteller and always had his slave bear him out in his lies. He told his fellow hunters that he had shot a deer and that when he and his slave examined it, they found that the bullet had passed through the ear and then through the hind foot and then through the head. The others asked how he had done that, and he told his slave to tell them. The slave scratched his head and then said, "When Master shot him, he was scratching his ear with his hind foot." On their way home he said, "Master, you tell your lies a little closer together from now on." (Brewer [1932], pp. 25–26; reprinted in Hughes and Bontemps [1958], p. 75)

6. (Texas: Mexican) Two travelling companions told of a river on fire, a gigantic bird, and a curious shot. The first companion said that he had but one cartridge, but shot a buck at the base of its right ear and through its left hind foot. When the *jefe político* said that he was insulting their intelligence, the second companion said that he had seen the buck and explained that when it had been shot it was scratching that ear with its hind foot on the other side. They were invited in and feasted for a week. When they left, the first companion asked, "What did you think of that last lie I fixed up?" The second companion replied, "The next time you had better be a little more careful or I may not be able to get you out." (Dobie [1944], pp. 36–41; see also Dobie's footnote to Brewer's tale [5])

7. (Alabama) A fellow told a crowd, "Today I shot a deer through the foot and head all at the same time, and killed it. Didn't I do that, Jack?" They asked Jack how it happened. Jack scratched his head and said, "The deer was chased by hounds and it stopped to listen where they were. Just as it put its foot up to its ear, Master shot it and the bullet went through the foot and through the head." When they were by themselves Jack said, "Look here, Master, I want you to get your damn lies closer together." (Fauset [1927], p. 266)

8. (Virginia) a man said that with one shot he shot a deer through its right hind hoof and its right ear and asked his slave to verify it. The slave did so, saying that the deer was scratching its ear with its hind hoof. Then he told his master that the next time he should get the shots a little closer together. (Bacon and Parsons [1922], pp. 291–92)

9. (North Carolina) Parsons reports that she failed to record this tale as told by Henry Smith, but that it was substantially as given by Jones [12] for Georgia. (Parsons [1917], p. 191)

10. (South Carolina) A man shot a deer through the hind leg and through the head with a single bullet. You might ask how it happened. The answer is that the deer was full of ticks and a tick bit him. He stopped, took up his hind leg, and scratched his head. And the hunter shot him through the head and the leg at the same time. (Parsons, "Sea Islands" [1923], p. 117)

11. (Georgia) John went hunting with his master, who shot a deer. He told a neighbor that he shot the deer in its ear and its hind leg at the same time. The neighbor said he couldn't see how he could do that. Master told John to tell him how he had done it. John said, "It's like this. As Master aimed his gun, the deer lifted its hind leg to scratch its ear, and the shot went through the leg and the ear at the same time." When the neighbor had gone John said, "Master, you must try to get your tale closer together next time." (Smiley [1919], p. 370)

12. (Georgia) A man told his friend that he had shot a deer and that when he examined it he found that the bullet had shot off a hind foot and hit it in an ear. His friend didn't believe him. The hunter asked his servant to prove what he had said. The friend asked the servant how the same bullet could hit the deer in a hind foot and an ear at the same time. The Nigger scratched his head and said that when his master fired, the deer must have been brushing a fly off the ear with its hind foot. The friend was satisfied. When the friend had gone the servant told his master that he was willing to back anything he said about deer hunting, but that next time he should put the holes closer together. (Jones [1925], pp. 134–35; reprinted in Courlander [1976], pp. 433–34)

13. (Cuba) Congo went deer hunting with his master and they saw a deer. Both shot, and Congo's shot hit a foot and his master's shot hit the head of the deer. On their way home they met the owner of a nearby farm who was also hunting. The neighbor said that they had had more luck than he had had. Congo's master replied, "Yes, and that is not the most important thing that happened. I shot a shot that hit the deer in the head, the foot, and the ear." The neighbor said that he did not believe it and asked how it could have happened. He was told to ask Congo, who said, "When he shot, the deer was scratching its ear with a hind foot on its head." The neighbor admitted that this was possible. When they went on Congo said, "Master, don't boast so much next time, it took much work to put it together." (Bascom [1948])

14. (Bahamas) Parsons reports that she heard this tale told by a native of New Providence, Bahamas. (Parsons [1917] p. 191)

15. (Argentina) One time I went hunting. I saw a deer at a distance and

shot and hit it. I ran to it and found the deer shot in an ear and a hoof. How could it have been hit in two opposite parts with a single shot? It was because the deer had been scratching its ear with its hoof at the very moment that I shot it. (Carrizo and Hidalgo [1948], p. 94)

Dog and Dog Head

In a footnote to her first version from South Carolina [9], Parsons says, "No tale appears to be more popular in the Sea Islands than this tale," and commenting on his version [17] Johnson says, "This is one of the most popular stories in the Sea Islands." Beckwith writes, "This story is told everywhere in Jamaica, but I find no African version and Mrs. Parsons says (JAFL 32: 391) that, although she heard it 'over and over again' in South Carolina, it was altogether unknown in North Carolina; see Sea Islands 1–5. Such a distribution argues a fairly modern origin for the complete form of the story." (Beckwith [1924], p. 243)

1. (Sierra Leone: Temne) Spider took a skull and Hare took a dog and they went hunting. They caught a fox and Spider said that his skull had killed it. This happened several times. Then the dog caught the chief's bull and Spider said that Hare's dog had injured it. Hare protested that Spider used to say that his skull caught the animals. Spider admitted that he had done so but said that this time it was Hare's dog. They were taken to the chief who said that Spider had stolen, because a skull could not catch a fox or even a rat. Spider was fined six cows, four for Hare and two for the chief. Other episodes follow. (Thomas, Part III [1916], pp. 72–74)

2. (Mali: Bambara) From selling firewood Hyena got twenty sous and Toad got twenty francs, and they decided to buy hunting dogs. Hyena bought a dog head and Toad bought a dog. Returning home they saw a deer in the bush. Toad sent his dog in pursuit and Hyena ran after it with his dog head in his hand. The dog reached the deer first and killed it. When Hyena arrived he opened the jaws of his dog head, forced the teeth into the place where the deer had been bitten by the dog, and waited for Toad to arrive. When he came Hyena cried, "It is my dog that killed it." Without a word of protest Toad told him to find someone to help carry the meat home. When Hyena left Toad splashed blood from the deer's wound on himself, and when Hyena returned with his wife and children Toad cried as if in pain. Hyena asked Toad who had wounded him. Toad replied, "It was the messenger of God who whipped me for having killed the Creator's deer. I told him that it was your dog that killed it, and he went to find another whip." "You lie," said Hyena, "Who has ever seen a dog head kill a deer. It is your dog that killed it." Hyena fled, leaving the deer to Toad. (Traoré [1944–45], pp. 26–27)

3. (Ivory Coast: Baule) After a visit to God Spider was given a skinny goat and Chameleon was given a fine hunting dog. On the way home Spider killed his goat and ate it, keeping the head; but Chameleon refused to kill his dog. The dog chased a gazelle and Spider threw his goat head at the

gazelle, crying, "Seize it! Seize it!" The dog killed the gazelle and Spider dragged it back to Chameleon, saying, "See what my goat head has caught." Chameleon said "What? Your dead head has killed a gazelle?" Spider said, "Yes, and therefore the gazelle belongs to me." They came to a village where the dog bit a goat's leg. "My dog doesn't hunt at all," Chameleon said, "Earlier Spider's goat head killed a gazelle, not my dog. It must have been the goat head that did this." "Nonsense!" said Spider, "If one kills a goat, what can its head do? Of course your dog captured the gazelle, but I tricked you." Chameleon said, "Then give me the gazelle," and Spider had to do so. Chameleon asked the goat's owner to forgive him and he had to pay nothing for the wounded goat, because the owner was happy to see Spider meet his downfall. (Himmelheber [1951], pp. 81–86; 2nd ed. [1955], pp. 78–83)

4. (Benin: Yoruba) Hyena and Hare each bought a hunting dog. Hyena ate hers and saved the skull. Hunting some days later, they saw a deer that ran off. Hare set his dog loose and Hyena ran after it with her skull. Finding the deer strangled by the dog, Hyena chased the dog away, opened the skull's jaws, and made it bite the deer's neck. Hyena said what a good catch her skull had made. Hare sent Hyena for fire to cook the deer and when she returned she found Hare on his side, moaning. Hare said that Hyena was lucky, because the deer was tame and its owner had thrashed him, crying, "Filthy Hyena!" until he saw that he was only a poor hare. He told Hyena that the owner was looking for her in order to beat her. Hyena fled and Hare kept the deer. (Guillot [1933], p. 23)

5. (Massachusetts) Although I cannot find the story in her published folktales, Parsons says that an immigrant from the Cape Verde Islands told her "the tale of 'Dog and Dog-Head'" in a garden on Cape Cod. (Parsons, "Sea Islands" [1923], p. xv)

6. (Alabama) Rabbit and Frog took their rice and went to buy hunting dogs. On the way Rabbit saw Frog's throat moving and thought he was eating his rice. Rabbit ate most of his rice and could only buy a dog head. On the way home Frog's dog caught a deer. Rabbit chased the dog away, put his dog head there, and claimed the deer. He sent Frog to the rising moon and then to a star for fire, but Frog could not get any fire. Rabbit went for fire and Frog hid the deer. He told Rabbit that a conjure man had taken it. Rabbit was frightened and said, "Any old fool ought to know that a dead dog head can't catch a deer." Frog said, "I knew my dog caught that deer, and I'm not going to give you any." (Showers [1898], p. 230)

7. (Virginia) Rabbit and Frog took their rice crop to town to sell it so that they could buy dogs to hunt deer. On the way Rabbit ate so much rice that he had left just enough to buy a dog's head, but Frog bought a dog. On the way home Frog's dog caught a deer, but Frog could not keep up with his dog. Rabbit could, and he drove the dog away and put his dog head by the deer. When Frog arrived, Rabbit said that his dog head had caught the deer. Rabbit sent Frog to moonrise and then to a star for fire. Then Rabbit went for fire and Frog hid the deer and began yelling that a man had taken it. Rabbit said

that he didn't care, that any fool ought to know that a dog head couldn't catch a deer. Frog said that he knew that Rabbit had been lying and that he carried the deer home and wasn't going to give Rabbit any meat. (Bacon and Parsons [1922], pp. 269–70)

8. (South Carolina) After another episode, Rabbit and Wolf went hunting in the woods. Wolf had his dog with him, but Rabbit couldn't afford a dog and had only a dog head. Wolf's dog caught a deer and Rabbit ran there, beat the dog off, set his dog head there, and waited for Wolf to come. He sent Wolf to the sunset for fire and took the deer home. Other episodes follow. (Christensen [1969] pp. 87–93)

9. (South Carolina) Fox bought a dog and Rabbit bought a dog head and they went hunting. Fox's dog caught a deer, but Rabbit ran and knocked it off and stuck his dog head on the deer. He said to Fox, "I told you to buy a dog head. See, my dog head caught the deer." Rabbit went home to get a cart to carry the deer. When he came back Fox was hitting a tree and shouting, "Oh Lord! I didn't catch the deer, Sir!" Rabbit heard him and shouted "Everybody knows that a dog head can't catch a deer." Rabbit left and Fox took the deer home. (Parsons, "Sea Islands" [1923], p. 1)

10. (South Carolina) Wolf had twelve biscuits and bought a dog and Rabbit, who had six biscuits, bought a dog head. They went to hunt deer in the woods where the white man didn't allow any hunters. Wolf caught a deer and went home to get a wagon. When Rabbit heard him returning, he began to whip a tree. Wolf heard him and went away, leaving the deer to Rabbit. (Parsons, "Sea Islands" [1923], pp. 1–2)

11. (South Carolina) Rabbit and Bullfrog went to buy dogs to hunt deer. Each had three biscuits to pay for his dog. On the way Rabbit saw Bullfrog's throat moving up and down and asked what he was eating. Bullfrog said he was eating one of his biscuits, and Rabbit ate one of his. Bullfrog's throat kept moving up and down, and he told Rabbit he was eating another biscuit. Rabbit ate a second biscuit, saying that he could buy a dog head with one biscuit, and that a dog head was just as good as a dog. Bullfrog bought a dog and Rabbit bought a dog head, and they went hunting. Bullfrog's dog caught a deer, but Rabbit can run faster than Bullfrog. He ran and knocked Bullfrog's dog off the deer and fastened his dog head on it. He ran back to Bullfrog and told him that he had said that a dog head was better than a dog. Soon the master came and asked who had killed his deer. Rabbit said it was Bullfrog's dog, but the master started to whip Rabbit. Rabbit went into the woods and whipped a tree, crying, "Please, Master! It wasn't my dog; it was Bullfrog's dog." The master came again and Rabbit said, "Master, you know that a dog head can't catch a deer. It must have been Bullfrog's dog." The master whipped them both. (Parsons, "Sea Islands" [1923], p. 2)

12. (South Carolina) Rabbit and Frog had their wives cook a dozen biscuits each so that they could buy dogs. On the way Rabbit saw Frog's throat moving up and down, and he ate half of his biscuits. Frog bought a dog with his dozen biscuits, and Rabbit bought a dog head with his half dozen. On their

way home they went hunting and Frog's dog caught a deer. But Rabbit can run faster than Frog, and he fastened his dog head onto the deer. When Frog arrived, Rabbit said that he had told him to buy a dog head, because a dog can't beat a dog head in running. Frog went for a wagon and on the way back he got off and began to whip a tree, crying, "Please, Master! Rabbit's dog head caught the deer." Rabbit cried out, "You lie! Frog's dog caught the deer." Frog said, "I know my dog caught the deer." Rabbit got mad and left, and Frog took the deer home. (Parsons, "Sea Islands" [1923], p. 3)

13. (South Carolina) Frog and Rabbit made dumplings to buy dogs. Rabbit asked what Frog was chewing and Frog told him dumplings. Rabbit began to eat his dumplings, but Frog was fooling him. Rabbit ate all but one of his dumplings and could only buy a dog head. Frog had all three of his dumplings and bought a dog. They went hunting and killed a hog and Rabbit fastened his dog head to it. While Rabbit went home for a cart, the hog's owner came and began to beat Frog. Frog said that it wasn't his dog, but Rabbit's that had killed the hog. Rabbit returned and said, "Who ever heard of a dog head catching a hog!" (Parsons, "Sea Islands," [1923], pp. 3–4)

14. (South Carolina) Rabbit told Frog that he knew of a man who would sell a dog for twelve biscuits and a dog head for six biscuits. They bought biscuits and started off. Rabbit saw Frog's throat working and, thinking Frog was eating a biscuit, ate one of his own. This happened again until Rabbit had only six biscuits. Frog had twelve biscuits and bought a dog and Rabbit bought a dog head. On the way back they hunted and Frog's dog caught a deer. Rabbit ran to it, knocked the dog away, and put his dog head on the deer. He said he had told Frog that a dog head was better than a dog. Rabbit went to get a wagon and when he returned Wolf, who was behind a bush, began to shout. Rabbit asked what was the matter and Frog told him that the boss said he was going to kill the one who caught the deer. Rabbit said, "Well, the Lord knows that a dog head can't catch a deer." Rabbit went off, leaving the deer to Frog. (Parsons, "Sea Islands" [1923], pp. 4–5)

15. (South Carolina) Partridge and Rabbit went to buy dogs to hunt deer. Rabbit bought a dog that cost lots of money, but Partridge had only enough to buy a dog head. They went hunting and Rabbit's dog chased a deer. Partridge flew to the deer and stuck his dog head on it. They went to the judge who said, "Dog head on the deer," so Partridge got half of the deer. (Parsons, "Sea Islands" [1923], p. 5)

16. (South Carolina) Parsons cites at least one other version. (Parsons, "Sea Islands" [1923], p. 3, n. 3, n. 4; p. 5, n. 2)

17. (South Carolina) Rabbit and Frog went to buy hunting dogs that cost twelve biscuits each. Frog had twelve biscuits, so he bought a dog. Rabbit had eaten six of his biscuits, so he bought a dog head. They went hunting and Frog's dog caught a deer. Rabbit ran ahead, knocked off the dog, put his dog head on the deer, and said it had caught the deer. Frog said that a dog head couldn't catch a deer, but Rabbit said of course it could and asked if Frog didn't see it on the deer. Frog cut the head off his dog and it never caught

any more deer. (Johnson [1968], pp. 136–37)

18. (South Carolina) Rabbit and Wolf wanted to hunt deer. Wolf had plenty of ginger cookies and he bought a dog. Rabbit had only one ginger, so he bought a dog head. They went hunting and Wolf's dog caught a deer. Rabbit said his dog head had caught it. He ran ahead, knocked off the dog, and fastened his dog head on the deer. Wolf said that a dog head couldn't catch a deer, that it took a dog to catch a deer; but Rabbit claimed it and went for a cart to carry it home. When Wolf heard Rabbit returning he beat on a tree, crying, "Please, Master! Please don't beat me. My dog didn't catch the deer. Rabbit's dog caught it." Rabbit listened and Wolf kept on hollering. Rabbit jumped down from the cart and called out, "Wolf, you lie! Who ever heard of a dog head catching a deer? Dog head can't catch deer; it takes a dog to catch a deer." Rabbit ran away, leaving the deer to Wolf. (Woofter [1930], pp. 48–49; reprinted in Courlander [1976], pp. 296–97 "from materials given to the author in manuscript form by Guy B. Johnson in 1931")

19. (South Carolina) Rabbit and Frog planned to exchange their peas for dogs. Frog was always swallowing and Rabbit thought he was eating. He decided to eat his peas too and ate a pea every time Frog swallowed. Frog bought a dog with his bushel of peas, but Rabbit had only enough to buy a dog head. Frog's dog caught a deer, but Rabbit drove the dog away and put his dog head on the deer. Frog claimed his dog had caught the deer and that a dog head couldn't do it; but Rabbit wouldn't give in. Frog went into the woods and called his dog. He took a stick and beat it against a tree, crying, "Master! It wasn't my dog! Rabbit's dog caught your deer." Rabbit heard and said, "It wasn't my dog. Who ever saw a dog head catch a deer!" Rabbit left and Frog took the deer home. (Works Projects Administration, South Carolina [1941], pp. 24–25)

20. (South Carolina) Fox and Frog went to buy dogs. Each had four pies. Fox saw Frog's throat working up and down and asked if he was eating pie. Frog said he ate one pie, and Fox said he would eat one of his. Fox bought a dog with his four pies, but Frog had only two pies and could only buy a dog head [*sic*]. On their way home Fox's dog caught a deer, but Frog drove off the dog and put his dog head on the deer. Frog said his dog head had caught the deer and sent Fox to bring a wagon to carry it. On the way back Fox stopped a short distance from the deer. He whipped a tree, crying, "Please, Master! My dog didn't catch the deer. Frog's dog caught it." Frog heard and fled with his dog head. Fox put the deer on the wagon and took it home. (Works Projects Administration, South Carolina [1941], pp. 23–24)

21. (Jamaica) Hanansi and Tacoomah went hunting with their two dogs. Hanansi ate his dog and put the dog head in his bag. Tacoomah's dog attacked a cow, but Hanansi drove it away, fastened his dog head onto a cow, and claimed it. Tacoomah knew that it was his dog that had caught the cow. He went away and got a whip. Cracking it he began crying, "It was not I, Sir!" Hanansi asked what was happening. Tacoomah cracked the whip again and cried, "It wasn't my dog that caught the cow. Hanansi's dog caught it."

Hanansi called out, "Tacoomah, you fool! Have you ever heard that a dog head can catch a cow?" Hanansi fled and Tacoomah got the cow. (Beckwith [1924] p. 22)

B I B L I O G R A P H Y

Anonymous
  1859 Editor's Drawer. *Harper's New Monthly Magazine* 19.
Bacon, A. M., and Parsons, E. C.
  1922 Folk-Lore from Elizabeth City County, Virginia. *Journal of American Folk-Lore* 35.
Bascom, Berta Montero
  1948 Field tape recording.
Beckwith, Martha Warren
  1924 Jamaica Anansi Stories. *Memoirs of the American Folk-Lore Society* 17.
Botkin, B. A.
  1949 *A Treasury of Southern Folklore.* New York, Crown.
Brewer, J. Mason
  1932 Juneteenth. *Publications of the Texas Folk-Lore Society* 10.
Carrizo, Jesus Maria, and Hidalgo, Guillermo Perkins
  1948 Cuentos de la Tradición Oral Argentina. *Revista del Instituto Nacional de la Tradicion* (Buenos Aires) 1.
Christensen, A. M. H.
  1969 *Afro-American Folk Lore.* New York, Negro Universities Press. [1892]
Courlander, Harold
  1976 *A Treasury of Afro-American Folklore.* New York, Crown.
de Zeltner, Fr.
  1913 Contes du Sénégal et du Niger. *Collection de Contes et Chansons Populaires* 40.
Dolbie, J. Frank
  1944 Tale of the Two Companions. *Texas Folk-Lore Society Publication* 19.
Fauset, Arthur Huff
  1927 Negro Folk Tales from the South [Alabama, Mississippi, Louisiana]. *Journal of American Folk-Lore* 40.
  1928 Tales and Riddles Collected in Philadelphia. *Journal of American Folk-Lore* 41.
Guillot, René
  1933 Contes d'Afrique. *Numéro spécial du Bulletin de l'Enseignement de l' A. O. F.*
Himmelheber, Hans
  1955 *AuroPoku.* Eisenach, Erich Röth-Verlag. 2nd ed. [1951]
Hughes, Langston, and Bontemps, Arna
  1958 *The Book of Negro Folklore.* New York, Dodd, Mead.
Johnson, Guy B.
  1968 *Folk Culture on St. Helena Island, South Carolina.* Hatboro, Pennsylvania, Folklore Associates. [1930]
Jones, Charles
  1925 *Negro Myths from the Georgia Coast.* Columbia, South Carolina, The State Company. [1888]

Parsons, Elsie Clews
   1917 Tales from Guilford County, North Carolina. *Journal of American Folk-Lore* 30.
   1923 Folk-Lore of the Sea Islands, South Carolina. *Memoirs of the American Folk-Lore Society* 16.
Showers, Susan
   1898 How the Rabbit and the Frog Caught a Deer. *The Southern Workman* 27.
Smiley, Portia
   1919 Folk-Lore from Virginia, South Carolina, Georgia, Alabama, and Florida. *Journal of American Folk-Lore* 32.
Thomas, Northcote W.
   1916 *Anthropological Report on Sierra Leona,* Parts I–III. London, Harrison and Sons.
Traoré, Dominique
   1944–45 Cinq Contes Africaines. *L'Education africaine. Bulletin de l'enseignement de l'Afrique* 33/34.
Travélé, Moussa
   1923 *Proverbes et Contes Bambara.* Paris, Paul Geuthner.
Woofter, T. J.
   1930 *Black Yeomanry. Life on St. Helena Island.* New York, Henry Holt.
Work Projects Administration, South Carolina
   1941 *South Carolina Folk Tales.* Compiled by Workers of the Writers' Program of the Work Projects Administration in the State of South Carolina. Bulletin of University of South Carolina.

S E V E N

✳

Holding the Rock

I have chosen this title to distinguish the tales presented here from AT1530 as described by Aarne and Thompson in *The Types of the Folktale:*

> 1530 *Holding up the Rock.* The rascal puts his shoulder under a great rock and pretends to hold it up. He persuades a man tō take his place and then runs away with the dupe's goods. [K125.1]. Cf. Types 9A, 1731.

In the tales that follow the trickster is usually holding up a rock or stone, but in two versions from Oaxaca [72–73] he is simply holding it, and in two others [75–76] he is on top of it holding it down. In other versions he holds a rock pillar, a cliff or precipice or mesa wall, a mountain or mountain's overhang, a cave or cave roof, a house or shelter or wall, the world or sky or fields of heaven, or a rock or tree or stalk that supports the world or clouds or sky. Saying that it will fall or that the world will come to an end, he usually persuades the dupe to take his place and runs away, leaving the dupe holding it. In two variants [20, 58] the dupe goes for a prop to hold it up and the trickster escapes. Although it often appears with other episodes, the tale has an independent existence [e.g., 8–10, 15, 18, 47].

Unlike AT1530, however, the motivation is usually escape from an enemy or sometimes simple trickery [18, 36, 86, 93] or revenge [47, 60, 78]; sometimes the motivation is not clearly indicated. It is not theft in any of these tales.

For AT1530 Aarne and Thompson cite Klipple's thirteen African tales, numerous New World versions, and four from Europe. Klipple's thirteen versions[1] and twenty-three[2] of Coffin's twenty-six versions are included here. Both Klipple and Coffin identify these as AT1530. Whether they belong under AT1530 and whether they are historically related to "Holding up the Rock" are legitimate questions, but questions that are irrelevant here. The point is that the American versions of "Holding the Rock" are closer to the African ones than they are to "Holding up the Rock" as described or to the European versions of AT1530 cited by Aarne and Thompson.

Reprinted from *Research in African Literatures*, 11 (1980), 479–510.

The four European tales cited are Turkish: Eberhard-Boratav No. 351 III and No. 352; Rumanian: Schullerus 1332*; and Hungarian: Dégh No. 46. None of these four tales fit the pattern of "Holding the Rock" and at least one does not even fit Aarne and Thompson's description of AT1530.

Eberhard-Boratav No. 351 III includes the following, after other episodes: "He [the hero] made a herdsman a beard of wool and recommended that he lie still in the sun; he told another herdsman that a rock would soon fall, and the herdsman propped up the rock. In both cases he stole the herdsmen's herds." Although this tale involves theft, Eberhard and Boratav do not cite AT1530; instead they cite AT1535 and AT1542.

Their second tale, No. 352, includes, among other episodes, "He met a priest and told him that a mountain was going to fall at once. He exchanged his horse for the priest's rested animal in order to bring a prop while the priest held the mountain."[3] The motive of theft is implicit here, and it was explicit in the first Turkish tale.

Schullerus 1332* translates,

> He is entreated to make a deceit, desires the coach to fetch his 'instrument' and goes off with it. Leaves the entreater there holding the rock. Dressed as bride. Mutilates the master's cow before the sale. Cuts off the goat's upper lip with which it laughs. Ties two horses in front and two behind. All the children with red hair are from the parson.[4]

Does this relate to AT1530 as described? It certainly does not relate to "Holding the Rock" as documented here.

The Hungarian tale, Dégh No. 46, concerns robbers who want to break into the house of an old woman and steal her treasure chest. Speaking to the prunes she is eating, she frightens the first two robbers as they peek in the window when she says, "I will gobble you up." When the next robber comes she says, "That's the third one," and so she frightens all eleven robbers. They flee, thinking that she is a witch.[5] This tale does not even remotely resemble either "Holding the Rock" or AT1530.[6]

Motif K1251 (there is no K125.1) in Thompson's *Motif-Index of Folk-Literature* is described as follows:

> K1251. *Holding up the rock*. Trickster makes dupe believe that he is holding up a great rock and induces him to hold it for a while. (Sometimes steals the dupe's goods). *Type 1530.

Additional citations are made to Africa (Kaffir) [19–20], (Hottentot) [21], (Suto) [25], and to Uncle Remus [57]. No European sources are cited except by reference to AT1530; and incidentally, no versions from India are cited under either AT1530 or motif K1251.

In the summary of AT1530, quoted above, reference is made to two other tale types, AT9A and AT1731, both of which have European versions.

> 9A *In the Stable the Bear Threshes*. The fox pretends to hold up the roof so that it will not fall on the bear's head. [K1251.1].

That this is a different tale type is made even clearer by the description of the motif cited.

> K1251.1 *Holding up the roof.* Fox pretends to be holding up the roof; hence cannot help the bear, who must do the threshing alone. *Type 9A.

The second tale type cited is even more obviously unrelated to "Holding the Rock."

> 1731 *The Youth and the Pretty Shoes.* By playing upon their desire for the pretty shoes he has stolen [T455.3.2], he betrays the wife, the daughter, and the servant girl of the parson [K1357] and finally the parson himself, who is standing by his side. Healing of the scab; holding the bung of the wine-cask. (Obscene).

Because "Holding the Rock" differs from AT9A, AT1731, and the four European tales cited under AT1530, I conclude that it did not come from Europe (or India). It must have come to America from Africa.

Again this is no new discovery. In his introduction to *Nights with Uncle Remus,* Joel Chandler Harris cites a Xhosa homologue [19] of his tale from Georgia [57].[7] Ten years later, in 1893, Gerber cited another African homologue of Harris's tale.[8] Dundes includes AT1530, "Holding up the Rock," among the folktales that he strongly suspects "will one day be shown to be African, not European."[9]

My twenty-eight African versions come from Sierra Leone (Limba and Kono), Liberia (Vai and Dan), Kenya (Mosiro and Kamba), Tanzania (Bondei, Zigula, Kaguru, and Mwanga), Zambia (Unidentified, Lamba, and Ndebele), Mozambique (Makua and Ndau), Zimbabwe (Nyungwe), South Africa (Venda, Xhosa, and Hottentot), Lesotho (Suto), and Namibia (Hottentot). The thirty-two versions from the United States come from Michigan, California, (Yokut Indians), Colorado (Spanish), Arizona (Hopi, San Carlos Apache, and Navaho Indians), New Mexico (Spanish; Taos, San Juan, Sandia, Laguna, and Isleta Pueblos; and Navaho, Jicarilla Apache, and Lipan Apache Indians), Oklahoma (Hitchiti Indians), Texas (Spanish), Georgia (Negro and Creek Indians). Thirty-three versions come from Mexico, Coahuilla, Sonora (Yaqui Indians), Jalisco (Unidentified and Tepecano Indians), Mexico D.F., Oaxaca, Morelos, Veracruz, and Nayarit (Cora Indians); and Guatemala, Dominican Republic, Puerto Rico, Peru, and Argentina.

   1. (Sierra Leone: Limba) After fishing with Fire Fly, Spider unexpectedly met Leopard in a cave. He gave Leopard his fishes for Leopard's newborn children but ate them himself during the night, leaving the cubs only the fish heads. When Leopard was about to seize him, Spider said that the cave was going to fall. He had Leopard hold it up while he went for timbers to support it, but he did not come back. Other incidents follow. (Finnegan [1967], pp. 316–19)

   2. (Sierra Leone: Kono) Leopardess found Spider and his cousin in a cave after Spider had killed her cubs. As she was about to kill Spider his cousin

called out, "The cave roof is falling." Leopardess put herself under it like a post, and Spider told her to stay there while they went to get posts to hold it up. They left and Leopardess waited, holding the cave roof until she died. (Thomas [1916], pp. 58–59)

3. (Liberia: Vai) After another episode, angry Leopard chased Hare and found him in a cave with his hands pressed against the rock ceiling. Hare said that the ceiling was falling and told Leopard to hold up the rock while he went for help. Leopard did so, and Hare ran away. Another episode follows. (Pinney [n.d.], pp. 120–23)

4. (Liberia: Dan) After pushing Leopard's wife into a pot of boiling water, Dwarf Antelope's son fled with Leopard in pursuit. He went into a small hole that Leopard could not enter in a large rock that hung over the path. He called to Leopard to prop his hands against the rock lest it fall on him. Leopard did so and Dwarf Antelope's son escaped, saying that the rock would fall if Leopard took his hands away. Leopard stayed there, growing hungrier and hungrier, but weak and tired as he was he pressed against the rock. Finally he was so weak that he let go of the rock. It did not fall, but Leopard was too weak to hunt and he died. (Himmelheber and Himmelheber [1958], pp. 245–46)

5. (Kenya: Mosiro) Wart Hog went to sleep in a cave and awoke to find that Lion was about to kill him. He stood on his hind legs and pretended to support the roof of the cave, calling out, "Lion, come and help me hold up the roof. It is falling and we shall both be killed." Lion supported the roof with his forepaws and Wart Hog told him to hold up the roof while he went for timber to prop it up. Lion agreed and Wart Hog made his escape. (Maguire [1927–28], pp. 263–64; [1948], p. 24)

6. (Kenya: Kamba) Carrying Lion's meat, Hare met a hyena who asked for a piece. Hare said that the meat did not belong to him. He went on and met another hyena, who also asked for a piece of meat. Hare said he would give him some and led him to a large, very high stone. He told Hyena to catch hold of the stone so that it would not fall on him. Hyena took hold of the stone and Hare went away. Hyena held the stone for ten nights, afraid to let it fall. Another hyena came and asked him why he was so thin. Hyena said that Hare had told him to hold the stone so that it would not fall. The other hyena said that Hare had lied. Hyena let loose of the stone and the two hyenas went away. (Lindblom [1926], pp. 28–29)

7. (Tanzania: Bondei) Lion met Boar and Boar ran into a rocky cave. Lion came in also and Boar said to him, "Prop up this stone; it will fall." Lion propped it up and Boar ran away. Lion propped it up strongly. Goat came and asked Lion what he was doing. Lion said that the stone would fall. Goat propped his horns against it and told Lion to go out. Then Goat went out and Lion said that Boar had betrayed him. Lion caught Boar and ate him. (Dammann [1937–38], pp. 300–01)

8. (Tanzania: Zigula) Wart Hog came to a cave to drink water. When Lion came to drink, Wart Hog said, "The stone can fall. Hold it up so I can drink.

When I am finished, you can drink." Lion propped up the stone and Wart Hog ran away. Lion stayed there three days. Then Goat came and asked what he was doing, and Lion said he was holding the stone. Goat put his head in and asked why the stone did not fall. Lion said that Wart Hog had gotten the best of him, but he would catch him and eat him. (Dammann [1937–38], pp. 155–56).

9. (Tanzania: Kaguru) Hunting for food, Boar came to a stony cave. He heard it creak like a tree and thought that it was falling. He held the rock so that it would not fall. On the third day Lion came by. Boar called to Lion to come and help him because he was dying, and Lion asked how he could help. Boar told Lion to help him hold up the cave so that he could get a joist, saying, "Listen how it creaks. Help me quickly." Lion held the rock and told Boar to cut the joist. Boar left and did not return while Lion stayed holding the rock. When Lion heard the creaking he tried hard to hold up the cave. On the fifth day Goat came and Lion called to him to help, promising not to eat him and telling him what had happened. Goat propped his horn under the rock and told Lion to leave. Goat also let go of the cave and went outside. He asked Lion if he saw the cave collapse and told him that Boar had betrayed him. Lion became the enemy of Boar. (Busse [1936–37], pp. 72–75)

10. (Tanzania: Mwanga) Hare took refuge from rain in a hole, but found Lion there and was frightened. To save himself he cried that a rock would fall and kill them. He told Lion to support it, and Lion did so. He told Lion to hold it fast because if he let loose he would die. Hare left, saying that he would bring a joist. Lion seized the rock and did not let loose, thinking that it would kill him. After seven days he let go and nothing happened. Lion said, "Such a deceiver." (Busse [1936–37], p. 259)

11. (Zambia) After other episodes Hare, overtaken by Hyena whose children he had eaten, pretended to be holding up a rock that would crush them both if it was not propped up. He persuaded Hyena to hold it up while he went to get a pole. Hare ran away leaving Hyena holding up the rock. (Worthington [1930], pp. 39 ff.; adapted from Klipple AT1530)

12. (Zambia: Lamba) After another episode, Little Hare tricked Hyena into trying to kill Lion. Hyena failed and hid in a burrow until he was very thin. When he became fat again Hyena caught Little Hare and said, "It is you who deceived me!" Little Hare led Hyena to a cave and told him, "Hold this rock. I'll cut a prop to prop it up. If you let go you'll die!" Hyena held the rock and Little Hare did not come back. Ony day Leopard found Hyena still holding the rock and told him to come away. Hyena said that Little Hare had told him that if he let go it would kill him. Leopard said that God had created the rock and it could not come loose. Leopard took Hyena, mere bones, away and gave him food. (Doke [1927], pp. 162–65)

13. (Zambia: Ndebele) After another episode Lion found Hare in a cave and threatened to eat him. Hare jumped across to a low hanging portion of the roof of the cave, where he pretended to hold up the rock. He cried, "Uncle, the cave is falling in! Come and help me hold it up. Come quickly or we will

both be crushed!" Lion placed his paws against the rocky roof, and both pushed upwards with all their strength. After a while Hare said, "My arms are very sore and tired. Let me collect some rocks to build a pillar to the roof. Then we can both sit down and rest. Please hold the roof up while I get the rocks." Hare vanished through the mouth of the cave and did not return. Lion began to think that he had been tricked again. He jumped backwards out of the cave. Nothing happened. The roof still stayed up and Lion *knew* he had been tricked again. (Savory [1962], pp. 46–52)

14. (Mozambique: Makua) After another episode Elephant chased Rabbit onto some rocks. One rock stood up and Rabbit held it saying, "The stone will crush you. Hold it!" Elephant held it and Rabbit went to cut a prop. He cut it short on purpose and Elephant was angry. Elephant said, "My arms hurt me," but Rabbit ran home leaving Elephant holding the rock. (Woodward [1935], pp. 132–34)

15. (Mozambique: Ndau) Lion accused Hare of murdering his children and Hare fled. When Hare began to tire, he saw a leaning stone. He went under it and held it up. Lion followed Hare under the stone and Hare told him to hold the stone lest it fall on them. Lion thought that if he let go of the stone it would crush them both. Hare ran away, but Lion stayed under the stone for many days. Hungry and tired, he let go of the stone, but it did not fall. Lion came out from under the stone and threatened Hare. (Boas and Simango [1922], pp. 170–71, 175)

16. (Mozambique: Ndau) After killing Lion's cubs Hare fled, pursued by Lion. When he became tired, Hare went under a leaning rock and held it up. Lion came and Hare told him to hold the rock, lest it fall on them. Lion held the rock and Hare came out from under it. He told Lion to hold onto the rock because it would fall on him if he let go. Lion stayed under the rock for many days. When he was tired and dying of hunger he let go of the rock. He was afraid that it would fall on him, but the rock did not fall. Lion went home and when he was strong again he tried to kill Hare. (Boas and Simango [1922], pp. 171–74, 175–79)

17. (Zimbabwe: Nyungwe) After another episode, Hare found Lion demanding the leg of a man's wife. He told them to come into a cave to get out of the wind and made them tell the whole story. While they were speaking Hare cried out, "The rock is tumbling down. Let's all hold it up." So they all supported the rock. Hare said that the man and woman should go and bring props to support the rock while he and Lion held it up. Hare told Lion to use all his strength to hold up the rock while Hare only rested his forefeet against it. The man and his wife came back with some props, but Hare said they were not satisfactory. When they had gone away again, they decided that Hare was helping them and they ran away. Hare told Lion to hold up the rock while he went to look for the man and woman and bring the props. Lion put forth all his strength to hold up the rock and Hare ran away. Lion became lean through hunger, but he was afraid to let go of the rock lest it fall on him. At last he let go of the rock and made a bound toward the mouth

of the cave, but he struck his head against a rock. Half stunned, he got out of the cave and ran away. (Posselt [1929], pp. 51–54; retold in Werner [1933], p. 270, n.2)

18. (South Africa: Venda) Sankhambi [the animal trickster] saw that the monkeys hated him. He offered to show them lots of honey and led them to a cave. When they were inside he made a noise and shouted, "The cave is falling. Support it!" The monkeys used all their strength to hold it up. Sankhambi told them to keep holding it up while he went to fetch some sticks. He ran away, leaving the monkeys still supporting the cave. Because they were starved that day their hips are thin. (Stayt [1931], p. 353)

19. (South Africa: Xhosa) In a lengthy tale about Hlakanyana [a boy trickster], he was pursued by Leopardess. He went under a big rock and cried for help, saying that the rock was falling. He told Leopardess to hold it up while he went for a prop to put under it. Leopardess held up the rock and Hlakanyana ran away. (Theal [1886], pp. 89–117; [1910], pp. 307–19)

20. (South Africa: Xhosa) After other episodes Lion tried to catch Jackal, but Jackal sprang away. He went under an overhanging rock and cried, "Help! Help! This rock is falling on me!" Lion went for a pole to prop up the rock so that he could get at Jackal, and Jackal escaped. Other episodes follow. (Theal [1886], pp. 186–90; [1910], pp. 97–99; retold in Honeÿ [1969], pp. 56–61; reprinted in Lee [1930], pp. 32–34; translated in Bautista Roca [1962], pp. 222–23; Pérez Arbeláez [1952], pp. 95–97)

21. (South Africa: Hottentot) After other episodes Lion chased Jackal and found him under an overhanging precipice. He was standing on his hind legs with his shoulders pressed against the rock. He called to Lion to help him, as the rock was falling and would crush them both. Lion put his shoulders to the rock and pressed with all his might. After some time Jackal proposed that he should fetch a large pole to prop up the rock, so that Lion could get out from under it. Jackal crept out, leaving Lion there to starve to death. (Bain [1879], pp. 69–73; translated in von Held [1904], pp. 72–76; reprinted in Theal [1910], pp. 88–91; retold in Honeÿ [1969], pp. 73–78)

22. (South Africa: Hottentot) Lion had a grudge against Jackal because Jackal had played a trick on him. One day he found Jackal at the foot of a rock with no way of escape. Quickly, Jackal sprang at the rock, placed his forefeet against it, and cried out for Lion to help him. Lion asked what was the matter. Jackal said, "Don't you see that the rock is falling? Come here. Place yourself against it and hold it until I get a stick to prop it up." Lion did so and Jackal escaped. (Bleek [1870], pp. 2–3; retold in von Held [1904], p. 142)

23. (South Africa: Hottentot) After other episodes Jackal fled, pursued by Lion. Jackal crept under a precipice that hung over, making a kind of cave. When Lion crept in Jackal called out, "Lion, the precipice is falling. If you don't hold it up, you'll be crushed to death. I'll run and get a pole to prop it up, but please wait till I come back." Jackal ran home laughing, leaving Lion holding up the precipice. (Metelerkamp [1914], pp. 101–07)

24. (South Africa: Hottentot) After other episodes Lion found Jackal sleeping

at the foot of a cliff. Jackal awoke and said, "Hold up this cliff and let me go and get a forked stick to prop it up." Jackal went away and did not come back. Some leopards found Lion and asked what he was doing. Lion answered, "I am holding this cliff." The leopards said, "God created this cliff and placed it there," but Lion believed Jackal. They told Lion to stop, but he said that the cliff would fall and crush him. Again they told him to stop, and Lion pushed the cliff away and fell on his back. (Maingard [1962], pp. 73–81)

25. (Lesotho: Suto) Overtaken in a cave by angry Rabbit, Hare told him that the cave was falling down. Rabbit tried to hold up the cave with his hands, enabling Hare to escape. (Sekese [1903]; summarized in Jacottet [1908], p. 44, n. 1)

26. (Namibia: Hottentot) After other episodes Jackal lay down under a rocky cave to sleep. The brother of the lion Jackal had killed found him and said, "Now I have you where I want you." Jackal said, "Look out! The stones will fall on us!" He grabbed the rock and told Lion to hold it fast while he went to find a piece of wood to put under it. Lion lay on his back and held up the rock. Jackal left and did not come back. Hare came, saw Lion holding up the rock, and said, "But grandfather, the rock has stood quietly from time immemorial!" Lion drew back, but he fell down from exhaustion and died. (Olpp [1888], pp. 3–4)

27. (Namibia: Hottentot) After another episode Jackal slept under an overhanging rock and was caught by Leopard. Jackal said, "Grandfather, stop! The rock is falling on us! Push against it so that we may not be killed." They both pushed and Jackal said, "Let me look for some wood to prop it up." Jackal went away and Leopard pushed against the rock. Jackal stayed away all day, and when he returned he found Leopard dead. (Schultze [1907], pp. 485–87)

28. (Namibia: Hottentot) Leopard sneaked up on Jackal and said, "Got you!" Jackal said, "The mountain's overhang is falling on us. Prop it up so that I can look for a piece of wood." Jackal left and Leopard propped it up until he died. (Schaar [1917–18], pp. 108–09)

29. (Michigan) After another episode, Fox and Deer were chasing Rabbit. Rabbit ran to a tall cypress tree and grabbed it, telling them to run fast because the world was falling. He told them to hold it up while he went to get a prop. They looked up and saw the tree wiggling against the clouds, and it looked as if it were falling. The low clouds made it look like the world was falling. Rabbit ran away and never came back. (Dorson [1958], pp. 163–64; [1967], pp. 92–94; reprinted in Haring [1972], p. 172; Edwards [1978], pp. 52–53)

30. (California: Yokut Indians) Coyote was hungry. He met Stink Bug and said that he was going to eat him. Stink Bug was scared. He was leaning against a big rock and he said that he was holding up the world so that it would not fall and kill him. He said that if Coyote took his place he would go and look for food for him. Coyote put his back against the rock and Stink Bug went off and hid. Coyote became very hungry, but he dared not move

lest the world fall. Finally, he took a great jump. The rock remained solid and he knew that he had been fooled. Another incident follows. (Rogers and Gayton [1944], pp. 199–200)

31. (Colorado: Spanish) After other incidents, Coyote found Rabbit in the shade of a rock and threatened to eat him. Rabbit said, "Don't eat me. I am holding this rock because if it falls the world will fall. But if you hold it, I will bring food for both of us." Coyote held the rock and Rabbit did not come back. Coyote said to himself, "I'm going to get out of here even if the rock falls. Maybe Rabbit will die too." He went in search of Rabbit, and other episodes follow. (Rael [n.d.], vol. 2, pp. 472–74, 782)

32. (Colorado: Spanish) After other incidents Coyote found Fox holding a rock. As the clouds were moving, it looked as if they were going to fall. Coyote asked what Fox was doing. She said that she was holding the rock because it was going to fall, but if he would hold it for her she would go for hens. She left and when Coyote was tired of holding the rock he let go, but the rock did not move. Coyote went looking for Fox, and other episodes follow. (Rael [n.d.], vol. 2, pp. 479–81, 783)

33. (Arizona: Hopi Indians) Grasshopper planted his field by himself. It became hot so he returned to his temporary shelter, drank, and lay down to rest, leaning his feet against the side of the shelter. Coyote came and asked what he was doing. He said that he was afraid the shelter would fall on him, and that he didn't know how to run away. Coyote said, "Let me lie down too." He did so, leaning his hind feet against the shelter. Grasshopper jumped up and said that he would go for water, leaving Coyote lying in the shelter with his feet against its timbers. Finally Coyote became tired and decided that Grasshopper had lied to him. He let go with his feet and jumped out quickly. The shelter was shaking but it did not fall. Coyote went after Grasshopper to eat him and his children, and another episode follows. (Voth [1905], pp. 212–13, 309)

34. (Arizona: San Carlos Apache Indians) After other episodes Coyote said he would kill Rabbit. When he saw him, Rabbit was standing against a rock. Coyote was about to knock him down when Rabbit said, "The sky is falling. Look up here." Coyote looked up and said, "It is so." Rabbit said that they had better stand against the stone. Coyote stood against it and Rabbit ran away. Another episode follows. (Goddard [1918], pp. 74–75; [1919], pp. 352–55)

35. (Arizona: Navaho Indians) Fox came to a rock pillar that seemed to be leaning against a cloud, and found Coyote pushing against it with all his might, as though he were trying to prevent it from falling over. Coyote called to Fox to help him. He said that their priest was on top of the pillar and that if it fell it would mean his death. He asked Fox to take a turn in holding up the pillar while he ran around to help the priest down. Fox agreed and leaned against the pillar with all his strength. After a time Fox looked up and saw that the cloud was gone and the pillar wasn't tipping at all. He walked away and looked back at the top of the pillar, expecting to see the priest, but all

he saw was a crow that flew away. Meanwhile Coyote had run away, laughing at the joke he had played on Fox. (Pousma [1934], pp. 115–16)

36. (Arizona: Navaho Indians) After other episodes Fox passed a tall slab of red sandstone that stood alone. On top of the rock Raven was eating corn, and at the bottom Coyote was holding on to the rock with his paws, waiting for Raven to drop a few kernels. He did not let go of the rock because he thought Fox might take his place. Fox said he had eaten much corn that Big Long Man had given him. Coyote decided to go to Big Long Man, but he was greedy and did not want Fox to go with him. He asked Fox to hold the rock while he went, saying that he dared not leave it lest it fall and kill somebody. Fox placed his paws against the rock and Coyote ran off. Fox became tired of holding the rock and decided to let it fall. He shouted to Raven, "Look out! The rock is going to fall!" Fox let go, jumped away, and ran off. (Hogner [1935], pp. 77–82)

37. (New Mexico: Spanish) As the final episode of a tale, Coyote met Fox and threatened to eat her. She told him not to but to come and help her hold a mountain that was falling. Coyote looked up and it appeared that the mountain was falling. He was fooled and Fox escaped. (Espinosa [1914], pp. 134–35)

38. (New Mexico: Spanish) After another episode, Coyote pursued Fox and found her making as if she were holding up a cliff. When Fox saw him, she cried, "Come here, Coyote! Christ told me that this cliff would fall and end the world. I've been holding it for two nights and I'm very tired." Coyote went to help her and Fox went away, leaving him holding the cliff. Coyote stayed there until he had a cramp and fell down, but the cliff did not fall and the world did not come to an end. Other episodes follow. (Espinosa [1937], pp. 181–82, 219)

39. (New Mexico: Navaho Indians) After other episodes, Coyote trailed Skunk in order to kill him. When Skunk saw Coyote approaching he put his hands against a high rock on which a crow was sitting. He looked up and saw clouds passing over the rock and thought that the rock was moving. Coyote saw Skunk holding up the rock and Skunk asked him to help him keep the rock from falling. Skunk said that there was a missionary [the crow] sitting up there and he did not know what to do because he had been holding it for a long time and was tired. Coyote came to help him and Skunk went away. Coyote pushed against the rock until he became tired. Exhausted, he ran away as fast as he could but the rock did not fall. Another episode follows. (Hill and Hill [1945], pp. 333–34)

40. (New Mexico: Taos Pueblo) Coyote found Fox holding up a mountain. Fox asked for help, saying that if the mountain fell the world would come to an end and that he had to relieve himself. Coyote stayed there holding up the mountain and Fox ran away. Other episodes follow. (Espinosa [1936], pp. 121–23)

41. (New Mexico: Taos Pueblo) After other episodes, when Yellow Fox saw Coyote coming up the mountain, he went under a rock. As he looked up, it

seemed that the cliff was falling and he began to push it, crying "Hurry up, help me!" If this cliff falls down it will be the end of the world for animals!" So they both pushed. Whenever he looked up, it seemed as if it were coming down. Yellow Fox said that he had to relieve himself and left Coyote holding the cliff. Coyote jumped away and saw that the cliff was still there. He said that Yellow Fox had fooled him and decided that it was of no use to follow him any more. (Parsons [1940], pp. 130–32)

42. (New Mexico: Taos Pueblo) Yellow Fox saw Coyote coming and stood close to a mountain. He said, "This mountain is going to fall. I am holding it up." Coyote offered to help him, and Yellow Fox said, "Look up at the clouds. Let me go and get a big stick to prop it up." Then Yellow Fox ran away. (Parsons [1940], p. 132)

43. (New Mexico: San Juan Pueblo) After another episode Coyote followed Fox's tracks, threatening to kill him. When Fox saw him coming, he leaned against a cliff and called, "Come quickly and help me! This cliff is falling! It will kill us both!" Fox looked up and saw the clouds passing over the cliff, making it look as if the cliff were really falling. Fox jumped to Coyote's side and leaned against the cliff as hard as he could. Coyote jumped away, making a big jump just as if the cliff might really fall on him. He told Fox to hold the cliff up while he went to get a stick to prop it up. Fox stayed there all day waiting for Coyote to come with the stick. Late that evening, when no clouds were passing, he saw that the cliff was not falling and knew that Coyote had tricked him again. Another episode follows. (DeHuff [1922], pp. 3–7; reprinted in Lee [1930], pp. 103–04)

44. (New Mexico: San Juan Pueblo) After other episodes Coyote set out to kill Grey Fox, but Grey Fox saw him coming. Grey Fox was under a mesa and he leaned against the wall as if holding it up. Mist was blowing across the sky, making the mesa look as if it were moving. He said to Coyote, "If this wall falls down, it will kill us. Look up at the sky, the mesa is moving. Come and help me." Coyote leaned against the wall and Grey Fox told him to hold it while he went to look for others to help. After Grey Fox left, Coyote said, "I am very tired holding up this wall. I am going to jump away. I had better jump four times so that the mesa won't catch me." He jumped to the north, to the west, to the south, and to the east. He looked back and saw that the wall was standing just as he had left it. He knew that Grey Fox had tricked him. (Parsons [1926], pp. 157–59)

45. (New Mexico: Sandia Pueblo) Coyote found Fox leaning against a rock and said that he would eat him. Fox said Coyote must not do so because he was holding up the rock and they were bringing him food. Coyote asked to help and got under the rock to hold it up. Fox ran away. No food came and Coyote grew tired. Finally he gave a big jump so that the rock would not fall on him and went away. Other incidents follow. (Espinosa [1936], pp. 120–21)

46. (New Mexico: Laguna Pueblo) Coyote was in a cave holding up the stone roof with his legs. Fox came and Coyote said that he thought that the roof was going to fall on him. Fox offered to help and then said that he would

get a stick to hold it up. Fox went away and did not come back. Coyote got tired and jumped out, but the stones fell on him and broke his leg. (Parsons and Boas [1920], p. 49)

47. (New Mexico: Laguna Pueblo) Wanting to get even with Fox, Rabbit went under an overhanging rock and called for help. He asked Fox to hold up the rock while he went for poles to prop it up. Fox grew tired and angry. Rabbit told him to push up the rock and run. (Espinosa [1936], p. 84)

48. (New Mexico: Isleta Pueblo) After other episodes, Little Blue Fox saw Coyote coming. He stood up on his hind feet and put his forepaws against a cliff. Coyote came and threatened to eat him. Fox said, "Oh, no! I saw this cliff falling and ran to hold it up. If I let go, it will fall and kill us both. Help me hold it." Coyote pushed the cliff with his forepaws and they stood there side by side. Fox said that he was thirsty and would bring water, because Coyote would soon be thirsty too, and he ran away. Coyote became tired and thirsty. He let go of the cliff slowly, made a great jump away backward, and ran as fast as he could. When he looked back and saw that the cliff had not fallen, he was angry and threatened to eat Fox. Another episode follows. (Lummis [1910], pp. 222–31)

49. (New Mexico: Isleta Pueblo) Rabbit told Coyote that the mountain was falling and got him to take his place holding it up. Other incidents follow. (Espinosa [1936], p. 117)

50. (New Mexico: Jicarilla Apache Indians) Lizard saw Coyote and was afraid. He ran up the stalk of a sunflower and told Coyote not to bother him because he was busy holding up the sky so that it would not fall on them. It was windy and the clouds were sailing past. Lizard said, "Look at that sky! It's going to fall on us! Keep looking and see if it isn't falling." Coyote looked and looked and became dizzy. When Lizard saw that Coyote was dizzy he ran away, and another episode follows. (Opler [1938], pp. 279–80)

51. (New Mexico: Lipan Apache Indians) Coyote saw Lizard on a stalk and was about to eat him; but Lizard said, "I've been put here to hold up this stalk. It's holding up the sky, and if I let go it will fall." Coyote watched him. When the wind blew the stalk began to sway. Lizard said, "See it is swaying! Help me hold it!" Coyote rushed up and held on also. Lizard said, "It still sways. Our hands might slip and the sky would fall on us. I'd better go and get some people to help." Coyote agreed and Lizard ran away. Coyote stood there, holding on and calling for Lizard to come back. The bottom of the stalk was rotten and began to break. Coyote was frightened. He let go and ran, and stalk fell after him. He thought that the sky was falling and he ran as fast as he could. (Opler [1940], pp. 149–50)

52. (New Mexico: Lipan Apache Indians) Coyote saw Lizard on a stalk and was about to eat him; but Lizard said, "Can't you see that I'm holding this stalk that supports the sky? I'm tired and you must help me. Take my place while I get my children to help us." Coyote caught hold and Lizard went among the rocks and watched. Coyote became very tired and called to Lizard to come, but Lizard watched him and laughed. Coyote saw a ditch. He let

go, ran for the ditch, and fell in. He waited for a moment and saw that the sky had not fallen yet, so he ran for the next ditch. When he had done this four times he realized that he had been fooled again. (Opler [1940], p. 150)

53. (Oklahoma: Hitchiti Indians) Rabbit lied to Wildcat saying, "If this tree falls on the road it will interfere with traffic. People said it must be braced up, so I have been standing here holding it. Help me so that we can brace it." Wildcat agreed and Rabbit told him to hold it while he hunted for something with which they could brace it. Rabbit left and did not return. After a long time Wildcat became angry and left. Other episodes follow. (Swanton, [1929], p. 108)

54. (Oklahoma: Hitchiti Indians) A man saw Rabbit eating peas in his garden and chased him. When Rabbi saw him coming he knelt down beside a tree, bracing himself against it. The man came and said that he was going to kill Rabbit. Rabbit said, "You can kill me but you will die also. This tree braces up the earth and is going to fall down. If it falls, the earth, the sky, and everything will be wiped out. I have sent people to bring others to help me brace it, and I am here holding the tree. If you kill me, the earth, sky, and all things will pass away." The man looked and the sky appeared as if it were going to fall. He looked closely and the tree appeared to touch the sky and be about to fall. The man ran away, and Rabbit ran off also. (Swanton [1929], p. 113)

55. (Texas: Spanish) In a tale of many episodes Coyote found Fox lying on her back in a cave beneath a cropping of boulders. Coyote said he would eat her up, but she said she had been told to hold the world on her feet to keep it from falling down. Fox said she was hungry and Coyote said he would hold the world on his feet if she brought a hen. He got under the rock and pushed it with his feet. Fox left and did not return. After several hours Coyote was tired. He said that if it is going to fall, then let it fall. He jumped out but the rock did not fall. (Aiken [1954], pp. 30–36)

56. (Texas: Spanish) After other episodes Coyote found Rabbit and threatened revenge. Rabbit said, "I am holding up this rock. They are going to bring me my dinner here, a great big meal." Coyote did not believe him, but Rabbit insisted he was telling the truth and asked Coyote to take his place. Coyote took his place and got stuck there holding up the rock. Fox came by and Coyote asked her to help him hold up the rock, but she ran away. He managed somehow to get out from under the rock, and other episodes follow. (Paredes [1970], pp. 54–58)

57. (Georgia) Rabbit killed Wolf's grandmother and fed her to him. When Rabbit told Wolf he had eaten her, Wolf chased him and found him under a leaning tree. Rabbit shouted to Wolf to come and hold up the tree before it fell, to hold it so that he could prop it up. Rabbit left and Wolf held up the tree until he became tired. (Harris [1883], no. 54; [1955], pp. 343–47)

58. (Georgia) After another episode, Rabbit escaped from Bear and ran under an overhanging rock. When Bear came Rabbit shouted that Bear should look out because he felt the rock falling. He told Bear to get something to

prop it up. Bear went off and brought a pole, but when he came back Rabbit was gone. (Harris [1910], no. 4; [1955], pp. 757–60)

59. (Georgia: Creek Indians) After other episodes Rabbit was lying under a bent-over tree when he saw Wolf coming. He stood up with the tree over his shoulder as if he were trying to hold it up. Wolf said, "I have you now," but Rabbit said, "They told me to hold up this tree all day and they would give me four hogs. I don't like hog meat but you might get it if you take my place." Wolf said he would hold up the tree. Rabbit said, "If you yield even a little it will give way, so you must hold it tight." Rabbit ran away and Wolf stood under the tree until he could stand it no longer. He jumped away so that it would not fall on him, but it did not fall. Another episode follows. (Swanton [1929], pp. 64–66)

60. (Georgia: Creek Indians) After other episodes Wolf tried to get even with Rabbit. When Rabbit saw him coming he ran up to a bent-over tree and said, "I am holding up this tree because if it falls the earth will pass away. Come and hold it while I go for help." Wolf held up the tree until he became tired, and Rabbit escaped. (Swanton [1929], pp. 66–67)

61. (Mexico) Lying in the shade of a tall rock, Fox saw Coyote coming. He jumped up and began pushing against the wall of the cliff. Coyote threatened to eat him, but Fox said that the cliff was falling and asked Coyote to help him. Coyote looked up at the top of the cliff and it did seem to be falling, so he jumped to Fox's side and pushed against the cliff. Fox said he would go for help and some food, promising to return in half an hour. A half hour passed but Fox did not return. Coyote pushed all night and in the morning he had no strength left. He jumped back from the cliff and raced away. When he looked back and saw that the rock was still standing, he knew that Fox had fooled him. (Storm [1938], pp. 32–34)

62. (Sonora: Yaqui Indians) Coyote found Rabbit and threatened to eat him, but Rabbit promised to bring him chicken to eat. Rabbit ran off but did not come back. Coyote followed his tracks and found him with his forepaws against a cliff. Coyote asked what he was doing, and Rabbit said, "I'm holding up this cliff." A rock fell and he held the cliff harder than ever. He told Coyote to hold it while he went for the chicken. Coyote pushed against the cliff while Rabbit ran off. Another rock fell and Coyote pushed harder. He grew tired and hungry. He let go of the cliff and ran away as fast as he could, but nothing happened. Another episode follows. (Giddings [1959], pp. 126–27)

63. (Jalisco) After another incident Monkey found Rabbit holding up a house and threatened to kill him. Rabbit said, "Don't kill me! I am holding up this house because if it falls it will kill us. Come and help me and I will bring you food." Monkey held it up with all his strength, and Rabbit ran away. Finally he said that Rabbit was a liar and decided to see if the house would fall. He jumped away and it did not fall. He found Rabbit holding up a rock and threatened to kill him. Rabbit said, "Don't kill me! Help me hold up this rock, because if it falls into the river it will drown us both." Monkey did not believe him and another incident follows. (Wheeler [1943], pp. 505–06)

64. (Jalisco) After another episode Coyote found Lamb holding up a rock and threatened to kill him. Lamb said, "How can you want to eat me when I am holding up this rock. If I let go, the world will come to an end. But if you hold it up I will bring you a hen." Coyote held up the rock and Lamb told him not to let go because the world would come to an end. Then Lamb ran away and did not return. Coyote was there three days holding up the rock and he was very hungry and thirsty. Finally he said, "I'm going to let go of the rock even if the world comes to an end." Coyote let go but the rock did not move and world did not come to an end. (Wheeler [1943], pp. 509-11)

65. (Jalisco) After other episodes Coyote found Fox holding a rock and said he was going to eat her. Fox said, "No. This rock is falling. If it falls it will crush me. If you hold it I will bring Burro to help you." Coyote held the rock until his limbs were trembling and he realized that he had been tricked. He ran after Fox and other episodes follow. (Robe [1970], pp. 74-77)

66. (Jalisco) After other episodes Coyote hunted for Fox. He found her pretending to hold up a rock and said he was going to eat her. Fox said, "Don't eat me. I will bring you many chickens, but I am here holding up this rock." Fox left Coyote holding up the rock and did not return. Coyote wondered what to do, thinking that if he jumped away the rock would fall and kill him. Finally, he jumped and the rock did not fall. He realized that Fox had fooled him again, and another episode follows. (Robe [1970], pp. 99-101)

67. (Jalisco: Tepecano Indians) As one of a tale's many episodes, Fox found Rabbit in a cave with his feet up, holding a large rock. She threatened to eat him, but Rabbit asked her to help him. Fox put her feet up against the rock and Rabbit went away. When Rabbit did not return Fox said, "Here I am holding the rock. If it falls it will smash me." She jumped out and ran away. (Mason and Espinosa [1914], pp. 150-53, 204)

68. (Coahuila) After other episodes Coyote found Fox lying on her back in a cave. Fox said that she had been promised a hen and had been told to hold the world on her feet to keep it from falling down. Coyote offered to hold up the world while Fox went for a hen, and Fox escaped. Coyote became tired and jumped out of the cave, but the rock did not fall and the world did not come to an end. Other episodes follow. (Aiken [1969], pp. 13-19)

69. (Mexico, D.F.) Coyote met Rabbit and threatened to eat him. Rabbit begged Coyote not to do so, promising to bring him a hen. Rabbit went for the hen but did not return. When Coyote knew that he had been fooled, he went looking for Rabbit. He found him and threatened to eat him. Rabbit said, "I didn't trick you. They told me to hold this rock, because if I let go the world will come to an end. You hold it while I go and get something to eat." Coyote stayed, holding the rock. When he was tired he let go, saying that it did not matter to him if the world came to an end, and he went looking for Rabbit. (Marden [1896], col. 43)

70. (Mexico, D.F.) In a tale of many episodes, Coyote found Rabbit hiding under a stone. Rabbit told him that he was holding the world and that if he let the stone fall the world would fall. He also said that he had not eaten for

five days. Coyote said he would help him if Rabbit brought him food. Coyote got under the stone and Rabbit left and did not return. After a day and a night Coyote was hungry and let go of the stone. He saw that it did not support the world and that this was one of Rabbit's lies. (Reid [1935], pp. 121–24)

71. (Oaxaca) As the final episode in a tale, Coyote searched for Rabbit who had gone under a stone. As Coyote passed by, Rabbit called to him. Coyote threatened to eat him, but Rabbit told Coyote to get under the stone, because if the stone were thrown down, the world would come to an end. Coyote went under the stone and Rabbit threw another stone on top of it, killing Coyote. (Mechling [1912], pp. 200–01)

72. (Oaxaca) In a lengthy tale Coyote told Rabbit that he would not escape, because he had tricked Coyote so much. Rabbit put a large stone in his hand as soon as he saw Coyote. He said that he had been there supporting the stone, because if he let go of it the world would be lost. Coyote believed him and Rabbit asked Coyote to help because he was very tired. Coyote took the stone and Rabbit told him not to let go of it lest the world be lost. Rabbit went away and did not return. Coyote became tired and let the stone down gradually, looking at the sky to see if it was coming down. When he saw it was not, he set the stone on the ground and went to look for Rabbit. (Boas [1912], pp. 204–14)

73. (Oaxaca) In another lengthy tale, Coyote found Rabbit on the slope of a great mountain and said he would eat him. Rabbit replied that he would not, because he was holding a rock and if he let go the world would come to an end. Rabbit asked Coyote to help him while he went for lunch. Coyote took hold of the rock and Rabbit escaped. After a while Coyote grew tired and said he would let go of the rock even if the world came to an end. He let go of it and it rolled, but nothing else happened. Coyote set out in pursuit of Rabbit again. (Boas [1912], pp. 235–41)

74. (Oaxaca) After another episode, Coyote found Fox in front of a rock and threatened to eat her. Fox said no, she would take him where there were chickens to eat. Coyote believed her and Fox left him holding the rock. Another episode follows. (Mechling [1916], pp. 553–54)

75. (Oaxaca) After another episode Fox pursued Monkey and found him on top of a rock. Monkey said, "I am so tired. If I let this rock go, it will be the Last Judgement. Hold it until I come back with food; but do not let it go." When Fox grew tired she said, "What does it matter if it is the Last Judgement?" She let the rock go, jumped, and ran away. When she looked back, she saw the rock in the same place, and other episodes follow. (Radin and Espinosa [n.d.], pp. 146–48)

76. (Oaxaca) Fox was sitting on top of a rock, holding it down, when Lion came and asked what she was doing. Fox said she was keeping the rock from rolling down. Lion was hungry and threatened to eat Fox. Fox said, "No. I will bring turkeys; but you have to hold the rock." Lion agreed, telling Fox not to delay. Fox went and ate a hen and told a friend about Lion. The friend

laughed and they went to get drunk. They went back to see Lion, who called for help, saying that he would have to let the rock go. Fox told him to do so and Lion asked for his turkey. Other episodes follow. (Radin and Espinosa [n.d.], pp. 149–51)

77. (Oaxaca) After other episodes Coyote hunted for Rabbit and found him holding a rock. Rabbit said, "Hold this. If not the hill will fall. I am coming back." Coyote grew tired and let go of the rock, and other episodes follow. (Radin and Espinosa [n.d.], pp. 153–54)

78. (Oaxaca) After other episodes, Fox wanted revenge and hunted for Monkey. She found Monkey holding a rock and asked why. Monkey said, "Because I don't want the world to be broken apart." Fox asked how long he had been there and Monkey replied, "Since it was made, and I've eaten nothing but flies. Will you hold it while I eat and come back?" Fox felt sorry for Monkey and stayed holding the rock. Three days passed and Monkey did not return, and Fox could not stand her hunger. Because Monkey had said that if she let go of the rock the world would be broken apart, Fox rolled the rock and nothing happened to the world. Another episode follows. (Radin and Espinosa [n.d.], pp. 182–83)

79. (Oaxaca) After another episode Coyote was hungry and found Rabbit near a rock. He asked what he was doing and Rabbit said, "I am holding this rock so it won't fall. If it falls we all will die." Coyote threatened to eat Rabbit, but Rabbit asked Coyote to take his place because he was going to a wedding. He told Coyote that if he heard firecrackers it was because they were playing music at the wedding. Coyote was happy because Rabbit promised to bring him food, and Rabbit was happy because he had escaped Coyote. When Rabbit was far away he lit fires all around, and Coyote thought that the wedding was taking place. Suddenly Coyote found the flames around him and jumped away, thinking that the rock would fall near him but it did not. Another episode follows. (Radin and Espinosa [n.d.], pp. 191–92

80. (Oaxaca) Coyote looked for Rabbit and found him at the foot of a large rock. He threatened to eat him, but Rabbit asked if he did not know that the world was going to come to an end. Coyote asked how he knew this, and Rabbit said that God had told his brother. Rabbit asked Coyote to help him hold up the rock to see if they could save the world. Coyote helped him hold up the rock and after several hours asked if Rabbit was hungry. Rabbit said yes and asked if Coyote could hold the rock by himself while he went to look for food. Coyote stayed and Rabbit went but did not return. Coyote became hungry but when he saw that the rock wanted to fall, he did not let go. He saw the clouds passing above but finally dared to let go of the rock and jumped away. When he looked the rock was still in the same place. (Parsons [1932], pp. 296–99)

81. (Morelos) After another episode Opossum and Puma came to a rock. Opossum said it was moving through the clouds and that Puma, who was seeking revenge, should hold onto it while Opossum went for food. Puma saw the clouds passing over the rock and thought that the rocks were moving.

He held onto it while Opossum ran away. After a while Puma saw that the rock was not moving but that the clouds were passing over it. (Boas [1912], pp. 246–47)

82. (Veracruz) After other episodes, Coyote found Rabbit under a big rock, pushing it up, and threatened to eat him. Rabbit said, "Don't eat me, because the world is going to end. I'm tired. Come and hold this rock." Coyote said, "No, because you're tricking me again." Rabbit said, "No. Hold it." Coyote held up the rock and it did not come down. Finally, he said to himself, "I am going to let go. Let me and Rabbit die. It's useless for him to trick me. In the end we both will die." Coyote let the rock go and it did not fall. Coyote said that Rabbit had tricked him again, and other episodes follow. (Robe [1971], pp. 23–27)

83. (Nayarit: Cora Indians) Opossum lay in a hole with his feet up against its wall, and Coyote came and asked what he was doing. Opossum said that he was blocking up the field of heaven that was about to fall and cover them. He said that everything in the world was about to fall and asked Coyote to help him. Coyote lay down holding up his legs and Opossum told Coyote to push hard while he went to look for a prop. Opossum left and did not return. Coyote waited and finally took heart and sprang away. Other episodes follow. (Preuss [1912], vol. 1, pp. 290–93)

84. (Guatemala) After other episodes, Rabbit went under a stone to hold it up. Coyote came and threatened to eat him, but Rabbit asked Coyote to help him. Coyote held the stone, but it fell and broke his balls. (Recinos [1918], pp. 472–73)

85. (Domninican Republic) After another episode in which Pedro was tricked by the king's daughter, he said he would get revenge. He found her with both hands against a cliff and asked what she was doing. She said that the king had sent her to hold onto it and that if she let go the world would come to an end. Pedro asked if she wanted him to help her and she accepted, saying that she would go to eat because she was hungry. When she did not return the next afternoon, Pedro let go of the cliff, expecting the world to come to an end, but it did not. Another episode follows. (Andrade [1930], pp. 43–44)

86. (Puerto Rico) Foolish John found a very large rock and when Clever John saw him, he asked what Foolish John was doing. He said he was holding up the world because the Virgin had told him to do so saying that, if he let it fall, the world would come to an end. Clever John offered to help and was left with the world in his hands. Other episodes follow. (Mason and Espinosa [1921], pp. 184–85)

87. (Puerto Rico) Pedro de Urdemalis promised to kill Juan el Astuto. When they met, Juan put a large stone on his head. He said that he was very tired, but if the stone fell the world would be finished. Pedro said that if Juan paid him twenty pesetas he would not let the world be finished. Juan told Pedro to hold the stone while he went home to look for the money and that he should not let the stone fall. Pedro agreed and took the stone, but Juan did not return. Pedro became more and more tired and finally said, "Let the world come to

an end," and threw away the stone. The world did not come to an end, and Pedro promised revenge on Juan. (Mason and Espinosa, [1922], p. 43)

88. (Puerto Rico) As one episode in "Trickster Seeks Endowments," Rabbit held up a rock. Alligator came by and asked him why he was doing so. Rabbit said that if the rock fell, it would destroy the city. Alligator held up the rock with his teeth, and Rabbit broke off a tooth with his hammer. (Mason and Espinosa [1927], p. 334)

89. (Puerto Rico) After other episodes Tiger pursued Hare. When she saw Tiger, Hare held a rock saying, "The world will fall if you don't help me hold up this rock." Tiger held it. When Tiger saw that Hare had gone, he let go of the rock and was surprised that the world did not fall. Another episode follows. (Mason and Espinosa [1927], pp. 334–35)

90. (Puerto Rico) After other episodes, Rabbit made a plan to kill Tiger and his mother. He held up a big rock and shouted to Tiger. When Tiger came, Rabbit told him that if he did not help him to hold up the rock, it would fall and destroy the world. To avoid this, Tiger helped him hold up the rock. Rabbit went above and threw a bigger rock, killing Tiger, and then killed Tiger's mother. (Mason and Espinosa [1927], pp. 335–36)

91. (Puerto Rico) After other episodes Lion looked for Kid to kill him, and he met Kid by a wall. When he saw Lion, Kid thought that he would not find a way to save himself, but immediately he put his front legs on the wall. When Lion came Kid said, "I am here holding up this wall that is falling, and if I let loose it will fall on us and kill us. You should hold it up while I look for a stake to hold it up." Kid went away and did not return. Lion stayed there and died of hunger because he was afraid to let go, believing that the wall would fall on him. (Mason and Espinosa [1927], pp. 371–72)

92. (Peru) After other episodes Fox found Mouse holding onto a rock and threatened to eat him. Mouse said, "No! You can eat me later. Hold onto this rock. It's going to flatten me and destroy the town if you don't hold it up." Fox agreed, saying that he was bigger, and grabbed the rock firmly. Mouse said he was going to bring a wedge. He climbed on top of the rock and it seemed to be moving. Fox gripped the rock harder and then let go. Nothing! The rock did not move. Fox said that he had been betrayed again, and other episodes follow. (MacLaughlin [1975], pp. 527–33)

93. (Argentina) Pedro decided to amuse himself with a person he saw coming. He put his shoulder against the wall, pretending that he could not hold it any longer. When the man came he called to him, "Come here, friend. Help me." The man ran to him and pressed against the wall. Pedro jumped back and said, "Wait until I bring a prop," and then disappeared. (Bustamente [1922], p. 134)

BIBLIOGRAPHY

Aiken, Riley
1954 A Pack of Mexican Tales. *Publications of the Texas Folklore Society* 21.

1969 A Pack of Mexican Tales. *Texas Folklore Society Publications* 12. [1935]

Andrade, Manuel J.
1930 Folk-Lore from the Dominican Republic. *Memoirs of the American Folk-Lore Society* 23.

Bain, Thomas
1879 The Story of a Dam. *Folk-Lore Journal* (Cape Town) 1.

Bautista Roca, José María
1972 Las razas de Africa. In *Las Raza Humanas.* Ed. Pedro Bosch Guimpera. Barcelona, Instituto Gallach. Vol. 2.

Bleek, W. H. I.
1870 *Reineke Fuchs in Afrika.* Weimar, Herman Böhlau.

Boas, Franz
1912 Notes on Mexican Folk-Lore. *Journal of American Folk-Lore* 25.

Boas, Franz, and Simango, C. Kamba
1922 Tales and Proverbs of the Vandau of Portuguese South Africa. *Journal of American Folk-Lore* 35.

Busse, Joseph
1936–37 Kaguru-Texte. *Zeitschrift für Eingeborenen-Sprachen* 27.
1936–37 Inamwanga-Texte. *Zeitschrift für Eingeborenen-Sprachen* 27.

Bustamente, Perfecto P.
1922 *Girón de Historia, Leyendas, tradiciones regionales y relatos históricos.* Buenos Aires: J. Crovetto & M. Carrio

Dammann, Ernst
1937–38 Bonde-Erzählungen. *Zeitschrift für Eingeborenen-Sprachen* 28.
1937–38 Zigula-Märchen. *Zeitschrift für Eingeborenen-Sprachen* 28.

DeHuff, Elizabeth Willis
1922 *Taytay's Tales.* New York, Harcourt Brace.

Doke, Clement M.
1927 Lamba Folk-Lore. *Memoirs of the American Folk-Lore Society* 20.

Dorson, Richard M.
1958 Negro Tales from Pine Bluff, Arkansas, and Calvin, Michigan. *Indiana University Folklore Series* 12.
1967 *American Negro Folktales.* Greenwich, Conn., Fawcett.
1972 *African Folklore.* Garden City, New York, Anchor Books, Doubleday; and Bloomington, Indiana University Press.

Edwards, Jay D.
1978 The Afro-American Trickster Tale: A Structural Analysis. Bloomington, *Monograph Series of the Publications Group* 4.

Espinosa, Aurelio M.
1914 New Mexican Spanish Folk-Lore. *Journal of American Folk-Lore* 27.
1936 Pueblo Indian Folk Tales. *Journal of American Folk-Lore* 49.

Espinosa, José Manuel
1937 Spanish Folk-Tales from New Mexico. *Memoirs of the American Folk-Lore Society* 30.

Finnegan, Ruth
1967 *Limba Stories and Story Telling.* Oxford Library of African Literature. Oxford, Clarendon Press.

Giddings, Ruth Warner
1959 *Yaqui Myths and Legends.* Tucson, University of Arizona Press.

Goddard, Pliny Earle
1918 Myths and Tales from the San Carlos Apache. *Anthropological Papers of the American Museum of Natural History* 34:1.
1919 San Carlos Apache Texts. *Anthropological Papers of the American Museum of Natural History* 34:3.

Haring, Lee
1972 A Characteristic African Folktale Pattern, in Dorson 1972.
Harris, Joel Chandler
1883 *Nights with Uncle Remus*. Boston and New York, Houghton Mifflin.
1910 *Uncle Remus and the Little Boy*. Boston, Small, Maynard.
1955 *The Complete Tales of Uncle Remus*. Compiled by Richard Chase. Boston, Houghton Mifflin.
Hill, W. W., and Hill, Dorothy W.
1945 Navaho Coyote Tales and their Position in the Southern Athabaskan Group. *Journal of American Folklore* 58.
Himmelheber, Hans, and Himmelheber, Ulrike
1958 *Die Dan, ein Bauernvolk im westafrikanischen Urwald*. Stuttgart, W. Kohlhammer.
Hogner, Dorothy Childs
1935 *Navajo Winter Nights. Folk Tales and Myths of the Navajo People*. New York, Thomas Nelson and Sons.
Honeÿ, James A.
1969 *South-African Folk-Tales*. New York: Negro Universities Press. [1910]
Jacottet, E.
1908 *The Treasury of Ba-Suto Lore*. Morija, Lesotho, Sesuto Book Depot.
Lee, F. H.
1930 *Folk Tales of All Nations*. New York, Coward-McCann.
Lindblom, Gerhard
1926 Kamba Tales of Animals. *Archives d'Études Orientales* 20:1.
Lummis, Charles F.
1910 *Pueblo Indian Folk-Stories*. New York, Century.
MacLaughlin, Jean
1975 Peru. In *Folktales Told around the World*. Ed. Richard M. Dorson. Chicago and London, University of Chicago Press.
Maguire, R. A. J.
1927–28 Il-Torobo. *Journal of the African Society* 27.
1948 Il-Torobo. *Tanganyika Notes and Records* 25.
Maingard, L. F.
1962 *Korana Folktales. Grammar and Texts*. Witwatersrand, University Press.
Marden, C. C.
1896 Some Mexican Versions of the "Brer Rabbit Stories." *Modern Language Notes* 11.
Mason, J. Alden, and Espinosa, Aurelio M.
1914 Folk-Tales of the Tepecanos. *Journal of American Folk-Lore* 27.
1921 Porto-Rican Folk-Lore: Folk-Tales. *Journal of American Folk-Lore* 34.
1922 Porto-Rican Folk-Lore: Folk-Tales. *Journal of American Folk-Lore* 35.
1927 Porto-Rican Folk-Lore: Folk-Tales. *Journal of American Folk-Lore* 40.
Mechling, William Hubbs
1912 Stories from Tuxtepec, Oaxaca. *Journal of Ameican Folk-Lore* 25.
1916 Stories and Songs from the Southern Atlantic Coastal Region of Mexico. *Journal of American Folk-Lore* 29.
Metelerkamp, Sanni
1914 *Outa Karel's Stories*. London, Macmillan.
Olpp, J.
1888 Aus dem Sagenschatz der Nama-Khoi-Khoin. *Mitteilungen der Geographischen Gesellschaft zu Jena* 6.
Opler, Morris Edward
1938 Myths and Tales of the Jicarilla Apache Indians. *Memoirs of the American Folk-Lore Society* 31.

1940 Myths and Legends of the Lipan Apache Indians. *Memoirs of the American Folk-Lore Society* 36.
Paredes, Américo
1970 *Folktales of Mexico.* Chicago, University of Chicago Press.
Parsons, Elsie Clews
1926 Tewa Tales. *Memoirs of the American Folk-Lore Society* 19.
1932 Zapotec and Spanish Tales of Mitla, Oaxaca. *Journal of American Folk-Lore* 45.
1940 Taos Tales. *Memoirs of the American Folk-Lore Society* 34.
Parsons, Elsie Clews, and Boas, Franz
1920 Spanish Tales from Laguna and Zuñi. *Journal of American Folk-Lore* 33.
Pérez Arbeláez, Enrique
1952 Folklore del Magdalena: La Cuna del Porro. *Revista de Folklore* (Bogota), Ser. 2, Vol. 1.
Pinney, Peter
n.d. Legends of Libera. Mimeographed.
Posselt, F.
1929 *Fables of the Veld.* London, Oxford University Press.
Pousma, Richard H.
1934 *He-Who-Always-Wins and Other Navajo Campfire Stories.* Grand Rapids, Michigan, Wm. B. Eerdmans.
Preuss, Konrad Theodor
1912 *Die Nayarit-Expedition.* Leipzig, B. G. Teubner.
Radin, Paul, and Espinosa, Aurelio M.
n.d. El Folklore de Oaxaca. *Annales de la Escuela Internacional de Arqueologia y Etnologia Americanas.* New York, G. E. Stechert
Rael, Juan B.
n.d. *Cuentos Españoles de Colorado y Nuevo Mejico.* Stanford University Press, Vols. I–II.
Recinos, Adrián
1918 Cuentos Populares de Guatemala. *Journal of American Folk-Lore* 31.
Reid, John Turner
1935 Seven Folktales from Mexico. *Journal of American Folk-Lore* 48.
Robe, Stanley L.
1970 Mexican Tales and Legends from Los Altos. *Folklore Studies* 20. Berkeley and Los Angeles, University of California Press.
1971 Mexican Tales and Legends from Vera Cruz. *Folklore Studies* 23. Berkeley and Los Angeles, University of California Press.
Rogers, Barbara Throll, and Gayton, A. H.
1944 Twenty-Seven Chukchansi Yokuts Myths. *Journal of American Folk-Lore* 57.
Savory, Phyllis
1962 Matabele Fireside Tales. Cape Town, Howard Timmins.
Schaar, W.
1917–18 Nama-Fabeln. *Zeitschrift für Kolonialsprachen* 8.
Schultze, Leonhard
1907 *Aus Namaland und Kalahari.* Jena, Gustav Fischer.
Sekese, Azariele
1903 *Mekhoa ea ba-Sotho.* Morija, Lesotho, Sesuto Book Depot. [1893]
Stayt, Hugh A.
1931 *The Bavenda.* London, Oxford University Press.
Storm, Dan
1938 The Little Animals of Mexico. *Texas Folk-Lore Society Publications* 14.
Swanton, John R.
1929 Myths and Tales of the Southeastern Indians. *Bureau of American Ethnology Bulletin* 88.

Theal, Geo. McCall
    1886 *Kaffir Folk-Lore*. London, Swan Sonnenschein, Le Bas & Lowrey.
    1910 *The Yellow and Dark-Skinned People of Africa South of the Zambesi*. London, Swan Sonnenschein.
Thomas, Northcote W.
    1916 *Specimens of Languages from Sierra Leone*. London, Harrison and Sons.
von Held, T.
    1904 *Märchen und Sagen der afrikanischen Neger*. Jena, H. W. Schmidt.
Voth, W. R.
    1905 *The Traditions of the Hopi*. Publication 96, Anthropological Series 8. Chicago, Field Columbian Museum.
Werner, Alice
    1933 *Myths & Legends of the Bantu*. London, George G. Harrap.
Wheeler, Howard T.
    1943 Tales from Jalisco, Mexico. *Memoirs of the American Folk-Lore Society* 35.
Woodward, H. W.
    1935 Makua Tales. *Bantu Studies* 9.
Worthington, Frank
    1930 *The Little Wise One*. London.

N O T E S

1. My numbers 5–6, 11, 15, 17–20, 21 (Held and Theal), 22–23, and 28.

2. My numbers 15–16, 30, 37, 39–40, 45–47, 49, 65, 70–74, 80–81, 84, 86–88, and 91. Three other tales (by Teit and Parsons) involve theft. Aarne and Thompson mistakenly say eleven tales for Africa (Klipple) and twenty-five tales for Coffin. Other New World tales cited by Aarne and Thompson are from the United States [31–32], Dominican Republic [85], Puerto Rico [86–91], and Mexico [72–73]. The tales from Argentina and Chile involve theft, as do others cited in Parson's comparative notes.

3. Wolfram Eberhard and Pertev Naílí Boratav, "Typen Türkischer Volksmärchen," Akademi der Wissenschaften und der Literatur, *Veroffentlichungen der Orientalischen Kommission*, vol. 5 (1953), 384–85, 422.

4. Adolf Schullerus, "Verzeichnis der Rumänischen Märchen und Märchenvarienten nach dem System der Märchentypen Antti Aarnes," *FF Communications*, no. 78 (1928), 69–70.

5. Linda Dégh, *Kakasdi Népmesék I*, Budapest, Akaémiai Kiadó, vol. 1 (1955), 441–42. I am indebted to Steve Deness for translating this tale for me, and to Linda Dégh for confirming my interpretation of it.

6. This instance clearly demonstrates the danger of accepting citations uncritically and the necessity of examining the tales themselves.

7. Joel Chandler Harris, *Nights with Uncle Remus*, (Boston and New York, Houghton Mifflin Company, 1883), p. xx.

8. A. Gerber, "Uncle Remus Traced to the Old World," *Journal of American Folk-Lore*, 6 (1893), 248. I have not yet been able to locate Gerber's South African tale in which, he says, Jackal asked Leopardess to support an inclining rock until he brought a prop.

9. Alan Dundes, "African and Afro-American Tales," *Research in African Literatures* 7 (1976), 188, 195.

E I G H T

✳

Taught an Incriminating Song (Saying)

In this tale type the trickster kills or steals the animal or children of a third party and then teaches the dupe to repeat a song or saying that incriminates him. I have found nothing like it in Aarne and Thompson's *The Types of the Folktale*, but Thompson's Motif K1066 is relevant: *"Dupe induced to incriminate himself.* Taught incriminating song or persuaded to wear incriminating clothes." Because it occurs by itself in both Africa [1] and the New World [13–17, 20–22, 24–26] it is a tale type and not simply a motif.

Because Thompson cites no references to Europe (or India) for K1066, I conclude that this tale type came to the Americas from (and originated in) Africa. His only references are to

> Hausa. Tremearne [1], but with incorrect page references;
> Georgia. Harris [19];
> South Carolina. Smiley [12], not Virginia;
> Jamaica. Beckwith [21];
> Bahamas. Parsons MAFLS 13 1918, pp. 70–72 [0], a different tale; and
> West Indies. Flower's index.

The incriminating song is found in twenty-one of the twenty-six versions, and the incriminating saying in the five others, all from Africa [1–2, 5–6, 10]. Incriminating clothes are found in one African version [1], in one from Jamaica [21], and in one from Haiti [23], but in each case there is also an incriminating song or saying. In one example from South Carolina [12] it is Rabbit, the trickster, rather than the dupe, who sings the incriminating song, but he is not believed.

In most of the African versions [2–10] this tale type follows that of the Murderous Nursemaid, with the dupe saying that he has killed the children of the third party. I have not found this combination in the New World. In four versions from the United States [11–12, 18–19] the dupe and the trickster

Reprinted from *Research in African Literatures*, 12 (1981), 203–13.

are courting the same girl. Baboons, apes, or monkeys are often the dupes in African versions [4-5, 7-10], and also in three tales from Jamaica [20, 22] and Surinam [24] in which the trickster has eaten Tiger's entrails. In two other divergent tales from Surinam the trickster teaches the incriminating song after setting a church on fire [25] and stealing the king's watch [26].

My ten African versions come from Nigeria (Hausa), Zaire (Kongo), Tanzania (Nyiha and Swahili), Malawi (Nyanja), Zambia (Lamba), Zimbabwe (Shona), Mozambique (Nyungwe), and South Africa (Venda). Nine from the United States come from Alabama, South Carolina, and Georgia. Seven come from Jamaica, Haiti, and Surinam. I have not had access to a Jamaican version reported to have been published by Wona (Mrs. Charles Wilson).

1. (Nigeria: Hausa) Lion had a ram named Babba Randam, and Spider asked to look after it. Spider killed and ate the ram, putting aside its bell, skin, and fat. He told Lion that someone had stolen the ram, but Lion said that Spider was lying and that he was going to summon all the animals to a dance. Spider told Hyena about the dance and gave him the ram's skin and bell to wear, and he rubbed her mouth with fat. Hyena was proud of her finery. When the animals had assembled, Spider came drumming, "Who has eaten Babba Randam? Hyena is the devourer of Babba Randam. The skin on her back is the skin of Babba Randam. The bell on her neck is the bell of Baba Randam. The fat on her mouth is the fat of Babba Randam." Dancing, Hyena said, "That is so. Beat your drum, Spider. That is so." Lion killed Hyena and the other animals ran away. (Tremearne [1910], pp. 352–53; [1914], pp. 180–81)

2. (Zaire: Kongo) After the episode of the Murderous Nursemaid, Gazelle went to the place where the animals were gambling. Pigeon gave him the dice, and Gazelle made a winning throw. Gazelle said, "I have eaten seven young leopards, and nothing has happened to me." The animals thought this was a lucky saying, so they repeated the words every time they threw the dice. Gazelle warned them not to repeat the words of others, but they thought that he wanted to keep his good luck to himself. Gazelle went back and brought Leopard, who heard one animal after another say, "I have eaten seven young leopards, and nothing has happened to me." Leopard killed all the animals except Gazelle. (Weeks [1911], pp. 376–78; [n.d.], pp. 376–78)

3. (Tanzania: Nyiha) After the episode of the Murderous Nursemaid, Hare told Lion that he would lie in wait for those who had eaten Lion's children. He found many animals playing ball and taught them a song, "We ate the six children of Lioness." He went back to Lion and said that he had found the murderers. Hiding Lion in grass, he carried him to the animals playing ball. He told them that they should build a big rampart, and when it was so high that Antelope could not jump over it he called to Lion who came out and killed all the animals. Another episode follows. (Kootz-Kretschmer [1929], Vol. 2, pp. 138–41; Vol. 3, pp. 122–24)

4. (Tanzania: Swahili) After a series of other episodes and that of the Murderous Nursemaid, Hare found the baboons playing a game and sold them

the skins of Lion's cubs. He told them that they were not playing the game right and showed them how, singing as he played, "We have eaten Lion's children on the quiet." The baboons wanted to learn the song, so Hare taught them the words. He went back to Lion's den and told Lioness that he had found the wild beasts that had carried off her children and who had their skins. He tied Lioness up in a bundle of grass, put some beans on top and carried the load to the baboons who were playing the game. Lioness could hear them singing, "We have eaten Lion's children on the quiet." Hare told the baboons that he had brought them a load of beans. He loosened the top of the bundle to show them the beans, and then he joined in their game. Lioness worked herself free and killed all the baboons, and Hare showed her the skins of her cubs. (Werner [1933], pp. 255–62)

5. (Malawi: Nyanja) After another episode and that of the Murderous Nursemaid, Rabbit said he would identify those who had killed Lion's cubs. He went to the village of the baboons, found them playing at throwing tops at corn cobs and joined the game. Rabbit told them that when he threw he would say, "Who ate Lion's cub?" and that they must say, "It was I, it was I." The next day Rabbit returned with Lion, who was wrapped up in a bundle. Rabbit and the baboons began to play. Rabbit threw, saying, "Who ate Lion's cub?" and they replied, "It was I, it was I." Lion burst out of the bundle and seized all the baboons. (Rattray [1969], pp. 57–59, 136–39)

6. (Zambia: Lamba) After the episode of the Murderous Nursemaid, Little-Hare left Lion and found some animals playing ball. He said, "What ate the lion-cub, and no case comes to light!" and they all said, "What a lovely proverb Little-Hare has put forth!" He returned to Lion and said that he had found animals saying, "What ate the lion-cub, and no case comes to light." The next day Lion and his wife went to the animals playing ball. They thought that the lions were dogs, and Little-Hare tied them to a stick and joined the game. When they threw the ball to Little-Hare, they all said, "What ate the lion-cub, and no case comes to light!" Little-Hare cut Lion and his wife loose, and they sprang on Eland, Zebra, and Buffalo and killed them. (Doke [1927], pp. 70–75)

7. (Zimbabwe: Rozwi Shona) After the episode of the Murderous Nurse-maid, Hare came to a party of baboons playing a game. He joined in the game and sang, "I killed the lion's children. What harm has come to me?" The baboons asked what this meant, and Hare told them that it was a new song. Being vain, they all sang it. Hare went back to the lions and told them that the baboons had killed their cubs. He offered to take them to the baboons. When they came near, they heard the baboons singing the song that Hare had taught them. Hare tied grass around the lions, telling them to wait. He invited the baboons to play their game near the lions, and they played and sang. Suddenly the lions rushed out and killed some of the baboons. Others escaped, and other episodes follow. (Posselt [1929], pp. 14–17)

8. (Zimbabwe: Jindwe Shona) After the episode of the Murderous Nurse-maid, Hare scratched himself with thorns. He told Lion that baboons had

taken his children and offered to find them. When he came to the baboons they were playing a game with beans, and he asked to join them. While playing he sang, "I ate Lion's child. What harm has come to me?" The baboons did likewise. Before leaving, Hare told them that he would come again and bring his beans. Hare returned to Lion and told him of the song the baboons sang. He tied up Lion in a bundle of grass and carried him back to the baboons. He found them still playing and suggested that they play inside the hut. The baboons asked what he had in his bundle and he asked, "Can't you see the beans?" They played, a baboon sang Hare's song, and Hare cried out for Lion to listen. One of the baboon children saw Lion's eye in the bundle, but the baboons would not listen to him. Hare suggested that they take some beans from the bundle, and when they opened it, Lion killed all the baboons. Other episodes follow. (Posselt [1929]. pp. 43–50)

9. (Mozambique: Nyungwe) After the episode of the Murderous Nursemaid, Hare wounded himself with thorns and told Lion that apes had beaten him and eaten Lion's children. Hare went to the apes and gave them nuts to eat. They played a game and Hare sang, "I have killed the lion and pulled off his skin." The apes repeated Hare's song. Hare returned to Lion and the next day they both went to the apes, carrying fruit and nuts for them. Hare made a trap and put the nuts in it, and Lion hid. Hare gave the apes the fruit, and they ate and began to sing Hare's song. A young ape saw Lion's eye, but the others paid no attention to him. They ate the nuts and were caught in the trap. Hare refused to free them and Lion threw off his covering of stems. They killed and cooked the young ape, and Hyena ate the others. Another episode follows. (von den Mohl [1905], pp. 24–30)

10. (South Africa: Venda) After the episode of the Murderous Nursemaid, Sankhambi, and animal trickster, told Lion that his cubs had been eaten by baboons. Sankhambi found the baboons playing a game and taught them to respond, "We have eaten Lion's cubs. What will become of us now?" He told them that he would bring them sweet potatoes wrapped in grass, and he brought Lion tied up in grass. He said they should play the game before eating the sweet potatoes. They played and the baboons gave the response. "We have eaten Lion's cubs. What will become of us now?" Sankhambi said that they should eat the sweet potatoes, and they cut the strings around the bundle of grass. Lion jumped out and killed the baboons, and Sankhambi cut off their tails. (Stayt [1931], pp. 355–56)

11. (Alabama) Rabbit and Bear were going to see Miss Reyford's daughter, and Miss Reyford didn't know Rabbit had been killing her hogs. She told Rabbit that if he told her who was killing her hogs, she would give him her daughter. Rabbit went to Bear and said some ladies were giving a social, and they wanted Bear to sing a bass solo. Bear felt proud and agreed. Rabbit said that he would sing, "Who killed Mr. Reyford's hogs? Who killed Mr. Reyford's hogs" and that Bear should answer, "Nobody but me." Bear did so and Rabbit flattered his voice. They went to Miss Reyford's party, and when Bear sang the refrain Mr. Reyford shot him. Bear was not killed, and another incident follows. (Fauset [1927], p. 224; reprinted in Hughes and Bontemps [1958], pp. 3–4)

12. (South Carolina) Wolf and Rabbit were in love with Kingdeer's younger daughter. Because she favored Rabbit, Wolf killed her goat and accused Rabbit, but Miss Kingdeer did not believe him. Wolf suggested that he and Rabbit serenade the girls. They sang, "Rabbit is a tricky man, and everybody knows. Did you kill Miss Kingdeer's goat, and everybody knows? Yes, yes, yes, yes, yes, yes, yes, and everybody knows." Wolf said, "I told you Rabbit killed her goat, and he's told you so." Rabbit said that Wolf had planned this because he was jealous. Miss Kingdeer didn't believe that Rabbit killed the goat and called her father. Wolf ran off very fast, while Miss Kingdeer and Rabbit laughed. (Smiley [1919], pp. 366–67)

13. (South Carolina) Rabbit stole McKinlaw's goose but denied it when he was accused. Rabbit told Wolf that he had been invited to a girl's house and that they must practice a song to sing there. They did so, and when they came to McKinlaw's house Rabbit sang, "Who stole, who stole, who stole McKinlaw's goose?" Wolf sang, "It's me, it's me, it's me who stole McKinlaw's goose." McKinlaw put Wolf in jail. (Parsons, "Sea Islands," [1923], pp. 145–46)

14. (South Carolina) Rabbit stole Brother Kinley's goose and had to appear in court. On his way there he met Fox and asked him to sing with him, teaching him a song. In court Rabbit sang, "Who stole Brother Kinley's goose?" and Fox sang, "It is me who stole Brother Kinley's goose." Kinley hit Fox on the neck. (Parsons, "Sea Islands," [1923], p. 146)

15. (South Carolina) Every night Mr. Gillerson lost one of his sheep. He asked Rabbit if he could tell him who was stealing them, and Rabbit said, "Yes. I will bring Wolf here if you give me some fresh milk." Rabbit told Wolf that Mr. Gillerson was inviting them to a frolic, and they should sing a song that Rabbit would select. Rabbit sang, "Didn't you steal Mr. Gillerson's goats?" and Wolf sang, "Yes, oh yes! I did it.' They sang the song all the way to Mr. Gillerson who chopped off Wolf's head. Rabbit got his milk. (Parsons, "Sea Islands," [1923], p. 146)

16. (South Carolina) Rabbit stole Kinlaw's goat and told Wolf that they would make thirty dollars if Wolf sang the refrain to a song. When they came near the court house, Rabbit sang, "Wolf stole Kinlaw's goat," and Wolf sang, "Yes indeed, indeed I did." The judge heard them and gave Wolf thirty days instead of thirty dollars. (Johnson [1968], p. 140; reprinted in Botkin [1966], pp. 665–66; retold in Cothran [1972], pp. 45–47)

17. (South Carolina) Rabbit stole Jonas' goat and became uneasy because Jonas was making so many inquiries about it. He told Jonas to come to a dance and he would prove who stole the goat. He also invited Wolf to the dance and asked him to join in a song. He said he would sing, "Who stole Brother Jonas' goat?" and that Wolf should sing, "I stole Brother Jonas' goat." Jonas came to the dance, heard the song, and had Wolf put in jail. (Adams [1938], pp. 174–76)

18. (South Carolina) Brother Ringo's best looking daughter was Wolf's girl and Rabbit was jealous. Brother Ringo was losing his hogs and he asked his friends to help him find the thief. He was giving a party and Wolf and Rabbit

were going to it. Rabbit said that he would sing a song if Wolf would sing the refrain, and Wolf agreed. At the party Rabbit sang, "I wonder who stole Brother Ringo's hog," and Wolf responded, "Nobody but me!" When Brother Ringo heard the song a second time, he took his gun and shot Wolf. All the girls were sorry that Wolf was dead. Rabbit said that Wolf had been stealing Brother Ringo's hogs, but the girls paid no attention. Rabbit lost his girl and his partner didn't get Wolf's girl. (Work Projects Administration [1941], pp. 41–42)

19. (Georgia) Rabbit and Fox were courting Deer's daughter, and Deer had almost decided to let Fox marry her. Rabbit killed two of Deer's goats and told Deer that he had seen Fox doing it. Deer investigated and saw the dead goats. Rabbit said that he could get Fox to confess, and Deer said that if Rabbit did so he could marry his daughter. Rabbit told Fox that he had promised that they would make music for Deer that night. They took their instruments and practiced their song. When they came to Deer's house Rabbit sang the call, "Some kill sheep and some kill shote, but Brer Fox killed King Deer's goat." Fox sang the response, "I did, that I did, and I'm glad that I did." Deer beat Fox with his cane until Fox fled, and Deer's daughter invited Rabbit in. (Harris [1883], no. 13; [1955], pp. 166–70)

20. (Jamaica) Annancy and Tiger went to the river to bathe. Annancy told Tiger to take out his fat before he went into the water and ate it while Tiger was swimming. Fearing Tiger, Annancy went to the town of the big monkeys and tried to teach them to sing, "Yesterday I ate Tiger fat," but they drove him away. Annancy went to the town of the little monkeys and taught them the song. He went back to Tiger and told them that the little monkeys were singing. They went to the little monkeys and Tiger heard them singing, "Yesterday I ate Tiger fat." He began to fight them, but they sent for the big monkeys who beat Tiger and Annancy. (Jekyll [1904], pp. 7–10)

21. (Jamaica) Anansi stole Mr. Mighty's two thousand sheep until only one was left. Mr. Mighty offered him his best daughter and two hundred pounds if he found how his sheep disappeared. Anansi said that the best way would be for him to give a ball. Then he told Tiger of the offer, gave him a coat, trousers, cap, and boots of sheepskin, and taught him a song. Anansi told Mr. Mighty that the thief would be wearing sheepskin clothes. At the ball Anansi played his fiddle and Tiger played his tambourine. Anansi sang the call, "Mr. Mighty lost his sheep, it looks like a tiger stole them." Tiger sang the refrain, "For true, Brother, for true. It looks like it made my clothes." Tiger was arrested and Anansi got the daughter and two hundred pounds. (Beckwith [1924], pp. 6–8)

22. (Jamaica) Anansi and Tiger went to bathe. Anansi told Tiger that they should take out their tripe. Anansi ate Tiger's tripe and told him that to find out how it had disappeared he must go to monkey town. He went to the monkeys and told them that when they saw Tiger they must sing, "This time we ate Tiger's guts!" When Tiger heard the song he killed all the monkeys

except one who told him that Anansi had taught them the song. (Beckwith [1924], p. 13)

23. (Haiti) After another episode, Malice exchanged the skin of the king's cow for shoes, hat, etc. and told Bouqui that he should put on the skin and eat all the cows. He taught Bouqui a song telling how he killed the cow in Monplaisir. The king heard the song and made Bouqui sit down in a hot basin. Another episode follows. (Parsons [1933–43], Part I, pp. 479–80; Part II, p. 56)

24. (Surinam) Tiger took out his entrails to bathe, and Anansi ate them. When Tiger asked where they were, Anansi said that he didn't know, but that he would show him who ate them. Anansi met some monkeys singing on their way to a wake. He told them that they musn't sing like that, but that they should sing, "We ate Tiger's belly. It was sweet." The monkeys agreed, but when Anansi took Tiger to the wake, they were singing a different song. Anansi asked if they had forgotten the song he had taught them, and they sang, "Tiger's belly is sweet." Tiger heard them and killed half of them. The other monkeys ran away and Anansi ran with them. Another episode follows. (Herskovits and Herskovits [1936], pp. 214–17)

25. (Surinam) Anansi set fire to the church. The king announced that whoever caught the person who had done it would be rewarded, and Anansi said he could do so if the king gave a party. Anansi invited Goat to the party and taught him to sing, "It is I who burnt the king's church." When the king heard the song, he had Goat imprisoned. (Herskovits and Herskovits [1936], pp. 282–85)

26. (Surinam) Anansi stole the king's watch. He told the king that if he were given a reward he would catch the thief, but the king must give a dance. Anansi asked Bobo to come to the dance with him and taught him a song. When Anansi sang, "The king's watch is lost, perhaps Bobo took it," Bobo was to reply, "Yes, yes, Anansi." When the king heard the song, he had Bobo locked up. (Herskovits and Herskovits [1936], pp. 284–85)

BIBLIOGRAPHY

Adams, E. C. L.
   1928 *Nigger to Nigger.* New York, Charles Scribner's Sons.
Beckwith, Martha Warren
   1924 Jamaica Anansi Stories. *Memoirs of the American Folk-Lore Society* 17.
Botkin, B. A.
   1966 *A Treasury of American Folklore.* New York, Crown. [1944]

Cothran, Jean
   1972 *The Whang Doodle. Folk Tales from the Carolinas.* Columbia, South Carolina,
      Sandlapper Press.
Fauset, Arthur Huff
   1927 Negro Folk Tales from the South: Alabama, Mississippi, Louisiana. *Journal of
      American Folk-Lore* 40.
Harris, Joel Chandler
   1883 *Nights with Uncle Remus.* Boston and New York, Houghton Mifflin.
   1955 *The Complete Tales of Uncle Remus.* Compiled by Richard Chase. Boston,
      Houghton Mifflin.
Herskovits, Melville J., and Herskovits, Frances S.
   1936 Suriname Folklore. *Columbia University Contributions to Anthropology* 27.
Hughes, Langston, and Bontemps, Arna
   1958 *The Book of Negro Folklore.* New York, Dodd, Mead.
Jekyll, Walter
   1904 Jamaican Song and Story: Annancy Stories, Digging Sings, Ring Tunes, and
      Dancing Tunes. *Publications of the Folk-Lore Society* (London) 55.
Johnson, Guy B.
   1968 *Folk Culture on St. Helena Island, South Carolina.* Hatboro, Pennsylvania,
      Folklore Associates. [1930]
Kootz-Kretschmer, Elise
   1929 *Die Safwa,* Vols. I–III. Berlin, Dietrich Reimer
Parsons, Elsie Clews
   1923 Folk-Lore of the Sea Islands, South Carolina. *Memoirs of the American Folk-
      Lore Society* 16.
   1933–43 Folk-Lore of the Antilles, French and English. *Memoirs of the American
      Folk-Lore Society* 26, Parts I–III.
Posselt, F.
   1929 *Fables of the Veld.* London, Oxford University Press.
Rattray, R. Sutherland
   1969 *Some Folk-Lore Stories and Songs in Chinyanja.* New York, Negro Universities
      Press. [1907]
Smiley, Portia
   1919 Folk-Lore from Virginia, South Carolina, Georgia, Alabama, and Florida.
      Journal of American Folk-Lore 32.
Stayt, Hugh A.
   1931 *The Bavenda.* London, Oxford University Press.
Tremearne, A. J. N.
   1910–11 Fifty Hausa Folk-Tales. *Folk-Lore* (London) 21–22.
   1914 *Hausa Folk-Tales.* London, John Bale, Sons & Danielsson.
von den Mohl, Alexander
   1905 Sammlung von kaffrischen Fabeln in der Ci-Tete-Sprache am unteren Sambesi.
      Mitteilungen des Seminars für Orientalische Sprachen zu Berlin, Dritte Abtei-
      lung: Afrikanische Studien 8.
Weeks, John H.
   1911 *Congo Life and Folklore.* London, Religious Tract Society.
   n.d. *Congo Life and Jungle Stories.* London, Religious Tract Society.
Werner, Alice
   1933 *Myths and Legends of the Bantu.* London, George G. Harrap.
Work Projects Administration, South Carolina
   1941 *South Carolina Folk Tales.* Compiled by Workers of the Writers' Program of
      the Works Projects Administration in the State of South Carolina. Bulletin of
      University of South Carolina.

N I N E

＊

Moon Splits Hare's Lip (Nose)

The most common African myth about the origin of death is referred to by Hans Abrahamsson in his classic study[1] as "The Message that Failed." There are two principal variants that may be told separately or be combined in the same narrative. In one a slow messenger is sent, usually by God, to tell men that when they die they will return to life, but a faster messenger is sent to tell them that when they die, they will remain dead because God has changed his mind. In the other version the message is falsified or perverted by the messenger or by the faster messenger if there are two.

Among the Hausa, the Bushmen, and the Hottentots the second version takes a distinctive form. Moon sends the message to men that as she "dies" and lives again so they will die and live again, but the message is perverted by Hare and death comes to the world. Also there is often a sequel. When Moon learns that Hare has told men that they will not revive after death, she strikes him, splitting his lip, mouth, or nose, causing his harelip; and in some versions Hare scratches, bites, or burns Moon's face, causing the dark spots that we see on the face of the moon.

One of the Uncle Remus tales, "The Rabbit and the Moon" or "Brer Rabbit Has Trouble with the Moon" [1] is a variant of this myth. The major difference is that Moon's message is garbled; it is not clearly the message about death, although there is the statement that "when Moon dies her feet get cold." The message is sent to Man by Moon; it is perverted by Rabbit; Moon splits Rabbit's lip; and Rabbit claws Moon's face, causing the dark streaks on the moon.

The Chitimacha Indian version from Louisiana [2] differs in that God, not Moon, sends the message and that Rabbit splits his own lip when he stumbles and falls, rather than being struck by God or by Moon. It also differs from the first pattern described in that, although God changed his mind, Rabbit is the only messenger. Nevertheless, it concerns the origin of death, as do all of the African versions cited.

Reprinted from *Research in African Literatures*, 12 (1981), 338–49.

This narrative may have become a folktale in Georgia, but it is clearly a myth in Africa and Swanton considers his Chitimacha Indian version to be a myth.[2] For this reason I am not including it in my series of articles on "African Folktales in America,"[3] but it is certainly relevant to the question of African contributions to the folklore of the United States.

It is always Hare, or Rabbit in the United States, who perverts the message. As in the United States, Hare or Rabbit is usually the only messenger, but in some versions he replaces a slow or forgetful messenger: Chameleon [4, 27–28], Tortoise [5, 7], Insect [20], Louse [22–25, 29], or Crocodile [26]. In some African versions there is no perverted message; Hare, again, simply contradicts Moon, saying that men will not return to life [8–10, 12, 16–17, 30]. Usually Moon splits Hare's lip, but in three Bushman tales [4–5, 7] a man does so, in another [17] an unidentified character bloodies Hare's head, and in the Chitimacha tale [2] Hare falls and splits his own nose. There is no mention of Hare being hit in two of the African narratives cited here [9, 18], but they are obviously related to the others. The sex of both Moon and Hare varies from one area to another.

The African versions closest to the Uncle Remus tale [1] come from the Hausa of Nigeria [3] and the Hottentots of South Africa [21]. Indeed, the differences between these three versions are less than the differences between the Bushman versions [4–17] or between the Hottentot versions [18–33]. Based on my findings to date, the African distribution of this myth is curious, to say the least.[4]

There are no references to this tale type in Aarne and Thompson's *The Types of the Folktale*, but the following three entries in Thompson's *Motif-Index of Folk-Literature* are relevant:

> A2216.3 *Moon splits hare's lip with hatchet; hence hare-lip.* (Cf. A2211.2, A751.5.1, A2342.1)—Hottentot: Bleek 72 No. 33.
> A751.5.1 *Man in the moon; moon's face scratched by hare* in retaliation for injury to hare. (Cf. A2216.3.)—Hottentot: Bleek 72 No. 33.
> A2234.4 *Hare weeps for mother when forbidden: moon hits him and cleaves lip.* (Cf. A2211.2, A2231.8, A2342.1.)—Bushman: Bleek and Lloyd 69.[5]

No sources from Europe or India are cited. Since the only references are to the Bushmen [16] and the Hottentots [21], I conclude that this narrative came to the United States from Africa.

Neither *Mr. Rabbit at Home* nor *Uncle Remus and the Little Boy* is one of Joel Chandler Harris's best known books, but his Uncle Remus tales are certainly widely known. This African myth has been published at least eighty-five times in what appear to be thirty versions, beginning nearly a century and a half ago [18], and there are these three citations in the motif index. I find it surprising that up to now no folklorist, to my knowledge, has recognized the African origin of this narrative.

1. (Georgia) Moon told Rabbit that it wanted to send a message to man. It said that it had caught a bad cold and wanted to take a rest, but it wanted

to let Man know that it wouldn't be gone long. Rabbit offered to go and Moon gave him the message, "I am growing weak to gather strength; I go into the shadows to gather light." When Rabbit gave the message to Man he said, "I'm growing weak and have no strength; I'm going off where the shadows are dark." Man sent back word that "Seldom seen and soon forgot; when Moon dies her feet get cold." Rabbit took man's message back to Moon and it made Moon angry. It hit Rabbit in the face with a shovel and made Rabbit angry. Rabbit jumped at Moon and used his claws. The fight was a hard one and you can see the marks of it today. All rabbits have split upper lips and Moon still has marks on its face where Rabbit clawed it. (Joel Chandler Harris, *Mr. Rabbit at Home,* Boston and New York: Houghton, Mifflin and Company, 1895, no. 17; retold in *Uncle Remus and the Little Boy,* Boston: Small, Maynard & Company, 1910, no. 2; and *The Complete Tales of Uncle Remus,* compiled by Richard Chase, Boston: Houghton Mifflin Company, 1955, pp. 750–53)

2. (Louisiana: Chitimacha Indians) "Anciently there was no death in the world; but finally a man fell sick, and the people sent Rabbit to God to inquire whether he would die. God said, 'No, he will not die, he will get well.' Rabbit started back with this answer; but in his haste he stumbled and fell on his face, and in doing so split his nose in the manner in which it is seen to this day. And unfortunately this caused him to forget the message he had received, so he retraced his steps and asked the question over again. This time, however, God was angry at being disturbed a second time, and he said, 'Tell them he will have to die.' Since then there has been death on earth." (John R. Swanton, "Some Chitimacha Myths and Beliefs," *Journal of American Folk-Lore,* Vol. 30, 1917, p. 476)

3. (Nigeria: Hausa) Moon sent Hare to tell men, "Moon dies and becomes alive again, so will you die and come to life again." Hare went to men and told them, "Moon dies and comes to life again, so will you die." Hare returned to Moon and told him what he had said to men. Moon was very angry and tried to split Hare's head with an ax but only struck his upper lip which until today bears the mark of their fight. Hare sprang at Moon's face and scratched it with his sharp claws. Since then one sees black stripes on the face of the moon, which are nothing other than the scars where Hare scratched. (T. von Held, *Märchen und Sagen der afrikanischen Neger,* Jena: H. W. Schmidt, 1904, p. 152; Hans Abrahamsson, "The Origin of Death: Studies in African Mythology," *Studia Ethnographica Upsaliensia* 3, 1951, pp. 7–8)

4. (Botswana: Bushman) God sent Chameleon to men with this message, "You will all die, but you will rise again." Chameleon was slow and forgot the message. He turned back to God and asked about it. God was angry and told Hare to take the message. Hare also forgot it and told men, "You will all die, but you will die forever." The men were angry and one struck Hare with a stone, splitting her lip; so Hare always has a cleft lip. (S. S. Dornan, "The Tati Bushmen (Masarwas) and their Language," *Journal of the Royal Anthropological Institue,* Vol. 47, 1917, p. 77; Abrahamsson 1951, p. 30)

5. (Botswana: Bushman) Moon sent Tortoise to men with the message, "As

I dying live again, so you dying will live again." Tortoise was very slow and kept repeating the message to himself so as not to forget it, but he did forget it and turned back to ask Moon to repeat it. Moon was very angry and she called Hare to deliver the message. In her great haste Hare also forgot the message, but she did not want Moon to know. She went on and told men, "As I dying live again, so you dying will die forever." Meanwhile Tortoise remembered the message and delivered it to men. When the men heard Tortoise's message they were very angry with Hare. One of them threw a stone at Hare, striking her on the mouth. It cleft her upper lip, and that is why every hare has a cleft upper lip. (Dornan 1917, p. 80; Abrahamsson 1951, p. 30)

6. (Botswana: Bushman) Hare was lying dead and Moon struck her son in the mouth with his fist, telling him to cry loudly as his mother was quite dead and would never return to life again as Moon herself does. Owing to Moon's blow, Hare has a cleft lip. (S. S. Dornan, "The Heavenly Bodies in South African Mythology," *The South African Journal of Science,* Vol. 18, 1921, p. 431; S. S. Dornan, *Pygmies & Bushmen of the Kalahari,* London: Seeley, Service & Co., 1925, p. 165; Abrahamsson 1951, p. 31, note 3)

7. (Botswana: Bushman) Moon sent Tortoise to men with the message, "As I dying am restored to life, so you dying will be restored to life." Tortoise went off repeating the message to himself so as not to forget it, but he was so slow that he forgot it. He returned to Moon to ask her again, but she was so angry that she called Hare and told her to take the message. Hare ran off, but on the way she stopped to eat and forgot the message. She told men that Moon's message was, "You will die, but you will die forever." Just then Tortoise arrived and gave the message correctly, and Hare and Tortoise began to fight. The men were so angry with Hare that one of them flung a stone at her. It struck Hare on the mouth and split her lip. So every hare has a cleft lip today, and all men have died ever since. (Dornan 1925, p. 172; Abrahamsson 1951, p. 30)

8. (Botswana: Bushman) Hare singed her hide garment in the fire and threw it at Moon's face. Moon said, "Men shall not die," but Hare said, "Men shall die." Moon took an ax and split Hare's mouth. (D. F. Bleek, *The Naron. A Bushman Tribe of the Central Kalahari,* Cape Town. Publications of the School of African Life and Language, University of Cambridge: University Press, 1928, p. 44; Abrahamsson 1951, pp. 31–32)

9. (Botswana: Bushman) Hare singed her hide garment in the fire and threw it at Moon's face. Moon's face was burned and is black from the garment. Hare said, "The man who marries many women shall be killed." Moon contradicted, "The man shall not die." (D. F. Bleek 1928, pp. 44–45, Abrahamsson 1951, p. 32)

10. (Botswana: Bushman) Hare threw her hide garment at Moon and burned his face. Hare said, "People shall die," but Moon said, "People shall live." Then Moon took an ax and split Hare's mouth. Hare singed her garment in the fire and threw it at Moon's face. Other episodes follow. (D. F. Bleek 1928, pp. 45–46; Abrahamsson 1951, p. 32)

11. (South Africa: Bushman) Moon struck Hare on the mouth with his fist, telling him to weep loudly for his dead mother because she would not return as Moon does but was quite dead. (W. H. I. Bleek, *A Brief Account of Bushman Folk-Lore and Other Texts,* London: Trübner & Co., 1875, p. 9; Abrahamsson 1951, p. 31)

12. (South Africa: Bushman) Moon told Hare that his mother would come back to life, so that he need not weep. But Hare did not believe Moon and continued to weep, saying that Moon was deceiving him. Moon became angry and threatened to beat Hare on the mouth. (W. H. I. Bleek 1875, p. 9; Abrahamsson 1951, p. 31)

13. (South Africa: Bushman) Moon sent Hare to mankind with the message of renewal of life, but Hare perverted it into a message of death. Moon heated a stone and burned Hare's mouth, causing the harelip. (W. H. I. Bleek 1875, p. 10; Abrahamsson 1951 p. 31)

14. (South Africa: Bushman) Hare perverted the message to men, causing Moon's mother to die. Moon split Hare's lip with a stick. (W. H. I. Bleek 1875, p. 10; Abrahamsson 1951, p. 31)

15. (South Africa: Bushman) Hare announced the death of Moon's mother causing Moon's wrath, etc. [as above]. (W. H. I. Bleek 1875, p. 10; Abrahamsson 1951, p. 31)

16. (South Africa: Bushman) Hare, who was then a human being, was weeping for his dead mother. Moon told him not weep because she would come back to life just as Moon himself did. Hare contradicted Moon, saying that his mother was completely dead. At this Moon became angry and hit Hare with his fist and clove his mouth, saying it would always be like that. Moon condemned Hare to be infested with vermin and killed by dogs and said, "You people, you shall die and vanish away. When I am dead, I return to life, and I had intended that men should resemble me. But Hare said that his mother was not just sleeping and that made me angry." It is because of Hare that we people die. (W. H. I. Bleek and L. C. Lloyd, *Specimens of Bushman Folklore,* London: George Allen & Company, 1911, pp. 56–65; Dorothea F. Bleek, "Bushman Folklore," *Africa,* Vol. 2, 1929, p. 305; I. Schapera, *The Khoisan Peoples of South Africa,* London: George Routledge & Sons, 1930, p. 160; Herman Baumann, *Schöpfung und Urzeit des Menschen im Mythus der Afrikanischen Völker,* Berlin: Verlag von Dietrich Reimer, 1936, pp. 276–77; W. H. I. Bleek and Lucy C. Lloyd, *Das wahre Geschichte des Buschmannes in seinem Mythen und Märchen,* Basel: Kommissionsverlag Zbinden & Hügin, 1938, pp. 29–32; Abrahamsson 1951, pp. 30–31; Geoffrey Parrinder, *African Mythology,* London: Paul Hamlyn, 1967, p. 67)

17. (Namibia: Bushman) Moon said that Bushmen should return like himself and not die outright. Hare objected saying, "No. The dead Bushman's wind smells bad," but Moon told Hare that Bushmen would return and not die outright. Hare said, "When you die, you do not smell bad. I will not listen to you," and he threw the dead Bushmen away. Hare cast his divining pieces and they said, "When Bushmen are a little ill they shall arise." Moon said to

Hare, "Your dead child shall return. It shall not die outright," but Hare said, "My son's wind smells bad," and threw his son away. And /xue laughed at Hare and beat Hare's head with a stick. Blood flowed and other episodes follow in this repetitive story, "as endless as the phases of the moon." (D. F. Bleek, "Kung Mythology," *Zeitschrift für Eingeborenen-Sprachen*, Vol. 35, 1934–1935, pp. 271–81; Abrahamsson 1951, p. 32)

18. (South Africa: Hottentot) Moon sent Hare to tell men, "As I die and am renewed, so shall you also be renewed." Hare deceived men saying, "As I die and perish, so shall you also perish." (James Edward Alexander, *An Expedition of Discovery into the Interior of Africa*, London: Henry Colburn, Vol. 1, 1838, p. 169; W. H. I. Bleek, *Reynard the Fox in South Africa*, London: Trübner & Co., 1864, p. 73; W. H. I. Bleek, *Reineke Fuchs in Afrika*, Weimar: Böhlau, 1870, pp. 56–57; Theophilus Hahn, *Tsuni-//Goam. The Supreme Being of the Khoi-Khoi*, London: Trübner, 1881, p. 52; James Honeÿ, *South-African Folk-Tales* [1910] New York: Negro Universities Press, 1969, p. 146; Abrahamsson 1951, p. 29)

19. (South Africa: Hottentot) Moon sent Hare to tell men, "As I die and rise to life again, so you also shall die and rise to life again." Hare went to men and said, "As I die and do not rise to life again, so you also shall die and not rise to life again." When Hare told Moon what he had said, she took a stick and in anger beat Hare on his mouth, slitting it. Hare fled. (H. C. Knudsen, *Grossnamaqualand*, Barmen, 1848, pp. 27–28; W. H. I. Bleek 1864, p. 71 and 1870, p. 55; René Basset, "Contes Populaires d'Afrique," *Les Littératures Populaires de Toutes les Nations*, Vol. 47, c. 1903, pp. 225–26; Baumann 1936, p. 276; Honeÿ [1910] 1969, p. 143)

20. (South Africa: Hottentot) Moon sent Insect to tell men, "As I die and dying live, so you shall die and dying live." On the way Insect was overtaken by Hare who asked where he was going. When Insect told him Hare said that he would take the message because Insect was an awkward runner. When Hare reached men he told them that Moon's message was, "As I die and dying perish, so you shall die and come wholly to an end." Hare returned to Moon and told her what he had said. Moon was angry and struck Hare on the nose with a piece of wood. Since that day Hare's nose is slit. (W. H. I. Bleek 1864, pp. 69–70; Theophilus Hahn, "Die Nama-Hottentoten," *Globus*, Vol. 12, 1867, p. 242; Theophilus Hahn, "Beiträge zur Kunde der Hottentotten," Verein für Erdkunde (Dresden), *Jahresberichte* Nos. 6–7, 1869, pp. 61–62; W. H. I. Bleek 1870, p. 54; A. Seidel, *Das Geistesleben der afrikanischen Negervölker*, Berlin: Alfred Schall, n.d., c. 1896, pp. 145–46; A. Seidel, *Geschichten und Lieder der Afrikaner*, n.d., pp. 145–46; T. v. Held 1904, pp. 95–96; Honeÿ [1910] 1969, pp. 141–42; Carl Seyffert, "Totengebräuche und Todesvorstellung bei den zentralafrikanischen Pygmäen, den Buschmännern und Hottentotten," *Archiv für Anthropologie*, Vol. 40 (N.S. Vol. 12), 1913, p. 206; Abrahamsson 1951, p. 28; Paul Radin and James Johnson Sweeney, *African Folktales & Sculpture*, New York: Bollingen Foundation, 1952, p. 63; L. Hughes, *An African Treasury of Stories, Poems, Essays and Articles by Black Africans*. New York: Crown

Publishers, 1960, p. 80; Harold Courlander, *The King's Drum and Other African Stories*, London: Rupert Hart-Davis, 1963, pp. 106–08; Susan Feldman, *African Myths and Tales*, New York: Dell Publishing Co., 1963, p. 107; Parrinder 1967, p. 67; Margaret Carey, *Myths and Legends of Africa*, London: Hamlyn Publishing Group, 1970, pp. 8–9; Paul Radin, *African Folktales*, Princeton: Princeton University Press, 1970, p. 63; Harold Courlander, *A Treasury of African Folklore*, New York: Crown Publishers, 1975, p. 499; Harold Courlander, *A Treasury of Afro-American Folklore*, New York: Crown Publishers, 1976, p. 585)

21. (South Africa: Hottentot) Moon sent Hare to inform men that as she died and rose again, so they should die and rise again. Out of either forgetfulness or malice, Hare told them that as Moon rose and died away, so they should die and rise no more. Hare returned to Moon and reported what he had said. Moon was so enraged that she took a hatchet to split his head, but the blow fell short and struck Hare's lip, cutting it severely. Hence it is that we see the "harelip." In retaliation Hare raised his claws and scratched Moon's face. The dark spots we now see on the surface of the moon are the scars that Moon received from Hare. (W. H. I. Bleek 1864, p. 72 and 1870, pp. 55–56; Edward B. Tylor, *Primitive Culture* [1871], London: John Murray, 2nd ed., Vol. 1, 1873, p. 355; O. Colson, "Ce qu'on voit dans la Lune," *Wallonia*, Vol. 1, 1893, p. 164; Honeÿ [1910] 1969, pp. 144–45)

22. (South Africa: Hottentot) Moon sent Louse to tell Men, "I die, and dead live on. You also will die and yet continue on." On the way Louse met Hare who asked where he was going. When Louse told him, Hare said that Louse walked clumsily and that he himself would go. Hare ran to Men and told them that Moon had said, "I die and dying perish; and you likewise will die and be put in the ground." Hare went back and told Moon what he had done. In anger Moon hit Hare on the nose with a stick. Since that time Hare's nose has been split. (Theophilus Hahn, *Die Sprache der Nama*, Leipzig: Johann Ambrosius Barth, 1870, pp. 57, 59; Friedrich Müller, *Grundiss der Sprachwissenschaft*, Vienna: Alfred Hölder, Vol. 1, Part 2, 1876, pp. 21–22; René Basset, c. 1903, pp. 229–30; I. Schapera, *The Khoisan Peoples of South Africa*, London: George Routledge & Sons, 1930, p. 357)

23. (South Africa: Hottentot) Moon sent Louse to Men to say, "As I die and dying live, so you also will die and dying live." But Hare, who met the messenger and took the message, told Men that Moon said, "As I die and dying perish, so you also will die and come to an end." When Hare told Moon the message he had delivered, Moon was angry and struck him on the mouth with a stick so that his upper lip was split. Hare fought back and scratched Moon's face with his paws, causing the dark spots as marks that remain until today. Hare, who still has a split lip, was hated by Men and they refused to eat his flesh. (Gustav Fritsch, *Die Eingeborenen Süd-Afrika's*, Breslau: Ferdinand Hirt, 1872, pp. 354–55)

24. (South Africa: Hottentot) Moon sent Louse to men with the message, "I die and come back from death; in the same way you will die and come

back from death." On the way Louse met Hare who asked what he was looking for, and Hare told him of Moon's message to men. Hare said that Louse went very haltingly and that he would take the message himself. Hare ran to men and told them that Moon's message was, "I die and remain dead; in the same way you will die and remain dead." Hare went back to Moon and told her what he had said. Angrily Moon took a stick and hit Hare on the nose. From that day on, his nose is split. (W. Planert, "Über die Sprachen der Hottentotten und Buschmänner," *Mitteilungen des Seminars für Orientalische Sprachen zu Berlin*, Vol. 8, Part 3, 1905, pp. 164–66)

25. (South Africa: Hottentot) Moon sent Louse to tell Men, "I die and still exist; so you also will die and continue on." On his way Louse met Hare who asked where he was going. Louse told him of Moon's message, and Hare said he would go because Louse was lame. Hare went to Men and told them that Moon's message was, "I die and become hollow-eyed; so you will also die and become hollow-eyed." Hare returned and told Moon what he had said. Moon was angry and struck Hare on the nose with a stick. From that day on Hare's nose is split. (Karl Meinhof, "Lehrbuch der Nama-Sprache," *Lehrbücher des Seminars für Orientalische Sprachen zu Berlin*, Vol. 23, 1909, pp. 170–71)

26. (South Africa: Hottentot) Long ago Lady Moon wanted to send a message to Men, but one creature after another refused. At last she called Crocodile, although he was very slow and not much good. She told Crocodile to tell Men, "As I die and dying live, so you shall die and dying live." Crocodile started off and met Hare, who asked where he was going. Crocodile told him Moon's message, and Hare said that Crocodile was too slow and that he would take it for him. Crocodile made Hare repeat the message and get it right, but when he reached Men Hare told them that it was, "As I die and dying perish, so you also shall die and come wholly to an end." The Men looked at each other in fright and Hare danced away, laughing at how he had cheated them. When he returned, Moon asked him what he had said to Men, and Hare told her. Moon was angry and took a club to Hare, but he ducked and it caught him only on the nose. Hare screamed and jumped at Moon with his four feet, scratching, kicking, and clawing Moon's face. That is why Hare goes about today with a split nose and why Moon's face has long dark scars. (Sanni Metelerkamp, "South African Folk-Lore Stories: As Told by Outa Karel," *The State*, Vol. 6, 1911, pp. 397–400; Sanni Metelerkamp, *Outa Karel's Stories. South African Folk-Lore Tales*, London: Macmillan and Co., 1914, pp. 70–77)

27. (South Africa: Hottentot) Moon sent Chameleon to Men with this message, "Oh Men, as I die and am renewed again, so you will die and be renewed again." Chameleon was slow and as he went he forgot the message. He returned to have Moon repeat it, but Moon was angry and called Hare, telling her, "You are a quick runner. Take this message to Men, 'Oh Men, as I die and am renewed again, so you will die and be renewed.'" Hare ran off, but she also forgot the message and said, "Oh Men, as I die and am not renewed, so you will die forever." When she returned, Moon questioned her about the

message she had delivered. When Moon heard what Hare had said, she seized a stick and struck Hare on the mouth, splitting her lip. And so every hare has a cleft lip to this day, and that is how death came into the world. (Dornan 1921, p. 433; Abrahamsson 1951, p. 28)

28. (South Africa: Hottentot) Moon sent Chameleon with the message, but Chameleon forgot it and turned back to get it. Moon was annoyed and called Hare who rushed off and also forgot it. Instead of turning back to get the correct version, Hare delivered it wrongly and death came into the world. In revenge Moon picked up a stone and split Hare's lip. (Dornan 1925, p. 215)

29. (South Africa: Hottentot) Moon said, "Men must die as I die," but Hare said, "They must die and die altogether." Moon struck Hare on the mouth, splitting it. Hare said to Moon, "You must become the shoulder-blade of a bush pig and ascend, sit in heaven, and light up the world." (L. F. Maingard, *Korana Folktales, Texts and Grammar,* Johannesburg: Witwatersrand University Press, 1962, p. 47)

30. (South Africa: Hottentot) Moon sent Hare to give mankind a message that Man would die and rise again as does the moon. Hare said to Man that he would die and never rise again. Hearing this, Moon was angry and struck Hare on the mouth, splitting it, hence, the "harelip." (Maingard 1962, pp. 47–48)

31. (Namibia: Hottentot) Moon commanded Hare to convey this message to Man, "As I die and am born again, so you shall die and be live again." Hare hastened to obey, but instead of saying, "As I die and am born again," he said, "As I die and am *not* born again." On his return Moon asked Hare what he had said. When Moon heard, he hurled a stick at Hare with such force that it split open his lips, giving him his peculiar mouth. Hare fled. (Charles John Andersson, *Lake Ngami,* London: Hurst and Blackett, 1856, p. 328; Anonymous, "Des schwedischen Reisenden Andersson Abenteuer unter den Damaras und Namaquas in Südwestafrika," *Globus,* Vol. 6, 1865, p. 349)

32. (Namibia: Hottentot) Moon sent Hare to announce to Men that they would do as he did—fade away and reappear. Hare told them this but they asked, "What are you saying?" Then Hare said, "As I do, so you will die goggle-eyed." Hare returned to Moon who asked him about the message; but Hare was silent, knowing that he had lied. Then Moon struck Hare on the mouth. [Since then Hare has had a harelip.] (Leonhard Schultze, *Aus Namaland und Kalahari,* Jena: Gustav Fischer, 1907, pp. 448–49)

N O T E S

1. Hans Abrahamsson, "The Origin of Death. Studies in African Mythology," *Studia Ethnographica Upsaliensia,* Vol. 3, 1951, pp. 4–34. Many of the African myths summarized here are also summarized by Abrahamsson.

2. In his introductory note (p. 474) Swanton says that during a recent visit, "I obtained fragments of a few myths. . . . The European connection of some, if not all, of them is apparent." For this one, however, he cites only Schultze [33], Bleek [20], and Dähnhardt III 1910, p. 22. Aside from one reference that I have not yet been able to check (Wood I, p. 322) Dähnhardt cites only one Canadian and eleven African sources, several of which are not relevant to "Moon Splits Hare's Lip (Nose)."

3. William Bascom, "African Folktales in America," *Research in African Literatures,* Vol. 8, 1977, pp. 266–91; Vol. 9, 1978, pp. 216–55; Vol. 10, 1979, pp. 59–74, 323–49; Vol. 11, 1980, pp. 175–86, 479–510. Another of Swanton's five Chitimacha "myths" is a version of "Trickster Seeks Endowments," a folktale which also must have come from Africa as I have already shown in this series.

4. I have some doubts about the source of the "Hausa" myth, not having yet found any homologues in the extensive literature on Hausa folklore. Abrahamsson, however, accepts it as a Hausa narrative.

5. Motif "A2211.2. *Rabbit laughs; cause of hare-lip*" and motif "A2231.8. *Toad refuses to weep over its dead children: dries up when dead. Cursed by Virgin Mary*" are not relevant. Motif "A2342.1. *Why hare's lip is split*" is too general, but Swanton's Chitimacha version [2] is cited.

T E N

✳

Dogs Rescue Master in Tree Refuge

Although the cannibal sister is lacking in this folktale, there is a relevant entry in the Aarne-Thompson tale type index. It is part IV of Type 315A, which reads as follows:

315A *The Cannibal Sister.*

I. *A Princess Becomes a Cannibalistic Ogress* and devours the animals, then the people at the court, and finally all the inhabitants of the city [G30, G346]. Her brother alone escapes.

II. *The Captive Brother.* (a) The brother returns to the city and is captured by his sister. (b) He gains a respite by sending her to sharpen her teeth or the like [K550]. (c) A helpful animal takes his place or warns him [B521].

III. *Magic Flight.* He flees, throwing behind him magic obstacles.

IV. *Escape on the Tree.* He climbs a tree but the sister gnaws it down. He escapes to another tree [R521]. (b) He calls his dogs who have been imprisoned. They break loose and kill the sister [B524.1.2].

India 5.

The most relevant motif is B524.1.3, "Dogs rescue fleeing master from tree refuge," from which my title is adapted. No Indian sources are cited for this motif, but references to India are irrelevant here since I am not concerned with ultimate origins. What is significant is that no European sources are cited in either the tale type or the motif index. For this reason I would usually have quickly concluded that the tale could not have come from Europe but came to the New World from Africa.

Both Boas and Parsons, however, cite two tales from Extremadura, Spain, in this connection.[1] Nevertheless Parsons says, "'Escape up the Tree' is a European tale brought over long since by immigrants from the west coast of Africa."[2] Dorson cites this statement without comment and apparently with approval[3] and thus seems to agree that his version [66] came to Michigan by way of Africa, not Europe.

Reprinted from *Research in African Literatures,* 12 (1981), 460–519.

In her comparative study of "Die Flucht auf dem Baum," Parsons again says, "The tale was brought by Spaniards and Portuguese to Africa," and "From Africa the story was brought to America by Negroes."[4] She also says, "Except for these Spanish tales I know of no other European variants; but it is highly probable that they occur."[5] Yet she does not cite any in her subsequent publications and Thompson found none.

One of these two Spanish tales can easily be dismissed because it is a different tale type, "The Dragon Slayer," AT300. A boy angered his mother by trading their three cows for three dogs named Sun, Moon, and Star. He left home and went to Madrid where he rescued a princess who was being sacrificed to a seven-headed serpent. He called his dogs who killed the serpent and then he cut out its seven tongues. An imposter cut off the serpent's seven heads and claimed that he had killed it and had the right to marry the princess; but the boy exposed him by producing the tongues as evidence and the boy and the princess were married.[6]

The other Spanish tale consists of two parts, the second of which is also "The Dragon Slayer" with three dogs killing a seven-headed serpent, the imposter cutting off its seven heads, and his exposure by the hero who produces the seven tongues. The first part, however, fits the pattern of "Dogs Resuce Master in Tree Refuge" and is included here [1]. Nevertheless this is the only known European version, whereas there are many from West Africa and many other parts of the African continent. Moreover, southern Spain, where this one European tale was recorded, was strongly influenced by Berbers and Arabs during the Moorish occupation; and a version from northern Algeria has been recorded among the Kabyle [2], an important Berber group. This suggests to me that regardless of its ultimate origin, "Dogs Rescue Master in Tree Refuge" is not a European tale brought to West Africa by the Spanish and Portuguese, but an African tale brought to Spain by the Berbers, but this is a side issue.

I should confess that in 1976 I stated that this would be the second article in this series,[7] so confident was I that it had spread from Africa to Spain. I decided, however, to wait until I had found a North African version, which I was convinced must exist. It was not until mid-1980 that I found one buried in the middle of a lengthy Kabyle narrative. Many Berber and Arabic folktales have not been translated, and I suspect that there may be other North African versions.

Andrade[8] has cited another Spanish folktale as an analogue of one of his tales from Dominican Republic. It consists of two parts, the second of which is again "The Dragon Slayer" with the rescue of a princess by a boy and his two dogs, the cutting out of the seven tongues of a serpent, and the exposure of an imposter who had presented the seven heads as evidence that he had killed the serpent. In the first part a one-eyed man, who had put a charm on a boy's sister, tried to poison him; but the boy was saved when his dogs defecated on the poisoned food. The boy was thrown into a room of poisoned spears but the dogs, named Break-Iron and Good-Winds, broke their chains and searched for him for thirty days above ground and underground. They saved him and he accused his sister. He told his dogs to kill her but the one-eyed man escaped to his underground home. The dogs chewed through seven iron doors and tore him apart.[9] This is a different tale and the tree refuge is lacking.

I have previously given an abbreviated analysis of twenty-six African versions of this tale type, but with only one text [34] and only page references to the others. I also cited the one Spanish version, four from Cape Verde Islanders, one from North Carolina, one from Georgia in the Uncle Remus tales, four from Bahamas, and two from Guyana [65, 112].[10] Dundes cites this study in suggesting that Dorson's tale entitled "Rangtang" [66] is African rather than European.[11]

Subsequently Dorson seems to have conceded that his tale is African, although he says only, "Very rarely does an African motif emerge in these nonanimal tales, such as in 'Talking Bones' [The Talking Skull Refuses to Talk] or, as Dundes points out, in 'Rang-tang' [Dogs Rescue Master in Tree Refuge]."[12]

The tree refuge and the rescue by the dogs form the core of this tale type, and I am considering only those folktales which include both. The many tales in which only one or the other is present are excluded because, even if they are historically related, they are different. My contention is that folktales in the New World are far more likely to have come from those that are the most similar, rather than from those that are different. It is also far more likely that either the tree refuge or the rescue by the dogs has been omitted or forgotten by some narrators than that it has been independently invented by over a hundred other narrators. The same argument holds for "Holding the Rock" [X, *Research in African Literatures* 11:4].

This is not really a tale about a flight or escape up the tree as Parsons called it, although the escape is present in many versions in both Africa and the New World [e.g., 11, 83, 86]. In many other versions the hero climbs the tree for nuts or fruit [e.g., 8, 69, 90] or does so for some other reason [e.g., 19, 80, 85]. Nevertheless, there is always a tree refuge, as Thompson aptly called it.

There are a number of recurrent motifs that may or may not be present, some of which deserve mention. Before leaving home the hero usually ties his dogs and they break their bonds when he calls to them [e.g., 5, 84, 93]. Sometimes he leaves behind a life token so that the dogs can be released when he is in danger; it is usually a liquid that turns red or turns to blood [e.g., 21, 83, 93].

He may produce the tree (or trees) magically [e.g., 3, 74, 96] and his attackers try to uproot it, gnaw it down with their teeth, or chop it down, often with axes produced magically. Magically he restores the tree to its original condition or makes it grow larger [e.g., 18, 68, 110], or, as successive trees are felled, he climbs or jumps into another tree [e.g., 37, 74, 88].

He calls to his dogs from his tree refuge, often by name. The names are unusual, to say the least, and sometimes they refer to the way in which the attackers are killed. Thus we have "Cut to Pieces, Swallow up, and Clear the Remains" from Nigeria [31], "Cut throat, Crack bone, and Drag it away" from South Carolina [82], and "Cut-Throat, Chew-Fine, and Suck-Blood" from Bahamas [87].

In both Africa and the New World a hunter marries an animal that has turned into a beautiful woman and he is attacked because he has killed many animals [e.g., 10, 84, 112]. In African versions the animal-wife may first demand to eat his dogs, but their bones are saved and the dogs revive in time to rescue him [e.g., 9]. The introductions of these tales are indeed varied, although some are fairly straightforward [e.g., 5]. Although often combined with other motifs and episodes this tale type does occur by itself [e.g., 19].

Two curious parallels have been recorded among the Shushwap and Thompson River Indians of British Columbia [60, 61]. In this connection Boas says,

> It seems rather remarkable that among the Indians of the Western plateaus apparently certain tales of European origin play an important part in their folklore . . . I am very much inclined to look for the origin of the Western group of tales in Spanish folk-lore. It is worth mentioning in this connection that the so-called 'Mexicans' (that is, Spanish-speaking half-bloods) still live as far north as British Columbia, and that the vocabulary of the Western plateaus relating to the horse contains a considerable number of Spanish expressions.[13]

I have yet to find a version from Mexico, while the American ones I have found are concentrated in South Carolina and the Antilles.

Perhaps this is an independent invention, or perhaps the tale, known in India, according to Aarne and Thompson, reached North America by a different route, from Asia. In the Thompson River Indian tale the man's two dogs are Grizzly Bear and Rattlesnake. In the Shushwap tale his four dogs turn out to be Grizzly Bear, Rattlesnake, Timber Wolf, and Panther. In her comparative study Parsons cites two Yukaghir tales from Siberia recorded by Bogoras. In one a boy in a tree refuge called for his wife to send his dogs and she sent two wolves and two bears who rescued him. In the other, where the refuge is not a tree but a storehouse on stilts, a woman and her son are saved by a horse and a fox. This slim evidence is unconvincing. Animal names and characters are readily substituted, particularly where a borrowed tale is adapted to a new environment. Possibly additional evidence will answer the question of whether these two versions are related to Asian or to African sources or whether they are historically unrelated.

My fifty-eight African tales come from Algeria (Kabyle), Senegal (Wolof), Mali (Malinke and Bambara), Sierra Leone (Temne and Limba), Liberia (Gola), Ivory Coast (Wobe and Guro), Upper Volta (Mosi and Bobo), Ghana (Ashanti), Benin Republic (Fon), Nigeria (Hausa, Angas, Yoruba, Bini and Ekoi), Cameroun (Gbaya), Zaire (Kongo, Chowke, Luba, Kanyoka, and Lia), Sudan (Zande), Tanzania (Haya, Digo, and Nyiha), Malawi (Yao),

Mozambique (Ndau), Lesotho (Suto), South Africa (Sotho, Venda, Zulu, and Xhosa), and Namibia (Hottentot). Twenty-five tales come from British Columbia (Shushwap Indians and Thompson River Indians), New England (Cape Verde Islanders), New Jersey, Michigan, Kentucky, Missouri (French), Texas, Alabama (Negro and Creek Indians), District of Columbia, North Carolina, South Carolina, and Georgia. Thirty-two tales come from Bahamas, Jamaica, Haiti, Dominican Republic, Puerto Rico, Guadeloupe, Les Saintes, Dominica, Martinique, Grenada, Trinidad, Guyana, Suriname, Argentina, and Chile (Spanish and Araucanian Indians). One tale comes from Spain.

Additional African versions are cited by Tauxier [14], Guilhem [15], Macdonald [48], and Stannus [49].

1. (Extremadura, Spain) A boy who had three dogs named Iron, Lead and Steel, disapproved of the giant who courted his sister. Because the giant knew this, he said that the boy must be killed. He told the sister to take him into the garden, delouse him under an orange tree, and ask him to pick an orange for her. Although the brother objected to climbing so high, he did as she wished. The giant came and shook the tree, and the boy called his dogs by name. They came and tore at the giant and he fled. The boy scolded his sister, but she said that she had not seen the giant. Then the giant told the girl to poison the boy's food, which she did. He gave a little to his dogs, who barked and refused to eat; but a cat ate the food and died. He told his sister that he would not risk a third attempt on his life and left home. Another episode follows. (Hernández de Soto [1886], pp. 249–57; summarized in Parsons [1922], pp. 8–9)

2. (Algeria: Kabyle) A hunter had two greyhounds named Scraper and Digger and another dog named Breaker of Doors. After intervening episodes he left his dogs at home and came upon the house of an ogress. She wanted to eat him, but he persuaded her to wait until he was fatter. She went out to look for other food, leaving him enclosed in the courtyard. He climbed into a tree that grew in the courtyard, believing that ogresses did not climb trees. The ogress took an ax and began to chop the tree. When it was about to fall he said, "Let me call three times." She said he could call ten times, not just three. He called out, "Oh Scraper! Oh Digger! Oh Breaker of Doors! Where are you?" He called thus three times. The dogs, who were closed in his house, heard his cries and began to pull at their chains. The hunter's wife was about to release them when his mother told her not to; but when the mother went into her room the wife released the dogs and they ran like the wind. When they reached the house of the ogress, Breaker of Doors broke down the door to the courtyard. The dogs threw themselves at the ogress and ate her. They saw the hunter in the tree and, pushing against it, held it up until the hunter came down and went home. One day his mother put the head of a snake in his food and blamed his wife for his death. After he was buried his dogs dug up his grave and licked him until all the poison was removed. He went home with his dogs and told them to eat his mother. The

dogs threw themselves at her and tore her up, each taking a piece. He stayed with his wife and became sultan. (Lacoste, vol. I, [1965], pp. 72–87; I have not had access to Mouliéras' original publication)

3. (Senegal: Wolof) On his deathbed a hunter left his dog to his daughter, saying that it would defend her. When he died, the animals that he had hunted said they would take their vengeance on the girl. She was beautiful and did not lack suitors. Forgetting the words of her father, she went to accompany them a little way on their way home. The dog tried to stop her but failed; so it said, "I will guard the house. Call me if you are in difficulty. Here are three spools. Take them and throw them on the ground if you are in danger." When they were deep in the forest the suitors turned into beasts and the girl found herself surrounded by lions, panthers, and tigers. As they were going to throw themselves at her she threw down one of the spools and was lifted to the top of a large palm tree where she called to her dogs. The animals attacked the tree with their teeth and it fell. She threw the second spool and another tree raised her up. The animals knocked it down and she threw her last spool and was again raised to a treetop. As the third tree fell, the dog arrived and tore the animals to pieces. (Guillot [1933], pp. 66–67)

4. (Senegal: Wolof) After other episodes, the animals met to find a way to get rid of a hunter and his dogs, named Fidelity, Betray Me, Promise, and Moderation. The animals changed themselves into women dressed in beautiful clothes and covered with jewels and went to visit him. He was enraptured and ridiculed his mother when she said that one resembled an elephant and another a hind. The women refused all food except dog meat and, against his mother's advice, the hunter ordered that his dogs be killed; but his mother had their bones and blood collected. After expressing satisfaction with their meal the women said that they would return home and suggested that the hunter accompany them on the way. His mother told him to take his gun, but the women asked why he needed it to accompany women. He left it and his mother said that he should take his bow and arrows, but the women asked why he should be equipped for battle. He left them and his mother gave him palm nuts to throw on the ground if he were in danger and told him to call her. Accompanied by the hunter the women departed and after a while they left him, asking him to wait for them. When they were out of sight, they turned into animals again, with the hind in their midst. When the hunter saw them, he threw a palm nut on the ground and called his mother. A giant palm tree arose and he climbed it just as the animals arrived. The hind dug up an ax and gave it to the elephant who attacked the tree while the hind sang. When the tree began to crack, the hunter threw the second nut, again calling to his mother. A second palm tree, three times higher than the first, arose and he climbed it. The elephant attacked it and when it began to fall, the hunter called his dogs by name. They came out of the pots that contained their blood and bones. One took his master's gun, one took his powder, and another took his shot, and they followed his track. As the second tree was about to fall the hunter threw his last nut and climbed up the third palm

tree, seven times larger than the one that fell. As the third tree was about to fall, the hunter heard the voices of his dogs. When they came he fell into their midst, took his gun, and loaded it. The hind and the other animals fled into the forest. (Diop [1947], pp. 135–53; summarized in Paulme [1976], pp. 33–34)

5. (Sierra Leone: Temne) Despite a warning that the forest spirit would kill him, a man went to pick kola nuts from the spirit's kola tree. He left his two dogs, named Kinkoyanduri and Kero, behind tied to a post. When he climbed the tree, the forest spirit came. It began to chop the tree with its ax, saying that it would eat him. The man climbed to the top of the tree and called his dogs who broke the rope and came running. The earth that they threw behind them as they ran and the chips from the tree became the mountains that we see in the world. The dogs took the forest spirit and divided it in the middle. The man came down and gathered all the kola nuts. That is why kola nuts are scattered in the world today. (Thomas [1916], Part III, pp. 58–60)

6. (Sierra Leone: Limba) While still in the womb, a girl told her mother that she would chose her own husband, a man who had no blemish, and she repeated this when of age. An ugly monster who heard of this borrowed the garments of snakes so as to appear blemish-free. When the girl saw him she insisted on marrying him and the next day she went home with him. When he returned the borrowed snake skins, she saw how hideous he was. Her husband gave her a room that she could not leave. One day her younger brother went to visit her, taking with him his three dogs named Kondeng-mukure, Sosongpeng, and Salialoho, which means "Jumping Well." She told him about her husband, who was away hunting. When the monster returned, he smelled human flesh and that night tried to kill the boy, but his dogs protected him. The next morning the monster asked the boy to leave his dogs behind and go with him to pick kola nuts. The boy tied his dogs and went with him to the kola tree. The monster made the boy climb higher and higher and then said he would shoot the boy. The boy sang the names of his dogs and they broke their fastenings and came running. They fell on the monster, bit him open, tore up all his flesh, split him all up, and scattered all the bits. The boy picked kola nuts and wove baskets for the dogs to carry them, and went home with his sister. The moral is that a woman's marriage should be arranged by a man, even if he is her younger brother. (Finnegan [1967], pp. 117–24)

7. (Sierra Leone: Limba) A hunter owned three dogs named Denifela, Sangsangso, and Tungkangbai. He saw a beautiful girl who was really a spirit and wanted to marry her. She said that he must first visit her home. He gathered the bridewealth, took his gun, and went with her. She led him to a cave where she turned into a breeze, entered six doors to her house, and then returned to him as a woman. She asked him to leave his dogs and gun behind, but he refused. They passed through the six doors and the hunter found a new world where he was fed strange food. The girl said that he should go

with her to pick kola nuts but not to bring his dogs. She tied up his dogs and said that he should not bring his gun. They went to the kola tree and the hunter climbed it. She made him climb to the top and then said that she was a spirit and would kill him. He shouted the names of his dogs and they broke their chains and came running. They fell on the girl, bit her in pieces, chewed her all up, and scattered her all. He found gold in the house and took it and everything else home. (Finnegan [1967], pp. 143–46)

8. (Liberia: Gola) In a lengthy tale twins rescued their sister from a forest devil she had married. It turned into a beautiful maiden and came to visit them. When she left she asked one of the twins to accompany her to a kola tree laden with nuts and pick them for her. When the boy climbed the tree she turned into a forest devil again. It blew powder and told the tree to come down. The boy blew his powder and told the tree to rise up. The tree went up and down until the boy's powder was finished. The boy called his two dogs, named Gobla and Kaba, and they ran to him. Gobla tore the forest devil in two and devoured the upper part, and Kaba devoured the lower part. The boy picked kola nuts and went home. (Westermann, "Gola," [1921], pp. 96–102; translated in Westermann, "Kpelle," [1921], pp. 486–92)

9. (Mali: Malinke) Two wild buffaloes turned themselves into beautiful women and went to find a great hunter who had killed many buffaloes and antelopes. They told him they ate only dogs, so he killed two of his dogs, but his mother rubbed their bones together and many young dogs appeared. That night the hunter slept with the two women. The next morning, when they said they wanted to leave, his mother gave him magic powder. The hunter took his gun to accompany them, but they said, "You want to kill us. Leave the gun." He put it down and took his sword, but they said, "You want to kill us. Leave the sword." He did so and they left together. Twice the women told him to turn back but he continued with them. They came to a baobab tree and the women wanted its fruit. When he climbed up the tree the women turned back into buffaloes and called all the antelopes and buffaloes. They tried to knock down the tree and kill the hunter. He called to his mother and put some of the powder on a lizard and the tree was set upright. Three times the animals almost knocked the tree down, and three times it stood up again. Meanwhile his mother had released his dogs. They came and killed the animals. (Frobenius, "Dämonen," [1924], pp. 48–50)

10. (Mali: Bambara) A hunter killed almost all the animals and those remaining met to decide his fate. Saying that she would bring him to them, a female buffalo changed herself into a young woman and went to live with the hunter. He offered her beef, mutton, and other kinds of meat, but she said she only ate dogs. The hunter killed his dogs one by one and gave her the flesh to eat. His aunt, suspecting that this woman was not human, gathered all the bones and saved them. When all the dogs had been killed, the woman said she was going home. The hunter took his gun to accompany her, but she said, "Are you going to kill me? Is it necessary to carry a gun to accompany a woman?" He left his gun and took his sword, and she asked if he was going

to cut off her head. He left his sword and took his hatchet, but again she objected. He left everything except his small hunting whistle. When they were far from his home he said that he wanted to go back, but each time she said no. Later she excused herself, went into the forest, changed back into a buffalo, and called the other animals. They came running and the hunter climbed a tree. The animals began to cut down the tree, taking turns and singing. When it came to Hare's turn he sang, "Don't you have your whistle, you idiot?" Finally the hunter understood and blew his whistle, calling his dogs, named Danfi. His aunt put the dogs' bones in a pot of boiling water; the dogs came to life and ran to the tree. The hunter told them not to harm Hare but to seize the female buffalo without killing her. The pack of dogs threw themselves at the animals and killed all but these two. The hunter came down from the tree, reproached the buffalo, and killed her himself. (Travélé [1923], pp. 129–35)

11. (Ivory Coast: Wobe) A man continually mistreated both wild and domestic animals despite the advice of his fellow villagers who said that animals were the friends of man and could rescue him. He beat his two dogs who supplied him with game, but they remained faithful to him. Walking in the forest he met the spirits of animals who recognized their enemy and gave chase. The man fled and climbed a tree while the animals waited below. The man called to his dogs who were in the village and they came running. When the spirits had fled, the dogs said, "We are dogs but we know all that you say and do, and we understand the language of animals." This was the man's first conversation with animals, but he could not keep it secret and he died. (Girard [1967], p. 141)

12. (Ivory Coast: Wobe) A man married a woman who ate only dogs. She refused the game he brought home and ate all his hunting dogs, but his mother saved their bones. One day he went hunting and met devils who said that he was the hunter who killed the wild animals. They pursued him and he climbed up a tree while they waited below. The man called his largest dog, Touho, who had also been eaten, but its bones reassembled and it came to the tree. Touho fell on the child of one of the devils and the others fled. The man came down from the tree, took barking from the dog's throat, and put it in that of the little devil. The little devil ran after his parents, barking for them to wait. They replied, "We do not want a child who barks." The man returned home and repudiated his wife. (Girard [1967], pp. 141–42)

13. (Ivory Coast: Guro) Two youths own a dog. One said to the other, "When we eat we must not give our dog the bone, but throw it to the others." One youth went hunting and the beasts of the forest said, "Kill the hunter." They chased him and he climbed a tree. He cried out and the dog heard. It ra, threw itself against a beast, killed it, and the others fled. The young man came down from the tree and carried the dead beast back to the village. He cooked it and gave the liver and the bones to the dog. Since then one gives food to dogs and they attack the beasts of the forest. (Tauxier [1924], p. 307)

14. (Upper Volta: Mosi) A hunter killed a young buffalo in the forest. Its mother changed into a pretty young woman and married the hunter. She told

him that she didn't like dogs and he killed his hunting dogs. His mother warned him that his wife was a wild beast, but he did not believe her. His mother collected the bones of the dogs and put them in a pot. One day the hunter and his wife were walking in the forest. She asked him to climb a large tree and pick some leaves for her. While he was in the tree she changed back into a buffalo and called to all the wild animals to help her kill him. The man in the tree blew his whistle; his mother heard it and threw water into the pot and boiled the bones. The dogs came to life and the mother showed them the way her son had gone. The dogs ran to the tree and the animals fled. When the hunter returned home, his mother told him that she had warned him. (Tauxier [1917], pp. 474–75)

15. (Upper Volta: Bobo) With a charm given him by a forest spirit a man created havoc among the animals of the forest, and they met to discuss how to get rid of the dreadful hunter. A wild sow turned herself into a very beautiful young woman, went to town, and married the hunter. He offered her a dinner of chickens, goat, and sheep, but she refused them, asking him to cook his two dogs. He did so and his mother saved the bones. The wife asked the hunter to accompany her to her distant village. When he took his bow, arrow, and ax, she asked, "Why? Do you want to kill me?" He said he wanted to hunt on the way back, but she said it was their honeymoon. He put them down and took his club, but again she asked if he wanted to kill her. He said he only wanted to defend them, but she said she was afraid of armed men. He put down his club and took only a little knife in his pocket and his hunting whistle. When they reached the forest, she asked him to climb the highest tree for firewood. When he was in the treetop she resumed her animal form and called all the animals of the forest. They came and began to fell the tree, some using their claws. When the tree was about to fall, a lizard gave a magic cry and the tree stood upright again. The hunter blew his whistle and his mother heard it. She pronounced incantations on meal and scattered it on the dogs' bones. The dogs revived, ran to the forest, and threw themselves on the animals, saving their master. (Guilhem [n.d.], Vol. I, pp. 146–51)

16. (Ghana: Ashanti) A hunter had four dogs called Sniff-sniff, Lick-lick, Tie-in-knots, and Gulp-down. One day he told his wife that he had seen a kola tree laden with nuts. She told him to pick some because they had none to eat and none to sell. Leaving his dogs at home he climbed the tree and picked some of the kola nuts. Then he was confronted by a forest spirit who owned the tree and who said he would kill the hunter. The hunter called his dogs by name and the third time they came running. Sniff-sniff sniffed the forest spirit, Lick-lick licked him, Tie-in-knots tied his throat in knots, and Gulp-down gulped him down. They returned home, and another incident follows. (Rattray [1930], pp. 164–69)

17. (Benin: Fon) After other incidents a man went to find a lion tail for his mother's funeral. As he left he told his wife that if he did not return the next day she should open the calabash he had placed behind the house, and if the blood inside it was boiling she should give tortoise meat to his dogs and free

them. After an intervening episode the man was pursued by lions. He climbed a tree and the lions surrounded it. Three days passed before his wife remembered to open the calabash. The blood had boiled until it spilled on the ground. She gave tortoise meat to the dogs and released them. They raced to help their master in his distress. The lions had gone to work with their teeth and claws and were almost master of the situation when the dogs arrived. They were not ordinary dogs; they had been protected ritually and could attack the lions without fear. The fight lasted about three hours and not a single lion survived. The man owed his life to his dogs. (Quénum [1938], pp. 45–47)

18. (Benin: Fon) The chief hunter told the king that he could kill a large sea animal that no one had been able to kill. He killed the animal, but its wife escaped. He cut off the animal's tail and showed it to the king. On the fifth day the animal's wife, in the form of a beautiful girl, came to the king. He said he would marry her, but she said he must shoot a calabash off her head. He failed, many others tried and failed, but the chief hunter succeeded and brought her home. Her relatives came during the night but the hunter's dogs drove them away. On the fifth day she asked him what transformations he made when he was in danger, but his mother stopped him from telling all. The next day she asked him to go with her to find leaves and, coming to the tall tree whose leaves she wanted, he climbed to the top. His wife called her relatives to kill him and they began to chop down the tree. The hunter had seven magical calabashes and when the tree was about to fall he broke the first and the tree stood firm. Finally he had only one left, but his dogs at home awakened and ran to save their master. As he broke the last calabash the dogs arrived and drove the woman and the other monsters away. (Herskovits and Herskovits [1958], pp. 186–90)

19. (Benin: Fon) A hunter told his mother that if he was not back before noon she should look at his medicine, and if it had turned to blood she should release his dogs. He went and climbed a tree to watch for animals, not knowing that it was the tree of monsters. Twelve monsters came, threatened to kill him, and began to cut down the tree. The hunter had three magic gourds with which he restored the tree. When he dropped the last one his mother who had been asleep woke up and saw that the medicine was all red. She called his dogs to eat then sent them running to their master. As the tree was about to fall they began to devour the monsters. They killed twelve monsters but the hunter told them to spare the thirteenth [*sic*], who was pregnant and who had told the others to let the hunter live. Among the hunter's dogs were some who ate only blood; others ate nothing but bones; others ate nothing but flesh. One ate nothing but skin; one took what fell; one went only for the rescue; and one ate only eyes. After the dogs had eaten the dead monsters, the hunter came down from the tree and took the pregnant one home with him. (Herskovits and Herskovits [1958], pp. 240–41)

20. (Benin: Fon) A twin had medicine that turned the color of blood when he was in danger. Leaving his three dogs he went hunting, after telling his

mother that if she found blood in his medicine she should feed his dogs and they would come to search for him. In the forest he met monsters who chased him. He climbed a tree and they chopped at it. He had seven small calabashes that held magic powder. When he broke them the tree swelled and grew large again. A pregnant monster told the others to leave the hunter alone. Then his mother found that the medicine had turned to blood and fed the dogs. They ran to the hunter, jumped on the monsters, and ate them all except the pregnant one whom the hunter had told them to spare. (Herskovits and Herskovits [1958], pp. 271–72)

21. (Benin: Fon) A twin in the forest saw a thirty-horned giant whose body parts separated to eat then reunited, but he said he had seen nothing. A beautiful girl came to his village and said she would marry the man who shot and pierced a pea in a calabash on her head. Many tried and failed, but the twin succeeded and they went to his house. That night she changed into a giant and tried to swallow him, but his forty-one dogs stopped it. While hunting he found a beautiful tree that changed into a woman and became his second wife. When his first wife, whom he had told, called her a tree, she went back to the forest. He was given a drum and told never to play it in the forest. When he did so monsters came and he climbed a tree. They chopped it down, but he changed into a partridge and flew home. His wife asked him how he had escaped and what other transformations he could make, but his mother stopped him from telling all. His wife asked him to go with her to find leaves. He told his mother that she should look at his medicine and if the water had spilled on the ground, red like blood, she should feed his dogs and tell them to find their master. In the forest his wife pointed out a large tree and he climbed it. She called and more than a hundred monsters came and began to cut down the tree. His medicine became troubled but his mother was not at home. He called to his friend who saved him with his gun. His friend was killed and he went again with his wife to find leaves. When he was up in a large tree, the monsters came and began to chop it down. When it was about to fall, he broke the first of his seven magic gourds and the tree became whole again. When the last gourd had been broken and the tree fell, the man changed into an ant, then a mound of earth, a partridge, a river, sand, and finally back into human form. He ran and climbed another tree, the one who had been his wife, and each time that the monsters cut at it the cut closed up. Finally his mother who had been sleeping awoke and looked at his medicine, which spread like blood on the ground. She fed the forty-one dogs, of whom seven were chiefs. The stongest was called Loka and the others were called Loke, Loki, Wesi, Wesa, Gbwlo, and Gbwloke. The twin sang to them, calling their names. The dogs came and caught the monsters, tore them in two, and swallowed them. The twin went home and buried his friend and buried his own dogs with him, because his friend and his dogs were the only things that were dear to him. (Herskovits and Herskovits [1958], pp. 275–84)

22. (Benin: Fon) A twin saw a monster whose body parts separated when

it ate, but he said he had seen nothing. One of the monsters changed into a young girl and came to his village. She said she would marry the man who shot and split a grain of corn in a calabash on her head. Many tried and failed but the twin succeeded. One day his bride asked him to go with her for wood. He told his mother that he had medicine and that when she found blood she should feed his dogs. His wife took him to the place where he had seen the monster and told him to climb a tree. When he did so she called to the thirty-horned monsters who came and began to cut down the tree. He had two magic gourds, which he broke as the tree was about to fall and it stood erect again. A bird flew to the twin's mother who was sleeping and woke her. She saw that the medicine had turned to blood and fed the dogs. They ran to their master with the bird showing them the way. They ate up all the monsters except a pregnant one who had asked the others not to fell the tree. (Herskovits and Herskovits [1958], pp. 284–87)

23. (Nigeria: Hausa) A man tied his two dogs to his house and told his two wives that if either released them he would send her back home. He took his flute, his game bag, and his ax and went into the forest. A dragon came toward him and he climbed a large tree. He blew his flute and his dogs leapt and barked. One of his wives saw this and against the advice of the other released the dogs. They came to the dragon who was uprooting the tree. The large dog seized the monster and threw it down, and the other killed it. The man went home and asked who had released the dog. The second wife told him. He repudiated her and kept the wife who had released the dogs. Schön [1968], Appendix, pp. xx–xxi; [1877], Appendix, pp. xx–xxi; [1885–86], Part I, pp. 151–52; Schön and Robinson [1906], pp. 118–19; translated in Basset [1886–87], columns 225–26; [n.d.], pp. 53–55)

24. (Nigeria: Hausa) A man tied up his dogs and went into the forest, telling his two wives that if either released them he would beat her when he returned. He met a monster and climbed a tree. He blew on his flute and the dogs heard him and began to whine. The senior wife released them against the advice of her cowife and the dogs raced to the tree. The monster fled, but the dogs caught it and killed it on the spot. When the man returned home he asked who had released them. The second wife said that the senior wife had done so. The man beat her and gave his senior wife a present. (Tremearne [1913], pp. 298–99)

25. (Nigeria: Hausa) A young man who had been sent for fire saw a woman feeding her hundred mouths. As he left with the fire he shouted what he had seen. The woman turned into a beautiful woman and went to the young man's town. She said she would marry whomever could open her little basket. All tried, but only the young man was successful. After they were married she asked him to visit her parents. In the forest she turned into a hyena. The man turned into a ring which she threw into a tree, where he turned into a man again. She began to dig at the roots of the tree and he called to his three dogs, named Blood-Drinker, Slasher, and Cold-Wind. The man had two other wives and the one that he didn't like let the dogs loose. They came and Slasher

slaughtered the hyena, Blood-Drinker drank up her blood, and Cold-Wind blew the rest of the blood away. When he returned home the man asked who had released the dogs. The wife that he liked said, "That damned woman did." He said, "Damned woman yourself! Get out of my house," and he thanked the woman whom he had not liked. (Edgar [1911–13], vol. II, no. 3; translated in Skinner [1969–77], vol. II, pp. 76–78)

26. (Nigeria: Hausa) A man saw a woman feeding her thousand mouths and heard the song they were singing. He promised not to tell what he had seen and went home; but he kept singing the song and soon everyone was singing it and the woman heard of it. She turned into a beautiful maiden, found the man, and they were married. She asked him to visit her parents and told his sister to tie up his dogs. When they were far from his home, she turned back into a woman with a thousand mouths and he was up a tree like a flash. She took an ax and began chopping at the tree, but just as she had nearly chopped through it, it was suddenly back just as it had been. The man took a flute from his pocket and blew it calling his dogs, "Yauwwa, Yauwale, Yajin, Daure, Ka-Fi-Dukiya." The dogs began to jump up and down, getting very excited, and his sister released them. They ran off, and when the woman saw them, all but one of her mouths vanished and she told the man that she had only been joking. He didn't believe her and his dogs gobbled her up. The man found her house full of silver and took it home. (Edgar [1911–13], vol. III, no. 6; translated in Skinner [1969–77], vol. II, pp. 78–81)

27. (Nigeria: Hausa) A hunter caught in a storm entered the house of two witches and ate some of their porridge. They thought someone was in the hut but could not find him. He escaped and went home. One of the witches changed herself into a maiden and went to his town. She found him and they were married. After a while she proposed that they visit her home. He tied up his dogs and told his two other wives not to let them go. When they got to her home she turned back into a witch and called her fellow witch. The hunter took one of the seven blades of grass that he had in his pocket and threw it down. It turned into a tree and he climbed it. The two witches began chopping the tree down with axes, and just as it was going to fall he took another blade of grass and waved it. It turned into another tree and from it he called to his three dogs, named Blood-Drinker, Squasher, and Sorcerer. When only one blade of grass was left, the wife he did not favor released the dogs. They came, felled the witches, and gobbled them up. He took riches from the witches' house and went towards home. Near his house he tied his dogs and left his wealth, and when he got home he asked, "Where are the dogs?" His favorite wife said, "There's the slut who let them go." When she admitted it, he said she must find them, telling her where to go. She brought back the dogs and he brought all his wealth and gave it to her. When the favorite wife saw her wearing bracelets and anklets, she left the hunter and went back to her family. (Edgar [1911–13], vol. II, no. 7; translated in Skinner [1969–77], vol. II, pp. 81–84)

28. (Nigeria: Angas) A man and his son went hunting, leaving his dogs

and other animals tied up. They met a woman with mouths all over her body and the boy cried, "What a terrible sight!" The woman began to chase them and turned into many birds, but the man and his son also changed into birds and escaped to their home. The woman changed into a beautiful girl and told the young men of the village that she would marry whomever knocked over a basket. All tried and failed until the boy knocked the basket over. After they were married, the girl said they should visit her village. The boy told the women in the compound to tie up all the animals but to release the dogs if they cried. That night in her village the leg of a man came from under the bed and told the boy to flee. He jumped on his horse and rode off but his wife turned into a mighty bird and then into a woman with mouths all over her body. She ate the horse's legs one by one, but the horse kept running. When she ate its body and there was nothing to ride on, the boy climbed a tree. The woman with her mouths waited beneath the tree, saying that they would eat him when he came down. At home the dogs began to cry and the women untied them. They rushed to their master, attacked the woman, and totally consumed every part of her. The boy came down from the tree, found his horse completely restored, and rode home with his dogs. (Vernon-Jackson [1963], pp. 35–39)

29. (Nigeria: Yoruba) A hunter sent his son to fetch fire but the boy went by a forbidden path. He met a beautiful woman who gave him a firebrand, but because of her beauty he extinguished it three times and returned for another. The third time she took it herself, returned with the boy, and offered to sleep with the hunter. Having done so, she asked the hunter to accompany her part of the way back, but she told him to leave his gun and to shut up his three dogs. When they were in the forest she asked him to pick some fruit. When he climbed a tall tree and did so she called out that she would eat him. He looked down and saw that she had changed into a snake that was coiled around the tree. The hunter called for his three dogs named Cutter, Snapper-and-Swallower, and Cleaner-of-the-Places. Cutter cut through the door and the three dogs ran to the tree. Snapper-and-Swallower bit off the snake's head and swallowed it; Cutter cut the snake into bits; Snapper-and-Swallower piled them up; and Cleaner-of-the-Places cleaned up the blood. The dogs offered to carry the meat home if the hunter promised not to tell even his wife, but he told her when she had made him drunk. The three dogs ran away into the forest, and another episode follows. (Frobenius [1926], pp. 233–38; translated in Frobenius [1971], pp. 182–87)

30. (Nigeria: Yoruba) A beautiful woman promised to marry the man who could throw three seeds into a calabash. Many tried and failed, but a hunter succeeded and took the woman home. She was a witch and three times that night she turned into a mass of teeth and prepared to eat the hunter, but his three dogs barked and awoke him. The next morning she suggested that she go hunting with him, leaving his dogs behind in chains. When they were in the heart of the forest she again turned into a mass of teeth. The hunter climbed a tree but the teeth started to chew it. As the tree was about to fall

the hunter recited an incantation, and another tree bent down to pick him up. The teeth felled tree after tree until only one was left. In the top of the last tree the hunter begged a bird to unchain his dogs and by chants conjured them to the scene. One of the dogs killed the witch; the second lapped up the blood; and the third cleaned up the spot. (Walker and Walker [1961], pp. 17–19)

31. (Nigeria: Yoruba) A hunter had three dogs named "Cut to Pieces," "Swallow up," and "Clear the Remains" and a magic flute by which he could call them wherever he was. He went hunting, leaving his dogs tied up in the compound, but telling his wife to release them if they became agitated. Every day a huge monster with her body covered with mouths stole all the meat he had killed the previous day. Finally he waited in his camp to confront her but she did not come. He tied up his loads and left, shouting an insult at her. She came with an angry roar and he fled, climbing to the top of a great tree and calling his dogs by name with his flute. The monster began to eat the base of the tree with her great mouths, but the hunter sprinkled magic powder on the tree and it became whole again. This continued until the powder was finished and the tree was nearly cut through. Suddenly the three dogs arrived, having broken their ropes. Living up to their names they devoured the monster completely. The monster's sister appeared to the hunter as a beautiful woman who offered to become his second wife, and he took her home. That night she resumed the form of a monster and tried to kill the hunter and his first wife but was torn to pieces by the three dogs. (Fuja [1962], pp. 155–61)

32. (Nigeria: Yoruba) I bought three puppies and raised them as fierce hunting dogs. One was named Sweeper because it ate without leaving any remnant; the second was named Cutter because it cut its victim to pieces; and the third was named Swallower because it never chewed bones or anything before swallowing them. I heard that there were many treasures in the village of the savage people and decided to get some. I left my three dogs locked in their room, although my mother advised me to take them with me. In the forest I was knocked down by a shadow that turned into a night person in the form of a woman six times as tall as I was. She was angry because I had entered her forest and pushed my nose with her finger as I backed away from her. Then she beat me with a stick, while I struck her with my gun. I ran to a mighty tree and climbed into its branches. She left and returned with two men who began to chop down the tree with their axes, and I called my dogs by name. Just as the tree was about to fall, the dogs came and drove the two men and the night woman away. "The entertainment of the fourth night" continues with other incidents and concludes with another rescue by the dogs and an escape with some of the treasures. (Tutuola [1962], pp. 53–66)

33. (Nigeria: Yoruba) A hunter who knew many charms had three dogs who went everywhere with him. One day he passed a village where a festival was going on and saw a group of men gathered about a beautiful woman. They were throwing seeds at a calabash that she held, and he learned that she had promised to marry the man who threw three seeds into it. The hunter

tried and his first three seeds landed in the calabash. The woman went home with the hunter and they were given a big welcome. A few nights later his wife, who was a witch, turned herself into a mass of teeth and tried to eat the hunter, but three times his dogs barked and she changed back into a woman. The next morning she said she wanted to go home with him and when they were about to leave, she persuaded him to chain his dogs and leave them behind. In the forest she again changed into a mass of teeth and the hunter climbed the nearest tree. The teeth began to bite the tree and when it began to sway the hunter said magic words and the branch of the nearest tree bent down and picked him up. This continued until only one tree was left. The hunter sent a bird to call his dogs and as their barking became louder the teeth turned back into a witch. The dogs pounced on her and tore her to bits. In gratitude, the hunter never again hunted little birds. (Akinsemoyin [1965], pp. 26–32)

34. (Nigeria: Yoruba) A hunter had three dogs named Cutter, Swallower, and Sweeper.[14] A woman trader regularly bought his meat, but he did not know that she was an evil tree spirit. He said that he wanted to marry her, and she invited him to her home. He called to his dogs, but she asked if he needed his dogs to visit his wife's home. She told him to lock his dogs in the house because she knew they were very fierce. He did so and took his gun, but she asked if he was going to make war at his wife's home. He left his gun and took his cutlass, but she asked if he wanted to cut off someone's head there, so he left it. When they entered the forest the trees began to greet them. The hunter was frightened and wanted to flee, but the trees blocked his path. When he saw that they were going to kill him, he climbed to the top of a tree and sang, calling his dogs by name. They came running and conquered the evil tree spirits for him. (Bascom [1969], pp. 416–23)

35. (Nigeria: Bini) A hunter's pregnant wife asked to eat lion meat so that she could deliver her child. Leaving his seven dogs to help his wives work his farms, the hunter searched for eight days. Finally he killed a lion cub with his knife and wounded its mother with his gun. The lioness pursued him and he climbed a tree. He blew his whistle to call his dogs and they came running. The lioness killed the first six dogs but the seventh killed the lioness. The hunter came down from the tree and revived the dead dogs by magic. The dogs agreed to carry the meat home if he told no one, but when he had drunk too much palm wine he broke his promise and told his wives. They called the dogs to carry their loads home from the farm, but the dogs jumped into a river and were drowned. The hunter struggled with the last dog which delivered a pup that he rescued. It grew up like the dogs that we know today, neither carrying loads nor working on farms as dogs once did. (Bordinat and Thomas [1973], pp. 19–22)

36. (Nigeria: Ekoi) A great hunter set out after elephants that had ravaged his farm. When he found them they turned into men whom he knew. They promised to pay for the damage to his farm and he spared them. He came to the hut of the Forest Woman, surrounded by human skulls and bones. A

lame girl warned him not to eat any of the cannibal's food and told him the sound she made when she was asleep. The Forest Woman failed to kill him and he escaped with the aid of charms that the lame girl gave him. The monster turned into a beautiful woman, sought out his house, and told him she had fallen in love with him. One of his wives knew that she was the Forest Woman and warned the hunter not to sleep with her, but he was obstinate. The wife told his two fiercest dogs to guard their master, which they did when the Forest Woman tried to kill him at night. The next morning the Forest Woman told him to chain his dogs and accompany her on the way. He did so and took the keys with him. On the way she asked him to climb a tree for fruit and then made the tree grow very tall by magic. She struck her belly and twenty armed men sprang out and surrounded the tree. They began to chop the tree down with axes, but a bird flew to the hunter's wife and told her what was happening. Unable to find the keys, she pounded the chains with a stone until they broke. The tree fell, but caught on another tree and the hunter climbed into it. When the second tree was about to fall the dogs arrived. The fiercest dog, named Oro Njaw, tore the Forest Woman to pieces and the others attacked her men, some of whom escaped. (Talbot [1969], pp. 247–54)

37. (Nigeria: Ekoi) A beautiful woman who was a witch said that anyone who wanted to marry her must hit a calabash with a stone. Many men tried and failed, but a hunter succeeded and took her home as his second wife. Soon she tired of him and decided to kill him. She told him to leave his five dogs and go with her into the forest to cut palm nuts. When he climbed the tree, she beat her breast and produced an ax. Calling out that she was going to kill him, she chopped the tree down. It fell against another tree and the hunter climbed into it. When she started to chop it, he sent a bird to call his dogs. They came and bit her until she died. He divided her body into five bundles which the dogs carried home. His first wife insisted that he tell her how he had carried the bundles and the next day she made the dogs carry five bundles of firewood home from the farm. As each dog placed its load on the ground it fell dead. (Dayrell [1913], pp. 11–13)

38. (Cameroun: Gbaya) A man had three dogs named Godongkela, Kilo, and Gbara. In those days many women had no husbands, and one of them asked him why he never married. He said that he loved no woman and that his dogs helped him in everything. One day when he went hunting with his dogs the woman changed into a cannibal to take her revenge. When the man saw her he fled and climbed a tree. The woman began to hew down the tree with her sex organ, but when it was cut half way through a toad called for the tree to come back together again. The woman tried to kill the toad but could not find it. She returned to the tree and began to hew it down again, but when it was half cut the toad cried again and the tree grew together. Meanwhile the man called to his dogs who were far away. They came running and threw themselves at the woman. One tore up her sex organ and the others mangled her face and body so that she died. The man took the toad back to

the village and forbad all Gbaya to eat toads. He never married, but some of the women changed themselves into men so that there were no women without husbands. (Tessman [1934], vol. I, p. 236)

39. (Zaire: Kongo) A hunter had four dogs. Mbwa-Ndombe, the eldest, had small teeth. Lusinga was all black and very small, but very strong. Mpembele and Kakalagoka were the youngest dogs. With their aid he killed an antelope and when night fell he found his way to the hut of an old woman who was a sorceress. She offered him food which he threw into the fire and brought him six fine kola nuts which he admired. She offered to take him to the kola tree in an abandoned village. The next morning she told him to leave his dogs and his gun behind and they started out. When he climbed the kola tree, she broke off its lower branches and called other sorcerers who surrounded the tree. One of them began to chop down the tree with an ax; at each blow the tree bent but then straightened up. The hunter sang, calling his dogs by name, and they came and bit and bit. Some sorcerers fled, but the old woman died. The hunter collected a basket of kola nuts, returned for his gun and antelope, and went home. (van Wing and Scholler [1940], pp. 61–66)

40. (Zaire: Chokwe) A man went hunting with his two dogs named Bullausumba and Bullaumao. He killed an antelope but after sunset lost his way. He came to the hut of a giant and asked for some tobacco. The giant gave him hair which he refused. The giant put the hair back on his head and gave him tobacco. That night the giant tried to kill him with a red hot iron, but the dogs growled and saved him. In the morning they went to pick fruit, leaving the dogs behind. The giant told him to climb a tree and he told the giant to take his belt and headband. When he was in the tree the giant told it to rise and the man told the bands to tighten. The giant cried that he was dying and told the tree to come down, and the man told the bands to relax. The tree was still too tall for the hunter to come down, so he called his dogs. They came and killed the giant. Then they tied a pole to the tree so that the hunter could come down, telling him that he must not tell how they had helped him. At home he gave the dogs half of his food. His wife asked him why he did so and he winked at her. The dogs ran away and never came back. (Frobenius [1928], pp. 262–63)

41. (Zaire: Luba) A youth hunted birds and traded them for two dogs. The dogs begat dogs of all kinds, the elephant dog, the lion dog, the hyena dog—all animals were represented. One day his father told him that his sister had married Big Tooth, a cannibal chief. Despite his mother's protests the youth set out to find his sister. When he reached her home, Big Tooth was away. When Big Tooth returned he welcomed his brother-in-law. That night Big Tooth tried to kill him, but the dogs growled and the youth was saved. In the morning Big Tooth told the youth to tie his dogs and go with him to gather nuts. When the youth was up the nut tree, Big Tooth began to cut down the tree with his tooth. The youth had a whistle with which he called his dogs and they cut their bonds with their teeth. When the dogs arrived, the youth told them to kill Big Tooth but to leave his tooth. When they had

done so, the youth came down from the tree, broke the tooth into little pieces, and tied them to the necks of his dogs. He took his sister home with him. (Peeraer [1937–38], vol. 4, 7–10)

42. (Zaire: Kanyoka) A hunter went hunting with his dogs. Caught in the rain, he took shelter in a shed where he met an ogre with two heads and another with three heads. The three-headed ogre asked, "Who is that one-headed ogre?" The two-headed ogre replied that he was the hunter. The three-headed ogre told him to tell the hunter that their master was coming. Other ogres, each with one more head than the one before, came and said the same thing, and finally their master with a hundred heads came. When night fell and the hunter slept, the ogres heated an iron in the fire to burn him, but the dogs growled at them and they withdrew. In the morning they told him to pick plums. They tied the dogs in the house and when he climbed the tree they chopped at it. He called to his dogs, Mulaji Kabwe. The dogs heard and tore down the door. They came and chopped up the ogres, and the hunter came down from the tree. (de Clercq [1909], pp. 85–86)

43. (Zaire: Lia) A woman lost in the forest found the house of a headless djinn who married her. Her family searched for her in vain, but her elder brother found her. With her help he escaped home safely, but when her younger sister visited her she was killed. Taking his twelve dogs her eldest brother went to see her. The dogs' barking drove off the djinn when it tried to kill him. The next day the djinn took him to gather kola nuts and the brother locked his dogs in the house. The djinn told him to climb the tree and then called djinns of all kinds, some without limbs and some without heads. They came with axes and began to chop down the tree. It began to crack and sway, but the brother slapped the tree and it became whole again. He called to his dogs, named Bakolo and Ibenga, and the djinns began chopping the tree again. It began to crack and the brother slapped it, making it whole again. Again he called to his dogs and this time they heard. They broke out of the house, ran to the tree, and tore the djinns to pieces. The brother came down from the tree and took his sister home. (Mamet [1960], pp. 114–19)

44. (Sudan: Zande) A woman had a beautiful daughter but she ate all her daughter's suitors. Ture took his dogs, named Karawandikiri and Nganguru, and went there and married the girl. That night the mother tried to kill Ture but the dogs drove her away. The next day the mother, the daughter, and Ture went to collect honey, but the mother said Ture must shut his dogs inside the house and tie the door securely. When they reached the bees' nest and Ture climbed the tree, the mother began to chop it down. Ture called his dogs by name and they tore down the door and came running. The old woman gave her daughter an ax and they both chopped at the tree. The dogs came and tore the old woman to pieces and Ture went home with his wife and his dogs. (Evans-Pritchard [1963–65], Part 4, pp. 31–34; [1967], pp. 155–56)

45. (Tanzania: Haya) A man's wife asked for a dry stick. He told his mother that if a leaf fell on her leg she should send his dogs to him. Then he and his wife went into the forest. They found a bird in a trap and he released it.

They went on and his wife told him to climb a tree for the stick. She turned into a lion and started to cut down the tree. A leaf fell on his mother's leg and she sent his dogs. The bird saw the lion cutting the tree and spit there, and the chips went back into place. The dogs came, killed the lion, and ate it. Then the dogs asked "When we get home, who will eat first?" The man said that he would, so his dogs killed him and ate him. But one of the dogs, a bitch, restored him to life. They went home, and since then dogs stay with men. (Rehse [1910], pp. 373–76)

46. (Tanzania: Digo) A woman gathering firewood met a monster that told her that it owned the place. It said that if she came there she must bring a child, and if not she herself would be eaten. She called her husband but the monster seized her and ate her up. A man came and the monster said it would eat him, but he climbed a tree and called his dogs, named Mimina. The dogs came, seized the monster, killed it, and ate it all up. When the man got home, he killed a goat for his dogs. (Dammann [1935–36], pp. 217–19)

47. (Tanzania: Nyiha) After other episodes a boy pursued by a wild man climbed a tree. The wild man felled it with his tooth, but a bird sang a song and it stood up again. While the man chased the bird, the boy climbed another tree and called his dogs. They came and bit the wild man until he died, and the boy went home. (Kootz-Kretschmer [1926–29], vol. II, pp. 120–23; vol. III, pp. 105–08)

48. (Malawi: Yao) While a man was hunting it began to rain and he went into a cave with his ten dogs. There he found an old man who chased him up a tree and began to fell the tree. When the tree was about to fall a bird said, "The tree of God shall never fall." The old man began to fell it again, and again the bird restored it. The hunter called to his dogs, but another bird said, "Puli!" and one dog died, "Puli!" and another dog died, and so until all the dogs were dead. The hunter called a dog at the village that wore beads. It came and said, "Puli!" and the old man died and the hunter was saved. (Macdonald [1882], Vol. II, p. 365)

49. (Malawi: Yao) A woman promised her unborn child to a monster in return for meat. When the monster came for her son the mother told it how to catch him, but three times the boy escaped. She said she would send him hunting in the forest so that the monster could catch him there. The boy went hunting with his four dogs, one of whom was named Mawalayenje. He met the monster and climbed a tree. The monster commenced to cut down the tree and the boy called his dogs. The first three dogs fell dead but Mawalanyenje flew at the monster and bit at it until it was dead. The boy came down from the tree and restored the three dead dogs to life. (Stannus [1922], pp. 335–36)

50. (Mozambique: Ndau) Abandoned with two dogs named Black and White, a brother and sister found a cave full of grain. The boy planted a tree nearby and told his sister that if it was dying she would know he was dead. Then he took one dog, leaving the other with his sister, and departed. He came to a kraal where there were no men because all of them had been eaten by one of the women. She invited the boy into her hut and that night tried

to kill him, but the dog bit her. She tried to poison him and to kill him in a pit, but each time the dog warned him. Then she told him to leave his dog behind and go with her to cut firewood. He climbed a tree and began to chop wood, and she began to cut the tree down, biting it with her big tooth. The boy called his dog and as the tree began to fall the dog came and bit the woman. The boy came down and killed her with his chopper. A great bird tried to kill the boy. It caught his dog, but the boy cut the bird to pieces and burned it and the woman to ashes. When he returned to the kraal the women made him their chief. He sent for his sister with the dog to lead the way, and they lived in the kraal together. (Kidd [1906], pp. 224–30)

51. (Lesotho: Suto) After other episodes a chief and a girl were pursued by her mother who was a cannibal with a huge thumbnail. When the mother came close to them the chief caused a row of trees to appear and he and the girl climbed into the nearest tree. The mother saw them and laughed, thinking she had them in her power. She started to cut the tree down with her thumbnail, but just as it was about to fall the chief and the girl jumped into the next tree. This continued until they were in the last tree, when the chief called to his warriors to bring their dogs. When the dogs attacked the woman, she used her thumbnail as a shield but it could not protect her. When the dogs were in front of her the warriors attacked from behind; and when the warriors were in front of her the dogs attacked from behind. When they had killed her, the dogs tore her apart and ate her flesh. Other incidents follow. (Postma [1964], pp. 136–41; translated in Postma [1974], pp. 136–41)

52. (South Africa: Sotho) An old woman told twin boys to call her if they killed the shaggy beast that had ravaged the land. One day one of the boys climbed a tree to eat fruit, and the shaggy beast came and asked him for some. He gave it all the ripe fruit, all the green fruit, all the leaves, and all the twigs. Then he blew on his flute, calling his brother to bring their dogs. The beast broke the branch the boy was sitting on and he jumped to another and another until he sat on the last branch. Then the dogs came and seized the beast and the twins killed it and called the old woman. When the beast was cut open, men, cows, sheep, and goats came out. (Hoffmann [1915–16], pp. 305–10)

53. (South Africa: Sotho) After another episode an old woman warned twin boys of a beast that had ravaged the land. One boy found a Thing in a pot that told him to put it on his back and then to let it down. He fled from the Thing and climbed a tree. It came and felled the tree with its teeth, but the boy swung into another tree and called for his brother to bring his dogs. He tried to kill the Thing with arrows and spears, but it swallowed them and cried the name of the beast. The brother came with the dogs, but it killed all but one mangy dog. The Thing grew as tall as the tree and broke off its branches, crying the beast's name. The beast came and the mangy dog killed it. When the beast was cut open, people, cattle, and weapons came out. (Hoffmann [1915–16], pp. 313–15)

54. (South Africa: Venda) A man searching for honey came to a deserted

village with a kraal full of goats. He was about to take the goats when a bird told him that there were better things ahead. The same happened at a sheep kraal and at a cattle kraal. Finally he came to a hut where an old woman threatened to kill him. He ran and climbed a tree, shouting for his dogs. The old woman tried to cut down the tree with her teeth. When the dogs came she killed them one by one, but a lame dog jumped on her back, seized her neck, and killed her. The man went home, taking the animals from the kraal [*sic*] with him. (Stayt [1931], p. 348)

55. (South Africa: Zulu) A woman who had a long toe was a cannibal. When she had eaten everyone except her two beautiful daughters, she tore flesh from the cheek of one daughter, but found it bitter. While she was out hunting, a youth who had left his dogs behind came and he and the daughters fell in love. The girls hid him that night, and the next day he and one of the girls went to get his dogs, leaving the one with the wounded cheek behind. When the cannibal returned, she found the other daughter gone and set out in pursuit. The youth and the girl saw her coming and climbed a tall tree, leaving the dogs at its foot. The mother came with an ax and began to hew the tree and the dogs bit her. As the tree was about to fall one dog tore off her head, another her arms, others tore off her limbs and other dragged her intestines away. Immediately the tree grew back to its original condition and the cannibal came to life. She began to chop at the tree again, and again the dogs tore off her head and limbs. They took the pieces to a river and ground them to powder which they cast into the water. The youth and girl came down from the tree and went to his people. (Callaway [1868], Vol. I, pp. 47–52)

56. (South Africa: Zulu) A youth went to court a girl. On the way a swallow warned him that the place would be dangerous and said it would protect him if he skinned it and took its skin with him. The boy did so and when he reached the girl's house her mother tried to kill him during the night, but the skin woke him. At dawn he and the girl fled with the mother in pursuit. The skin told him to climb a tree and leave his dogs below. The mother came and hewed at the tree, but when it was about to fall the dogs tore her to pieces and scattered them. The skin told them to descend and flee because the mother would come to life again. Although the dogs had ground her to powder and thrown it into the water she came to life again, but the couple had escaped. (Callaway [1886], vol. I, pp. 53–54)

57. (South Africa: Zulu) After another episode a girl pursued by cannibals climbed to the top of a tall tree. The cannibals came and sat beneath the tree to rest, but water leaked from a vessel that she carried and they saw her. They began to hew at the tree with their axes, and the tree wavered but became firm again. The girl's brother dreamed that she was being eaten by animals and set out with his very great dogs to look for her. He found the cannibals and asked what they were doing. They told him to hew but he saw his sister and tried very little to hew. He gave snuff to the cannibals and set his dogs on them. The dogs laid hold of them and killed all of them, and he took his sister home. (Callaway [1868], pp. 142–47)

58. (South Africa: Xhosa) A mean father sent his two daughters to fetch water in the finest pots in the village. The young sister fell and broke her pot. She was afraid to go home to her father and persuaded her sister to leave home with her. They came to house of their father's sister, but they did not know it. Her son was at home alone and he told the girls that their aunt was a cannibal. He hid them that night and the next night they ran away. The aunt pursued them with her ax and they climbed up a tree. She started to chop the tree, but three times a bird sang and the chips went back into place again. The aunt caught the bird and swallowed it, but one feather fell to the ground and continued to sing. Finally the aunt fell to the ground, exhausted. From the treetop the girls saw their father's three dogs and called them by name. The dogs came running and ate up the cannibal. The girls returned to their father who was so glad to see them that he forgave them for breaking the pot and for running away from home. (Theal [1886], pp. 122–26; [1910], pp. 327–29)

59. (Namibia: Hottentot) A woman who was a cannibal had a daughter whom many men tried to marry, but the mother killed them while they slept. A man with two lion-dogs came and put a stone where he was to sleep. That night the cannibal came with a hatchet, but the dogs drove her off. The man woke up and replaced the stone where he had slept and fled. The cannibal came and began to hack at the stone. Then she hurried after him, but he climbed up a tree. She chopped off the branches until only one branch was left. The man winked at his dogs and they came and caught her. The man fled to his kraal where he slaughtered three cows for his dogs. When they came to the third cow he killed them, fearing they had become bloodthirsty. (Schultze [1907], pp. 397–99)

60. (British Columbia: Shushwap Indians) After another episode a woman and her son were pursued by cannibal women. The mother pulled out four hairs from her body and threw them on the ground. They turned into four tall trees in which she and her son took refuge. The cannibals tried to fell the tree with hammers and chisels, but when it was about to fall the mother and son jumped to the next one. When the last tree was about to fall the boy urinated on it and the wood swelled, closing the notches that had been cut. The father's four dogs, Grizzly Bear, Rattlesnake, Timber Wolf, and Panther, were tied up at home. They became restless and tried to break loose. Suspecting that something was wrong the father released them. As the last tree was about to fall they attacked the cannibals, killed, and ate them. Because these dogs killed and ate the cannibals, the grizzly bear, rattlesnake, wolf, and panther kill people today. (Teit [1909], pp. 635–37)

61. (British Columbia: Thompson River Indians) After other episodes two sisters and the son of one of them were pursued by a cannibal. One woman pulled out four pubic hairs and threw them on the ground. Immediately four tall trees grew from them and they climbed into one of them. When the cannibal arrived, he began to chop it down. When it tottered the three fugitives jumped into the second tree. The cannibal chopped it down and then the

third tree, and the fugitives took refuge in the fourth one. As the cannibal began to chop down the last tree the women cried for help, and their two dogs that had been left at home became restless. These dogs were fierce and strong, for they were the Grizzly Bear and the Rattlesnake. The Grizzly Bear growled and pawed the ground and the Rattlesnake shook its rattles. The women's husbands knew that their wives were in danger and let the dogs loose. While they ran to their mistresses the boy urinated down the heart of the tree, causing the wood to become elastic and the cannibal could make only slow progress in cutting it. The Grizzly Bear and the Rattlesnake arrived as the tree was tottering, attacked the cannibal fiercely, tore him to pieces, and killed him. The women and the boy returned home. Having once killed a human being, the Grizzly Bear and the Rattlesnake acquired the habit and still sometimes kill people today. (Teit [1898], pp. 34–36)

62. (New England: Cape Verde Islanders) Three brothers set out in turn to find a cure for their father's illness. The first two lost an eating contest with an old woman's three daughters and were pushed into a pit. The third son had three dogs named Flower, Hour, and Moment. He told his father that when he saw them pulling on the warp-line he should release them because he would be in danger. On his way he was given salt, briar seeds, and three *polon* seeds. He won the eating contest, pushed the old woman into the pit, and rode away with his two brothers. When the old woman pursued them on her goat he threw down his gifts in turn, causing a sea, a briar thicket, and three *polon* trees to appear. Apparently the brothers climbed one of the trees, because the old woman started to cut it down. The hero sang to his dogs, calling their names. They came, seized the old woman, and killed her and her goat. (Parsons [1922], pp. 1–3; "Cape Verde" [1923], Part I, pp. 121–25, Part II, pp. 75–78)

63. (New England: Cape Verde Islanders) Three brothers left home in turn with their lions. The first two were thrown into a pit by an old woman with whom they sought lodging. The third was given salt, ashes, three *polon* seeds, and a gourd seed. He left his three lions, named Hour, Wait, and Moment, tied up at home and told his sister to release them when they foamed at the mouth and his garden dried up. He escaped from the old woman's house and when she pursued him he threw down three of his gifts causing a sea, a snow storm, and a *polon* tree to appear. Apparently, again, he climbed the tree because the old woman and her children began to cut the tree down, but as it was about to fall he threw the second *polon* seed and a second tree grew up. When he had thrown the third seed and the third tree was about to fall, his sister found his garden drying up and released his three lions. When the lions came they did not leave a particle of the woman or her children; they all became farina. He went back to the old woman's house and released his two brothers and many other people. On the way home he was killed by his brother, but a gourd grew from the seed he had been given. It revealed the murder and when it was opened, he came out. (Parsons [1922], pp. 3–7; "Cape Verde" [1923], Part I, pp. 125–31, Part II, pp. 79–85)

64. (New England: Cape Verde Islanders) A man was married to a witch who wanted to kill him. She said she wanted to show him her garden. He started to get his dog, but she said she wouldn't go with him. When he started to get his stick, she said she wouldn't go with him. He hid three *polon* seeds on his person and they left. After a while she asked him if his dog could hear him if he called. At first he said yes, but, becoming suspicious, he said no. She told him to say his prayers and he sang, calling to his dog, "Little lion!" The dog broke its chains and came running. He dropped a *polon* seed and a tree sprang up and he climbed into it. She took out a tooth, turned it into a machette, and began to chop the tree down. When it was about to fall he dropped the second seed; another tree sprang up and he climbed it. When he had thrown the third seed and the third tree was about to fall, his little dog rushed against her. He told it to seize her and not let a drop of blood fall on the ground. The dog seized her and ate her up. (Parsons [1922], p. 8; "Cape Verde," [1923], Part I, pp. 131–32)

65. (New Jersey) Harris cites a version similar to one of his own [84] from Mr. Richard Adams Learned of New Jersey whose grandfather had heard it from his old nurse in Guyana. Cf [112]. In it the dogs are named Yarmearoo and Gengamaroto. (Harris [1892], pp. v–vi)

66. (Michigan) A boy had two dogs named Dan and Rangtang. His mother sent him to his grandmother but wouldn't let him take his dogs that were tied to her bed. On the way he met some witches. He climbed a tree and called to Rangtang by name. The witches started to cut the tree down and he called again. When the tree was about down the dogs began to bark and the boy's mother turned them loose. The dogs came and cut off the witches' arms, cut off their legs, and cut off their necks. (Dorson [1956], pp. 198–99; [1967], pp. 249–50)

67. (Kentucky) A boy's sister was carried away by a bear and no one could find her. A year later two women with long tails asked that the boy lead them to the forks of the road. He didn't want to, but his mother told him to go. He tied two willow limbs beside two pans of water and tied his two hound dogs to the limbs. He told his mother to release the dogs when the water got as red as blood and the willow limbs began to shake. After they started down the road and the boy was frightened and climbed a tree. The women turned their tails into axes and began to chop the tree down. When it was almost cut down the boy dropped one of the six eggs that he always carried and filled the hole up. When only one egg was left his mother saw the water as red as blood and the willow limbs waving and she turned the dogs loose. The boy dropped the last egg and yelled to his dog, "Get them, get them!" One of the dogs got one woman and slung her over the ground. The other dog got the other woman and soon both women were dead. On the way home he found his sister and went home with her (Roberts [1955], pp. 19–21)

68. (Kentucky) Two witches who looked like dogs asked to have a boy show them the way to another road. The boy didn't want to go but finally

he agreed. He stuck a willow switch in a basin of water and told his mother to release his dogs when the water turned to blood and the willow shook. After they started down the road he looked back and saw the women following him like dogs. He ran and climbed a tree. They turned their tails into axes and began to chop the tree. When the tree was nearly chopped down, the boy dropped one of his three eggs and said, "Fill up!" and the tree became normal. When he was down to his last egg his mother saw the willow shaking and the water turned to blood. She turned the dogs loose and they came as the tree was about to fall. The boy said to his dogs, "Drag them around and around for a mile! Drag them around for three miles!" Then the two witches were dead. (Roberts [1955], pp. 21–22)

69. (Missouri: French) A brother and sister vowed never to marry, but the son of a fairy fell in love with the girl. Because the brother would not permit him to court his sister, the fairy directed the girl unwittingly to poison her brother's soup, but his three dogs upset the bowl. He left home in anger and met the fairy. She asked him to climb an apple tree and pick the apple of her choice, but she kept asking for a different one. He threw an apple at her head and she summoned little devils. He called his dogs, named Madouza, Liba, and Boustapha, and they chased the fairy and her dogs away. The next day his sister again poisoned his soup and the dogs spilled it. She told him to keep his dogs locked up and he did so. The next day he was poisoned and his sister could marry the fairy's son. (Carrière [1937], pp. 119–20)

70. (Texas) A great hunter had two dogs named Sambo and Ringo. One day he left them with a pan of milk shut up behind a picket fence and went into the woods. Suddenly he found himself face to face with the Poopampareno! He threw down his gun and climbed to the top of a tree, but the Poopampareno began to saw down the tree with his teeth. The hunter called three times for his dogs. They saw that the milk had turned to blood and finally heard their master's call. They jumped over the fence and raced into the woods. Just as the tree was about to fall they grabbed the Poopampareno by the throat before he could take his teeth out of the trunk. (Beazley [1938], pp. 252–54; reprinted in Botkin [1949], pp. 518–19)

71. (Texas) A boy put his twelve dogs in their pen and told his mother that if he was in trouble he would whistle to them and if they barked a long time she should let them out. Then he and his sister went to visit their grandmother, a witch who ate children. That night they tiptoed toward home after putting their white sheet over the witch's children, whom she killed by mistake. A magic ball showed her the road the children had taken and she set out in pursuit. They heard her coming and climbed a tree and the boy whistled for his dogs. They began to bark and bark and the mother let them out. The witch came with her ax and began chopping the tree singing, "Wham, Jam, Jenny-Mo-Wham." The boy sang for the tree to grow big at the bottom and little at the top. Every time that a chip fell out another one grew back. Soon the dogs came running and tried to bite the witch, but she killed all but one

with her knife. The last dog jumped at her throat, sank his teeth in, and killed her. The children cut out the witch's heart and rubbed it on the dead dogs' noses, and they all came back to life (Hendricks [1953], pp. 217–19)

72. (Alabama) A wild man captured a little girl, reared her, and married her. Her brother took his three dogs named You-Know, I-Know, and God-Knows and went hunting. He found his sister in a house in the woods. Her husband was kind to him and offered to accompany him part way home. On the way the wild man told the boy to climb a tree and pray while he sharpened his knife. When the boy called to his dogs, saying God-Knows, the man thought he was praying. The boy called again and the dogs came. They took the wild man and tore him to pieces. (Richardson, Work, and Parsons [1919], pp. 399–400)

73. (Alabama) Wiley took his hounds to the swamp but they ran away after a shoat. The Hairy Man came and Wiley climbed up a big tree. The Hairy Man took Wiley's ax and began to chop down the tree, but at Wiley's command the chips flew back into place. The Hairy Man kept chopping and Wiley kept hollering to the chips. Wiley called for his dogs, but the Hairy Man said that he had sent the shoat to draw them off. Wiley called again and they both heard the hounds yelping. The Hairy Man ran off through the swamp, and other episodes follow. (Botkin [1966], pp. 682–87; reprinted in Courlander [1976], pp. 482–86)

74. (Alabama: Creek Indians) A boy had three dogs named Simursitty, Jeudawson, and Ben-boten. He loved to hunt and he killed many buffaloes. Because of this, two buffaloes turned into pretty maidens and went to kill him. When they came, the dogs growled and his mother warned him against them. That evening the maidens asked the boy to tie up his dogs and the next morning they invited him to go home with them. His grandmother said no, but he went. They came to a herd of buffaloes and the maidens turned back into buffaloes. Frightened, the boy stuck an arrow in the ground and it became a tree. He climbed up the tree but the buffaloes butted it down. He threw a second arrow on the ground and it became another tree, and when the first tree fell he sprang into the second one. This continued until all his arrows were gone. He threw his bow down and it became another tree. When he sat in it he called his dogs. His grandmother was sleeping but she woke up when the dogs began to howl. She ran to them and saw that they were trying to break their chains. Then she heard the boy's voice in a distance and she burst the chains. The dogs ran and drove the buffaloes away, saving their master. (Parsons [1922], pp. 18–19; Swanton [1929], pp. 72–73)

75. (District of Columbia) Possum found some grapes for his children but saw Coon coming. He hid the grapes in leaves and climbed a tree. Coon found the grapes and saw Possum in the tree. Fearing that he would be eaten, Possum refused to come down. Coon began to chop the tree with an ax. The tree began to sway and Possum called to his dogs, Longie, Sonnie, Billie, Gone Away, and Buckena. The second time he called the dogs came running and caught Coon. Buckena shook him by the throat until he was dead. Possum

took Coon home and made soup for his hungry children. (Crimmins [1931], pp. 165–66)

76. (North Carolina) Two mean boys were given to a witch, but that night they avoided being killed by staying awake. They fled from her house and climbed a tree. The witches took an ax and began to chop down the tree. The little boy prayed and his dogs, named King Kilus and King Lovus, came and killed the witches. (Parsons [1917], pp. 189–90)

77. (North Carolina) A boy's mother gave him some seeds and told him to throw some out of his pocket if he got into trouble. He went to a country where they didn't like him and some men chased him until he climbed up a tree. The men fetched axes and began to chop the tree down. The boy threw some seeds on the men and the chips from the tree flew back into place. As fast as the men chopped the tree he threw seeds and the chips flew back into place. They boy called his dogs, Bark, Berry, Jupiter, Kerry, and Darker-in-the-Morning. Just as he was dropping his last seed the dogs came and flew at the men and ate them up, head and feet. The boy went home with his dogs. (Hendricks [1943], pp. 178–79; reprinted in Cothran [1972], pp. 60–63)

78. (South Carolina) I had two dogs, Jimmie Bingo and Jim Bolden. I told my mother to turn them loose if they started to holler and went into the woods but she went to sleep. I climbed up a tree to escape from a wolf and called to my dogs. The wolf gnawed at the tree, trying to fell it. I told the tree to grow larger and called for my dogs again. When they came the wolf turned into a witch. They began to eat the witch and cut it up. I went home. (Parsons, "Sea Islands," [1923], pp. 80–81)

79. (South Carolina) A boy tied his dogs, put some water in a basin, and told his mother that when the water turned to blood she must turn the dogs loose. Then he set out in search of his sister. He met an old man and climbed up a tree. The old man started up after him and the boy called his dogs. They came running and he said, "Take um, Cut-Throat and Suck-Blood." That was the last of the old man. (Parsons, "Sea Islands," [1923], p. 81)

80. (South Carolina) A giant wanted to eat Johnny and his sister, Mary. He came to their house while Johnny was away and slowly climbed the steps to get Mary. Johnny came back and the giant told him to tie his dogs and climb the tallest tree in the woods. The giant began cutting the tree with his teeth, and Johnny called his dogs by name, Cut-er-Throat, Suck-er-Blood, Crack-er-Bone, and Smash-er-Meat. The second time he called they jerked loose and came running. The tree was just about to fall, but Cut-er-Throat cut the giant's throat, Suck-er-Blood sucked his blood, Smash-er-Meat smashed his meat, and Crack-er-Bone cracked his bones. (Parsons, "Sea Islands," [1923], pp. 81–83)

81. (South Carolina) After other episodes, a brother and sister were warned not to sweep dirt into the well because a beast would come out and destroy them. While the boy was away, the girl swept dirt into the well. The beast came out and told her to have her brother keep his two dogs at home to protect her. The dogs were named Cut-the-Throat and Suck-the-Blood, and

the boy left them at home. The beast came to him and he asked to be allowed to climb a tree and shoot five arrows to call his dogs. His sister was driving a stake to fasten the dogs and they didn't come, so he sang, calling them by name. Cut-the-Throat broke loose and cut off Suck-the-Blood's chain. They came and the boy said, "Cut his throat! Suck his blood!" and they did so. He came down and went home, and other episodes follow. (Parsons, "Sea Islands," [1923], pp. 83–88)

82. (South Carolina) A boy visited his sister, not knowing that her husband was a giant who ate people. The giant found the boy hidden under a bed and made him climb a tree and then began to cut the tree down with his teeth. The boy had three dogs named "Cut throat," "Crack bone," and "Drag it away." Before he had left home the boy had told his mother that if his dogs growled she should turn them loose. Up in the tree the boy called for his dogs and they growled. When he called again, his mother remembered and released them. When the dogs came one cut the giant's throat, one cracked his bones, and one dragged him away. (Penn School Pupils [1925], pp. 223–24)

83. (Georgia) A boy's sister was carried away. One day two fine ladies with animal features asked to have the boy lead them to the forks of the road. He didn't want to go, but his mother told him to do so. He got a pan of water and stuck a willow limb in the ground and told his mother that when the water turned to blood and the willow began to shake she should untie his two dogs, Minnyminny Morack and Follerlinsko. After a while the two ladies dropped on all fours and ran after the boy. He climbed a big pine tree and refused to come down. The ladies took off their dresses and he saw they were panthers. They turned their tails into axes and began to chop down the tree. When it was about to fall, the boy broke an egg and the tree was restored. When he had only one egg left, his mother released the dogs and they came. The boy told them, "Shake them and tear them. Drag them round and round till you drag them two miles." The dogs did so and he told them, "Shake them and tear them. Drag them round and round till you drag them ten miles." The dogs did so and the panthers were killed. The boy came down and went to look for his sister. He found her living with a bear and combed her hair. The bear wanted its hair combed and the boy told it to put its head in boiling water, and he took his sister home. (Harris [1886]; [1889], no. 5; [1955, pp. 420–27)

84. (Georgia) A hunter killed many wild animals with his bow and arrows and his two dogs, Minny-Minny-Morack and Follamalinska. The wild cattle held a meeting to decide what to do about it. A white cow turned into a pretty woman, met the hunter, and married him. He gave up hunting for a long time but finally went hunting again. The woman tied up his dogs and he went alone. He found the cattle and killed many, but when he called his dogs they did not come. When he had only three arrows left the cattle charged him. He stuck an arrow in the ground and it grew into a big tree with him in the top limbs. Some of the cattle got axes and began to chop down the tree. The hunter called his dogs again, but they did not come. When the tree

fell he stuck another arrow into the ground and was carried to the top of another. He called to his dogs again. By this time they had gnawed through the strong ropes by which they were tied and they arrived just as the third tree fell. The dogs destroyed nearly all of the wild cattle and among their corpses the hunter saw a snow-white cow. He took its hide with him and when he reached home his wife was gone. (Harris [1892], no. 12; [1955], pp. 524–29)

85. (Bahamas) After his brother had been killed by a witch a boy told his mother that at twelve o'clock a basin of water would boil into a basin of blood and that when she saw them in a rage she should release his three dogs, Watchman, Lion, and Tiger. Then he went to look for his brother and to seek his fortune. His mother went to sleep. The boy climbed a tree to rest and the witch came and sang as she chopped at the tree. The boy called for his dogs. As the tree began to lean, the dogs jumped across a river and one took the witch and the others took her two children. They destroyed them, and the boy took the money in the witch's bag and went home. (Parsons [1918], p. 66)

86. (Bahamas) The king offered his daughter in marriage to the man who killed Mad Bull, an animal that had killed thousands of people. A little boy told his mother that he was going hunting and that when a pot of water boiled to blood she must turn loose his dogs, Cut-Throat, Chaw-Fine, and Suck-Blood. In the forest Mad Bull chased him up a tall tree and the boy sang to make it grow taller. Mad Bull tried to bite the tree down and, just as it was about to fall, the dogs broke loose and came a mile at each jump. When they arrived, the boy told Cut-Throat to cut Mad Bull's throat, Suck-Blood to suck its blood, and Chaw-Fine to chew it up. The dogs killed Mad Bull and the boy took its teeth to the king and married the king's daughter. (Parsons [1918], pp. 66–67)

87. (Bahamas) Two boys sent their younger brother for fire. He came to the house of a witch who struck her side, and twenty-four men came out and then she struck her other side, and twenty-four more men came out and ate with their hands, feet, and chins. When the boy whistled, she struck her sides again and the men jumped back into her belly. The boy denied seeing what he had seen and stole fire. The witch chased him, but he got home safely. The witch dressed up as a pretty woman and said she would marry the boy if he shot a coconut off of her head, which he did. They went home and that night she tried to kill the boy with a razor. He turned into a bucket of water, a kettle of hot water, and then climbed a tree. Twenty-four men came out of the witch to cut down the tree, but the boy sang to make the tree stand up. The boy's dogs, named Cut-Throat, Chew-Fine, and Suck-Blood, came and killed the witch. They cut her into four pieces and threw them to the north, south, east, and west. (Parsons [1918], pp. 67–68)

88. (Bahamas) A boy told his mother that he was going to look for a livelihood and that when she saw a pot boil until the water turned to blood she must turn loose his six dogs. He took three arrows and traveled until he met an old woman who asked to marry him. When he refused she said she

would kill him. He threw one of his arrows and sang for it to grow and climbed to the top. The woman spanked three men out of the right side of her ass and three axes out of the left side. The men chopped at the tree and when the ax became dull she told them to sharpen it on her cunt. When the tree was about to fall,the boy threw another arrow, sang to it, and climbed to the top of a second tree. The men chopped at it and when it was about to fall the boy threw his last arrow, sang, and climbed to the top of third tree, and the men chopped at it. Fearing that his mother was sleeping, the boy asked a hummingbird to tell her that she should release his dogs, and as the last tree was about to fall they came. The boy said, "Sue boy, Ring-Wood; catch him, Cut-Throat; chew, Chew-fine; suck, Suck-Blood; stow it, Stow-it-All." They killed the men and the old woman and the boy took her treasure. (Parsons [1918], pp. 69–70)

89. (Bahamas) Traveling in the woods a boy met three ladies who said they were going to kill him. He told his mother and, when he went again, he instructed her that if she heard him call she should release his three dogs. When he met the three ladies they rushed at him and he climbed up a tree. The ladies began to cut down the tree and he called for his dogs, Crack-bone, Suck-blood, and Tearer-eat-all. His mother was asleep but one of the dogs heard his master's voice, broke his rope, and woke her up. The mother cut the other dogs loose and they ran to the rescue of their master. He told them to do their duty and in no time they had the three ladies torn to pieces. (Parsons [1928], pp. 503–4)

90. (Jamaica) A boy went to find fire and saw a witch cooking. She hit her side and many people come out. She gave him fire and he and his younger brother ran home. The old woman came to their house and said she would marry whoever could knock a package off her head. The younger brother failed but the elder succeeded. That night the witch tried to kill her new husband but his three dogs, named Blum-blum, Sinde, and Dido, drove her away. The next day he told his mother to chain the dogs but to let them go if a white basin boiled up in blood. He left with his witch-wife and far from his house she asked him to pick an apple. When he had climbed the tree she struck herself and ten men with axes came out to fell the tree. He sang, calling the names of his dogs, and she sang for the tree to fall. When it was about to fall he called for it to bear him up. His mother was deaf, but the basin boiled over and the blood flowed to her. She released two dogs and the third broke its chains and they galloped away. The dogs destroyed the ax men and the old witch herself. The boy came down from the tree, cut the witch up, and scattered the pieces all over the earth. That is why cow-itch weeds are everywhere (Beckwith [1924], pp. 96–98)

91. (Haiti) A boy told his mother to cut the chains of his three dogs if they panted with their tongues out. He went to a savannah and climbed up an apple tree. Devils began to chop down the tree. As it was about to fall, he threw down a seed and prayed that God would let the tree become bigger than a house. He threw another seed and prayed that the tree would become

bigger than a hill. The boy sang to his dogs. His mother had forgotten to attend to them, but she remembered and set them loose. They came and broke the necks of all the devils. The boy reproached his mother but she said that she had forgotten because of all the work she had to do and that it would not happen again. (Parsons [1933–43], Part II, p. 546, Part III, p. 172)

92. (Haiti) A boy wanted to be a hunter and his mother tested him by having him shoot at a pin. She gave him a pin to stick in any girl he met to see if she was a she-devil or a young lady. She also gave him seven grains. He pricked a girl he met and drew pus but he invited her to come with him. She asked him to climb a tree for an apricot and throw it down on her left breast. Three hundred and ninety little devils with axes came out of her belly. As the tree was about to fall, the boy asked for a tree the size of Port-au-Prince. The she-devil sang and the boy sang for his four dogs, Vego, Saltata, Mi-un-valorai, and Baille-sang-nodé. He threw a grain and the woman swallowed the three hundred and ninety little devils. She beat on her belly again and five thousand and ninety-five little devils came out, but the dogs arrived and killed them and the she-devil. (Parsons [1933–43], Part II, pp. 546–48, Part III, p. 172)

93. (Haiti) On the way to market twin boys met two sisters. One girl had each boy throw a golden apple into the air. She rejected the boy whose apple fell on the ground but went home with the one whose apple fell on her left breast. She said she was pregnant and could only eat an apricot they had seen on the way. Before they started for it the boy told his grandmother to tie up his three dogs, Adiantedianto, Bon bowtimboli, and Jolsalibolo, but to turn them loose if water in a bowl turned to blood. They went to the tree and he climbed it. The woman, who was a she-devil, told the boy to drop the apricot on her head. Two hundred little devils with axes came out and attacked the tree. He threw down grains his grandmother had given him and the tree became a hundred and fifty times bigger. He climbed to the top of the tree and called for his dogs. The water turned to blood and the dogs broke their chains. As the tree was about to fall again he dropped a second grain and the tree became three hundred times bigger. He climbed higher and called his dogs again. They killed all the little devils and he cut off the she-devil's head and buried it after showing it to his grandmother. She was still eating the ear of corn that the she-devil had given her to make her forget to free the dogs. (Parsons [1933–43], Part II, pp. 548–51, Part III, pp. 172–73)

94. (Haiti) A she-devil who had refused a hundred suitors finally married. Her husband had three dogs, named Akang, Anhosay, and Andilo. The wife became pregnant, wanted dog flesh, and ate the dogs, and the man tied their bones above the hearth. The wife wanted to visit her mother and told the man to accompany her. Before leaving he told his mother that if a pan of water turned to blood she would know that he was in danger. The mother gave him seven seeds to throw away when he was in danger. On the way the wife told him to climb an acacia and make it fall on her breast. When it did, she struck her belly and two hundred small devils with axes came out.

The man threw a seed and the tree became as wide as the sky and earth. The wife struck her belly again and two hundred more devils with axes came out and began to chop the tree. The man threw another seed and a sea appeared. The wife struck again and four thousand more devils came out. At home the mother saw that the pan was full of blood and she released the bones and they became living dogs. When the devils with their axes had crossed the sea and arrived at his tree the man threw another seed, but six thousand more devils came out of his wife. The tree fell but the man changed into an ant. They found him but he threw another seed and found himself on top of another tree. Then he sang, calling his dogs by name. The wife sent forth twenty thousand more devils with axes, but the dogs came and broke the necks of all the devils. Then they broke the wife's neck and the man went home. (Comhaire-Sylvain [1938], pp. 300–4)

95. (Dominican Republic) After another episode a hunter who was the Devil fell in love with a boy's sister. She said that she would marry him but that he must kill her brother. The boy went out after tying his dogs, named Wind Breaker, Chain Breaker, and Bomber. He told his sister that if they howled she should release them because he would be in danger, but she plugged up their ears. They boy climbed a fruit tree and found his sister's lover there. The Devil threw him a fruit and from it came many little devils that began to chop the tree. The boy called his dogs by name but, although they howled, they could not hear him because their ears were plugged. Finally, Wind Breaker heard something and the dogs howled louder. The wicked sister did not release them, but they got loose and ran to the tree. The boy told them to kill the little devils. They did so and the boy went home. While he was asleep his sister stuck a poisoned pin in him. He died and was buried but the dogs dug him out of the grave and took out the pin, and he revived. The dogs turned into three angels and made the boy realize that a dog is man's best friend. The sister lived with the Devil and the boy stayed happily with his father. (Andrade [1930], pp. 106–9)

96. (Dominican Republic) A man who had three dogs went hunting and found a lady whom he liked very much, but soon he found that she was the Devil's wife. Because he had an erection he took her home. His mother told him to take her back where he had found her. The mother bugged him so much that he told the woman he would take her to the bush. She agreed but told him to leave his dogs behind. She gave him three hairs to tie the dogs with, saying that they could break them and come to him if he needed them. When they left the three hairs turned into three thick chains. When they got to the bush she said that she was the wife of the Devil and that she was going to eat him. The man's mother had given him three twigs to throw when he was in danger. He threw one and it turned into a big tree and he climbed it. The woman called her people to fell the tree. He called his dogs, Parsley, Snake, and Cutter Dog, but they could not get away. He threw another twig and it became another tree after the little devils had cut down the first one. He kept calling the dogs and threw the last twig, which became an even bigger

tree. While the little devils were chopping at it the dogs broke loose and scared them away. The man went home with his dogs and lived happily ever after. (Andrade [1930], pp. 139–40)

97. (Dominican Republic) A young man lived with his mother and his three dogs. He fell in love with a young woman who came to his house. His mother warned that she might cause his death but he married her. His bride tied his three dogs with three of her hairs and stuffed their ears. They went for a walk in the woods, but before leaving he put corn kernels in his pocket. When they reached a mamey tree that had only one fruit, she told him to pick it and see what would happen. He climbed the tree and she pulled out a guitar and sang. Little devils appeared with axes and began to chop at the tree. When it began to fall he threw nine kernels of corn and the tree became bigger. The woman kept singing. When the corn was finished and the tree was about to fall, he called to his dogs, "Indifor, Caricatéi, Jenabronbrón, and Bronbrón." The dogs heard his voice, broke their chains, and arrived when the tree was about to fall. They took the Devil's wife who said she would marry the man if he let her go, but he told the dogs to tear her to pieces. He went home with his dogs and later married a young woman. (Andrade [1930], pp. 140–41)

98. (Dominican Republic) A brother and sister came to a witch who gave them three dogs saying, "This white one is Ramilallé. This black one is Ondifó. This yellow one is Caricaté." The witch disappeared as if charmed. The boy told his sister to turn loose his dogs if they barked because he would be in danger. A woman with long hands, feet, and teeth, and big eyes came to the house and carried the sister away. The boy met a serpent with seven heads and climbed a tree. He sang, calling his dogs, but they could not break loose. From the seven heads of the snake seven men with axes appeared and began to chop down the tree. As it was about to fall the dogs broke loose. They came to the seven Blacks and tore them to pieces. The boy went home and found that his sister was not there. He searched for her and came to a cave where an old woman sang, saying that to save his sister she must have his three dogs and three fingers from the boy's right hand. He sang back that she must first fight him and his dogs. He sang to his dogs that they must not leave a bone of the old woman, promising each a pearl necklace. When the dogs attacked her, she turned into a lion, a tiger, and then a piece of paper that said, "Whoever gets this paper, if a man he will marry the king's daughter, if a woman she will marry the king's son." The brother and sister took the paper and married the king's daughter and the king's son. (Andrade [1930], pp. 141–42)

99. (Puerto Rico) A girl married against her brother's advice. When her mother learned from a priest that her daughter's husband was the Devil, she asked the brother to find her. Before leaving he told his mother that if his rose lost its petals she should release his two dogs, named Cajón and Cajonero. At the house of the Devil he asked for water from the well, but each bucketful that the Devil pulled up became empty. The brother and sister took a horse

and fled, but the cock crowed and the Devil knew they had left. The Devil took another horse and pursued them. The boy threw down salt, salt water, and a leaf, and a salt mountain, salt water, and a palm grove appeared. The Devil felled all the palm trees except the one in which the children were. The mother saw the rose and let the dogs loose. They came and killed the Devil and his wife, and the children came down from the tree and went home. Another incident follows. (Mason and Espinosa [1926], pp. 314-15.)

100. (Puerto Rico) After another episode a boy had three dogs named Cancuerno, Canflor, and Caniyera. His sister fell in love with a giant. Wanting to trick her brother she told him to leave his dogs behind to kill the giant while the brother went hunting. When the giant came she sent him to her brother. As a last request the boy asked to climb a tree and say goodbye to his family and his dogs, but he called his dogs and they killed the giant. The sister asked to see the giant's body and she took out his two eyeteeth. The boy married a princess and on the wedding night his sister put the teeth under their bed and the boy was killed. After he was buried, the dogs dug up his body and sucked out the teeth. The boy revived, his sister was killed, and the dogs became angels. (Mason and Espinosa [1926], pp. 330-33)

101. (Guadeloupe) A boy had three dogs named Quatiquati, Tinedé, and Boiyé. He told his mother that he was going hunting and that she should release his dogs if she saw a rose fade. He met the Devil and climbed a tree. The Devil chopped at the tree and when it was about to fall the boy prayed and God made it seven times bigger. He called to his dogs, but his mother was talking and did not notice the rose until it was faded. Then she turned the dogs loose. Each time the tree was about to fall, the Devil hit his belly and brought out ten thousand little devils with axes. When the dogs came the boy told them to eat all the devils but to keep the Devil's tongue for him. He gave the tongue to his mother and it stuck in her throat, but he slapped her on the back and it came out. (Parsons [1933-43], Part II, pp. 137-38, Part III, p. 170)

102. (Guadeloupe) After escaping from an old woman, a little boy went home. The old woman dressed up as a pretty girl and asked him for an apple. He told his mother that when a bowl of water turned to blood she should turn loose his three chained dogs, named Longo, Laidoux, and L'Allemand. He climbed a tree for the apple but the higher he climbed the taller the tree grew. The woman gave birth to ten thousand little devils who chopped at the tree with axes. The boy sang for his dogs and when the tree was about to fall, he said, "Fall, rise!" When the tree was really about to fall, he plucked a hair from his head and whistled on it; it fell on the dogs' chains and they broke. The dogs ate all the devils and the old woman. The boy took a piece of a devil's tongue to his mother. It stuck in her throat but he slapped her back and it came out. The boy and his dogs drowned in a well. (Parsons [1933-43], Part II, pp. 138-41, Part III, pp. 70-71)

103. (Guadeloupe) A boy's mother told him to test his girl by pricking her. If blood came she was a Christian; if matter came she was a devil. The boy

showed his own blood to his mother and married the girl. The boy had three dogs, named Fifi, Fioumise, and Filomene. He told his mother to release them if a plate of water turned to blood. He left with his wife, who told him to climb a tree for an apple. She hit her belly and out came a lot of little devils; and she defecated tools for them to cut down the tree. The boy prayed that God would make the tree a thousand times bigger, and he sang for his mother to let his dogs loose. The water turned to blood but the mother was sleeping because of a potion her son's wife had given her. The dogs came and ate all except the tongue which the boy gave to his mother. It stuck in her throat, but he slapped her on the back and it came out. (Parsons [1933–43], Part II, p. 141, Part III, p. 171)

104. (Les Saintes) A boy had three large dogs named Guele Filo, Sandalo, and Baillelo. He told his mother to release them if a bowl of water began to boil. She gave him seven lice and he went into the forest. He climbed a tree to eat apples and the Devil ordered him down. The Devil beat his belly and defecated little devils with axes. They sang and began to chop at the tree, and the boy sang to his dogs. When the tree was about to fall he cracked a louse and the tree became twice as big. The water began to boil but the mother did not notice. The dogs broke their rope. When the lice gave out and the tree fell, the dogs arrived and killed the Devil. He gave the Devil's tongue to his mother. It stuck in her throat but he slapped the back of her neck and it came out. (Parsons [1933–43], Part II, pp. 247–50, Part III, pp. 171–72)

105. (Dominica) A boy had three dogs named Quat'e-t'ou'cawé, Méblé, and Enri. He told his mother to release them if a basin of water turned red. He met a lot of little devils and climbed a tree. The devils started to chop it down to kill the boy. He took an egg from a nest in the tree and broke it, praying that God would make the tree bigger, and sang to his dogs. The water had turned to blood but his mother was busy cooking. When the tree was about to fall, he broke another egg and the tree became bigger. When he broke the last egg, the dogs broke their chain. They arrived as the tree was falling and ate up all the devils. The boy threw down his hat and clothes and the dogs recognized their master. He took the tongue of a devil to his mother; it caught in her throat and she strangled to death. (Parsons [1933–43], Part I, pp. 434–35, Part III, p. 170)

106. (Martinique) A black boy wanted to marry a white girl, but white Martiniquans do not marry Negroes. A white girl proposed to him and they were married. She became pregnant and suggested that they visit his mountain estate, telling him to tie up his dogs, named Coléfala, Dimilaroi, and 'Tit Poliment. He put a bowl of water in his mother's room and told her to release his dogs if the water turned to blood. After they started his wife returned on a pretext and tied the three dogs with three hairs from her head and gave his mother a sleeping potion. At the plantation she asked her husband to climb a tree for an apricot, making him climb higher and higher until he threw one down. The apricot hit her on the belly and when she beat on her belly little

devils came out with their axes. The bowl of water turned to blood but the boy's mother was asleep. The more that the devils chopped at the tree the larger it grew. The boy called to his dogs by name and they broke their chains and came singing. They destroyed the woman and the devils. (Parsons [1933–34], Part I, pp. 326–29, Part III, p. 169)

107. (Martinique) A boy's mother was dead and all he had was three arrows and three dogs. When he was three days old he met a beautiful woman with a red bouquet. She said she would give it to the one who shot his arrow into it and the boy succeeded and married her. His godmother appeared, warned him that his wife was a devil, and gave him a bottle of milk. She told him that if he ever went anywhere with his wife he should tell his grandmother to release his dogs if she saw the milk turn to blood. His wife proposed that they look at her mountain property after first tying his dogs. She sent him up a tree for an apricot and he threw it down on her belly. Little devils came out with axes, cutlasses, and knives and began to cut the tree. The milk turned to blood but the grandmother was sleeping. He sang to his dogs calling them by name, Goudou Missa, Bomba Sala, and 'Tit Poliman. When the tree was about to fall, the boy threw an arrow and the tree became a thousand times bigger, and so also with the second and third arrow. The dogs cut their chains and came. One swallowed the devil's mother but she came out its behind. The same thing happened again, but the third time the boy told the dog to swallow her and squat down. When she came out again he cut off her head, ears, fingers, and toes. He cooked them for his mother [sic] when he returned home. A bone stuck in her throat and he slapped her on the back to relieve her. (Parsons [1933–43], Part I, pp. 329–37, Part III, pp. 169–70)

108. (Grenada) After another episode a boy told his sister not to touch the grave of an old woman they had killed. When she did so, the woman arose from the grave and told the girl that she didn't want her, only her brother. She took an ax and found the boy in a tree. She started to chop the tree down, and, when it was about to fall, the boy called his dogs, named Scandale, Dash, and Carlu. When they came he killed the old woman and the boy took all of her property home. (Parsons [1933–43], Part I, pp. 80–81, Part III, p. 169)

109. (Trinidad) A boy who loved hunting tied his dogs and told his mother to release them if she saw water in a basin turn to blood. He went out and climbed a tree and a witch with some little devils tried to cut it down to kill him. He asked God to make the tree bigger and sang for his dogs, named Tintin, Passe-pa'to', Appilleloto, and Carouma. The mother did not notice that the water had turned to blood, but his dogs bit through their ropes. They came and devoured all the little devils, leaving the witch to the last. The first dog swallowed the witch but she came out its behind, and the same thing happened with the second and third dog. The fourth dog swallowed her and sat down. The boy asked God to make the tree small again and came down. He went home and told his mother that it would have been her fault if he had lost his life. (Parsons [1933–43], Part I, pp. 33–34, Part III, pp. 167–68)

110. (Trinidad) A young man who loved every passing woman was about

to escort a fine looking Carib woman to her home, and she told him to tie his dogs. He told his mother to release them if she saw the pot on the fire boiling and the water turning to blood, but she forgot. The Carib woman sent the man up a tree for a golden apple and told him to shake the tree. Every leaf that fell became a young she-devil, ax in hand. When they started to cut down the tree the man turned into a tree, but she turned him into a man again. He had previously told her the things he could turn into, but when he started to say he could turn into a needle his mother hushed him. Whatever the man turned into the Carib woman turned him into a man again. Then he made the tree seven times larger and turned himself into a needle. She couldn't turn him into a man and she couldn't cut the tree until she did so. A blue frog offered to help cut the tree, but it made the tree seventy times larger, and a white frog made it fifty times larger still. The man's strongest dog broke its chain and the chains of his other dogs. They came and devoured all the young devils but the old one hid in a hole. The man spit on a leaf and threw it to his dogs; they recognized their master and lay down. When he came home I told him that a man who loves every woman he sees will always get into danger. (Parsons [1933–43], Part I, pp. 34–36, Part III, p. 168)

111. (Trinidad) A boy had three dogs named Oh-me-boy, Ah-me-enge, and Shoo-me-boy. He told his mother to release them if water in a basin turned to blood, but his mother was a witch and stuffed the dogs' ears with cotton. The boy found an orange tree with one orange at the top and a pretty girl asked him to get it. When he climbed the tree the girl struck her right side and seven devils came out, then her left side and seven more devils came out. They chopped at the tree and their ax sang. The boy sang for his dogs. He prayed and the tree was whole again. The dogs' footfalls sang as they came. They tore up the devils and the girl who had hidden in a hole. The boy threw down his jacket and hat and the dogs recognized them. When the boy up-braided his mother she sang. (Parsons [1933–43], Part I, pp. 36–38, Part III, p. 168)

112. (Guyana) A hunter had three magic arrows and two fierce dogs named Ya-me-o-ro and Con-ga-mo-ro-to. He killed many white cows. The cows hated the hunter but feared to attack him because of the dogs. One evening he heard groans coming from the woods and taking his dogs with him he found a beautiful woman lying on the ground, apparently in great distress. She begged him for food and shelter and he carried her home and nursed her until she was well again. He begged her not to leave and she became his wife. One day he started to go hunting and his wife begged him to leave his dogs to protect her. He tied them up and for the first time went hunting alone. He heard a great noise and saw all the cows gathered to kill him. He ran for home, but, seeing that the cows would catch him, he stuck one of his arrows in the ground and put his foot on top of it. At once he found himself on top of a tall palm tree that had sprung from the ground. The cows butted the tree but could not fell it. They rushed away and returned with axes and began to chop the tree down. He called his dogs by name but they did not come.

When the tree was about to fall he shot his second arrow into the ground and an even larger tree sprang up. The hunter leaped to it and the cows began to chop at it. He called his dogs again, shot his last arrow, and leaped into the third tree. He called again to his dogs and saw his wife come and turn into a white cow. When he called a fourth time his dogs came, having gnawed through their ropes. First they attacked his wife, the queen cow, and tore her to pieces. Then they turned on the others, killing many and putting the rest to flight. (Wells [1892], pp. 46–49)

113. (Suriname) A wise boy was apprenticed to a devil because he was bad. The devil tried various ways to kill him but failed and sent him to work with a master carpenter. When the devil decided he must look for the boy he changed into a beautiful woman and said that she would live with the one who knocked a basket from her head. Many men tried and failed, but the boy succeeded and lived with her. She said that they should go and look for fruit. Before leaving the boy chained his three dogs and told his mother to release them when the water in a pot on the fire became red. They went into the bush, found a fruit tree, and the boy climbed it. His wife turned into a tall man. At home the water became red but the mother did not notice it. The devil sang and many people came. The boy dropped a bottle of magic and the tree grew so large that they could not cut it. The water in the pot turned to blood but the mother was gossiping with a neighbor. The dogs chewed at their chains. When the tree was about to fall the boy dropped a bottle again. The devil sang and many more devils came with axes to cut the tree. The dogs broke loose and came to the tree. They killed all the devil's helpers and wanted to kill him also, but the boy stopped them. He dug a hole and put the devil in it. Back home he told his mother that his dogs must not eat canned things, but one day she cooked salmon and left the can. The dogs smelled the can and killed the boy. (Herskovits and Herskovits [1936], pp. 324–27)

114. (Argentina) Abandoned in the forest by their parents, a boy and his sister found three dogs and named them Chain of Gold, Chain of Silver, and Long Balls. A giant fell in love with the girl and taught her to cry and ask her brother for apples. When the boy climbed the tree to get them the giant told him to come down to be eaten. The boy called his dogs by name and they came and attacked the giant. Another day the giant told the girl he was going to turn himself into a serpent. He gave her three bristles and told her to tie the dogs with them and ask for apples again. When the boy was in the tree the giant came and told him to come down to be eaten. The boy called his dogs by name and finally they broke the bristles and came running. They seized the giant and left him unrecognizable. Another episode follows. (Chertudi [1960–64], vol. I, pp. 104–8)

115. (Argentina) Abandoned in the forest by their parents, a boy and a girl found three huge dogs and named them Come Soon, Cut Iron, and Faster than Wind. They found a witch baking cakes and the boy climbed a tree and stole cakes from the oven with a stick. The witch noticed that some cakes

were missing and, thinking that her cat was taking them, she said, "I'll give you some when I eat." When the girl heard this she laughed, and the witch discovered the boy in the tree. She had a fork that grew longer and longer until it reached the boy. He called to his dog, "Iron Cutter." The dog came and cut the fork with a bite. "Come Here Soon," the boy shouted. The second dog came and pushed the witch to the ground. "Faster than Wind," he called. When the third dog came the boy and girl climbed on its back and disappeared in the air with the two other dogs. Another episode follows. (Chertudi [1960–64], Vol. II, pp. 90–91)

116. (Chile) An orphan brother and sister grew up and the boy became a hunter. One day his dogs attacked a giant, but the boy spared his life in return for his palace and wealth. He locked the giant in a room, telling his sister never to open it, but she opened the room and fell in love with the giant. The giant proposed that they kill her brother and suggested that she ask for a plant to cure her illness and that she tie his two dogs with strands of hair. The giant followed the boy and was about to kill him. The boy asked to climb a tree to bid good-bye to the world. In the tree he called to his dogs, "Break Iron, Break Chain." The dogs heard him, broke their bonds and ran to him. He told them to kill the giant and they did so. Other episodes follow. (Pino Saavedra [1960–63], Vol. I, pp. 124–29; [1967], pp. 40–46)

117. (Chile: Araucanian Indians) A monster was the lover of the sister of a small Indian. The youth traded his herd of sheep for two dogs named North and South. His sister was angry and wanted the monster to kill him. She pretended to be sick and sent her brother for pears for medicine. He put his dogs and his gun in a box and went to a pear tree. When he had climbed it the monster came and said it would kill him. He asked to pray first, climbed down from the tree, and called his two dogs. They came running and killed the monster. Another episode follows. (Lenz [1895–97], pp. 242–49; [1898], pp. 187–92)

BIBLIOGRAPHY

Akinsemoyin, 'Kunle
1965 *Stories at Sundown*. London, George G. Harrap.
Andrade, Manuel J.
1930 Folk-Lore from the Dominican Republic. *Memoirs of the American Folk-Lore Society* 23.
Bascom, William
1969 *Ifa Divination: Communication Between Gods and Men in West Africa*. Bloomington, Indiana University Press.
Basset, René
1886–87 Contes haoussas. *Melusine* 3.

n.d. Contes Populaires d'Afrique. *Les Littératures Populaires de Toutes les Nations* 47, c. 1903.

Beazley, Julia
1938 The Poopampareno. *Texas Folk-Lore Society Publications* 14.

Beckwith, Martha Warren
1924 Jamaica Anansi Stories. *Memoirs of the American Folk-Lore Society* 17.

Boas, Franz
1912 Notes on Mexican Folk-Lore, *Journal of American Folk-Lore* 25

Bordinat, Philip, and Thomas, Peter
1973 Revealer of Secrets. *African Reader's Library* 24. Lagos, African Universities Press.

Botkin, B. A.
1949 *A Treasury of Southern Folklore.* New York, Crown.
1966 *A Treasury of American Folklore.* New York, Crown [1944]

Callaway, Canon
1868 *Nursery Tales, Traditions, and Histories of the Zulus.* Springvale, John A. Blair; Pietermaritzburg, Davis and Sons; London, Trübner.

Carrière, Joseph Médard
1937 *Tales from the French Folk-Lore of Missouri.* Evanston and Chicago, Northwestern University.

Chertudi, Susana
1960–64 *Cuentos Folklóricos Argentina,* Vols. I–II. Buenos Aires, Instituto Nacional de Filología y Folklore.

Comhaire-Sylvain, Suzanne
1938 Creole Tales from Haiti. *Journal of American Folk-Lore* 51.

Cothran, Jean
1972 *The Whang Doodle. Folk Tales from the Carolinas.* Columbia, South Carolina, Sandlapper Press.

Courlander, Harold
1976 *A Treasury of Afro-American Folklore.* New York, Crown.

Crimmins, Martin L.
1931 Mr. 'Possum and Mr. Coon *Publications of the Texas Folk-Lore Society* 9.

Crowley, Daniel J.
1977 *African Folklore in the New World.* Austin & London, University of Texas Press.

Dammann, Ernst
1935–36 Digo Märchen. *Zeitschrift für Eingeborenen-Sprachen* 26.

Dayrell, E.
1913 Ikom Folk Stories from Southern Nigeria. Royal Anthropological Institute, *Occasional Papers* 3.

de Clercq, Aug.
1909 Quelques légendes des Bena Kanioka. *Anthropos* 4.

Diop, Birago
1947 *Les Contes d'Amadou-Koumba.* Paris, Fasquelle.

Dorson, Richard M.
1956 *Negro Folktales in Michigan.* Cambridge, Mass., Harvard University Press.
1967 *American Negro Folktales.* Greenwich, Conn., Fawcett.
1977 The African Connection. In Crowley 1977.

Dundes, Alan
1976 African and Afro-American Tales. *Research in African Literatures* 7.

Edgar, Frank
1911–13 *Litafi na Tatsuniyoyi na Hausa,* Vols. I–III. Belfast, W. Erskine Mayne.

Evans-Pritchard, E. E.
1963–65 *Zande Texts,* Parts 1–5. Oxford, The Author.
1967 *The Zande Trickster.* Oxford, Clarendon Press.

Finnegan, Ruth
1967 *Limba Stories and Story-Telling.* Oxford Library of African Literature. Oxford, Clarendon Press.
Frobenius, Leo
1924 Dämonen des Sudan. *Atlantis 7.*
1926 Die Atlantische Götterlehre. *Atlantis 10.*
1928 Dichtkunst der Kassaiden. *Atlantis 12.*
1971 *African Nights. Black Erotic Folk Tales.* New York., Herder and Herder.
Fuja, Abayomi
1962 *Fourteen Hundred Cowries. Traditional Stories of the Yoruba.* London and Ibadan, Oxford University Press.
Girard, J.
1967 Dynamique de la Société Ouobé. *Mémoires de l'Institut Fondemental d'Afrique Noire 78.*
Guilhem, Marcel
n.d.–1962 *50 Contes et Fableaux de la Savane,* Vols. I–II. Paris, Ligel
Guillot, René
1933 Contes d'Afrique. *Numéro spécial du Bulletin de l'Enseignement de l'A. O. F.*
Harris, Joel Chandler
1886 The Little Boy and his Dogs. *Louisville Courier-Journal,* February 18.
1889 *Daddy Jake, The Runaway: And Short Stories Told After Dark,* New York, The Century Company.
1892 *Uncle Remus and his Friends.* Boston, Houghton Mifflin.
1955 *The Complete Tales of Uncle Remus.* Compiled by Richard Chase. Boston, Houghton Mifflin.
Hendricks, Peggy
1953 Wham, Jam, Jenny-Mo-Wham. *Publication of the Texas Folklore Society 25.*
Hendricks, W. C.
1943 *Bundle of Troubles and Other Tarheel Tales.* Durham, North Carolina, Duke University Press.
Hernández de Soto, Sergio
1886 Cuentos Populares de Extremadura. *Biblioteca de las Tradiciones Populares Españoles 10.*
Herskovits, Melville J., and Herskovits, Frances S.
1936 Suriname Folklore. *Columbia University Contributions to Anthropology 27.*
1958 Dahomean Narrative. *Northwestern University African Studies 1.*
Hoffman, C.
1915–16 Märchen und Erzählungen der Eingeborenen in Nord-Transvaal. *Zeitschrift für Kolonialsprachen 6.*
Kidd, Dudley
1906 *Savage Childhood.* London, Adam and Charles Black.
Kootz-Kretschmer, Elise
1926–29 *Die Safwa,* Vols. I–III. Berlin, Dietrich Reimer.
Lacosta, Camille
1965 *Traduction des Légendes et Contes Merveilleux de la Grande Kabylie recueillis par Auguste Mouliéras,* Vols. I–III. Bibliothèque de l'Ecole des Langues Orientales Vivantes. Paris, Librairie Orientaliste Paul Geuthner.
Lenz, Rodolfo
1895–97 *Estudios Araucanos.* Santiago de Chile, Imprenta Cervantes.
1898 Araukanische Märchen und Erzählungen. *Verhandlungen des Deutschen Wissenschaftlichen Vereins zu Santiago de Chile 3.*
Macdonald, Duff

1882 *Africana; or, The Heart of Heathen Africa*, Vols. I–II. London, Simpkin Marshall; Edinburgh, John Menzies; Aberdeen, A. Brown.

Mamet, M.
1960 Le Langage des Bolia (Lac Léopold II). Tervuren, *Annales du Musée Royal du Congo Belge* 33.

Mason, J. Alden, and Espinosa, Aurelio M.
1926 Porto Rican Folk-Lore: Folk Tales. *Journal of American Folk-Lore* 39.

Parsons, Elsie Clews
1917 Tales from Guilford County, North Carolina. *Journal of American Folk-Lore* 30.
1918 Folk-Tales of Andros Island, Bahamas. *Memoirs of the American Folk-Lore Society* 13.
1922 Die Flucht auf dem Baum. *Zeitschrift für Ethnologie* 54.
1923 Folk-Lore from the Cape Verde Islands. *Memoirs of the American Folk-Lore Society* 15, Parts I–II.
1923 Folk-Lore of the Sea Islands, South Carolina. *Memoirs of the American Folk-Lore Society* 16.
1928 Spirituals and Other Folklore from the Bahamas. *Journal of American Folk-Lore* 41.
1933–43 Folk-Lore of the Antilles, French and English. *Memoirs of the American Folk-Lore Society* 26, Parts I–III.

Paulme, Denise
1976 *La mère dévorante. Essai sur la morphologie des contes africains.* Bibliothèque des Sciences Humaines. Paris, Editions Gallimard.

Peeraer, Servais
1937–38 La Littérature Orale Muluba. *Bulletin des amis de l'art indigene du Katanga* 3–4.

Penn School Pupils
1925 Folklore from St. Helena, South Carolina. *Journal of American Folk-Lore* 38.

Pino Saavedra, Yolando
1960–63 *Cuentos Folkloricos de Chile*, Vols. I–III. Santiago de Chile, Instituto de Investigaciones Folklóricas "Ramón A. Laval."
1967 *Folktales of Chile.* Folktales of the World, Richard M. Dorson, ed. Chicago, University of Chicago Press.

Postma, Minnie
1964 *Litsomo.* Johannesburg, Afrikaanse Pers-Boekhandel.
1974 Tales from the Basotho. Translated by Susie McDermid. *American Folklore Society, Memoir Series* 59.

Quénum, Maximilien
1938 *Au Pays des Fons. Us et Coutumes du Dahomey.* Paris, Larose, 2nd. ed. [1935]

Rattray, R. S.
1930 *Akan-Ashanti Folk-Tales.* Oxford, Clarendon Press.

Rehse, Hermann
1910 *Kiziba Land und Leute.* Stuttgart, Strecker & Schröder.

Richardson, Clement; Work, Monroe N.; and Parsons, Elsie Clews
1919 Folk-Tales from Students in Tuskeegee Institute, Alabama. *Journal of American Folk-Lore* 32.

Roberts, Leonard W.
1955 *South from Hell-for-Sartin.* Lexington, University of Kentucky Press.

Schön, James Frederick
1877 *Hausa Reading Book.* London, Church Missionary Society.
1885–86 *Magana Hausa*, Parts I–II. London, Society for Promoting Christian Knowledge.
1968 *Dictionary of the Hausa Language.* Farnborough Hants, Gregg Press. [1876]

Schön, J. F., and Robinson, Charles H.
   1907 *Magana Hausa*. London, Society for Promoting Christian Knowledge.
Schultze, Leonhard
   1907 *Aus Namaland und Kalahari*. Jena, Gustav Fischer.
Skinner, Neil
   1969–77 *Hausa Tales and Traditions. An English Translation of Tatsuniyoyi Na Hausa, Originally compiled by Frank Edgar*. London, Frank Cass, Vol. I, 1969; Madison, The University of Wisconsin Press, Vols. II–III, 1977.
Stannus, Hugh
   1922 The Wayao of Nyasaland. *Harvard African Studies* 3.
Stayt, Hugh A.
   1931 *The Bavenda*. London Oxford University Press.
Swanton, John R.
   1929 Myths and Tales of the Southeastern Indians. *Bureau of American Ethnology Bulletin* 88.
Talbot, P. Amaury
   1969 *In the Shadow of the Bush*. Westport, Conn., Negro Universities Press. [1912]
Tauxier, L.
   1917 *Le Noir du Yatenga*. Paris, Emile Larose.
   1924 *Nègres Gouro et Gagou*. Paris, Librairie Orientaliste Paul Geuthner.
Teit, James
   1898 Traditions of the Thompson River Indians of British Columbia. *Memoirs of the American Folk-Lore Society* 6.
   1909 The Shushwap. *Memoirs of the American Museum of Natural History* 4:7.
Tessman, Günter
   1934 *Die Baja. Ein Negerstamm in Mittleren Sudan*, Vols. I–II. Stuttgart, Strecker und Schroeder.
Theal, Geo. McCall
   1886 *Kaffir Folk-Lore*. London, Swan Sonnenschein, Le Bas & Lowrey.
   1910 *The Yellow and Dark-Skinned People of Africa South of the Zambesi*. London, Swan Sonnenschein.
Thomas, Northcote W.
   1916 *Anthropological Report on Sierra Leone*, Parts I–III. London, Harrison and Sons.
Travélé, Moussa
   1923 *Proverbes et Contes Bambara*. Paris, Paul Geuthner.
Tremearne, A. J. N.
   1913 *Hausa Superstitions and Customs*. London, John Bale, Sons & Danielsson.
Tutuola, Amos
   1962 *Feather Woman of the Jungle*. London, Faber and Faber.
van Wing, J., and Scholler, Cl.
   1940 *Legendes des Bakongo-Orientaux*. Brussels, Bulens.
Vernon-Jackson, Hugh
   1963 *More West African Folk Tales, Book One*. London, University of London Press.
Walker, Barbara K., and Walker, Warren S.
   1961 *Nigerian Folk Tales*. New Brunswick, New Jersey, Rutgers University Press.
Wells, Davis Dwight
   1892 Evolution in Folklore. *Popular Science Monthly* 41.
Westermann, Diedrich
   1921 Die Gola-Sprache in Liberia. Hamburgische Universität, *Abhandlungen aus dem Gebiet der Auslandskunde* 6, Reihe B, Völkerkunde, Kulturgeschichte und Sprachen 6.
   1921 Die Kpelle. Ein Negerstamm in Liberia. *Quellen der Religions-Geschichte*, Gruppe 10, Band 9.

NOTES

1. Boas [1912], p. 259, n. 1; Richardson, Work, and Parsons [1919], p. 397, n. 6.

2. Richardson, Work, and Parsons [1919], p. 397.

3. Dorson [1956], pp. 232–33; [1967], p. 249.

4. Parsons [1922], pp. 9, 11. In most of the American Indian tales cited in this study the hero is not rescued by his dogs. For the same reason I exclude one of her two Hausa versions, the one from Angola, the one from Louisiana, and one of the two from Georgia. "Escape up the Tree" and "Dogs Rescue Master in Tree Refuge" are not the same.

5. Parsons [1922], p. 9.

6. Hernández de Soto [1886], pp. 258–70.

7. William Bascom, "Afro-American Studies. Introduction," *Actes du XLII Congrès International des Américanistes, Paris, 2–9, Septembre 1976,* Vol. 6, 1979, p. 594.

8. Andrade [1930], p. 141.

9. Aurelio M. Espinosa, "Cuentos Populares Espanoles," *Stanford University Publications, University Series, Language and Literature,* Vol. 3:2, 1924, pp. 336–41.

10. Bascom [1969], pp. 134–36; 417–23.

11. Dundes [1976], p. 191; reprinted in Crowley [1977], p. 45.

12. Dorson [1977], p. 90.

13. Boas [1912], p. 259.

14. This version is from an Ifa divination verse. The Yoruba names of the dogs (Okemokerewu, Osopakagbomomi, and Ogbalegbarawe) could be only partially translated by the informant. Okemokerewu was said to mean "One who cuts child of kerewu." Kerewu means cotton seed or bracelet but its meaning in this context is not known. Compare Frobenius [29] who transcribes the name as Oke Makeren and translates it as *Abschneider.* Osopakagbomomi was translated as "Osopaka takes the child and swallows it," with the meaning of Osopaka unknown. Frobenius gives Osoquako Gwenini and translates it as *Zuschnappende und Verschlucker.* Ogbalegbarawe was translated as "One who sweeps the ground and sweeps dry leaves." Frobenius gives Ogballe Gbarawes and translates it as *Reiniger des Platzes.* Compare also Fuja's "Cut to Pieces," "Swallow up," and "Clear the Remains," and Tutuola's Cutter, Swallower, and Sweeper.

✳

ELEVEN

Agreement to Sell Mothers;
Agreement to Kill Mothers; "Cutta Cord-La!"

"Agreement to Sell Mothers" requires little discussion. The trickster and the dupe decide to sell their mothers or other relatives, usually to buy food. On the way to market the trickster's mother usually escapes, frequently because he has tied her with a weak rope, but the dupe ties his mother with a strong rope and sells her. This tale is usually combined with other episodes, frequently with that of the buried tails as in the two Uncle Remus versions [22-23], but it is a tale type because it has been recorded by itself [10-11].

I have found no references to this tale type in either Aarne and Thompson's tale type index or Thompson's motif index.[1] Therefore I conclude that it came to America from (and originated in) Africa.

Calame-Griaule and Lacroix have published a very helpful comparative study of this tale type under the title "La mére vendue," citing a number of the African versions included here as noted. Three of their versions,[2] however, are clearly a different tale type and belong in the following section, "Agreement to Kill Mothers."

My sixteen African tales come from Senegal (Wolof, Serere-None, and Fulani), Mali (Fulani, Malinke, Bozo, Dogon, and Twareg), and Upper Volta (Bambara, Mosi, and Gurma). Seven come from New England, Louisiana, South Carolina, and Georgia. Two come from Bahamas and Guadeloupe.

1. (Senegal: Wolof) Hare told Hyena that his aunt was so ill that she was only skin and bones. He suggested that they sell their aunts in a country where there was lots of grain and cattle. Hyena said it was too good to be true. Hare told him to tie his aunt with a strong rope, but he tied his own aunt with a cotton thread. On the way they tied their aunts to trees and took a little walk. When they returned Hare's aunt was not there. Hyena's aunt said that she had broken her cord and fled and that she herself had tried to do the same but had been unable to break her cord. Hare said he would go

Reprinted from *Research in African Literature*, 13 (1982), 181-95).

and look for his aunt, but Hyena said that his aunt would suffice. They sold Hyena's aunt and bought a donkey loaded with two huge sacks of grain and a large fat cow. They started home and other episodes follow. (Senghor and Sadji [1965], pp. 39–48)

2. (Senegal: Serere-None) Hare and Hyena were going to cultivate a field of millet, but Hare stole the seeds and hid them. Hyena suggested that they sell their mothers as slaves and buy millet with the money. They tied their mothers to a tree and awaited the sale, but Hare cut the bonds of his mother and she fled. Hare pretended to be very angry, but Hyena said that the price of her mother would be sufficient to buy millet. The next day, with the price of Hyena's mother, they bought millet to replace that which Hare had stolen. (Basset [n.d.], pp. 187–188)

3. (Senegal: Fulani) Hyena, Lion, Panther, and Hare grew millet and put it in a storehouse. Hare returned and emptied the storehouse, leaving only some hyena dung. When the animals returned to the storehouse, Hyena found only the dung. She was accused but denied doing it. They went to a river for a test. The other animals jumped over without touching the water, but Hare fell in. Hare said it was because his paws were short. As another test they said they would sell their mothers. The other animals used weak cords to tie their mothers; they went only a little way and the cords broke and they went on. But Hyena used a strong cord and it did not break. The animals said, "She has sold her mother. It is Hyena who ate the millet." (Gaden [1913], pp. 236–239; adapted in Calame-Griaule and Lacroix [1970], p. 1370)

4. (Mali: Fulani) After other incidents Hyena and Hare were told to sell their mothers. Hyena tied his mother with large ropes, but Hare tied his with a thread. Hare told his mother to break the thread when they came to a hollow tree and hide in it. When she did so Hare complained that she had spoiled his fortune, but Hyena said to let her go, that they would sell his mother. They did so and bought a cow. They slaughtered the cow near the hollow tree, and another episode follows. (Brun [1919–20], pp. 180–184).

5. (Mali: Malinke) Hare told Hyena that he had dreamed that a terrible tornado was coming. He said that to escape he must tie his mother with a strong cord and beat her until she broke it; if the cord did not break, he should sell his mother. Hare said that he was going to do this so as not to die. Hare showed Hyena a large cord with which to tie his mother. Hare tied his mother with a slender string and beat her with all his force, and the string broke; Hyena tied his mother solidly and beat her, but she could not break her bonds. Hare told Hyena to sell her. They went to a Fulani camp and exchanged Hyena's mother for a cow, and other episodes follow. (Monteil [1905], pp. 135–138; adapted in Calame-Griaule and Lacroix [1970], pp. 1370–1371)

6. (Mali: Malinke) Hare suggested to Jackal that they sell their mothers and buy cows, and Jackal agreed. Jackal tied his mother with a thick strong rope, but Hare tied his with a thin cord. Hare told his mother to break the cord when they were near the market and hide in a hollow tree. When she

did so Hare cried out that she had escaped, but Jackal said it did not matter because they still had his mother and could buy a fine cow. They sold Jackal's mother, bought a sick cow and killed it, and other episodes follow. (Frobenius, "Erzählungen" [1922], pp. 110–114)

7. (Mali: Bozo) Hare and Hyena decided to sell their mothers. Hare tied his mother with a cotton thread and Hyena tied hers with a *Bauhinia* bond. Hare's mother escaped, but Hyena exchanged her mother for a sick cow, and another episode follows. (Daget, Konipo, and Sanankoua [1953], p. 139; adapted from the resume in Calame-Griaule and Lacroix [1970], p. 1369)

8. (Mali: Bozo) Hyena and Hare decided to sell their mothers in order to buy cows. They went to find hibiscus fibers to make rope. Hare said that his mother was not strong and one fiber would suffice. Hyena made a stout rope. Hare pierced his mother's nose and put one fiber through it. Hyena did the same with his rope, tying his mother well. Hare told his mother to escape. When she did Hare complained, but Hyena said, "Your mother is worth nothing. Mine will suffice for two." They went to Fulani who wanted to buy their mothers. He told them to take what they wished from his herd. Hyena took an old, weak cow and Hare took a bull, and another episode follows. (Calame-Griaule and Lacroix [1970], p. 1358)

9. (Mali: Bozo) Hare and Hyena took their mothers to market. Hare's mother escaped but Hyena said that her mother would suffice. They found a Fulani who gave them a cow and an ox. Hare asked for the ox, but Hyena took it, saying that she was the one who had sold her mother. Another episode follows. (Calame-Griaule and Lacroix [1970], p. 1361)

10. (Mali: Dogon) Hare and Hyena agreed to sell their mothers. Hyena tied her mother firmly with a rope, and Hare tied his firmly with a thread. When they went to sell them Hare's mother cut the thread and fled, but Hyena's mother remained captive. (Calame-Griaule and Lacroix [1970], p. 1356)

11. (Mali: Dogon) Hare and Hyena agreed to sell their mothers. Hare hid his mother under a basket. Hyena tied her mother with a rope and went to sell her for food. When God told them to show Him their mothers, Hare uncovered his mother and showed her to God. When God asked Hyena where her mother was, Hyena said that she had sold her mother and had eaten. God said, "Hyena is too greedy. Go away, I am not going to give you food." Hyena looked everywhere for food but did not find any. The intelligent one found food but the glutton did not. (Calame-Griaule and Lacroix [1970], p. 1357)

12. (Mali: Twareg) Jackal told Hyena, "We are going to sell our mothers." Jackal went to his mother and told her to escape that night, but in the morning she was still there. They took their mothers and went off with them. When they were in the bush they made an enclosure. Hyena tied her mother with a leather strap and Jackal tied his with a thread. Jackal told his mother to escape when they were asleep, and when they awoke and they saw only Hyena's mother. They followed Jackal's mother for a while, but returned so that Hyena's mother would not leave them also. They sold Hyena's mother

for a donkey and sack of millet, and other episodes follow. (Calame-Griaule and Lacroix [1970], pp. 1362–1366)

13. (Upper Volta: Bambara) Hyena suggested to Hare that they sell their mothers and buy food. Hare agreed and tied a thread to his mother's neck, telling her to break it on the way. Hyena tied a large, strong rope to her mother's neck and they left with Hyena in front. On the way Hare's mother broke the thread and fled. Hare told Hyena that he was going home because his mother had escaped, but Hyena told him not to, saying that the price for her mother would suffice. At the first village Hyena sold her mother and bought a cow. They started home, and other episodes follow. (Equilbecq, vol. 42 [1913–1916], pp. 261–268; adapted in Calame-Griaule and Lacroix [1970], pp. 1371–1372)

14. (Upper Volta: Mosi) During a famine both Hare and Hyena were hungry. Hare said to Hyena, "It is necessary for us to sell our mothers for millet." Hyena agreed and the next morning Hare tied his mother with a weak thread, telling her, "When we are in the bush break the thread and escape." Hyena tied his mother stoutly with a strong cord. On the way Hare's mother broke her thread and fled. Hare pretended to run after her, but Hyena said, "After we have sold my mother, then we can look for yours." Hyena sold his mother for millet and divided it in two, but Hare refused his share saying, "My mother has shamed me. I cannot accept your millet." They started home, and another incident follows. (Tauxier [1917], pp. 430–431)

15. (Upper Volta: Mosi) During a famine Hare said to Hyena, "We are going to sell our mothers, or else we will die of hunger." Hyena agreed, saying that Hare was very intelligent. For five days Hyena made a very stout, solid rope and tied it to her mother. Hare tied a thread to his mother, telling her to break it when they were in the bush. She did so and escaped. Hare cried, "My mother is gone," and Hyena said, "You are a fool. You did not take a good rope. I tied my mother well." Hare went home and Hyena sold her mother for a donkey and a load of millet. Another episode follows. (Calame-Griaule and Lacroix [1970], pp. 1359–1360)

16. (Upper Volta: Gurma) During a famine Hyena suggested to Hare that they sell their mothers. Hare told his mother about the plan but promised to release her on the way, telling her to run away as fast as she could. Hyena saw that Hare had bound his mother with a short rope and warned that she might escape. Hyena's mother was bound tightly. Nearing the market, Hare released his mother and she fled. Hyena sold her mother and bought salt. They started for home, and another episode follows. (Guilhem, vol. II [1962], pp. 28–32)

17. (New England: Cape Verde Islanders) During a famine Wolf and his nephew, Pedro, agreed to sell their mothers for corn. Pedro said, "Your mother is stronger than mine. Tie her with a rope. I'll tie mine with ravelings." Pedro told his mother about their plan, saying that when they reached a certain place she should escape and go home. When she did so, Pedro told his uncle that they would eat the corn that they would get for his mother, and then

they would catch his own mother and sell her. They sold Wolf's mother for four sacks of corn, and another episode follows. (Parsons [1917], pp. 230–231; "Cape Verde" [1923], Part I, pp. 109–110, Part II, pp. 72–73)

18. (New England: Cape Verde Islanders) Parsons cites a variant of the above. (Parsons, "Cape Verde" [1923], Part I, p. 109, notes 3 and 4)

19. (Louisiana) Bouqui asked Rabbit if he didn't know that all creatures were selling their mothers so as to have something to eat. Rabbit said yes and that he was going to sell his mother for hominy and gumbo. When they were ready to go, Bouqui tied his mother with a rope and Rabbit tied his mother with a cobweb, telling her to jump down from the cart when they reached the briars and run home. She did so, Bouqui sold his mother for hominy and gumbo, and other episodes follow. (Fortier [1888], pp. 125–126, 151–152; [1895], pp. 109–110)

20. (South Carolina) Rabbit told Wolf that their grandparents were of no use and proposed that they take them to town and sell them for a keg of butter. Wolf agreed and they caught their grandparents and tied them to their cart to carry them to town. Wolf tied his grandparents with a strong rope, but Rabbit tied his on the back of the cart with some little trifling yarn. They started off and heard the yarn break. Rabbit said that his granduncle had gotten away, but Wolf said they should go on because they had enough without him. They heard the yarn break again, and Rabbit said that his grandaunt had gotten away. Wolf said that Rabbit should watch them because he had to drive. Again they heard the yarn break, and Rabbit said that his grandfather had escaped. Wolf said that Rabbit must not have tied them tight enough. Rabbit said that he would tie them tighter but that Wolf must be driving too fast. Instead Rabbit loosened them and soon they heard the yarn break again. Rabbit said that his grandmother had gotten loose, and Wolf was angry. Rabbit said it was no use to try to catch them now, and they went on and sold Wolf's relations and bought a keg of butter. Another episode follows. (Christensen [1969], pp. 73–80; summarized in Levine [1977], p. 109)

21. (South Carolina) Rabbit and Wolf agreed to sell their mothers and buy bread and butter. They tied them to their wagon and started off to the auction. Rabbit told Wolf to look at something good and released his mother while Wolf was driving. When they got to the auction Wolf had to sell his mother alone, but he bought the bread and butter with the money. Another episode follows. (Parsons, "Sea Island" [1923], p. 11)

22. (Georgia) During a famine Rabbit and Wolf agreed to sell their mothers and buy food. Wolf agreed to sell his mother first and then Rabbit could sell his. Wolf put his mother in a wagon and drove off to town with Rabbit. He sold his mother and they started for home with a wagon load of food. Another episode follows. (Harris [1883], no. 39; [1955], pp. 284–289)

23. (Georgia) During a drought Rabbit and Fox agreed to sell their families. They tied them up, put them in Fox's wagon, and drove off. Rabbit got in back and untied his wife and seven children and then sat on the seat with Fox. One by one he told them to jump off until all were gone. Fox noticed

that they were gone and Rabbit began to cry. He blamed Fox's family for eating his family, but Fox's wife said that she hadn't touched them. Fox traded his family for corn. They started for home, and another episode follows. (Harris [1883], no. 41; [1955], pp. 293–297)

24. (Bahamas) Times were hard and Boukee and Rabby couldn't get anything to eat; so they agreed to sell their mothers. Rabby said, "You tie your mother with a chain and I will tie mine with a string." They did so and started off. When they were in the bush Rabby told Boukee to beat his mother to make her walk faster, saying he would beat his mother too. Rabby beat his mother, the string broke, and his mother ran away. Rabby cried and told Boukee to go on and sell his mother. Boukee told Rabbit to wait until he came back. Boukee sold his mother for a horse and a cart loaded with provisions. He went back to Rabby, and another episode follows. (Cleare [1917], pp. 228–229)

25. (Guadeloupe) During a famine Zamba said to Rabbit, "Let's sell our mothers for corn." Zamba tied his mother with a big cord, but Rabbit tied his with a thread. When they arrived at the king's house Rabbit put his mother on the ground and she ran away. Zamba sold his mother, and another episode follows. (Parsons [1933–1943], Part II, p. 27; Part III, p. 72)

Agreement to Kill Mothers

Beidelman has made this folk tale famous by his analysis of how a Kaguru version fits the Kaguru matrilineal society.[3] It is, however, found widely in Africa, in patrilineal as well as matrilineal societies.

Two or more animals agree to kill their mothers or other relatives. One hides his mother in a treetop, the sky, the forest, or a cave and eats there with her or brings her food. The other animal, who has killed his mother, finds the hidden mother of the first and kills her or falls when the rope on which he is ascending breaks, is cut, or is dropped. In Beidelman's version Hyena starves to death after killing his mother.

This is a tale type because it occurs by itself, but it does not appear in the tale type index. The most relevant motif is K231.1.1 "Mutual agreement to sacrifice family members in famine. Trickster refuses to carry out his part of the bargain," but K944 "Deceptive agreement to kill wives (children). Trickster shams the murder; dupe kills his" is also relevant because examples of "Agreement to Kill Mothers" are cited (e.g., Dennett). Both motifs have references to Africa and the Americas; both also have references to India, but none to Europe. Therefore, I conclude that this tale type came to the New World from Africa.

I depart here from my practice of summarizing all the known versions and I do so for two reasons. First, since Alan Dundes and I have found some one hundred African versions of this tale type, this article would be unduly long. Second, Dundes has undertaken a comparative study of it and I do not wish to preempt his work. I will cite only three African versions to show something of their variations, one from the United States, and one from the Caribbean.

1. (Nigeria: Efik) During a famine Leopard ordered all the other animals to bring him their grandmothers in turn for him to eat and, then, to bring their mothers. The animals agreed to do so because Leopard threatened to eat them if they did not. One animal after another brought his grandmother, but Tortoise produced evidence that his grandmother was dead. The animals then brought their mothers for Leopard to eat, but Tortoise hid his mother in a palm tree. He gave her a basket tied to a long string so that she could let it down for him to fill with food for her to eat. The string was strong enough that she could pull Tortoise up whenever he wished to visit her. Squirrel remembered that Tortoise had not given his grandmother to Leopard and decided to watch him. He saw Tortoise putting food in the basket, climbing in himself, and being pulled up. He told Leopard and took him to the tree. Tortoise's mother had already let down the basket and Leopard got into it; but he was too heavy for her to pull up. Being an expert climber, Leopard climbed the palm tree and found Tortoise's mother; but her shell was too tough to eat, so he threw her to the ground and went home. When Tortoise found his mother dead, he knew that Leopard had killed her. He decided to live by himself and have nothing to do with other animals. (Dayrell [1910], pp. 86–90)

2. (Nigeria: Yoruba) During a famine Tortoise suggested to Dog that they kill and eat their mothers. They killed Dog's mother and divided her flesh. Tortoise put his mother in the sky and when he wanted to have something to eat he pulled on a rope that hung down to earth. Then his mother pulled him up, he ate, and she let him down again. Dog came and said that they should kill Tortoise's mother since his own mother's flesh was finished. Tortoise said that he had not seen his mother since morning and Dog agreed to wait until she returned. Tortoise went to the rope every day and ate with his mother. One day Tree Bear [Ọfafa] saw him being pulled up. Tree Bear was a friend of Dog and told him what Tortoise was doing. Dog hid by the rope until Tortoise came to be pulled up. Dog hung on under Tortoise, but the rope was not strong enough. It broke and Tortoise and Dog fell to the ground. Another episode follows. (Frobenius [1926], pp. 265–66)

3. (Nigeria: Yoruba) In a time of great strife the animals met to decide what to do. They concluded that their mothers were the cause of all their troubles and agreed to kill them. The great slaughter began but Dog, who greatly respected his mother, sent her to heaven. She was grateful and taught him a song to sing if he were in trouble. The next season brought famine, and Dog sang to his mother to send down a cord with a bench on the end and take him up to be fed. He feasted with her every day. One day Tortoise asked Dog how he was getting fatter when everyone else was growing thinner. Dog said he would show him if Tortoise kept his secret. The next morning Dog sang to his mother and they both were pulled up on the little bench on the end of the cord. They ate and returned to earth, Tortoise promising not to divulge Dog's secret. But Tortoise told king Lion that there was a place where there was plenty to eat, and the next day they went to the place. Lion

had brought his wife, his friends, and his followers so that there was quite a crowd of animals. Tortoise sang Dog's song and he and Lion sat on the bench; but the other starving animals hung onto the cord or onto the tails of other animals. Dog's mother noticed that something was wrong and looked down. When she saw all the animals she thought they were coming to kill her. She cut the cord with a knife and all the animals except Tortoise were killed. Tortoise was blamed for the death of the king and was executed because the other animals did not believe his story. When Dog sang to his mother the cord reached only half-way to earth and he could not eat with her. As the famine continued in the Country of Animals, Dog went to the Country of Man and has been fed by man ever since. (Fuja [1962], pp. 119–24)

4. (Georgia) During a famine Rabbit suggested to Wolf that they kill their grandmothers. Wolf agreed, killed his grandmother, and sold her for food which they ate. When his turn came Rabbit hid his grandmother in the top of a big coconut tree and gave her a cord with a little basket tied to it. Every day Rabbit came to feed her. When he shouted, "Granny! Jutta cord-la!" she let down the basket and he filled it with food. Wolf heard Rabbit and saw the basket come down and go back up. He went to the tree and shouted, "Granny! Shoot-a cord-la!" She said to herself that her son didn't talk like that and she didn't lower the basket. When she told Rabbit what had happened he laughed. Wolf came back and shouted, "Granny! Jutta cord-la!" but she noticed that his voice was rough. She looked down, saw Wolf, and told him to go away. Wolf went to a blacksmith and had him change his voice by running a red-hot poker down his throat. When Wolf called again, Granny thought it was Rabbit and let the basket down. Wolf put some food in the basket and got into it himself. Granny found the basket heavy but thought that Rabbit loved her a lot and had given her lots of food. When the basket was almost to the top she stopped to rest. Wolf looked down, saw Rabbit, and jerked on the rope. Rabbit shouted, "Granny! Cutta cord-la!" Granny cut the cord and Wolf fell down, breaking his neck. (Harris [1883], no. 40; [1955], pp. 289–292)

5. (Haiti) During a famine Malice proposed to Bouqui that they eat their mothers. He said that they should first eat Bouqui's mother and the next day eat his own. After they ate Bouqui's mother Malice hid his own mother in the woods. He told Bouqui that his mother had run away when she saw that they killed Bouqui's mother. Bouqui began to fight and Malice put out his eyes, but Rabbit gave him a leaf and his sight was restored. (Parsons [1933–1943], Part II, p. 484; Part III, p. 72)

"Cutta Cord-La!"

I take this title from that of Harris' Uncle Remus tale [XIV:4] in the previous section. Although it is appended to "Agreement to Kill Mothers" in that instance, it is a separate tale type because it is found by itself. The only reference to it in the indexes is to this same Uncle Remus tale under Motif K231.1.1, so I conclude that it also came to the New World from Africa.

My citations here are probably incomplete because it was only recently that I recognized this as a separate tale type, but I do not consider it necessary to recheck the many versions of "Agreement to Kill Mothers." In addition to Harris's tale from Georgia, they include Sierra Leone, Cameroun, and Jamaica.

1. (Sierra Leone) During a famine Hare asked Spider how he kept so fat and well. Spider said that when it got dark he would show Hare where he got his food. That night Spider took Hare to his farm, stood under a tree, and sang, "Mother! I have come! Send down our rope." A large rope came down and they both took hold of it. Spider sang, "Mother! Pull up our rope," and they were pulled high up into the tree where they found all kinds of food. They ate, said good-bye to Spider's mother, and went down the rope to the ground. Hare was so happy that the other animals asked him where he got his food. He said that Spider had told him not to tell anyone but that he would show them. That evening when Spider was asleep Hare, Elephant, Camel, Porcupine, and Tortoise went to Spider's farm. Hare sang, "Mother! I have come! Send down our rope," and the rope came down. All the animals took hold of it and Hare sang "Mother! Pull up our rope." As the rope slowly went up the animals shouted and the noise woke Spider. He ran outside and when he saw what was happening he sang, "Mother! Cut our rope quickly!" She cut the rope and the animals fell to the ground. Hare fell into a hole and he still lives there. Elephant fell and got his long trunk, Camel got the hump on his back, Leopard got his spots, Porcupine got his quills, and Tortoise got his shell. (Clarke [1963], pp. 7–11)

2. (Cameroun) During a famine the animals agreed to eat their mothers, but Tortoise hid his mother in the clouds. He gave her a basket tied to a long chain and every day he brought her some meat, calling to her, "Mammy, send down the chain." When he had put the food in the basket he called, "Pull up the chain, Mammy." Every day the animals ate one of their mothers. Knowing that his turn would soon come, Tortoise announced that his mother had starved to death, and he showed the animals the place where he said he had buried her. Hare was suspicious and noticed that Tortoise did not eat all of his share of meat but put some of it aside. Hare followed Tortoise and saw him call for the chain to come down and to be pulled up. Hare told the other animals and they decided to get into the basket when Tortoise was asleep and eat his mother when she pulled them up, but when Leopard called, "Send down the chain, Mammy," she noticed that it was not the voice of Tortoise. Leopard went to a blacksmith who hit and hit his voice, but it did not become small enough and again Tortoise's mother knew that it was not the voice of her son. Leopard went back to the blacksmith who knocked and knocked his voice until the animals said it would do. When Leopard called again, Tortoise's mother let down the chain and all the animals jumped into the basket. When she pulled up the chain the basket was heavy and she stopped to rest. Tortoise woke up and found that Leopard and Hare were not at home. He ran to his mother and saw her struggling to pull up the basket. Tortoise shouted, "It's not me, Mammy! Don't pull, Mammy! Cut the chain, Mammy! Cut the chain!"

She found a weak link and broke it with a stone. All the animals fell and were killed, and Tortoise and his mother had plenty of meat to eat. (Todd [1979], pp. 52–59)

3. (Jamaica) Anansi lived in a tree with his family. He went around robbing people and they couldn't find where he lived; but Tiger and Tacoomah saw the rope come down and how he sent provisions up for his family. Tiger went to a tinsmith to get a fine voice. He went to the tree and sang, "Mama, send down the rope"; but the mother heard how coarse his voice was. Tiger went to a goldsmith and got a voice like Nansi's, and when he sang again the mother let down the rope. Nansi came and saw her pulling Tiger up. He said, "Mama, cut the rope!" She cut the rope and Tiger fell, breaking his neck. (Beckwith [1924], p. 20)

4. (Jamaica) Rabbit and the children were going up to heaven to eat. They got in the merit and sang, "Mammy and Harry, pull up the merit." Anansi wanted to go along with them and they heard him singing, "Pull up the merit." They recognized his voice and Rabbit said, "Mammy and Harry, cut down the merit." They cut it down and since that day Anansi's waist is almost cut in two. (Beckwith [1924], p. 20).

BIBLIOGRAPHY

Basset, Réne
　n.d. Contes Populaires d'Afrique. *Les Litteratures populaires de toutes les nations* 47. c. 1903.
Beckwith, Martha Warren
　1924 Jamaica Anansi Stories. *Memoirs of the American Folk-Lore Society* 17.
Brun, Joseph
　1919–20 Recueil de fables et de chants en dialect *Hal Poular. Anthropos* 14–15.
Calame-Griaule, Geneviève, and Lacroix, Pierre-Francis
　1970 La "mère vendue," Essai d'analyse d'un thème de conte africain, in Pouillon, Jean, and Maranda, Pierre, Echanges et communications, Melanges offerts à Claude Lévi-Strauss, *Studies in General Anthropology* 5.
Christensen, A. M. H.
　1969 *Afro-American Folk Lore.* New York, Negro Universities Press. [1892]
Clarke, W. R. E.
　1963 *Some Folk Tales of Sierra Leone.* London, Macmillan.
Cleare, W. T.
　1917 Four Folk-Tales from Fortune Island, Bahamas. *Journal of American Folk-Lore* 30.
Daget, J., Konipo, M., and Sanankoua, M.
　1953 La Langue Bozo. *Etudes Soudaniennes* (Dakar) 1.
Dayrell, Elphinstone
　1910 *Folk Stories from Southern Nigeria.* London, Longmans, Green.
Equilbecq, F. V.

1913–1916 Essai sur la littérature merveilleuse des Noirs, suivi de contes indigènes de l'Ouest-Africain Français. *Collection de Contes et Chansons Populaires* 41–43.

Fortier, Alcée
1888 Bits of Louisiana Folk-Lore. *Transactions of the Modern Language Association of America, 1887* 3.
1895 Louisiana Folk-Tales in French Dialect and English Translation. *Memoirs of the American Folk-Lore Society* 2.

Frobenius, Leo
1922 Erzählungen aus dem West-Sudan. *Atlantis* 8.
1926 Die Atlantische Götterlehre. *Atlantis* 10.

Fuja, Abayomi
1962 *Fourteen Hundred Cowries. Traditional Stories of the Yoruba.* London and Ibadan, Oxford University Press.

Gaden, Henri
1913 *Le Poular. Dialecte Peul de Fouta Sénégalais. Vol. I.* Collection de la Revue du Monde Musulman. Paris, Ernest Leroux.

Guilhem, Marcel
n.d.–1962 50 Contes et *fableaux de la savane*, vols. I–II. Paris, Ligel.

Harris, Joel Chandler
1883 *Nights with Uncle Remus.* Boston and New York, Houghton Mifflin.
1955 *The Complete Tales of Uncle Remus.* Compiled by Richard Chase, Boston, Houghton Mifflin.

Levine, Lawrence
1977 *Black Culture and Black Consciousness.* New York, Oxford University Press.

Monteil, C.
1905 Contes Soudanais. *Collection de contes et chansons populaires* 28.

Parsons, Elsie Clews
1917 Ten Folk-Tales from the Cape Verde Islands. *Journal of American Folk-Lore* 30.
1923 Folk-Lore from the Cape Verde Islands. *Memoirs of the American Folk-Lore Society* 15, Parts I–II.
1923 Folk-Lore of the Sea Islands, South Carolina. *Memoirs of the American Folk-Lore Society* 16.
1933–1943 Folk-Lore of the Antilles, French and English. *Memoirs of the American Folk-Lore Society* 26, Parts I–III.

Senghor, Léopold Sédar, and Sadji, Abdoulaye
1965 *La belle Histoire de Leuk-le-Lièvre.* London, George G. Harrap. [1953]

Tauxier, L.
1917 *Le Noir du Yatenga.* Paris, Émile Larose.

Todd, Loreto
1979 *Some Day Been Day, West African Pidgin Folktales.* London, Routledge & Kegan Paul.

N O T E S

1. Thompson does cite Fortier's Louisiana tale and Harris's two Georgia tales under motif K231.1.1, but this motif refers to "Agreement to Kill Mothers."

2. Calame-Griaule and Lacroix [1970], pp. 1367–1368, 1372, 1372–1373.

3. T. O. Beidelman, "Hyena and Rabbit: A Kaguru Representation of Matrilineal Relations," *Africa* 30 [1961], pp. 61–74.

T W E L V E

✳

Knock Dust (Water) Out of Rock;
Waiting on the Lord

Since neither of these tales appeal in the Aarne-Thompson tale type index or in Thompson's motif index, I conclude that they came to the New World from (and originated in) Africa. I am not aware that this has been previously suggested for either tale. Both have an independent existence and thus they are tale types.

In the first there is a contest to see which suitor will win a girl in marriage. The winner must knock dust or water out of a rock, and the trickster wins by deception. With some reservations I have included the two tales from southern Africa [3–4] in which the deception is lacking.

My four African versions come from Upper Volta (Bobo-Fing), Ivory Coast (Guro), Tanzania (Jita), and Zimbabwe (Jinda Shona). Five come from the United States: Unidentified, Arkansas, Virginia, and Georgia.

1. (Upper Volta: Bobo-Fing) The king had a very beautiful daughter. Men and animals of all species came to court her, but the king did not know which of her suitors to choose. On the advice of an elder he announced that she would be given to the one who danced until his sweat flooded the rock under which the village ancestors lay. On the day of the contest a crowd gathered to watch. Many danced, but the rock remained dry. Hare came with bags of water hidden under his large gown. He danced poorly and the crowd laughed at him. No one noticed him prick small holes in the bags. The water trickled down his legs and wet the stone. He signalled for the musicians to pick up with the beat. He pressed on the bags and the water streamed down. People saw that the rock was all wet and acclaimed Hare as the victor. The king presented his daughter's fiancé to the crowd, and some days later the marriage was celebrated. (Guilhem vol. II [1962], pp. 7–10)

2. (Ivory Coast: Guro) Red Doe told the animals that she would give her pretty daughter to the man who could jump so strongly that he could make

Reprinted from *Research in African Literatures*, 13 (1982), 196–207.

dust spring out of a flat stone. Spider put some corn flour in his loincloth and when he jumped it flew out. It was mistaken for dust from the stone, and Red Doe gave her daughter to Spider. (Tauxier [1924], p. 274)

3. (Tanzania: Jita) During a drought a man said that whoever stamped on the ground so that water came out could marry his daughter. All the animals except Rabbit tried, but only dust flew up. Lion told Rabbit to stamp, but Rabbit protested that his paws were too small. When he stamped on the ground, however, moisture appeared. Lion claimed that he had made it come and Rabbit told him to stamp again. Lion and the other animals had another try, but only dust flew up. Elephant told Rabbit to stamp, and again he protested that his paws were too small, but when he stamped on the ground water flowed forth. All the animals bent down to drink and Rabbit went off with his wife. Another episode follows. (Sillery [1932], pp. 290–292)

4. (Zimbabwe: Jinda Shona) After another episode the animals sought for water but found none. They began dancing, stamping on the ground, and singing, "Stamping, ever trampling. Clear waters we shall drink." They kept on dancing until a great dust arose, and they asked when the water would come. They tried dancing while some rested, but no water came. Tortoise offered to try alone, but the other said that his feet were too small. He did so, singing a song, and a little water came out of the ground. The others told him to stop, but when they danced only dust came up. They told Tortoise to dance again, and when he did water came up until there was a great pool of it. Other episodes follow. (Posselt [1929], pp. 43–50)

5. (United States) The king of the forest wanted his daughter to get married. All the animals wanted to marry her, but he did not know which animal he liked best. He invited them all to a big party and announced that he would marry his daughter to the one who could dance until dust came out of the floor. Rabbit ran home and put ashes in his pockets, his shoes, and his cap, and then went back to the party. Fox, Bear, and Wolf danced but could raise little or no dust. Rabbit began to dance and the ashes began to fly. He stood on his head, shook himself, and turned round and round. The dust got so thick that no one could see Rabbit. It got into the king's eyes and he called for Rabbit to stop, telling him to marry his daughter. (Love [1964], pp. 43–45)

6. (Arkansas) There was a contest. The one who danced dust out of the rock won the girl. Everyone had danced but Rabbit. Rabbit dipped himself into ashes but no one paid attention to him. When he was told that his turn had come he pretended he didn't care, but he went there, shook himself a little bit, and the ashes flew. He jumped onto the girl's lap and said, "That's my girl." (Dorson [1958], pp. 30–31)

7. (Virginia) Rabbit and Fox were courting the king's daughter. The king said he would give her to the one who could dance sand out of the rock. Fox danced and danced, but could not dance any sand out of the rock. Before Rabbit began he tied a bag of sand with a little hole in the bottom in each of his trouser legs, and when he danced the sand flew. Rabbit won the king's daughter. (Bacon and Parsons [1922], p. 278)

8. (Georgia) Miss Meadows and the girls were tired of the animals courting them, and they didn't want to marry any of them. Miss Meadows told the animals that the one who could knock dust out of a big rock with a sledge hammer could have his pick of the girls. Rabbit borrowed Coon's slippers, filled them with ashes, and was the last to arrive. The other animals tried their three licks at the rock, but no dust came. Then Rabbit grabbed the hammer, leaped up in the air, cracked his heels together, and came down on the rock at the same time that the hammer did. Ashes flew up so that Fox sneezed and the girls coughed. Rabbit said, "Stand back, ladies! Here comes the dust!" Sure enough the dust came and Rabbit got one of the girls. (Harris [1880], no. 30; [1955], pp. 98–101)

9. (Georgia) Coon, Wolf, Rabbit, and Possum were courting Fox's daughter but she didn't want to marry any of them. Fox told them that the one who could pound dust out of a rock with a hammer could marry her. Rabbit was depressed because the others were stronger than he was, but he filled his slippers with ashes. He was the last to try, after the others had failed. Rabbit raised the big hammer, standing on tiptoes, and when the hammer came down his heels came down and the dust flew so that they couldn't see him. Rabbit thought that was just one of his courting tricks. (Backus [1899], pp. 113–114; abstracted in Levine [1977], p. 111)

Waiting on the Lord

In this tale type Hawk, who works for a living, is killed when he dives to earth for food; he is eaten by Buzzard, who waits on the Lord or on the salvation of the Lord to provide him with food.

In all but two [3, 6] of these twenty-two versions it is a kind of hawk that is killed; the other bird is a buzzard, turkey buzzard (a kind of vulture), vulture, or John Crow (a vulture-like bird). In all but two of the versions [5, 13], it is clear that Hawk is eaten by the other bird. The concept of salvation, which is European, has replaced God or the Lord in five versions [5–7, 9, 20].

A bet replaces "Waiting on the Lord" in one tale from South Carolina [14], but five other versions from that state [12–13, 15–17] are clearly homologues. In the Brazilian version Turkey Buzzard says, "I eat on the misfortune of others," but otherwise this appears to be a homologous tale. In another version [4] Buzzard simply waits for his meat.

This folktale is of interest because Dorson has said that "African analogues are lacking for the buzzard and poll parrot cycles."[1] The most divergent of all the versions is Dorson's "Why the Buzzard Went South" [6] in which Seagull is not killed and Buzzard wants to eat a cow killed by a train. It may be, as Dorson says, a separate tale type, yet in it Seagull hustles for a living while Buzzard waits on salvation. His other two versions [5, 7] conform closely to the pattern. Dorson cites W. J. Faulkner's "Bre'r Turkey Buzzard Waits for Dinner" from the United States, but I have not been able to locate the record.[2]

My three African versions come from northern Nigeria (Hausa and Bura).

Sixteen come from the United States: Unidentified, Michigan, Alabama, Virginia, South Carolina (Negro and Catawba Indians), Georgia, and Florida. Two come from Jamaica and Brazil.

1. (Nigeria: Hausa) Vulture alighted at the town gate, waiting for someone to defecate so that he might eat. Hawk asked what he was doing and Vulture replied, "I'm waiting for what God will bring me." Hawk said, "You look for what God gives you; but I look for what my strength will bring me." Vulture said, "We wait for what God brings us." Hawk flew up and saw a lizard on a tree stump. He swooped down at it, but the stump broke off both of his wings. Vulture saw Hawk lying there and went to him. When Hawk asked where he was going, Vulture said, "I have come to eat you." Hawk asked Vulture to wait until he was dead, but Vulture replied, "I won't wait until you are dead. You came here to kill another creature. Now God has given you to me and you are my meat." Vulture ate up every bit of Hawk. (Edgar, vol. III [1911–1913], no. 20; translated in Skinner, vol. I [1969–1977], pp. 281–282)

2. (Nigeria: Hausa) Hawk found Vulture on a house top and asked what he was doing. Vulture replied, "I'm seeking what God sends." Hawk said, "I seek what I want with force, come what may." Hawk saw a rat far below, near a trap. He swooped down, fell into the trap, and could not get out. Vulture flew down and Hawk asked, "Are you not waiting till I've breathed my last?" Vulture replied, "You wanted to take the life of another. You are what I was awaiting from God. Today where is that force of yours?" (Abraham [1959], pp. 39–40)

3. (Nigeria: Bura) Eagle asked Buzzard what he was doing, sitting in a tree. Buzzard answered, "I am sitting here waiting for the shoulder of God." Eagle said, "I eat by my strength." A quail alighted on a stump and Eagle made a dash at it, but it flew away. Eagle's breast struck the stump and was cut open and he could not fly. Buzzard came and Eagle asked what he was doing. Buzzard said, "I am going to eat you. Or did I not tell you that I was waiting for the shoulder. This is what God has given me." Buzzard ate Eagle. (Helser [1930], p. 155; [1934], p. 54)

4. (United States) Buzzard and Hawk had a talk. Hawk said he had the hardest life; he borrowed and lent; he watched the chickens hatch; but hard work wasn't easy. Buzzard said he took life easy and ate what he found; he trusted that he would live and eat. Hawk said such talk would starve any hawk; but Buzzard said his way was best, since it gave him a chance to study and rest. Hawk saw a hen and her chicks walk out of the poultry yard to the edge of the woods. He darted down and landed on an osage. A thorn stuck him and held him tight. Buzzard glided down to the top of the hedge and said, "Didn't I tell you? I wait for my meat and when it comes I eat." Hawk hung there, meat for a meal. I don't say what Buzzard did, but Hawk's and Buzzard's families haven't been friendly since that day. (Young [1912], pp. 123–124)

5. (Michigan) Hawk and Buzzard were sitting in a tree discussing food. Hawk asked Buzzard, "What do you do for something to eat?" Buzzard replied,

"I sit and wait on the salvation of the Lord. He'll send something to eat." Hawk looked down and saw a bird. He said, "I don't wait on the salvation of any man to send me something to eat. You watch me. See that bird yonder? I'm going to get it and I'll have something to eat." Hawk dove down and when the bird flew around a tree Hawk drove his head into a fork and broke his neck. Buzzard came down and ate him. The good Lord had sent him something to eat. (Dorson [1953], pp. 208–209)

6. (Michigan) Seagull said he hustled for a living, but Buzzard said, "We wait on salvation," meaning that buzzards wait until something dies. A cow was killed by a train but Buzzard didn't like fresh meat. He went away to wait until it smelled bad but returned to find that the cow had been buried. Buzzard went down South, where they never buried the dead. (Dorson [1956], p. 42; [1967], pp. 112–113)

7. (Michigan) In his note to this last tale [6] Dorson says, "The idea of the buzzard waiting on the salvation of the Lord occurs in a separate tale, where the impatient hawk kills himself diving after a bird, and buzzard eats the hawk. I have texts of this form from E. L. Smith and Sam Wilder." Presumably one of these two versions has already been cited [5]. (Dorson [1956], p. 206; [1967], p. 112)

8. (Alabama) During a famine Buzzard told Hawk that he was going to wait on the Lord. Hawk saw a bird alight on a limb and made a dive for it, but he got caught on the limb. Buzzard flew up to him saying, "I told you I was going to wait on the Lord," and ate Hawk. (Browne [1954], pp. 133–134)

9. (Alabama) Hawk saw Buzzard sitting on the ground, looking miserable. Hawk asked what he was doing, and Buzzard said he was starving to death. Hawk asked what he was waiting for and Buzzard said, "I'm waiting for the salvation of the Lord to feed me." Hawk laughed at him and said he was going to hunt Rabbit for dinner. Buzzard said he couldn't eat fresh meat and Hawk said he was sorry for him. Hawk sailed down out of the sky, but Rabbit ducked into a hollow stump. Hawk couldn't stop. He hit the stump and broke his neck. Rabbit called to Buzzard, "Come and get him. I and God will feed you." Buzzard said, "Thank you, Lord, for answering my prayer. I'll just let Hawk lie there a day or two, and then I'll eat him." (Courlander [1957], pp. 11–14; [1976], pp. 474–475)

10. (Virginia) Hawk found Buzzard sitting in a tree and said, "You look like you haven't got anybody in the world." Buzzard didn't reply. Below them a sparrow went under a fence. Hawk tried to catch it but got hung up in the wire. Buzzard still hadn't said anything. After a while Hawk started to smell. Buzzard flew down saying, "It's a good thing to wait on the Lord." (Dance [1978], p. 248)

11. (Virginia) Buzzard was sitting on a post, half-starved. Hawk lit near him and said, "Aren't you something, Old Buzzard? You sit here waiting for something to die. If something doesn't die pretty soon, you'll die. Aren't you something?" Buzzard said, "Well, Hawk, I'll wait on the Lord. We can't all

be alike." Hawk said, "Why don't you do like I do? When I get hungry I kill something." Buzzard said, "I told you we can't all be alike. I'll just have to wait on the Lord until something dies." A flock of partridges flew across the field and Hawk said, "I'm going to show you how I get my food. Now watch this." Hawk dove at one of the partridges but hit a tree and broke his neck. Buzzard said, "It's good to have patience. Something is dead now. I can eat." (Dance [1978], p. 248)

12. (South Carolina) During a fasting contest Buzzard was getting weak but he held to his pledge and waited on the Lord. Hawk made a dodge and killed himself against a fence. Buzzard went down and ate him saying, "It's a good thing to wait on the Lord." (Parsons, "Sea Islands," [1923], p. 118)

13. (South Carolina) Hawk found Buzzard sitting on a stake and asked what he was waiting for. Buzzard said he was waiting for something to eat. He showed Hawk a sparrow sitting on a sharp stick. Hawk darted at the sparrow and fastened himself to the stick. Buzzard came and said, "Hawk, it's a good thing to wait upon the Lord." (Parsons, "Sea Islands," [1923], p. 119)

14. (South Carolina) Buzzard bet Hawk that he could fly down onto a sharp stake with all his weight and not be pierced. Hawk bet that he could too. Buzzard flew at the stake but went off to one side. Hawk flew, and the sharp stake went right through his body and killed him. Buzzard got Hawk for dinner. (Parsons, "Sea Islands," [1923], p. 119)

15. (South Carolina) Hawk met Buzzard and asked him how he ate. Buzzard replied, "I wait on the Lord." Hawk saw a sparrow sitting on a fence and made a dive at it, but his beak got stuck in the fence. Buzzard said, "I'll let you stay there until you rot and then I'll come and eat you. It's good to wait on the Lord!" (Work Projects Administration, South Carolina [1941], p. 7)

16. (South Carolina: Catawba Indians) Hawk said to Buzzard, "How do you make your living?" Buzzard said, "I wait for God (to take care of me)." Hawk said, "You will always be hungry. See what I do." Hawk flew off to catch a chicken and was killed. Buzzard ate him up completely. (Speck [1934], p. 19)

17. (South Carolina. Catawba Indians) Hawk saw Buzzard sitting on a fence and asked how he made his living. Buzzard said he waited on the Lord. Hawk said, "I don't wait on the Lord. I'll show you how I make my living." A little bird flew in the crack of a fence and Hawk sailed down to catch him. In his haste he struck his head against the fence and was killed. Buzzard flew down and commenced picking on Hawk, saying to himself, "Our law is better, to wait on the Lord." (Speck and Carr [1947], p. 82)

18. (Georgia) Turkey Buzzard said that when the wind and rain stopped, he would make himself a house; but when the sun shone he didn't need a house. He's a foolish bird, but one time Hawk found him sitting on a tree and asked him what he was waiting for if he was hungry. Buzzard said, "I'm awaiting on the Lord." Hawk said he was going to get a chicken. He flew off and darted down, but instead of hitting a chicken he hit the sharp end of a

fence rail and was stuck there. Buzzard watched him, getting hungrier, and said, "I knew the Lord would provide." He flew down from the tree and had Hawk for breakfast. (Harris [1883], no. 64; [1955], pp. 378–380)

19. (Georgia) Food was scarce, and Hawk and Turkey Buzzard were flying around looking for food. They met and Hawk asked Buzzard how he was making out. Buzzard said that he was dying of hunger but that he would keep on going and wait on the Lord. Hawk said that he was smart enough and that, Lord or no Lord, he managed to find all he wanted to eat. When they met again Hawk said, "See that chicken down yonder. I'm going to catch him for my dinner." He left Buzzard and lunged at the chicken, but it turned out to be a sharp pointed stump instead of a chicken. Hawk hit his breast against the stump and killed himself. Several days later Buzzard flew by and smelled something dead. He flew down and found Hawk. He said, "Didn't I tell you it's better to wait on the Lord instead of trusting your own luck?" Then he ate Hawk up. (Jones [1925], pp. 27–28; retold in Levine [1977], p. 92)

20. (Florida) Sitting in a tree Hawk asked Buzzard how he was doing. Buzzard replied, "Pretty good. I wait on the salvation of the Lord." Hawk said he didn't wait on anybody, he took his own food. Buzzard said he would live to pick Hawk's bones. Hawk saw a sparrow sitting on a dead limb and dove down at it, but he ran the sharp end of the limb into his breast and hung there. Buzzard flew by him and said, "I told you I would live to pick your bones. I wait on the salvation of the Lord." (Hurston [1969], pp. 153–154; reprinted in Botkin [1966], pp. 672–673)

21. (Jamaica) Hawk invited John Crow to go for a chick that Fowl had promised him. John Crow was reluctant, but he went with Hawk to the fowl yard and they perched in a tree. Fowl saw them and asked Dog to shoot them when they came down. Hawk said they should fly down, but John Crow refused saying, "I will wait upon God's leisure." Hawk said, "All the time you wait upon God for him to give you, you will never get it. I'm going." Hawk flew down, singing, and Dog shot him. John Crow laughed, saying he would go down and see what happened to Hawk. He found Hawk dead, pecked out his eyes, and began eating him. Another episode follows. (Jekyll [1904], pp. 140–143)

22. (Brazil) Hawk, who was fat and happy, met Turkey Buzzard who was thin and sad. Hawk asked, "What do you have, Turkey Buzzard, that you are so thin?" Turkey Buzzard replied, "So it is, and why are you so fat?" Hawk asked, "Why don't you get fat also?" Turkey Buzzard replied, "I cannot, because no one around here is dead." Hawk said, "Do what I do. Eat the live ones." Hawk invited Turkey Buzzard to go hunting and they flew around. Hawk was catching little birds and giving some to Turkey Buzzard to eat. They found a flock of doves and Hawk said, "Let's go and catch them." They went up and down and here and there, until the doves went into the forest. Vulture went to the top of a tree. He was very confident, but Hawk kept chasing the doves. He chased them so much that he pierced himself on the point of a stick and died. Turkey Buzzard jumped on his corpse and began

to eat it, saying, "I eat on the misfortunes of others." (da Silva Campos in de Magalhães [1939], p. 323)

BIBLIOGRAPHY

Abraham, R. C.
1959 *Hausa Literature and the Hausa Sound System*. London, University of London Press.
Backus, Emma M.
1899 Tales of the Rabbit from Georgia Negroes. *Journal of American Folk-Lore* 12.
Bacon, A. M., and Parsons, E. C.
1922 Folk-Lore from Elizabeth City County, Virginia. *Journal of American Folk-Lore* 35.
Botkin, B. A.
1966 *A Treasury of American Folklore*. New York, Crown. [1944]
Browne, Ray B.
1954 Negro Folktales from Alabama. *Southern Folklore Quarterly* 18.
Courlander, Harold
1957 *Terrapin's Pot of Sense*. New York, Henry Holt.
1976 *A Treasury of Afro-American Folklore*. New York, Crown.
Crowley, Daniel J.
1977 *African Folklore in the New World*. Austin, University of Texas Press.
Dance, Daryl Cumber
1978 *Shuckin' and Jivin'! Folktales from Contemporary Black America*. Bloomington: Indiana University Press.
de Silva Campos, João
1939 Contos e Fábulas Populares de Baía, In de Magalhães 1939.
de Magalhães, Basílio
1939 *O Folclore no Brasil*. Rio de Janeiro, Imprensa Nacional.
Dorson, Richard M.
1953 A Negro Storytelling Session on Tape. *Midwest Folklore* 3.
1956 *Negro Folktales in Michigan*. Cambridge, Mass., Harvard University Press.
1958 Negro Tales from Pine Bluff, Arkansas, and Calvin, Michigan. *Indiana University Folklore Series* 12.
1967 *American Negro Folktales*. Greenwich, Conn., Fawcett.
1977 The African Connection. In Crowley 1977.
Edgar, Frank
1911–1913 *Litafi na Tatsuniyoyi na Hausa*, Vols. I-III. Belfast, W. Erskine Mayne.
Guilhem, Marcel
n.d.–1962 *50 Contes et fableaux de la savane*, Vols. I-II. Paris, Ligel.
Harris, Joel Chandler
1880 *Uncle Remus: His Songs and His Sayings*. New York, D. Appleton.
1883 *Nights with Uncle Remus*. Boston and New York, Houghton Mifflin.
1955 *The Complete Tales of Uncle Remus*. Compiled by Richard Chase. Boston, Houghton Mifflin.
Helser, Albert D.
1930 *African Stories*. New York, Fleming H. Revell.
1934 *Education of Primitive People*. New York, Fleming H. Revell.

Hurston, Zora Neal
1969 *Mules and Men.* New York, Negro Universities Press. [1935]
Jekyll, Walter
1904 Jamaican Song and Story: Annancy Stories, Digging Sings, Ring Tunes, and Dancing Tunes. *Publications of the Folk-Lore Society* (London) 55.
Jones, Charles, C., Jr.
1925 *Negro Myths from the Georgia Coast.* Columbia, South Carolina, the State Company. [1888]
Levine, Lawrence W.
1977 *Black Culture and Black Consciousness.* New York, Oxford University Press.
Love, Rose Leary
1964 *A Collection of Folklore for Children in Elementary School and at Home.* New York, Vantage Press.
Parsons, Elsie Clews
1923 Folk-Lore of the Sea Islands, South Carolina. *Memoirs of the American Folk-Lore Society* 16.
Posselt, F.
1929 *Fables of the Veld.* London, Oxford University Press.
Sillery, Anthony
1932 A Sketch of the Kikwaya Language. *Bantu Studies* 6.
Skinner, Neil
1969–77 *Hausa Tales and Traditions. An English Translation of Tatsuniyoyi Na Hausa, Originally compiled by Frank Edgar.* London, Frank Cass, Vol. I, 1969; Madison, the University of Wisconsin Press, Vols. II-III, 1977.
Speck, Frank G.
1934 Catawba Texts. *Columbia University Contributions to Anthropology* 24.
Speck, Frank G., and Carr, L. G.
1947 Catawba Folk Tales from Chief Sam Blue. *Journal of American Folklore* 60.
Tauxier, L.
1924 *Nègres Couro et Gagou.* Paris, Librairie Orientaliste Paul Geuthner.
Work Projects Administration, South Carolina
1941 *South Carolina Folk Tales.* Compiled by Workers of the Writers' Program of the Work Projects Adminstration in the State of South Carolina, Bulletin of the University of South Carolina.
Young, Martha
1912 *Behind the Dark Pines.* New York, D. Appleton.

NOTES

1. Richard M. Dorson, "The African Connection" in Crowley [1977], p. 89.
2. W. F. Faulkner, "Dean Faulkner Folk Story Series," *World of Fun Records,* S251-B, Nashville, Methodist Publishing House; cited in Dorson [1956], pp. 203, 206; [1967], pp. 112, 380.

T H I R T E E N

*

Birds' Fasting (Singing) Contest

In this tale type two birds usually have a contest to see which one can go without food longer. One bird eats without being observed, but the loser gets no food and dies. Often the birds sing to each other to show how they are doing. In one of the Uncle Remus tales [14] the contest is to see which bird can sing longer, but again the winner eats while the loser goes without food.

There is no relevant entry in Aarne and Thompson's tale type index, but Thompson's motif index has the following:

K53. *Deceptive contest in fasting.*

The first reference cited under this motif is to Tom Peete Cross, *Motif-Index of Early Irish Literature* (Bloomington, 1952). I have been able to locate only two of the references cited by Cross (in O'Donovan and in Plummer), but these are tales about humans and are not at all the same. I expect that Cross's two other references are also quite different. Thompson also gives a reference to Indonesia, but it is not relevant here.

Thompson's remaining references under motif K53 are to Louisiana [10], Nigeria [5], Bahamas [16], Jamaica [19], and Georgia [13], all of which are considered here. Since I believe that there are no European versions of this tale type, I conclude that it came to the Americas from Africa. It is clearly a tale type rather then simply a motif; in fact, in most of the twenty-four versions it has been recorded by itself.

Dundes has previously noted the similarities between a Seminole Indian tale from Florida [15], an Uncle Remus tale from Georgia [13], and a Kongo tale from Zaire [7], and he speaks of "probability of its African origin."[1] In this Seminole verison one of the birds is replaced by Rattlesnake, but the loser is Owl, the most frequent loser in these tales [6–8, 10, 15–16].

My eight African versions come from Nigeria (Edo, Igbo, and Efik), Gabon (Tsogo), and Zaire (Kongo and Luba). Seven come from the United States:

Reprinted from *Research in African Literatures*, 13 (1982), 499–507.

Unidentified, Louisiana, South Carolina, Georgia, and Florida (Seminole Indians). Nine come from Bahamas, Cuba, Jamaica, Haiti, Puerto Rico, and Nevis.

1. (Nigeria: Edo) Plantain Eater said to another bird that they should not eat anything for seven days. Plantain Eater ate no food, but on each of the seven days the other bird went to the farm and ate pepper. He did not die, but Plantain Eater died of hunger. The other bird found Plantain Eater rotten and laughed at him. He told the others that Plantain Eater had died because he ate no food. (Thomas [1910], Part II, pp. 44–45)

2. (Nigeria: Igbo) Nwanza, a small bird, accused Obu, the Sneak Hawk, of greed, but Obu denied it. They agreed to eat nothing for four weeks, and to sing all the time so that each might know if the other flew away in search of food. Obu sat on a nest of black ants, and since he does not eat them, he died of hunger. Nwanza sat on a nest of flying ants and ate them. When Obu's song ceased, Nwanza found him dead, and another episode follows. (Anonymous [1930], Book III, pp. 24–27; translated in Anonymous [1949] Book III, pp. 20–22)

3. (Nigeria: Igbo) Hummingbird and Cuckoo agreed to fast for seven days. Hummingbird found black ants that bite like fire in his nest, and Cuckoo found brown ants in his nest, and neither told of his discovery. Every morning Cuckoo sang and Hummingbird replied with the same song. On the sixth day Cuckoo did not sing; so Hummingbird sang, but there was no reply. He flew to Cuckoo's nest but found nothing but bones. Another episode follows. (Ekwensi [1965], pp. 5–6)

4. (Nigeria: Igbo) There was a great argument between Sunbird (Nwanchi) and Cuckoo (Obu) about which had the greater power of endurance. They wanted to decide which would be the first to die of fasting. Therefore the other birds decreed that they should be confined to their nests for a week, and that if either of them was seen outside their nest he would be killed. Cuckoo was confident that he would win because he was bigger, but Sunbird left his nest at night when the other birds were asleep and ate and drank. At the end of the week the other birds assembled. Ostrich called for Cuckoo to come out, but he had died and there was no response. When Ostrich called Sunbird he came out and was declared the winner. Another episode follows. (Bordinat and Thomas [1973], pp. 49–53)

5. (Nigeria: Efik) The king said that he would make the animal or bird that could endure hunger for a long period the chief of his tribe. The 'Nsasak bird is small with a green and red breast and with blue, yellow, and red feathers around his neck. The Odudu bird is much larger, with black and brown feathers and a cream-colored breast. They were great friends, but they decided to compete for the chieftainship. The king told them to build houses that he would inspect and then he would shut them inside. The 'Nsasak bird made a tiny hole in the wall of his house that the king did not notice, and every morning he escaped through it and flew away. At sunset he would go back into his house and call out, asking the Odudu bird if he was hungry.

The voice of the Odudu bird grew weaker and weaker every night until he could no longer reply. At the end of seven days the king had the houses opened and the Odudu bird was found dead, but the 'Nsasak bird flew out singing merrily and was appointed chief of all the small birds. (Dayrell [1910], pp. 153–55)

6. (Gabon: Tsogo) Hornbill said to Owl, "You claim to be stronger than I am. Let us try to fast all day." Owl agreed and the next morning Hornbill knocked on Owl's door saying, "I come for our bet of yesterday." They perched near each other on the branch of a tree. After a little while Hornbill asked if he couldn't revive his limbs. Owl agreed and Hornbill flew off, swallowing some insects in his flight, and then returned to the branch. A second time he flew off and again swallowed some mosquitoes. Thus it went until the end of the day. All this time Owl stayed motionless on the branch. When evening came she was overcome with hunger and unable to hold onto the tree. She fell heavily to earth and everyone laughed saying, "Owl has lost her bet. She could not withstand hunger." Triumphant, Hornbill cried, "What did I tell you? Now you see that I am stronger than you, and therefore your senior." Owl was carried home, half dead, and from then on did not dare to open her mouth to argue with Hornbill. (Walker [1967], pp. 265–66)

7. (Zaire: Kongo) Owl and Kingfisher argued about who could go longer without food, and they agreed to try for ten days. They tied a rope across a stream and sat on the middle of it, looking into the water. On the third day Kingfisher saw a fish below him and, pretending to fall, caught and ate it. Coming out of the water he said his head had turned giddy. Owl said, "Never mind. Let us continue our contest." Kingfisher continued to have giddy fits whenever a fish came under his perch, but Owl did not notice the fish. In a few days Owl lost his strength and fell into the water and was drowned. Kingfisher flew away. (Weeks [1911], p. 415; [n.d.], p. 415)

8. (Zaire: Luba) Owl asked Hummingbird how his appetite was, saying that he was always eating. Hummingbird denied it, saying that if anyone deserved that reputation it was Owl. Hummingbird challenged Owl to see who could go longer without eating and they sat on lianas over a river. Hummingbird saw a flying ant, flew to it, and swallowed it. Owl could not see well in the daytime, and only noticed that Hummingbird moved on his liana. Then Hummingbird caught a butterfly and Owl asked why he moved so much. Hummingbird said that he was so small that the wind moved him. Hummingbird caught a fly. Owl asked if he had heard it and where it had gone. Hummingbird said it was sitting near him, but he would not eat it because he would lose the bet. Owl did not feel hunger until night when he usually hunted. The following days were the same as the first. Owl had little to eat. A rat came along on his liana, but Owl did not eat it; he preferred to win his stupid bet. Exhausted, Owl finally fell into the river and was drowned. (de Bouveignes "Ecoutant," [n.d.], pp. 91–94)

9. (United States) Dove and Partridge had a dispute. Partridge said she wasn't obliged to farm like Dove, because Bob White brought her food. Dove

said she wouldn't plant corn next year as she had been doing. Partridge said that if Dove was willing to eat pickings and leavings she might survive, and Dove said picking and stealing keep one from starving. Partridge asked who could starve longer than she could and they decided to have a starving match. Partridge went into the sedge field and Dove perched on top of a fence where all the birds could see her. On the first day Dove called out and Partridge whistled back. The sedge field joined the berry hedge on one side and the corn patch on the other. Partridge ate without being seen, but Dove ate nothing. The next day Dove called out weakly, but Partridge whistled back as lively as the first day. The third day Dove called out still more weakly and fell from the fence, dead, but Partridge whistled back as lively as ever. (Young [1912], pp. 198–202)

10. (Louisiana) Mockingbird and Owl were courting Miss Mockingbird who said she would marry the one who stayed longer in a tree without eating. Every day Mockingbird sang and flew down to her, making as if to kiss her, and she gave him food. Every day Owl sang his song and flew down to her, making as if to kiss her, but she turned him away. When Owl was dying of hunger she gave him a slap, and he was so weak that he died. Mockingbird flew away with his bride. (Fortier [1895], pp. 34–37)

11. (South Carolina) Hawk told Buzzard, "Let's fast and see who can live longer without eating." They sat side by side on a limb, but every now and then Hawk would dart down and catch a bird. Buzzard thought he had gone to sleep and fallen off the limb. After the third day Buzzard was getting weak, but he held to his pledge and waited on the Lord. Hawk made a dodge and killed himself against a fence. Buzzard went down and ate him saying, "It's a good thing to wait on the Lord." (Parsons "Sea Islands," [1923], p. 118)

12. (South Carolina) Rabbit and Buzzard agreed not to eat for two weeks, but Rabbit is very tricky. He shut Buzzard up and went home and ate his supper. When he came back he said, "I am starving, starving all day long." Buzzard would say the same thing. The next day Buzzard did not answer. He had starved to death. Rabbit said, "He won't eat me." (Parsons "Sea Islands," [1923], p. 118)

13. (Georgia) Smart Bird said, "Let's see how long we can go without food and drink," and Fool Bird said he would win. Each took a horn, and when Smart Bird blew his horn Fool Bird blew his to answer. Fool Bird stayed by the stream but Smart Bird went into a tree where there were many ants and bugs. He ate them and drank dew from the leaves while Fool Bird became weak and died. (Harris [1883], no. 66; [1955], pp. 384–86)

14. (Georgia) Crow bet Buzzard that he could sing longer than Buzzard could. They began to sing, each singing the same refrain in turn until he was out of breath. They began to get hungry and Crow saw his wife flying by. Crow sang, "Go tell my children to bring my dinner, to bring it quickly." Crow's family came flying with more food than he knew what to do with. Buzzard sang until he was famished and fell from the tree. Since then there

has been no more singing in the Buzzard family. (Harris [1889], pp. 1009–10; [1948], no. 1; [1955], pp. 847–50; retold in Harris [1894], pp. 139–46)

15. (Florida: Seminole Indians) Owl said he could go longer without eating than Rattlesnake could. Rattlesnake said, "All right. You go up in that tree and don't go away. Every thirty days I'll come out of my hole and rattle. You shout, 'Owl'". They did so for three months. After four months Snake rattled but there was no reply. After thirty days more Snake rattled again. Again there was no reply and another episode follows. (Capron [1953], pp. 164–65)

16. (Bahamas) Pigeon and Owl were competing for the queen's daughter. They agreed to have a trial to see who could stay hungry longer from Monday to Friday. Pigeon ate berries from a berry tree, but Owl was in a dry tree. Each day Pigeon sang and Owl answered in song, but by Wednesday Owl was getting hungry and caught a couple of roaches. Pigeon kept on eating berries and drinking water. On Saturday Pigeon sang, but Owl didn't answer. Pigeon found him dead, carried him to the king, and married the king's daughter. (Parsons [1918], pp. 97–98)

17. (Bahamas) Pigeon and Mourning Dove made a bet on who could stay in the woods longer. Mourning Dove ate food like people, but Pigeon ate berries. Each day Pigeon sang and Mourning Dove answered in song, but by Thursday Mourning Dove didn't answer. Pigeon found him dead and married Frog. (Parsons [1918], pp. 98–99)

18. (Cuba) Two birds were arguing about whether it was better to be smart or to be honest and loyal. Cotunto said that smartness was worthless, but Pitirre said that in difficulty you needed cleverness. They argued without agreeing and decided to make a bet. Each would go to a branch of a tree and stay there without sleeping, eating, or drinking. They placed themselves so that they could not fly without being seen by the other, and every so often they would sing so that the other would know that they were awake. Cotunto sang, and Pitirre answered with the same song. This went on until both were weak. Pitirre saw a passing butterfly and ate it without moving from his place and Cotunto did not notice. Pitirre sang better. Cotunto tried to sing, but he died of hunger, tiredness, and thirst because he was loyal to the bet. Pitirre told his brothers, "See how it is better to be clever in difficult situations." From then on Cotunto had to follow Pitirre because Pitirre was the winner. (Guirao [n.d.], pp. 67–71)

19. (Jamaica) Jumping Dick said he would bear hunger longer than White Belly.[2] White Belly went up a tree where a grape dropped, and Jumping Dick picked it up on the ground. They sang to each other. (Beckwith [1924], p. 67)

20. (Jamaica) After explaining the talk of birds and animals, Hopping Dick went up on a sharp stump and White Belly went up a tall tree. They bet as to which one could stay longer without eating, speaking, or singing to each other. Hopping Dick went down to the ground and picked up a worm, but White Belly stayed in the tree and died. (Beckwith [1924], p. 178)

21. (Haiti) When both Hummingbird and Guinea Fowl asked for his daughter, the king said he would put them in a tree to stay ten days without food or drink. The birds sang to each other day after day. On the tenth day the king took them down and gave each a daughter. (Parsons [1933–43], Part II, pp. 506–07, Part III, p. 92)

22. (Haiti) When both Pigeon and Guinea Fowl asked for his daughter, the king put each in a hutch to stay for a year and a day without food or drink. The girl loved Guinea Fowl and carried him food, but Pigeon had corn and ate ten grains each day. The birds sang to each other day after day. One day the king sent his daughter to a festival, and while she was gone Guinea Fowl died. (Parsons [1933–43], Part II, pp. 507–08, Part III, p. 92)

23. (Puerto Rico) Guinea Fowl and Water Fowl agreed to guard a man's wheat that was being eaten by animals. After flying around they sat on a branch and began to sing. Guinea Fowl sang her song and Water Fowl answered with his. Then they flew around the field again and Guinea Fowl, who was intelligent, ate her fill while Water Fowl, who was careless, did not eat. Again Guinea Fowl sang and Water Fowl answered. That is the way that Guinea Fowl beat Water Fowl. (Mason and Espinosa [1929], p. 149)

24. (Nevis) Ground Dove and Mountain Dove wanted to see who could live longer. Mountain Dove went to a coconut tree where there were blossoms, but Ground Dove went to a cedar tree where there were none. They took turns going to the other to say good morning. One morning Mountain Dove found Ground Dove dead. He went home and another episode follows. (Parsons [1933–43], Part II, pp. 336–37, Part III, p. 111)

B I B L I O G R A P H Y

Anonymous
   1930 *African Folk Tales,* Books I–III. Lagos, Church Missionary Society's Bookshop; London, Longmans, Green.
   1949 *Itan Arosọ ti Afrika,* Iwe Kini-Kẹta (Books I–III). London, Longmans, Green.
Beckwith, Martha Warren
   1924 Jamaica Anansi Stories. *Memoirs of the American Folklore Society* 17.
Bordinat, Philip, and Thomas, Peter
   1973 Revealer of Secrets. *African Reader's Library* 24. Lagos, African Universities Press.
Capron, Louis
   1953 The Medicine Bundles of the Florida Seminole and the Green Corn Dance. *Bureau of American Ethnology Bulletin* 151, Anthropological Papers 35.
Dayrell, Elphinstone
   1910 *Folk Stories from Southern Nigeria, West Africa.* London, Longmans, Green.
de Bouveignes, Olivier (non-de-plume of Léon Guébels)
   n.d. *En écoutant conter les Noirs.* Namur, Grand Lacs

Ekwensi, Cyprian O. D.
   1965 *The Great Elephant Bird*. London, Thomas Nelson and Sons.
Fortier, Alcée
   1895 Louisiana Folk-Tales in French Dialect and English Translation. *Memoirs of the American Folk-Lore Society* 2.
Guirao, Ramón
   n.d. *Cuentos y Leyendas Negras de Cuba*. La Habana, Ediciones "Mirador."
Harris, Joel Chandler
   1883 *Nights with Uncle Remus*. Boston and New York, Houghton Mifflin.
   1889 Mr. Crow and Brother Buzzard. *Dixie* 6, No. 12.
   1894 *Little Mr. Thimblefinger and His Queer Country*. New York, McKinlay, Stone & Mackenzie.
   1948 *Seven Tales of Uncle Remus*. Ed. Thomas H. English. Atlanta, Emory University.
   1955 *The Complete Tales of Uncle Remus*. Compiled by Richard Chase. Boston, Houghton Mifflin.
Mason, J. Alden, and Espinoso, Aurelio
   1929 Porto Rican Folk-Lore: Folk Tales. *Journal of American Folk-Lore* 42.
Parsons, Elsie Clews
   1918 Folk-Tales of Andros Island, Bahamas. *Memoirs of the American Folk-Lore Society* 13.
   1923 Folk-Lore of the Sea Islands, South Carolina. *Memoirs of the American Folk-Lore Society* 16.
   1933–43 Folk-Lore of the Antilles, French and English. *Memoirs of the American Folk-Lore Society* 26, Parts I–III.
Thomas, Northcote W.
   1910 *Anthropological Report on the Edo-Speaking People of Nigeria*, Parts I–II. London, Harrison and Sons.
Walker, André Raponda
   1967 *Contes Gabonais*. Paris, Editions Présence Africaine, 2nd. ed.
Weeks, John H.
   1911 *Congo Life and Folklore*. London, Religious Tract Society.
   n.d. *Congo Life and Jungle Stories*. London, Religious Tract Society.
Young, Martha
   1912 *Behind the Dark Pines*. New York, D. Appleton.

N O T E S

1. Alan Dundes, "African Tales among the North American Indians," *Southern Folklore Quarterly*, 29 (1965), 214–15.

2. Beckwith says that both Jumping Dick or Hopping Dick and White Belly are birds (1924), pp. 261–62.

F O U R T E E N

❋

Diving Contest

In this tale the trickster and a dupe have a contest to see who can stay under water the longer. During the contest the trickster steals their food.

The most relevant entry in the tale type and motif indexes is motif K16.2 which reads:

K16.2. *Diving match: trickster eats food while dupe is under water.*

This description fits all of the New World versions [15–18] and one of the African versions [14] considered here; but in most of the African versions [1–13] the motif might be described as:

K16.2* *Diving match: trickster eats food while dupe waits on the bank.*

I count these two variants as a single tale type. It is a tale type, rather than simply a motif, because it has an "independent existence" [e.g., 1, 17]. Incidentally, Chatelain's version [4] cited byThompson under motif K16.2 would belond under K16.2*.

Except for Beckwith's Jamaican tale in which Dog steals Hog's mouth, all others cited by Thompson under motif K16.2 are considered here [13, 4, 17, 15, 16]. Since none of these are from Europe or India, I conclude that this tale type came from (and originated in) Africa.

Again this is no new discovery. Nearly a century ago Joel Chandler Harris[1] noted the similarity between Theal's Xhosa story [14] and his own from Georgia [17], and the same parallel has been cited by Gerber.[2] It has also been cited by Dundes[3] who noted that "References for motif K16.2, Diving match: trickster eats food while dupe is under water, include only African and American Negro texts with no mention of the American Indian versions. There can be no question as to the African origin of this element in American Indian folklore." It is also significant for our purpose that there is also no mention of versions from Europe or India here, or elsewhere in the motif or tale type indexes.

My fourteen African versions come from Nigeria (Tiv), Gabon (Benga and

Reprinted from *Research in African Literatures,* 13 (1982), 508–17.

Lumbu), Angola (Kimbundu), Zaire (Unidentified, Kongo, Mbala, Mongo, and Luba), and South Africa (Xhosa). Three come from the United States: South Carolina and Georgia. One comes from Cuba.

1. (Nigeria: Tiv) Hare and Cricket agreed to help each other on their farms and that Hare's wife should provide lunch. One day Cricket said, "Let us have a dip in the stream. That will give us an appetite for lunch." When they got to the pool Cricket suggested that they should hold their breath and stay underwater. Hare could hold his breath for only a short time and kept popping up to the surface. Cricket stayed under for a long time, and on the last occasion Hare thought that he would never come up again. But this was just a trick on the part of Cricket, who had snapped off the lower joint of his legs and left them sticking out of the water while he went to Hare's farm and ate all the food. This went on for some days and Hare kept beating his wife for not bringing them food. But one day a mischief-maker told Hare to take hold of Cricket's legs and pull him up when he dived. Cricket was eating the food on Hare's farm as usual when Hare appeared and said, "I suppose you are holding your breath *here?*" Cricket begged for mercy but Hare forced his head into the fire. That is why a cricket has a black neck. (Abraham [1940], pp. 79–80)

2. (Gabon: Benga) Cuckoo invited Tortoise to dinner and she accepted. But before sitting down at the table, Tortoise said that she never ate without having taken a bath. Cuckoo said that he would accompany her to a nearby river, and on the way Tortoise cut a long liana and took it with her. At the river she told Cuckoo to attach it to his foot while she held the other end, so that the current would not carry him away. Cuckoo did so and jumped into the water. When Tortoise's turn came she tied the liana to her foot and jumped into the river while Cuckoo held the other end. At the bottom of the river Tortoise untied the liana from her foot and tied it to a root. Then she swam underwater to a path and, hidden from view, went to the house of Cuckoo and devoured the whole dinner. Then she returned to the river, dived in again, retied the liana to her foot, and returned to Cuckoo. Cuckoo asked why she had stayed so long and Tortoise said it was because she had been speaking to the big fish of the river. When they went back to the house Cuckoo saw that nothing was left of the food that she had prepared. Tortoise said, "It is not very good. You invited me to dinner and there is nothing to eat. It is very bad on your part." Tortoise went home pretending to be very discontent. The same thing happened a second time, but before inviting Tortoise a third time Cuckoo consulted a diviner. He gave Cuckoo a wooden figurine smeared with birdlime, and Tortoise was caught on the Tar Baby. (Walker [1967], pp. 131–33; summarized in Paulme [1975], pp. 576–77)

3. (Gabon: Lumbu) Food was scarce in the land and the animals went hunting in the forest. Leopard killed nothing, but each day he appropriated the game that Tortoise killed. Tortoise plotted revenge. He proposed to Leopard that their families bathe in a nearby river. Leopard's children plunged into the water but came out quickly, saying that the water was deep and the current

was strong. Tortoise said that he and his children would teach them how to swim. The plunged into the river and came out on the other bank and then returned, to the astonishment of Leopard and his children. Then they dived in together and disappeared under the waves. They came out far downstream a long way from Leopard and his children. They climbed up the bank and returned to camp where they quickly ate all the food Leopard had left on the fire. After waiting for a long time Leopard returned to camp. He was hungry and wanted to eat, but he found nothing. He accused Tortoise of having stolen his food, but Tortoise said, "You yourself are the thief." Tortoise and Leopard became enemies. They abandoned not only the hunting camp but also the village in which they had lived together. And now, who do you decide was wrong? And who do you decide was right? (Walker [1967], pp. 47–50)

4. (Angola: Kimbundu) Fox caught a cock and Mole stole flour and they cooked them. Fox said, "Let us go to have a bath. When we come back we will eat well." Mole agreed and they went to the river. Mole had made a tunnel from their house to the river. Fox swam to the middle of the river and came back. Mole said, "When I get in the water you won't see me so soon." He dived into the river, swam underwater to the tunnel, and went into the house. He ate the food and returned to Fox saying, "Let us go now." They went into their house and found the food gone. Fox asked who had eaten their food and Mole said, "I don't know. We both went to bathe. How can I know who ate it?" The same thing happened the next day. On the third day, when Mole went for flour, Fox stayed behind and found Mole's tunnel. He set a trap in it and then caught a fowl. They cooked their food and went to bathe. Fox entered the river and came ashore. Mole dived under the water and died in the trap. Fox went home, found the food, found Mole dead in the trap, and ate him. (Chatelain [1894], pp. 202–07)

5. (Zaire) Leopard and Gazelle lived together. Leopard killed three hares and Gazelle cooked them. They ate part of the meat and kept the rest in a pot. The next morning they went to the river to bathe. Gazelle told Leopard to go in first. He agreed but stayed only a short time. Gazelle mocked him, saying that he didn't know how to bathe. Leopard told Gazelle to dive into the river. She said, "Now you will see how I dive. Count the time that I stay underwater." She dived in and came out farther away. She went to the village and ate the rest of the food. Then she went back into the river and came out where she had left Leopard. He said, "Truly, you know how to dive." They returned to the village and found the pot empty. Leopard was angry, but Gazelle calmed him. This happened again and again until Leopard consulted a diviner. He gave Leopard an amulet to put under the pot to catch Gazelle. The next day when the went to the river, Leopard went into the water first but didn't stay long. Then Gazelle went in, came out farther away, and went to the village to eat the remaining food. When she licked the bottom of the pot her muzzle stuck to it. When Leopard found her he threatened to drown her, and another episode follows. (Siwa [1956], pp. 121–23)

6. (Zaire: Kongo) To celebrate their new farm, Leopard and Gazelle cooked

a large pig. When it was done Gazelle suggested that they bathe in the river first and then eat their feast. Leopard jumped into the river but came out quickly. Gazelle said, "You don't know how to dive," and Leopard replied, "You dive and show me how." Gazelle dived into the water, ran along the bottom of the river, and came out near the town. He ate up all the pig, returned to the river, and came out of the water puffing and blowing at the feet of Leopard. "There," said Gazelle, "that is the way to dive." When they returned to Leopard's house they found the pan empty. Leopard was ashamed because the food had been left in his house and beat his wife. Leopard took one of his goats, and when it was cooked Gazelle again suggested that they bathe before eating. Gazelle played the same trick on Leopard and he did so several times. Each time Leopard's wife received a beating and Leopard killed another goat. Another episode follows. (Weeks [1911], pp. 429–32; n.d., pp. 429–32)

7. (Zaire: Mbala) Tortoise caught birds and Long Head stole manioc and they prepared a meal. Tortoise suggested that they bathe because it was very hot, and eat when they returned. At the river Long Head dived into the water and sang. Tortoise cried, "You don't know how to bathe. Come out of the water and I will show you how." Long Head came out and Tortoise sang. Tortoise dived into the river and swam underwater far enough downstream. He came out, went to the house, and ate all the food that they had prepared. Then he returned by the same route and came out where Long Head was waiting. Long Head said that she was hungry and asked what Tortoise had been doing under the water. Tortoise said that was the way his parents had taught him to bathe. They went home and found that someone had taken their meal, leaving only sauce without meat. Tortoise asked what they were going to do and Long Head said that they should eat the sauce. The same thing happened again and again. Long Head grew thin, but Tortoise was fat. Long Head consulted a diviner who told her that Tortoise had eaten the food and said that Long Head should set a trap for him. The next time Tortoise was caught in a trap and could not come to the surface of the water. Long Head found him dead. (Mudindaambi [1973], pp. 130–33)

8. (Zaire: Mongo) Tortoise and Cuckoo were hunting in the forest. Cuckoo caught an antelope and Tortoise, who had caught nothing, said that she had caught one too. Cuckoo cooked his antelope and Tortoise suggested that they go bathing and eat afterwards. Tortoise said Cuckoo should bathe first because she wanted to see how he bathed. Cuckoo dived into the water and came out immediately. Tortoise laughed, "Cuckoo, you know nothing. Watch and see how a child of Crocodile swims." Tortoise dived into the depths and came out by their hut. She ate all the meat that Cuckoo had prepared, leaving only bones and skin. Then she dived into the water and came out by Cuckoo saying, "Did you see what a dive is?" Cuckoo was astonished and proposed that they return home. There he found the pot empty and he yelled. Every day the same thing happened until one day Cuckoo set a trap and Tortoise was caught. She cried for help, saying she had come to spy on the one who

ate their meat, but Cuckoo understood and told Tortoise to go home. Other episodes follow. (Hulstaert [1970], pp. 476–83)

9. (Zaire: Mongo) Tortoise and Cuckoo went fishing. Cuckoo found his net full of fish, but Tortoise's net was empty. When the fish were cooked Tortoise said that they should bathe and eat afterward. Cuckoo dived in first, sang, and came out. Tortoise said, "Cuckoo, you do not know how to bathe because you do not dive deep. Watch me." She dived in and came out at another place and went back to their camp. She ate all the fish, leaving only the heads and bones. Then she dived in again and came out near Cuckoo. Cuckoo said, "Oh! That was long." Tortoise asked if he did not see her belly was full of water. Cuckoo said it was full because she had eaten. They went back to camp and found only fish heads and bones. The next day Cuckoo put resin on the pot and Tortoise's arms stuck to it. She fell into the pot and died. Cuckoo found her and took her and the fish home. (Hulstaert [1970], pp. 494–99)

10. (Zaire: Mongo) Tortoise and Turtle Dove gathered fruit with edible seeds. Tortoise suggested that they go to bathe and then divide the seeds. At the river Tortoise told Dove to go first. Dove went into the water and came out immediately. Then Tortoise dived in, came out elsewhere, and ate all the seeds. She rubbed the skins on Dove's children. She went back in the water and came out near Dove, saying that they should go eat the seeds. When they found the seeds finished, Tortoise accused Dove's children of having eaten them. Another day they gathered fruit again, but Dove set a trap and Tortoise was caught. She called for help, but Dove left her in the trap and she died. (Hulstaert [1970], pp. 500–03)

11. (Zaire: Mongo) Tortoise and Bat found fruit with edible seeds. Tortoise suggested that they go to bathe before they ate the seeds, and at the river he told Bat to dive first. Bat did not know how to dive and immediately came ashore. Tortoise said, "Is that all that you dive? Watch me." Tortoise dived and swam underwater to the place where their camp was. She came out and ate all the seeds. She put palm oil on Bat's children and then swam back to Bat saying, "Now you have seen what is called a dive!" Finding the food gone when they returned, Tortoise accused Bat's children; but they told how Tortoise had come to eat the seeds and had put palm oil on them. Tortoise and Bat quarreled, and other episodes follow. (Hulstaert [1970], pp. 508–15)

12. (Zaire: Mongo) Tortoise and Bat caught four rats in their trap and cooked them in leaves over the fire. Tortoise suggested that they go to bathe and told Bat to bathe first. Bat bathed but did not go under the water. Tortoise said, "You don't know how to swim. When I go I eat shrimp, I will return with my stomach full of shrimp." She dived in, swam underwater, and came out at their house. She ate the four rats, leaving only the heads. When Bat asked who had eaten the rats, Tortoise said she had been bathing with him. Every day it was like this, but one day Tortoise was caught in a trap and she yelled. Bat said, "So it was you who always ate the animals." and other episodes follow. (Hulstaert [1970], pp. 534–37)

13. (Zaire: Luba) Tortoise suggested to Hawk that they dive into the water to see who could hold their breath longer. Hawk dived into the water and came out after about a minute. Tortoise dived in and drifted to the ford where people came to the river. She went to Hawk's house as quickly as she could and ate the fish that Hawk had caught. She dived into the water again and returned to Hawk. Hawk accused her of stealing the fish and another episode follows. (de Bouveignes "Levres," [n.d.], pp. 90–96)

14. (South Africa: Xhosa) After other episodes Hkakanyana, the boy trickster, and another boy hunted birds. In the evening he said that it was time to roast their birds. They were at a river and he told the boy, "We must go under the water and see who will come out last." They went under the water and Hlakanyana came out last. They tried again and Hlakanyana came out quickly and ate all the birds, leaving only the heads. Then he went under the water again and the boy came out before he did. When Hlakanyana came out he said that they should eat their birds. They found that the birds had been eaten and Hlakanyana accused the boy, saying that he had come out of the water first. Other episodes follow. (Theal [1886], pp. 89–117; [1910], pp. 307–19)

15. (South Carolina) Rabbit and Wolf had half a bag of tallow. Rabbit said, "Let's go down to the stream and see which of us can dive longer. Rabbit dived in but came up and sneaked back to the house and ate all the tallow. Then he sneaked back to the stream and dived under. Then Wolf came up and Rabbit came up a little after him. Rabbit said, "I told you I could dive longer." They came out of the water and went to the house. Rabbit told Wolf to divide the tallow. Wolf went for it, came back, and asked Rabbit who ate the tallow. Rabbit said, "I don't know, but I know that I didn't eat it. Some one must have stolen it while we were diving." Another episode follows. (Stewart [1919], p. 395)

16. (South Carolina) Rabbit and Wolf had half a bag of tallow. Rabbit proposed that they go to the stream and see who could dive longer. As soon as he was underwater, Rabbit sneaked back out, went to the house, and ate all the tallow. Then he went back to the stream and dived under the water. After a while he came up again and claimed that he had won. When they went back to the house Rabbit told Wolf to divide the tallow. Wolf went for the tallow but came back and asked Rabbit who had eaten it. Rabbit said that someone must have stolen it while they were diving, and another episode follows. (Parsons "Sea Islands," [1923], p. 40)

17. (Georgia) Walking along with a string of fish, Mink met Terrapin. Terrapin proposed that they go down to the stream and that the one who could stay underwater longer could have the string of fish, and Mink agreed. They waded in, dived, and stayed underwater a long time, until Mink had to come up to catch his breath. After a while Terrapin stuck his nose out of the water and Mink said that Terrapin had won. Terrapin said that it should be the best two out of three, so they dived in again. This time Terrapin came up, ate all of the fish, and slipped back underwater again. He came up and

accused Mink of eating the fish. Mink denied it, but Terrapin repeated his accusation and then went away laughing. (Harris [1883], no. 67; [1955], pp. 386–89)

18. (Cuba: Congo) Turtle said she could take longer baths in the river than Dog could. While Dog was swimming underwater, Tortoise went to the house and ate all the food. She returned and told Dog that he didn't know how to bathe and that she took long baths. When they went home Tortoise assured Dog that a thief had eaten the food. Tired of this, Dog went to a diviner who advised him to make a tar baby, and this episode follows. (Guirao [n.d.], pp. 57–60)

BIBLIOGRAPHY

Abraham, R.C.
  1940 *The Tiv People.* London, Crown Agents for the Colonies, 2nd ed.
Burton, W. F. P.
  1961 *The Magic Drum. Tales from Central Africa.* London, Methuen.
Chatelain, Heli
  1894 Folk-Tales of Angola. *Memoirs of the American Folk-Lore Society 1.*
de Bouveignes, Olivier (nom-de-plume of Léon Guébels)
  n.d. *Sur des Levres Congolaises. Contes.* Collection Lavigerie. Namur, Grand Lacs.
Harris, Joel Chandler
  1883 *Nights with Uncle Remus.* Boston and New York, Houghton Mifflin.
  1955 *The Complete Tales of Uncle Remus.* Compiled by Richard Chase. Boston, Houghton Mifflin.
Hulstaert, G.
  1970 Fables Mongo. *Académie royal des sciences d'outre-mer, classe des sciences morales et politiques,* NS 37, 1.
Kohl-Larsen, Ludwig
  1956 *Das Zauberhorn. Märchen und Tiergeschichten der Tidinga.* Eisenach und Kassel, Erich Röth-Verlag.
Mudindaambi, Ng. Lumbwe
  1973 Pourquoi le Coq ne chante plus? Myths mbala 2.*Ceeba Publications* Series 2, Vol. 8.
Parsons, Elsie Clews
  1923 Folk-Lore of the Sea Islands, South Carolina. *Memoirs of the American Folk-Lore Society 16.*
Paulme, Denise
  1975 Typologie des contes africains du Décepteur. *Cahiers d'Etudes Africaines 15.*
Siwa, Remi-André
  1956 Le léopard et la gazelle. *La Voix du Congolais 12,* no. 119.
Smith, Edwin W., and Dale, Andrew Murray
  1920 *The Ila-Speaking Peoples of Northern Rhodesia,* Vols. I-II. London, Macmillan.
Stewart, Sadie E.
  1919 Seven Folk-Tales from Sea Islands, South Carolina. *Journal of American Folk-Lore 32.*

Swanton, John R.
 1913 Animal Stories from the Indians of the Muskhogean Stock. *Journal of American Folk-Lore 26.*
 1929 Myths and Tales of the Southeastern Indians. *Bureau of American Ethnology Bulletin 88.*
Theal, Geo. McCall
 1886 *Kaffir Folk-Lore.* London, Swan Sonnenschein, Le Bas & Lowrey.
 1910 *The Yellow and Dark-Skinned People of Africa South of the Zambesi.* London, Swan Sonnenschein.
Walker, André Raponda
 1967 *Contes Gabonais.* Paris, Editions Présence Africaine, 2nd. ed.
Weeks, John H.
 1911 *Congo Life and Folklore.* London, Religious Tract Society.
 n.d. *Congo Life and Jungle Stories.* London, Religious Tract Society.

NOTES

1. Harris (1883), p. xix.
2. A. Gerber, "Uncle Remus Traced to the Old World," *Journal of American Folk-Lore,* 6 (1893), 248–49.
3. Alan Dundes, "African Tales among the North American Indians," *Southern Folklore Quarterly,* 29 (1965), 214. Dundes cites American Indian tales in which the trickster steals the dupe's clothing while the dupe is under water, and such tales are also told in Africa; however, I do not find the similarities convincing and the distribution is somewhat curious. All the American versions known to me come from Southeastern Indians in the United States; none come from New World Negroes. I give references to these tales involving the theft of clothing below; but, for the present at least, I am content to rest my case on tales that involve the theft of food:

1. (Zaire: Luba) de Bouveignes "Levres," (n.d.), pp. 78–82.
2. (Zaire: Luba) Burton (1961), pp. 103–06.
3. (Tanzania: Hatsa) Kohl-Larsen (1956), pp. 105–06.
4. (Zambia: Ila) Smith & Dale Vol. II (1920), pp. 361–63.
5. (Oklahoma: Natchez Indians) Swanton (1913), pp. 204–09; (1929), pp. 234–39.
6. (Oklahoma: Natchez Indians) Swanton (1929), pp. 230–34.
7. (Texas: Alabama Indians) Swanton (1929), pp. 134–35.
8. (Texas: Alabama Indians) Swanton (1929), pp. 136–38.
9. (Texas: Koasati Indians) Swanton (1929), pp. 178–81.
10. (Georgia: Creek Indians) Swanton (1929), pp. 10–13.
11. (Georgia: Creek Indians) Swanton (1929), pp. 13–15.

INDEX

WILLIAM BASCOM (1912–1981) was Professor of Anthropology and Director of the Robert L. Lowie Museum of Anthropology at the University of California at Berkeley. He was the author of *Ifa Divination: Communication between Gods and Men in West Africa* and *Sixteen Cowries: Yoruba Divination from Africa to the New World;* he coauthored *Continuity and Change in African Cultures* and *A Handbook of West African Art.*